MARCH 1917

On the Brink of War and Revolution

WILL ENGLUND

W. W. NORTON & COMPANY

Independent Publishers Since 1923

New York | London

For information about permission to reproduce selections from this book,
write to Permissions, W. W. Norton & Company, Inc.,
500 Fifth Avenue, New York, NY 10110

For information about special discounts for bulk purchases, please contact
W. W. Norton Special Sales at specialsales@wwnorton.com or 800-233-4830

Manufacturing by LSC Communications Harrisonburg
Book design by Chris Welch
Production manager: Julia Druskin

ISBN 978-0-393-29208-4

W. W. Norton & Company, Inc.
500 Fifth Avenue, New York, N.Y. 10110
www.wwnorton.com

W. W. Norton & Company Ltd.
15 Carlisle Street, London W1D 3BS

1 2 3 4 5 6 7 8 9 0

To Theo and August

May the coming century be distinguished by good sense

CONTENTS

NOTES ON THE TEXT

English spellings of Russian names a hundred years ago were variable. I have changed spellings throughout, even from printed material, to conform to modern usage. Thus, in Chapter 6, we have the mentally unstable chief Russian minister Alexander Protopopov, instead of Protopopoff. But not to be too consistent, I have adhered to the traditional spelling of "czar," which was universal in 1917, rather than the more accurate transliteration of "tsar."

In 1917, Russia was still on the Julian calendar, which at that time was thirteen days behind the Gregorian calendar used in the rest of the world. This is why the uprising in Petrograd, which broke out the second week of March by our way of thinking, is called the February Revolution. To avoid confusion, I have rendered all dates, even in quoted material, in the now-universal Gregorian calendar.

Today, Ukraine is a country in its own right, but in March 1917 it was part of the Russian Empire. In that era it was universally referred to in English as "the Ukraine," and I have retained that usage—as in Chapter 3, where the Cantacuzène estate at Bouromka is described.

"Colored," "Negro" and "negro" were all considered acceptable terms in 1917. In passages where I am trying to present the thinking of a century ago, I have used those words. My intent is to avoid what might seem to be infelicitous anachronisms, and I don't want to appear to be trying to be more correct than, say, W. E. B. Du Bois, a founder of the National Association for the Advancement of Colored People, when he appears in Chapter 17. Where, on the other hand, we are clearly looking back from the vantage point of the twenty-first century, I have used "black" or "African-American."

In writing this book, I have made one very arbitrary assumption: that the quotes in newspaper articles are accurate. I know from experience that even today this is not strictly the case. But rather than clutter up the text with qualifications, let me offer this caveat here, just once. I am reasonably certain, moreover, that public addresses were rendered in the press as delivered, because then as now politicians and other speakers handed out advance copies of their speeches. In a few instances I have been able to compare newspaper reports with the speaker's text, and they are faithful accounts. Impromptu remarks are harder to gauge. In some cases—when, for instance, Jeannette Rankin arrived at Washington's Union Station to take up her seat in Congress (see Chapter 21)—they were covered by more than one newspaper, and, again, comparisons show little variation. Where there was just one reporter present, I take it on faith that at the very least the tenor of the speaker's words was well captured. Thus, we have Teddy Roosevelt exclaiming, in Chapter 15, "That's the stuff—no fifty-fifty there!" Could anyone doubt that?

MARCH
1917

CHAPTER I

"Go! Go! Go!"

You have to see the libraries they have here, said Nikolai.

We just got off the boat, said Leon.

Come quick. They're free and open all evening.

We've been up since 3.

They're amazing. It's America. You'll see.

And so they did. Leon and Natasha and their two boys, tired and cranky as they were, made a public library their first stop in the city of New York, down near Astor Place. Look at what the state provides, said Nikolai. Think of it!

LEON WAS LEON TROTSKY—revolutionary by trade, an exile from the clutches of czarist Russia, expelled in turn from Austria, France and Spain. Nikolai, who had preceded him to America by several months, was Nikolai Bukharin, the eager 28-year-old editor of the call-to-arms newspaper *Novy Mir*, or *New World*, which was published out of a brownstone on St. Mark's Place. Safe at last, with an ocean between them and the great war that had been tearing Europe apart since 1914, they could begin the methodical work of preparing for revolution in Russia. It was coming, no doubt about that, but there was so much to do to make ready. It was January 1917.

New York was full of Socialists, though Trotsky thought they lacked ferocity. What kind of Socialist owns a car? He enjoyed the thought of New York as the bastion of capital—leading the way toward a more advanced stage of capitalism, as Marx would have it, but capitalist nonetheless. He liked the idea of living in the heart of the beast.

"My only profession in New York was that of a revolutionary socialist," he would write later.

"In those days mine was a profession no more reprehensible than that of a bootlegger."

And yet. They found an apartment in the Bronx, on Vyse Avenue. It came with electric lights, a gas stove, a bath, a telephone (the two boys, Seryozha and Lev, loved the telephone), an elevator and even a chute for the garbage. It had a Negro superintendent who, Trotsky wrote approvingly, stole from the landlord but not from the tenants. The boys went to school, picked up English just like that, loved everything about this big bursting city in a land far from war.

New York had so much to offer and there were powerful reform movements pushing it ever more forward. Trotsky was unimpressed. He wrote in *Novy Mir*: "I left a Europe wallowing in blood, but I left with a profound faith in a coming revolution. And it was with no democratic 'illusions' that I stepped on the soil of this old-enough New World."

You couldn't reform your way to a better life. You needed to disrupt the whole system, then the whole world. You needed a revolution. And the Great War in Europe had softened the ground, so to speak. It had accelerated the tide of history. Europe was where the future lay— however tempting the illusions might be in New York.

So every day, while his sons were picking up the latest slang from their new friends in the Bronx, the professional revolutionary rode the Interborough Rapid Transit train all the way from 174th Street down to Astor Place.* He preferred to think of New York in the abstract, as a "city of prose and fantasy, of capitalist automatism, its streets a triumph of cubism, its moral philosophy that of the dollar." He did write of watching one day as an old man in tatters fished a stale crust of bread out of a garbage can on St. Mark's Place but didn't take that thought anywhere. He wasn't keen on personal observation. "New York impressed me tremendously because, more than any other city in the world, it is the fullest expression of our modern age," he wrote.

So what was really happening in New York in the early months of 1917? Food riots, for one thing. Trotsky noticed them, but left the rabble-rousing to others. A combination of factors had led to widespread food shortages, followed, naturally enough, by price gouging. It wouldn't have happened but for the distant war in Europe. At the same time, American trade with Europe had boomed since the war had begun in 1914, and wealth was pouring into New York. Total U.S. exports had increased from $2.3 billion in 1913 to $4.3 billion in 1916, and would reach $6.3 billion in 1917. That year America enjoyed a trade surplus of more than $3 billion. The value of American exports to the United Kingdom was 1,000 times greater than of those to Germany.

Europe had been at war for thirty-one months—a sustained eruption of violence worse than any the world had ever seen. A war psychosis, as one Russian put it, had the continent in its thrall. Millions of refugees, millions of wounded, millions of dead. From Belgium to Switzerland, from the Baltic to the Black Sea, even across the southern rim of the Alps—the ground itself was torn asunder by the high explosives of an industrial age. But here in New York, the seasons turned, the bright lights shone, and life went on, restless, contentious, good-natured, ambitious. The war was an ocean away, a distant spectacle. But how broad was an ocean, really, and how much longer

---

* That was one ride. Until 1918, all IRT trains from the Bronx and northern Manhattan came down Broadway, then cut across 42nd Street to Grand Central—where the Shuttle runs today—and made a sharp right turn to head downtown toward City Hall.

could Americans think that it would keep them safe from the agonies of the world?

The city was a jumbled mass of contradictions, certainly. It boasted the world's tallest skyscraper—the four-year-old, 57-story Woolworth Building—and the rank tenements of the Lower East Side. Row upon row of chocolate-hued brownstones lined Manhattan's cross streets. It was the natural place of business for both J. P. Morgan, the financier, and Max Eastman, the radical editor of *The Masses*. Southern blacks were settling in uptown Harlem even as the flow of Catholics from Italy and Jews from Russia had been closed off by the war. In Yorkville, on the Upper East Side, German-Americans read German-language newspapers and ate sauerbraten and strudel in German restaurants. Irish-Americans vied for political power; Sicilian mobsters had started to amass a different kind of power. The Catskill Aqueduct, a huge public works project that would carry clean fresh water to the city from upstate, was months away from opening. Real estate developers were casting their eyes on the uncrowded outer boroughs.

New York was filthy, jostling, physically unencumbered by seemingly any controlling vision, and always on the make. Only six years earlier the Triangle Shirtwaist Factory fire had killed 145 Jewish and Italian men and, mostly, women, who worked, and died, under appalling conditions. The mansions on Fifth Avenue were as grand as any urban dwellings in the world. Sinclair Lewis referred to the city in 1917 as "this madness of multiform energy."

IN THE WINTER, skaters flocked to Central Park; in the summer, Coney Island drew its millions of visitors. New Yorkers had a choice of three baseball teams to root for, one in Brooklyn and two in Manhattan. Only the Giants were any good. People elsewhere in the country looked askance at New York's social reforms, its immigrants, its high life, its art, its power, its New York values. Across the nation, Wall Street was loathed.

When he wasn't putting out *Novy Mir*, Trotsky raced from meeting to meeting—up to Harlem, down to the Lower East Side, once even to Philadelphia. He sparred with Morris Hillquit, head of the Socialist Party in New York. He had a friendly meeting with Eugene V. Debs, who had run for president on the Socialist ticket in 1912. He poured out articles in Russian, gave speeches in both Russian and German, trying to build socialism in the shadow of Wall Street and to foment revolution in Russia. The empire of the czar—autocratic, corrupt, characterized at the top by a sort of brazen stupidity—had spawned a generation of revolutionaries at home. Americans had learned the word *pogrom* from Russia's treatment of its Jews. But outside émigré circles, American indifference to the fate of Russia was profound.

All that was to change abruptly, unexpectedly, shockingly, in the middle of March. Revolution erupted in the Russian capital, Petrograd, without any assistance from Trotsky or the other Red revolutionaries, who had taken to calling themselves Bolsheviks. The people themselves had risen up, and this would remake Russia. It also presented Americans with what many saw as an opportunity—to remake the world. On this side of the ocean, the downfall of the old regime was hailed as a great leap forward in the struggle to make the world safe for democracy.

TROTSKY HAD TO catch up. The excitement was back in Russia, and this revolution needed to be pushed forward—hard—toward its second act. Nine-year-old Seryozha had had diphtheria, but now he was better and he had caught his parents' enthusiasm at the thought of return.

It was March 26, the day before their departure. Seryozha went for a walk—and didn't come back. Trotsky was beside himself. For years, he had been working in exile toward this moment, toward the hour when he could finally devote himself to the construction of a new world on earth. And now Seryozha was nowhere to be found. Trotsky's wife, Natalia Sedova, kept packing, and worrying, as she had so many times in the past.

They planned to take one of the few ships still daring a transatlantic run—daring that it could evade the German U-boats now prowling the sea. If Trotsky couldn't make that ship, the revolution might proceed without him. Three anxious hours passed, as Trotsky would describe them—but he may have been as anxious for his own revolutionary ambition as he was for the safety of his son.

Then the phone rang. "I am here." It was Seryozha, at a distant police station. He had, remarkably, remembered his parents' telephone number. As they later found out, the boy had decided that before leaving New York he would settle a question that had been bothering him: If there was a 174th Street, just around the corner from Vyse Avenue, were there 173 streets leading up to it? Could he walk all the way down to 1st Street? But the cops got this son of a revolutionary before he could find out. Seryozha told his parents where they could find him, they rushed down to retrieve him, and there he was—playing checkers with a big New York City policeman in blue tunic and brass buttons and happily chewing a stick of black gum. The Americanization of Seryozha—Sergei Lvovich Sedov—ended that day, though neither he nor his parents could have known that for sure. The next morning they sailed for Canada, and from there they made their way onward to revolutionary Petrograd and the remaking of the world. Even as he left, Trotsky hoped one day to return.

THE FOOD RIOTS in New York in early March were an eerie reflection of the beginnings of the strife that unseated the czar in Petrograd. Angry women attacked pushcarts on Stanton and Houston streets. A mob got out of control at 114th Street and First Avenue. Another mob forced its way into a synagogue at Broome and Norfolk streets, but were dispersed by police. Ten were arrested. A boycott was launched against grocers accused of gouging. At a meeting of delegates from two hundred women's organizations, it was decided to urge the city to sell food to consumers directly, bypassing retailers. Thousands of appeals were sent to Mayor John Purroy Mitchel, some declaring that people were starving. George Perkins, head of the mayor's food committee, and a friend of Theodore Roosevelt's, urged the city's well-to-do to economize on their food purchases so there would be more for everyone else. When the health commissioner addressed 2,000 housewives from the east side in Clinton Hall, on Lafayette Street, just steps away from Trotsky's office, and suggested they feed their families rice and hominy, he was nearly hissed off the stage. "The Commissioner grabbed his hat and coat, but Jacob Panken, Socialist lawyer, quieted the women," a newspaper reported.

Some officials wondered aloud if "foreign" agents—that is, Germans—were behind the shortages. The United States and Germany had broken off diplomatic relations in February, and since then the Germans had sent a few unlucky American ships trading with the Allies to the bottom. The American Railway Association denied that a lack of freight cars was causing the food crisis—but that was almost certainly the real explanation. By 1917, American railroads were staggering under the huge increase in freight traffic that the war had brought about. As the year began, there were more miles of track in service, 254,000, than ever before—or ever since. (Today the number stands at about 140,000.) But there weren't enough boxcars, and those that existed were stacking up in East Coast ports, as American exports to Europe that had leaped every year of the war were now stalled because of the U-boat campaign. The lack of railcars forced Pillsbury to close two of its flour mills in Minnesota, and there was a real fear that New England would run out of flour in a matter of weeks.

In much of the country—and much of New York—the wartime boom had had its ameliorating effect. But now Wall Street itself was worried; stock prices had nearly doubled since late 1914 but had recently begun a steep decline, as fears began to gather that the Allies would be forced to seek a peace, ending the good times.

It was as though a great flood tide was setting in, pulling a roiled and perplexed America toward war. The determination in the early years to stay out of it was eroding. With the war dragging on, Americans began to acknowledge that they did indeed have a stake in the outcome. The question was how best to exert American influence on the course of distant events, and what result would best serve American interests. The United States had size and wealth; Americans were beginning to ask themselves what role that should give their country in the affairs of the world. And all the while they were enjoying a strangely jubilant sort of prickly peace.

AT A STUDIO on East 48th Street, a young vaudeville star named Buster Keaton was making his first film, *Butcher Boy*, directed by the comedian Fatty Arbuckle. At the end of his first day on the set, Keaton brought the camera home, where he took it apart so he could fully understand how the magic was made. Men of uncertain propriety called "lounge lizards" were showing up in cafés along Broadway, on the lookout for rich women to sponge off. The highest-paid baseball player in America passed through New York; he was Grover Cleveland Alexander, who for three seasons past had dominated the National League while pitching for the Philadelphia Phillies, and was now making an unheard-of $12,500 a year. The *Philadelphia Evening Ledger* called him "our local pitching Croesus." In 1917 the Phillies went to spring training in St. Petersburg, Florida, and got there on a coastwise steamer from New York, amid much wisecracking about German submarines.

New York was undergoing a sexual revolution, too. The cover of the March issue of *Vanity Fair* (price 25 cents) featured a painting of a nude standing on green grass, with purple hills in the background. She holds one arm above her head, her palm strangely horizontal. A drape of perfectly diaphanous material harkens back, perhaps, to ancient Greece, in a nod to Art. It hides nothing.

The previous fall Margaret Sanger had opened a birth-control clinic in Brownsville, Brooklyn. As she expected it might, this led to her arrest and conviction, and a transfer to the women's section of the Queens County Jail. When she was released in March, her supporters sang "The Marseillaise." Delmonico's refused to seat them for lunch, so Sanger and her allies went to the Lafayette Hotel instead. At the end of March she bought John Reed's cottage in Provincetown, Massachusetts; the dashing radical journalist, who had made his name covering a silk workers strike in Paterson, New Jersey, in 1913, and the opening months of the war in Europe, for *The Masses*, used the money to finance a trip to Russia to report on this revolution.

H. L. Mencken, editor of *The Smart Set*, spent the early war years making it one of the country's most influential journals, publishing Edna St. Vincent Millay, Theodore Dreiser, Aldous Huxley, Sinclair Lewis, Eugene O'Neill and Dashiell Hammett. Mencken was a strong advocate for Dreiser in particular. In May 1915, *The Smart Set* introduced James Joyce to American readers, running two stories from his *Dubliners*. Mencken was caustic, insightful and sophisticated. He detested Woodrow Wilson's high-mindedness, and described the president as "the self-bamboozled Presbyterian, the right-thinker, the great moral statesman, the perfect model of the Christian cad."

A DANCE CRAZE was sweeping the city, and much of America. Public dancing—in places that served cocktails, no less—was shocking, exciting and, as young couples discovered, fun. Vernon and Irene Castle set the pace—they were the Fred Astaire and Ginger Rogers of this earlier generation. Their careers ignited when they broke the color bar and hired a black composer and impresario named James Reese Europe to lead their band.

Popular music had been rooted not a decade earlier in the theater and vaudeville. Black musical theater had occupied a vibrant niche, but one that was especially hard hit by the advent of the movies. Black musicians who lost their jobs began to find work in cafés instead. Jim Europe, who grew up in Washington four doors down from John Philip Sousa, the March King, rode that wave to success. For him, the only truly American music was African-American. Only black musicians could play it as it really should be played. By 1917 he had persuaded the Castles and a large part of the sophisticated audience for music that he was right.

"I don't think it too much to say," Europe told the *New York Tribune* (which mangled his name as "Jesse Rees Europe") that the black musician "plays this music better than the white man simply because all this music is indigenous with him. Rhythm is something that is born in the negro, and the modern dances require rhythm above all else." The Negro, he said, "is peculiarly fitted for the modern dances."

Jim Europe was what people called a "race man." He believed that America's black population must someday stand as equals to the white majority—and he understood that this was not going to be a gift from the whites, but something that blacks would have to achieve. Once, talking about the smaller royalties he received as a composer because he was black, he said, "I am not bitter about it. It is, after all, but a slight portion of the price my race must pay in its at times almost hopeless fight for a place in the sun. Someday it will be different and justice will prevail."

Europe grew disenchanted with the word "ragtime," though that's what everyone called his music. He had come to think of ragtime as something white songwriters turned out when they were trying to copy black music. By March of 1917 the great black ragtime composer Scott Joplin was dying of dementia caused by syphilis, forgotten, locked away in Manhattan State Hospital on Wards Island. Jim Europe wanted to push music forward.

He had conducted an all-Negro orchestra in Carnegie Hall in 1912, and dreamed of a day when he could manage large ensembles, playing serious music derived from Africa. Yet something new was in the air. That March saw the release by Victor of a record by a small band from New Orleans. They called themselves the Original Dixieland Jass Band, and they were white. It was the first commercial jazz record.

Europe had noticed this new sound, which turned music into a performer's art, not a composer's. In 1917 its popularity suddenly took off. He would later have ideas about where jazz could go, but right at this moment he had other plans, other worries.

In 1916 a long-stalled effort to form a National Guard regiment among Harlem men finally got underway. Though in his mid-30s, Europe believed he had to take part. If America were to enter the war, blacks would have to prove themselves, he believed. But even if it didn't, the regiment offered a chance to organize a body of Harlem men, instilling pride and discipline. Europe enlisted in the 15th Regiment as a private on September 18, 1916. He was made a sergeant a week later. Soon he would be a lieutenant, in charge of a machine-gun squad.

But the regiment's white commander, Colonel William Hayward, who was running into one difficulty after another in getting the regiment equipped, and who feared the consequences for his men if they failed to meet Army standards, had another idea. He asked Europe what it would take to create the best band in the United States. Europe told him he'd need $10,000 altogether—a lot of money back then. Europe later said he'd picked such a high figure hoping that Hayward would give up the idea. But the colonel pressed forward and raised the money from his well-to-do friends. So now Europe had a band to put together. A military band.

OTHER NEW YORKERS, suspecting that entry into the war was coming, were joining National Guard regiments as well. William J. Donovan, a Wall Street lawyer from Buffalo known as "Wild Bill" from his college days, had signed up with the Fighting 69th, the predominantly Irish regiment that had won fame in the Civil War. There he would get to know the poet Joyce Kilmer, the author of "Trees."

America was neutral and at peace, but hostility toward Germany was rife, and ripening. Some of the strongest voices for war were raised in New York. Newspapers were prowar, Wall Street was prowar, men such as Elihu Root, the former secretary of state and of war in Republican administrations, and the winner of the Nobel Peace Prize for his work as head of the Carnegie Endowment for International Peace, organized rallies for war. They exalted the former president, Theodore Roosevelt, of nearby Oyster Bay, who was itching to get into the fight.

But there were strong New York voices against war, too. The city had a large German population, and its political machines were controlled by the Irish, many of whom opposed the idea of going to war alongside England. New York was home to pacifists and radicals, like John Reed and Margaret Sanger, who viewed the war as a criminal clash of imperial powers.

AT THE END of February, a 36-year-old Montanan named Jeannette Rankin came to New York. The previous November she had become the first woman ever elected to the U.S. Congress. She was difficult, ornery and effective. For two years, she had led the campaign for suffrage in Montana, and as soon as the vote was extended to women, by referendum on November 3, 1914, she decided to run in the next election for one of the state's two at-large congressional seats. She campaigned from one end to the other of what was then the third-largest state in the nation. She met with Lutheran farmers' wives on Montana's eastern plains, and danced with Irish copper miners in Butte, a hard-bitten, strife-torn city on a hill, known then as the "Gibraltar of unionism." She rode horseback when she had to, but loved cars. In Montana's wide open spaces, where ranges frame broad scrubby valleys and from a height you can see a town twenty miles away, where boosters talk about the Big Sky but what's really impressive is the realization of how big the air is—in a landscape like that, what is a horse at walking pace compared to a car at 30 miles an hour? A 1913 photo shows Rankin standing in the back of an open, mud-splattered car, with chains on the rear wheels. (Even in town, in

Missoula, the streets weren't paved until 1911.) In her hand she holds a flag, snapping smartly in the breeze.

Rankin's father had become well-to-do by running a sawmill at a place called Grant Creek back when Montana was still a territory, and wealthier still as he took a controlling interest in several banks. He had dealt with the U.S. Army often in the early days—the Indian wars were still sputtering—and it had given him a jaundiced view of the military mind at work, a view his daughter inherited. "I grew up knowing that the military was a crooked thing," she once told an interviewer.

She had lived first at the ranch on Grant Creek, then in a mansard-roofed brick house on Madison Street in nearby Missoula, on a lot just up from the Clark Fork River and backing on Rattlesnake Creek. Missoula is an absolutely flat city, hemmed in by hills, and in her childhood there would have been days when the whole town was blanketed in unstirring coal smoke from the Northern Pacific steam locomotives and the coal stoves in nearly every home. She was an indifferent student: Her first-quarter marks as a sixth-grader included a 76 in reading, a 74 in writing, a 64 in geography, a 90 in language and a 98 in deportment. Her grades changed little over the course of that year, except that deportment fell to an 84 by spring.

At the age of 22, so it was said, she had written in her diary, "Go! Go! Go! It makes no difference where, just so you go! go! go! Remember at the first opportunity go." In 1908 she left for New York and spent two formative years as a student at the New York School for Philanthropy, mixing with progressives and radicals. She made friendships then that would be important to her the rest of her life. From New York she embarked on a career as an organizer for women's suffrage. In Helena in 1911, she addressed the Montana House of Representatives on the suffrage question.

"She neither begged for support, threatened, cajoled or appealed to the chivalry of man, but simply advanced her argument and asked merely for sincere and earnest consideration of it," reported the *Helena Independent*.

"It is beautiful and right," she said that day, "that a mother should nurse her child through typhoid fever, but it is also beautiful and right that she should have a voice in regulating the milk supply from which the typhoid resulted."

She went on to direct campaigns in Albany—where she was condescended to by a young state senator, Franklin D. Roosevelt—as well as in Delaware, Florida, New Hampshire and North Dakota. In 1913 she lobbied Congress.

She was strong-minded and had an unshakable belief in the power of shoe-leather organizing as more fruitful than publicity-seeking and charismatic leadership. She was supported, financially and emotionally, by her brother Wellington, who was far more conservative and had his own political ambitions. He kept a careful eye on her image. In the early days she made her own clothes and she always made a point of dressing well. She took care never to appear in public as priggish or manly.

In 1915 she had traveled to New Zealand to see what a country that gave women the vote, had worker's compensation laws, old-age pensions and child protection laws looked like. She supported herself while she was there as a seamstress.

In 1916 she ran for the House on the Republican ticket, though she later claimed she never registered as a member of the party. In a year when Montana and the nation gave Wilson and the Democrats a landslide victory, she easily coasted to a win as one of the two at-large representatives, out of a field of seven men and one woman. As a progressive, she was naturally an opponent of the Anaconda Copper Mining Company, controlled by Standard Oil—the Rockefellers, in other words. For the better part of twenty years, Anaconda had been able to have its way with the state legislature and most of the local newspapers by wielding what people in Montana called "the copper collar." Rankin campaigned on a platform calling for increased support for mothers and children, for prohibition, for easier credit for farmers, and for tax reform. But she had only one real objective, and that was to represent the women not just of Montana, but of the nation. She didn't talk about the war.

"Doesn't it make you feel dizzy to realize that you have become a historical character?" wrote a friend, Mary Atwater, a few days after the election. "It is a big job we have helped hand you, and we all feel confident you will be equal to it. Three cheers for 'Our Jeannette.'"

An admirer from Cairo, Illinois, read in the paper that Rankin was avoiding photographers because Republican leaders of Montana felt that the publicity she was receiving "might classify her as a freak." The admirer, Winifred Warder, was appalled. "Might not an Illinois girl say that she does not agree with 'Republican leaders of Montana' if such is their opinion, for one so honored as you have been need not be afraid of any kind of newspaper notoriety for in truth no matter how lightly treated it emblazons the fact of suffrage recognition and to the women of America your picture personifies 'Hope.'"

The whole country was fascinated by her—the spunky woman from the West. Much of America still lived according to a saloon-and-spittoon culture, and most American women were confined to a few narrow choices: They could be schoolteachers, or nurses, or nuns, or work as seamstresses in sweatshops—or, of course, they could stay at home to raise families. The boundaries were starting to loosen, but now suddenly here was a woman joining the halls of political power. And from way out in Montana, that wild, rugged, honest, nearly mythological and wide-open state.

Now she was to begin a twenty-city speaking tour, starting at Carnegie Hall. "Of course I am excited over the immediate prospects of speaking to a big New York audience," she wrote to a friend in Red Lodge, Montana. "And it's also new to me this being courted by the public, and urged to speak when heretofore it has always been my part to urge people to listen to me, that I scarcely know how to take it."

It was March 2. She stood before an audience of 3,000, curious and eager to show their support for a female politician in the flesh. The speech in her hands had been written by Wellington, who, then and later, tried to deflect some of his sister's more radical tendencies.

"Her white chiffon dress fluttered in the breeze of her own eloquence," the *New York Tribune* reported in its account of her Carnegie Hall speech. Newspapers were always remarking on her appearance. "Her white satin cloak lay over the back of the chair, and her white satin pumps were small and dainty. She was a debutante on her way to the coming-out party of women into the class of real people. But there was nothing white-chiffony about the Hon. Jeannette's opinions, as she laid them before the crowd last night."

The meeting was presided over by Carrie Chapman Catt, one of the most important leaders of the suffrage movement. Rankin, speaking without notes, made virtually no reference to the war in Europe and only one glancing reference to the possibility of America's entering it. She didn't talk about the U-boats torpedoing American ships. Nor did she do so in any of her other appearances that month.

"A slip of a young woman," the *Tribune* reported, "looking just like a high school graduate about to read the valedictory, but not quite sure she remembered the last word of the first sentence, stepped out before the applauding crowds at Carnegie Hall last night."

Rankin declared: "There's nothing else for the women of New York to think about, nothing else for them to talk about, nothing else for them to work for, until they get the vote. Until then they haven't taken the first step to freedom."

This was her most important message; this was what she believed was the most immediate need. To think, to talk—and then to *work* for the vote.

In the mainstream of Western progressivism, she spoke in favor of the referendum, the ballot initiative, proportional representation, direct primaries, and a popular vote for president. She endorsed prohibition. She described the wonders of Montana to her New York audience: 58 bushels of No. 1 wheat to the acre, enough flour to make

18 loaves of bread for every American, free land still being given away. (Harry Truman had gone up there from Missouri two years earlier to have a look and decided he wasn't interested.) She talked about cheap electricity thanks to an abundance of water power and natural gas, and she told of traveling 16 miles in a lumber wagon during her campaign, and 60 miles on horseback. (She probably traveled several thousand miles by train and car.)

"I'm proud of the West!" she said. "I'm glad that it belongs to me!"

Rankin's years of campaigning against Anaconda had given her a new way of looking at economic power.

"Industrial democracy is more important than political democracy," she said. This was what she meant when she said that getting the vote was only the first step toward freedom. She wanted Americans to take control of their lives and move beyond what she called the "money system."

Theodore Roosevelt sent a telegram that night, which was read out to the audience. "I most earnestly hope that you and those like you will make and keep the Republican party loyal to the spirit of Abraham Lincoln," he wrote, "and in very truth the party of nationalism and genuine democracy; the party which stands for the right of every man, woman and child within our national borders, and which in return exacts from every full grown man and woman the fullest performance of duty to the nation both in peace and in war."

Before she left New York, she had lunch with another newly elected Republican member of Congress: Fiorello LaGuardia, representing a district that included the West Village. They struck up a close friendship that was to last for years. She once told a friend that he had proposed to her, which he, in a good humor one day, acknowledged.

From New York she headed to Bridgeport, Connecticut, then back to Brooklyn, then to Hartford, where she addressed the state legislature. From there it was Trenton, New Jersey, and then westward. People everywhere were curious about her, as if they wanted to get a sense of how someone could be both a woman and a member of Congress.

She told one interviewer that she liked going to the movies, yet didn't consider herself frivolous. The *Daily Gate City and Constitution-Democrat*, of Keokuk, Iowa, ran an approving editorial, drawing on accounts of her Carnegie Hall speech. "She was dressed in distinctly feminine style, with none of the severities commonly credited to women of brains," it read.

"'Her shoes were notably small, with French heels.'. . . 'Her chestnut hair was prettily coiffed.'. . . 'Her gown was soft and clingy, showing a pleasantly rounded throat and neck.'. . . There is every indication that Miss Rankin is a normal, feminine twentieth century woman. There is still much to be learned of her character and ability as a legislator, but the public appears to be willing to take her for granted. There isn't going to be so much fun with the congresswoman idea, after all."

A progressive Republican, like Roosevelt, she met with the former Rough Rider on March 1, before the Carnegie Hall debut. Earlier that day, he had told a reporter that a fight "must be won by hitting, and if we go to war with Germany we must strike hard at Germany." Just two days earlier, he had scornfully written, "The entire pacifist movement in this country, during the past two and a half years, has really been in the interest of German militarism . . . and against our own honor and vital national interests." But Rankin was determined to use her position to extend universal suffrage to women, and she kept her thoughts about war to herself.

"I don't even know if she's a pacifist," wrote an interviewer from the *New York Evening World*, in an article under the headline "First Congresswoman in U.S. Is Good Cook and Knows How to Make Own Clothes; Won't Commit Herself on War Question." After admiring Rankin's pleasure in baking pies, and expressing disappointment that her hair wasn't, as rumored, red, the reporter asked her how she would vote if there were a war resolution in Congress.

"She would only say, 'I believe women are patriots in the best and highest and truest sense, and that they will do what they think best for their country, whatever personal sacrifice is entailed.'"

In any case, her brother Wellington had persuaded the Lee Keedick speaker's agency, which was sponsoring her tour, to threaten cancellation if she spoke out against going to war.

ROOSEVELT HAD BEEN trying to muzzle himself, with little success. He was hopping mad. On February 1, Germany had announced that it was resuming unrestricted submarine warfare in a zone surrounding western Europe and the Mediterranean. Now even ships flying neutral flags—the American flag included—would be targets. President Wilson had broken off diplomatic relations, but Roosevelt argued that the United States was hiding disgracefully behind the might of the Royal Navy. Without British warships in the Atlantic, he said, the Germans would be in New York.

Germany had made itself an enemy, in his view, and how much better it would be to fight Germans over there, rather than here at home.

Earlier in the year he had labeled as "wickedly false" the assertions of Secretary of State Robert Lansing that the war aims of the belligerent powers were similar. He had said that President Wilson had "earned for this nation the curse of Meroz,* for he has not dared to stand on the side of the Lord against the wrongdoings of the mighty."

He had accused the Germans of carrying out a policy of murder on the high seas. And he had warned that the United States was in danger of becoming the "helpless spoil of any alien that envies us because of our wealth and despises us because of our soft weakness."

His name was cheered in the Senate when Warren G. Harding of Ohio said the Germans wouldn't have threatened with their U-boats if TR was still president. He hammered away at the country's lack

---

* Meroz, a city mentioned in the Book of Judges, was cursed by the angel of God because its inhabitants did not help the Israelites in battle.

of preparedness, and hours before he met with Rankin he had gone up to Hartford, where he was delighted with what he found. Connecticut was the first state to institute a "military census," and it was registering every male of military age, noting health and occupation, as well as completing an inventory of all industrial plants. A *New York Times* reporter was astonished to learn that all the information was being recorded by way of punching holes in cards according to a code—cards that could then be read by sorting machines.

Roosevelt applauded the implication of "universal obligatory service."

He told reporters: "It means that every young man who is fit and can best render that service in the army shall be sent to the front. It means that if any man can best render that service by cultivating the soil or doing work on a railroad or in a munitions factory he shall do so. It means, in short, that every man and every woman in the country in time of war shall be held absolutely liable to render service to the country in whatever position the country feels that service will be most valuable."

Roosevelt, then 58, had been dreaming of putting together a glorious force of a quarter million volunteers that he would lead to France to redeem American honor. It would be the Rough Riders, the heroes of the Spanish-American War, once more. He saw it as a unit of the best sort of men, black as well as white, gathered from around the country—and letters poured in to Sagamore Hill, his Long Island home, from as far away as Alaska, asking to join. It would take the fight to the Western Front as an expeditionary force while the regular Army was building up and preparing—if Congress would declare war. He acknowledged in private correspondence that, if the United States didn't enter the war, he might take the division to France after organizing it in Canada.

He kept the French ambassador, Jules Jusserand, informed of his plans. Jusserand was enthusiastic, not surprisingly, and conferred with Paris about the proposed division, though he had to keep the sensibilities of the White House in mind as well. On February 23 he closed a letter to TR this way: "Great events are ahead of us and Liberty shall conquer."

Reporters loved Roosevelt. They trailed him daily. He knew he could never get permission from Washington to organize his division if he dwelt too much on Wilson, who had promised to keep America out of the war. But his letters show what he was thinking.

"I am sick at heart at the shilly-shallyings of Wilson in this great crisis," Roosevelt wrote. "He is playing an utterly contemptible part." In the presence of danger, he said, the president was a coward.

America, the former Rough Rider believed, had gotten rich and soft. It was time for Americans to show what they were made of.

CHAPTER 2

"A Crime Against Civilization"

On August 6, 1914, the Great War was just nine days old. The Austro-Hungarian Empire declared war on Russia, and Serbia declared war on Germany. The French army was preparing to attack German-occupied Alsace the next morning. The German assault on Liège, Belgium, was in its third day. In Britain, the War Office gave notice that it was about to begin the requisition of horses. Europe's huge standing armies were mobilized and swinging into action.

In Washington, Ellen Axson Wilson died of what was then called Bright's disease—kidney failure. She was 54 years old, and her husband, the president of the United States, was adrift in his grief. Ellen—warm, loving, talented—had been his pillar, the woman who had helped him successfully surmount one crisis after another, from his years as Princeton's president, then New Jersey's governor, then candidate for the White House, and finally as the nation's chief executive.

"I cannot express to you the loveliness of life in [the Wilson] home," a cousin, Mary Hoyt, once wrote. "It was filled with so much kindness and courtesy, with so much devotion between Ellen and Cousin Woodrow, that the air always seemed to have a kind of sparkle."

It had been a marriage where "love [was] always law," Ellen's brother Stockton Axson wrote. With his family, Wilson could give his affection free rein, and his humor. He loved nonsense rhymes and atrocious puns. He and Ellen, a Georgia girl who had gone to New York to study at the Art Students League, were perfect complements to each other. They had three daughters, and Wilson was always happier to be home with his family than anywhere else, or with anyone else. His brother-in-law remembered times when Wilson would venture an opinion, and Ellen would exclaim, "Woodrow, you know you don't think that!" and he would smile and reply, "Madam, I was venturing to think that I thought that until I was corrected."

After she died, Wilson wondered out loud if she had been taken to spare her the spectacle of some awful calamity that might arise from the war in Europe. "He was the loneliest man in all the world," Axson wrote. "I can see the lonely figure of the president now, walking down the long hallway, the hair so much whitened in the few months."

Now Wilson told his closest adviser, Colonel Edward M. House—a wily, manipulative, scheming yet principled realist—that he doubted he could remain in the White House beyond the end of his first term. His gigantic achievements of 1913, which had come out of the most productive session of Congress up to that time and encompassed a sweeping array of domestic reforms, were behind him. What more could he do, especially now that Ellen was dead?

House saw an opportunity for Wilson, in a field to which the president had devoted little attention up to then—foreign affairs. But Wilson had a deep distaste for what he saw as the clash of grasping empires on Europe's battlefields. He hated the self-interest and ignorance that lay behind balance-of-power theories. Like most American idealists, he had become deeply disenchanted with America's own imperial fling against Spain in 1898. He was not a pacifist but held that war was brutal and generally unnecessary. He did send the Marines to occupy Haiti in 1915. But he genuinely believed in the possibility of building a new system of international relations based on natural harmony, justice and fair play.

Distracted by grief, the widower in the White House could not stir himself to do the hard work that would get others to his side, or to appeal to the self-interest of the warring nations.

Americans stood by in those early years. Jeannette Rankin was in a little town in Montana when the news came in 1914 that war had broken out. "We sat there and we couldn't believe it," she remembered years later. She felt foolish for not knowing it was coming, and then realized that no one in America did. Kings, kaisers, czars; royal courts and royal intrigue; the maneuverings of empires in Africa, the Balkans, East Asia—who'd want to get mixed up in that? The war was interesting, appalling—and very far away. Wilson asked Americans to be neutral in spirit as well as in deed. Americans who cared about the war were divided between those who were pro-German, or anti-British, and those who felt strong ties of history and culture to England. Hardly anyone was pro-Russian. But a very large number of Americans—probably the majority, at least according to the assessments of members of Congress in those prepolling years—didn't much care at all.

Some went to fight. James Rogers McConnell, a University of Virginia student, was so taken with the Allied cause that he joined the Lafayette Escadrille—a group of Americans flying for the French. He was shot down and killed in March 1917. Julier Chevalier, orphaned at the age of 17, looked after a shipload of mules from Texas bound for the Western Front. The English valued American mules because they were less skittish than horses when artillery was firing, and as a result mules had become one of America's largest agricultural exports. In 1914, 4,883 were exported; in 1916, 111,915 were, and that was to rise to more than 136,000 in 1917. With nothing to do once he got off the ship, Chevalier joined the Royal Artillery, and by 1917 he was a gunnery sergeant serving in a mud-mired stalemate against the Bulgarians on the Macedonian front.

From 1914 to 1917, the American economy boomed. The war was good for farmers, manufacturers and financiers (who could weather a stock market dive). The decline in the Russian wheat harvest—which happened because so many peasants had been drafted—sent world prices high enough that farmers were tempted to move out into the High Plains to grow wheat, where it had once been thought there wasn't enough rainfall to make a go of it. Exports of condensed milk increased more than sixfold during the first three years of the war. Cured beef and bacon exports nearly doubled. The amount of cotton sold abroad declined by a third, yet cotton growers saw their export earnings go up nearly 50 percent as the price went higher and higher.

American railroads employed 285,000 engineers, firemen, conductors and brakemen to run the country's trains; the average pay was a little over $1,300 a year. Engineers in passenger service made an average of 90 cents an hour; in freight service, just 60 cents. Between 1915 and 1916 the railroads' operating income was up 43 percent, on $3.7 billion in revenue. Orders for new locomotives increased from 1,491 in 1914 to 5,487 in 1916.

The Baltimore & Ohio Railroad opened what was said to be the world's largest export coal pier in March 1917, in the Curtis Bay section of Baltimore, to meet the demand for coal abroad, particularly in Europe. Costing $2.5 million, it could handle 40 hopper cars an hour, or 12 million tons of Appalachian coal a year. That same month, the Hell Gate Bridge across the East River opened for trains, finally enabling New Englanders to reach Washington and points south in one trip.

In early 1917 the French government had placed orders for 350 locomotives with Baldwin Locomotive Works, of Eddystone, Pennsylvania. The British government had ordered 705, from various American manufacturers. The Russians, 735.

Besides locomotives, Baldwin was making artillery shells for the Russians, at 25,000 a day. It was turning out 8,000 daily for the French. American wire companies were selling hundreds of thousands of miles of copper telephone wire to the Allies.

The money the war brought into the country caused such prosperity, unevenly distributed as it was, that it was all Detroit could do to turn out enough cars to meet demand. The movies flourished.

Over time, sentiment began to shift toward the Allies. All those billions of dollars' worth of munitions and locomotives and tins of beef and mules on the hoof were going principally to England and France, and almost none to Germany or Austria. What did get through to the Central Powers had to be disguised as cargo bound for Scandinavia, then transshipped to Germany, in order to bypass a British naval blockade that had been established in 1914 and strengthened in 1915. But it wasn't all about money. Tales of German atrocities that had once been dismissed as British propaganda started to make a dent in Americans' attitudes. By 1915, the Western Front had settled into a static war, and the British blockade of German ports didn't outrage most Americans as much as the German response, which was to deploy U-boats to start sinking ships indiscriminately. In May 1915, the *Lusitania* was sunk off the coast of Ireland, killing 128 Americans, and the shock was deep. Wilson sent several strong notes to Berlin; Roosevelt, naturally, didn't think they were strong enough, and began around this time to think the United States should join the war. Finally, the Germans backed off. But now a great number of Americans saw them as the villains of the conflict.

The war shook things up in ways no one could imagine, even thousands of miles away. In 1914, Tom and Marguerite Harrison had had no wants, no insecurities. He was a seemingly successful young businessman; she was the daughter of a steamship magnate. She had grown up in Catonsville, outside Baltimore, at a house called Ingleside, whose broad grounds swept down a hill toward the distant B&O railroad tracks. Marguerite had had a lively, adventurous childhood, went to the right sort of schools, and after an extended tour to Italy and Austria designed to end her scandalous affair with her landlady's son, she married, settled down, and had a son of her own, Thomas II. Propriety reasserted itself.

And yet, despite America's tremendous collective growth in prosperity and confidence, Harrison, approaching her late 30s, felt trapped—by expectations, by respectability, by her station in Baltimore society. Not long after the war broke out in Europe, her husband began acting unpredictably, given to rages and swept by sudden mood changes. Doctors at Johns Hopkins Hospital diagnosed him with a brain tumor. When he died in the fall of 1915, she discovered that his erratic judgment had left her debts amounting to $70,000, equivalent to well more than $1 million today.

At 36, Marguerite was a widow with a 13-year-old son and no money. Her social and professional life remained circumscribed; she had no business experience and few marketable skills. Faced with making ends meet while maintaining the forms of genteel society, she took in boarders, including newly hired government workers who were brought on to carry out Wilson's ambitious programs, and who commuted to Washington. She started a florist business with a friend, but barely made enough to cover the expenses. Fortunately, she knew Van Lear Black, the publisher of the *Sun*, the newspaper that served the elite of Baltimore and had gained a reputation far beyond Maryland with its strong coverage of Washington and national politics. The *Sun* had played an important role during the 1912 Democratic convention, held in Baltimore, when it had come out strongly, and persuasively, for Wilson. In 1910 its proprietors had started an afternoon paper, the *Evening Sun*, and, now, with the war on, it could take advantage of the transatlantic time difference and offer increasingly interested readers same-day war news. The paper was growing as never before, but it needed staff. Black was from one of Maryland's more distinguished merchant families, and that put him and Harrison in the same social circle. She got in touch, and he asked her to come in the following Monday.

Journalism had been almost entirely a man's pursuit, but that culture was starting to change, helped in some part by the war, and the prosperity it brought to newspapers. Even if they thought it didn't

concern them, people loved reading about it. The war was entertainment, and the newspapers were happy to oblige. That meant bigger
staffs, and a broader array of stories to try to keep some of these new
readers.

As it happened, the *Sun's* society pages needed help. Harrison
knew everyone who counted in the city, and though she had never
touched a typewriter before, the paper put her to work. She came
to savor the wisecracking in the newsroom, the energy, the noise,
the bravado, the adrenaline that flowed with a good story. Her $20
weekly salary didn't go far, but she impressed her bosses and soon
persuaded them to let her write about the theater and movies—and
to give her a raise. Now she was interviewing stars, and getting a
firsthand look at America's burgeoning film industry. Her brother-
in-law was Albert Ritchie, Maryland's attorney general, and he
arranged her appointment to the state's film board, which was set up
to review and censor any film that a distributor wished to exhibit. In
the early going, the film board had been concerned only with kisses
that lingered too long, or sinners who went unpunished, but as the
war drew closer, that was to change. Harrison's appointment with
her brother-in-law's help, while she kept her day job writing about
movies for the *Sun*, would strike people today as embodying at least
two separate conflicts of interest, but she unapologetically accepted
it. She said she needed the money. She didn't actually believe in censorship, she wrote years later, and in fact none of the other members
of the board did either. But the annual stipend of $2,500 was too
attractive to pass up.

Harrison had fond memories of her trip to Austria before the war,
when she was sent away to forget the landlady's son, and in 1914
she had knitted socks for Austrian soldiers fighting the Russians.
But she had been shocked by the sinking of the *Lusitania*. As 1916
became 1917, and she became more and more conversant with the
movies, she saw how the British were developing sophisticated films
that could sway American audiences. This was something new—

a direct appeal by a foreign power to Americans, and, with the ability of the movies to work on an emotional level, a visceral one as well. German propagandists, by contrast, never found a light touch and, she thought, probably did their cause more harm than good. H. L. Mencken, who spent time in Germany, and liked the Germans, agreed: "The more one observes their method of propaganda, the more one is amazed by their stupidity. They are wholly devoid of any sense of publicity. The English put it over them every time."

BY THE SUMMER of 1915, a year after the war started, President Wilson had love on his mind. He was courting Edith Galt, a Virginia widow, and she had swept him off his feet. In the mornings he found himself singing the hit song of 1911, "Oh, You Beautiful Doll." After first turning him down, Edith accepted his proposal of marriage. "She is wholly delightful and lovable," Wilson wrote to a friend. "She is known here for everything that is fine and for nothing that is touched with the small spirit of the society folk of the place." Edith, in turn, was struck by his "splendid, fearless eyes." On November 22, House complained in his diary that Wilson was so engrossed with his fiancée that he was neglecting business. In December they married.

Edith saw in him a "boylike simplicity" that was at odds with the formality of official life. She believed he was "starving for the bread of human companionship," and she was eager to provide it.

Both of Wilson's wives were southerners, as he was himself. Born in Virginia, he had grown up in Georgia and South Carolina. He was eight when the Civil War ended, and was the last American president to have been cared for by slaves as a child. In Staunton, Virginia, the Shenandoah Valley town where he was born, and where his father was the Presbyterian minister, the church leased three slaves from a local farmer to work for the family. As president, he ordered the segregation of the federal workforce.

The loving husband and father, the progressive president whose

far-reaching reforms—including the income tax and the establishment of the Federal Reserve—had been designed to broaden American prosperity to the middle classes, nurtured a deep belief in the
separation of the races. He was not a vicious race-baiter, though
some of the men around him were. Shortly after Woodrow and Edith
met, introduced by his cousin Helen Bones, they fell into a conversation about their childhoods, "and found many things in common
regarding the South, the poverty of all our own people after the Civil
War and the faithfulness of the old negroes to their masters and mis-
tresses."

In 1915, he enjoyed a White House showing of D. W. Griffith's
Birth of a Nation, about heroic Klansmen turning back Reconstruc-
tion. He chose it—the first film ever to be shown at the White
House—despite a protest campaign by the National Association for
the Advancement of Colored People and large demonstrations in
Boston by African-Americans.

Several decades of immigration from Europe had made men like
Wilson acutely sensitive to the standing of Anglo-Saxons in America.
The 1910 census found that one in seven Americans, 13.5 million
people, had been born abroad. In 1914 alone, 1.2 million immigrants
entered the United States. The Jim Crow laws that had proliferated
since the 1890s—and that Wilson supported—were a manifestation
of insecurity at the top. This was the era when it was felt that the old
Union and Confederate enemies must reunite in spirit as well as in
practice. Though he came by way of New Jersey, and his father was
from Ohio, Wilson was counted the first southerner to be elected
president since before the Civil War. But like the Democrats who followed him, he had an unwieldy coalition to keep together, one that
embraced both southern gentry and Irish cops, country lawyers and
Polish coal miners, Baptist preachers and Jewish dressmakers.

No good could come of the war in Europe, he was sure. Until 1915,
his secretary of state had been the pacifist William Jennings Bryan.
Wilson saw what was happening in Europe as threatening civiliza-

tion itself—and by that he meant, threatening the future of the white race. What, he wondered, would happen to the whites of the world if Europe destroyed itself? Japan, having tasted victory over Russia in a war in 1905, would surely be ascendant.

At a cabinet meeting, Wilson said "that he had been more and more impressed with the idea that 'white civilization' and its domination in the world rested largely on our ability to keep this country intact, as we would have to build up the nations ravaged by the war." That meant staying out of the war.

Wilson saw himself as a righteous man. Though he could deliberate over a policy decision, once his mind was made up there was no changing it and no hope that he might compromise. By his definition any opposition must be self-interested, mean and dissembling. This characteristic was to be his undoing at war's end.

Yet when it came to his own career moves, he showed he could evolve. By nature a conservative, he ran as a machine candidate for governor of New Jersey in 1912 against a liberal opponent. But as soon as he was elected—with an eye on a bigger prize—he denounced the political bosses who had put him in office, trumped them in the legislature, and became a standard-bearer for clean politics.

Edith Wilson didn't care for House, and was jealous of the way Wilson relied on him. She was quite certain he had tried to stop their marriage in 1915, thinking it would hurt his boss politically. House had a strong tendency to be sycophantic. When he wrote to Wilson, he always found something Wilson had done to be brilliant. But his advice wasn't off the mark and he was able to see the world without the righteousness that colored Wilson's perceptions. He went off to Europe to try to find a peace deal, largely in cahoots with the British, but nothing came of it. Eventually the president's wife pushed him out of the White House. He moved to New York, to a house on East 53rd Street, but kept up a steady correspondence from there, talked to someone in the State Department nearly every day, and was a go-between with British officials who were trying to work around the high-strung and ineffective British ambassador to Washington, Cecil Spring Rice. House thought Spring Rice, who once screamed insults at Secretary of State Robert Lansing, was unfit for the job.

In 1916, having decided he would seek a second term in the White House after all, Wilson backed a package of progressive reforms and won reelection on the slogan "He Kept Us Out of War." But by the end of that year, British gold reserves were nearly exhausted, and when the Germans renewed their submarine campaign, the shipment of gold bullion to New York as payment for war supplies became unacceptably risky in any case. If Britain fell, it would leave America without the protection of the Royal Navy and almost certainly spell an end to the wartime economic boom the United States had been enjoying. The U.S. ambassador to Great Britain, Walter Hines Page, wrote to Wilson in March 1917. "France and England must have a large enough credit in the United States to prevent the collapse of world trade and of the whole of European finance," he warned. "Perhaps our going to war is the only way in which our present prominent trade position can be maintained and a panic averted."

But Wilson, in his own mind, wouldn't be persuaded by appeals to self-interest. In fact, as 1917 began, it had seemed to House that Wilson was hardly engaging at all. The British, for their part, let House know that they were starting to grow impatient; if Americans believed in democracy the way they said they did, they needed to get in the fight. Frank Polk, the State Department counselor, told House that Wilson "thinks he is for peace almost at any price," but wasn't doing much about it.

But on January 3, House took the train to Washington—"as usual it was late"—and had dinner with the Wilsons at the White House. Afterward he and the president had a long conversation. First they talked about the appointment of federal judges, then the pros and cons of coordinating foreign relief societies. Wilson made fun of an overly melodramatic telegram that Ambassador Page had sent from London. Then he turned serious. House had sent him a memoran-

dum by Josiah Wedgwood, an English politician,
tic," by which he meant, too much of a fantasy. V
Was it because Wedgwood thought President
man who could lay down terms for ending the war? 1.
agreed with Wedgwood on that point, but didn't think the U..
ernment had the power, on its own, to resolve the fundamental problem of territories that had been conquered by the warring powers.

Here was an issue that would bedevil the world and obstruct
peaceful settlements for the next hundred years, and will probably
continue to do so for another hundred at least. In 1917, Germany
had occupied Belgium and part of northern France, and its forces
had moved east as far as Lithuania. Russia had moved on Austria in
Galicia; Austria had lost ground to Italy, but had taken all of Roma-
nia and most of Serbia. The British were driving toward the Ottoman Vilayet of Baghdad. Sorting that out would have been a gigantic
undertaking, and resolving issues of reparations, the return of refu-
gee populations, the sorting of mixed ethnic groups, could only add
to the complexity.

Wilson brushed that aside. He said he was thinking about making
a public statement outlining what the general terms of a settlement
should be, and proposing a mechanism by which the world could
secure itself against future war—a league of democratic nations. The
territorial disputes were secondary, he said. House was enthusiastic
about the idea, as well he might have been, because he had proposed
just that course to Wilson about a week earlier. Wilson, House noted
in his diary, had characteristically forgotten where the notion came
from, but since it was such a good idea, House was willing to let it go.

"You are playing with what the poker players term the blue chips,
and there is no use sitting by and letting great events swamp you,"
House told Wilson. "It is better to take matters into your own hands
and play the cards yourself."

The next day, House saw Lansing, who said that Wilson never
discussed foreign affairs with him. In fact, he said, Wilson rarely

ɔke much with anyone, and he said the president's mind was "a vacuum" when House wasn't in Washington. Later that day, William McAdoo, the secretary of the treasury and one of Wilson's sons-in-law, complained to House that the president was allowing things to drift aimlessly and was paying no attention to departmental business or to whether things "are well or badly done."

The colonel returned to the White House for lunch, where he prodded Wilson about American lack of preparedness in case it got into the war.

"There will be no war," Wilson replied. "This country does not intend to become involved in this war. We are the only one of the great White nations that is free from war today, and it would be a crime against civilization for us to go in."

A WEEK LATER, House again took the train from New York down to Washington. ("Strangely enough, the train was on time.") He went into Wilson's office and the president closed the door. He showed House a draft of the speech he was planning—he had shown it to no one else. House offered a few tweaks in language but was mightily pleased. Best of all, he thought, Wilson would clearly be aiming his address at the people of the warring nations, not at their governments.

This was when he realized that Wilson was determined to end the war. House believed that "the president at last seems to have awakened to the importance of the foreign situation," though he was fairly confident that hardly anyone else in Washington was aware of it. "The little circle close to the president seems to have dwindled down to the two of us, Mrs. Wilson and myself."

Time was of the essence. If a path toward peace couldn't be laid out in the next two months—by mid-March—the spring offensives on the Western and Eastern fronts would commence and Wilson's initiative would be dead. That would leave the European powers fighting for another year, with an even greater potential for unimaginable global catastrophe. The early months of 1917 offered an opportunity that might never come again. House knew from his conversations with European diplomats, on both sides, that a settlement was not out of the question. But neither side was eager to acknowledge that the millions of deaths and casualties up to that point had been in vain. It would be a tough sell, but maybe Wilson, of all men, had the moral presence to pull it off. He had until March.

ON JANUARY 15, back in New York, House received a visit from the German ambassador, Johann Heinrich Graf von Bernstorff, a "jaunty, carefree, man of the world" who, by 1917, had trimmed off the formerly upturned, Germanic corners of his mustache. Germany was open to arbitration to end the war, Bernstorff told him, and interested in a peace conference if Wilson would lead one. House thought this was the most important communication any belligerent had sent since the war began. Germany must be tottering, House thought. And France was clearly close to exhaustion. Russia, still under the czar, was uncertain. Great Britain—firm in its course and deaf to outside appeals—might be the biggest obstacle to peace.

Sir William Wiseman, who was House's best British contact, told him that the British people were sure that victory was close at hand. Captain Guy Gaunt, an Australian-born officer in the Royal Navy who ran an intelligence-gathering network in the United States, told House that if the United States didn't enter the war soon it shouldn't count on British help in the future if Germany and Japan teamed up against the Americans. "I told him we were not afraid of both Germany and Japan and did not need Great Britain's help."

On January 20, Wilson had his message ready. He had written out a final draft in longhand. Now he and Edith went to his study; she read it aloud to him, while he copied it on his typewriter. He had chosen to deliver his appeal two days later, in an address to the Senate. Wilson called for Europeans to lay down their arms: The only solution to the conflict, he said, was "Peace Without Victory." America was prepared to broker a solution and to impose its terms if necessary on the combatants.

It was a deadly serious proposal. It forced both sides to assess what Peace Without Victory would mean. What would be the political consequences at home, in Paris and Vienna and London and Berlin? How would the armies react?

In the days that followed, House told Wiseman that Wilson was convinced the war must end in a draw. The president worried out loud at a cabinet meeting about the consequences for Europe if Germany should be destroyed. Bryan, from his retirement in Miami, where he had moved to escape the licentiousness of his native Omaha, wrote a letter of fulsome praise for Wilson's "brave and timely appeal to the war-mad rulers of Europe." His proposal will place Wilson among the "Immortals," Bryan predicted.

The days ticked by. March, and the spring thaw, were approaching. "If Germany really wants peace she can get it," Wilson wrote to House. Then the British sent word, through House, that they didn't think much of Wilson's idea. By their calculation, the war was still winnable. A few days later, Bernstorff's peace feeler to House was overtaken by a decision that had been in the works for some time in Berlin. Germany answered Wilson's appeal by resuming unrestricted submarine warfare in the Atlantic.

CHAPTER 3

"Rich Earth, Rotting Leaves"

Years earlier, back when the czar was secure on his throne and Russia looked forward confidently to a century of progress—the Twentieth Century!—Princess Cantacuzène arrived at a small, private ball in St. Petersburg, at the palace of the Grand Duke Vladimir. It was the winter of 1901. A newlywed, and a foreigner, the princess was still finding her way in the upper reaches of Russian society, but she knew that a private ball was less formal than a public one. She chose one of her favorite dresses, with a deep square-cut neckline, and set off with great anticipation. The ball was everything she imagined it would be. And then who should arrive unexpectedly but Empress Alexandra herself. Grand Duchess Marie took the princess by the hand, and presented her to the monarch. In this one act she leaped over the dictates of protocol one usually had to endure before a presentation at court. It seemed she had arrived, or so she thought.

But afterward word went around that Alexandra had criticized the young princess to others for wearing the wrong dress to such a function, rather than one cut straight across, in a more dated Edwardian fashion that left the shoulders exposed. Other women had been in square-cut dresses, but only the princess had been presented to the empress. The princess tried to shrug off the gossip, but then came the reaction of Petersburg society. Well-bred women of noble standing rallied to her defense. She was, after all, not only new to the city, not only a foreigner, but an American, born Julia Grant 25 years earlier in the White House, where her grandfather was at that time president of the United States. It showed a lack of tact and perhaps even of breeding on the part of the empress to criticize her. At the next court ball, a far more formal affair, four or five young Russian women showed up in square-cut dresses, just to show their solidarity—and their disdain for their German-born monarch. "Gossip and bitterness followed, all of which seemed both amazing and unnecessary, but showed how the wind blew already in 1901," the young princess wrote years later.

Princess Cantacuzène (who also held the title of Countess Speransky, though everyone called her Joy) was a perceptive observer of the dying days of the Russian Empire. She was impressed by nobility and wealth, and not much of a republican, her background notwithstanding. The peasants on her husband's huge estate in the Ukraine struck her as loyal, conscientious, superstitious, and vaguely comical salt-of-the-earth figures who needed someone of intelligence and strength to guide them. They were, at least, not drunkards like the riffraff in the nearby villages.

Joy's father, Frederick Grant, had played a role in Republican politics in New York City, and before she married, she had met both Elihu Root, then a senator, and Theodore Roosevelt, the city's police commissioner, at her parents' dinner table. "Amusing, interesting, with a quick, warm sympathy and a charm innate, Roosevelt was the keenest, the most intense and urgent personality imaginable." She remembered how rapidly he spoke, and how persuasively.

She and Mikhail Cantacuzène, a dashing prince whose name betrayed a Romanian family background, decided a few weeks after they met, in Italy, that they would marry. Up until then she had greatly enjoyed flirting with young men but hadn't been serious about any of them. The wedding took place at the Episcopal Church in Newport, Rhode Island, with a Russian priest co-officiating, and from there they sailed to Europe on a private yacht.

When they arrived at Bouromka, the Cantacuzène-Speransky estate, after a long journey by carriage from the nearest train station, 70 versts away, all the servants turned out to meet them, a band played, ceremonial bread and salt were offered. She was lucky, she thought, to have come from a seaside house on the Jersey Shore and a brownstone in mid-Manhattan, and not to have preconceived ideas about the running of a vast Russian estate. Her mother-in-law was French, which made things a little easier.

There were servants who spent all day pumping and carrying water. Two men worked full-time doing nothing but polishing and filling kerosene lamps. Others devoted themselves, on their knees, to the application of beeswax to the intricately inlaid wooden floors. Once, when she slipped, a servant said the problem was with the American shoes she wore, not the Russian wax.

She spent the winter months in St. Petersburg, and the long drowsy summers in the Ukraine, which seemed to sum up her life's destiny. She had a son and two daughters. They were Prince Mikhail, Princess Bertha and Princess Zinaida. She called them Mike, Bertha and Ida.

A memory from childhood haunted her. "I recall suddenly being waked up and dressed in the night on a train which moved slowly amid shouting crowds. . . . Torches, quantities of them, burned, flared up and smoked, then flickered down, throwing changing lights on faces which to my child's imagination looked wild with excitement." She was lifted into a carriage as jostling men and women reached out. Terrified by the noise and the emotion of the crowd, she shrieked and clung to her mother.

It was in Colorado, and she was with her grandparents as they were making a triumphant tour of America, home from a year in Europe after grandfather Ulysses' retirement from the presidency. This crowd was roaring with approval for the general who had saved their nation at its moment of peril, but it was frightening and bewildering to a little girl. The next time she saw such a mob was nearly forty years later, in disintegrating Russia, and it wasn't a friendly one.

LIVING AT HIS club at 31 Bolshaya Morskaya in Petrograd, not far from Palace Square with its towering granite monument to Alexander I, whose army had stopped Napoleon and then marched across Europe to France a century before, Roman Rosen was in deep dismay. He was not naturally an optimistic man—being too much of a clear-eyed realist, and a witness to decades of Russian bungling—but in the late winter of 1917 the hopelessness of his country's position was glaringly obvious. Nicholas II had gone to the front, to take personal command of the army. It was a foolish, self-defeating move.

Rosen turned 70 on February 24; he was a slight man, with a touch of arthritis in his shoulders. His Van Dyke beard had turned white, but the mustache above it remained dark, and the effect was to make him appear permanently disapproving. Rosen was a conservative, a baron from the Baltic nobility, a believer in government service. He felt that the great Russian bureaucracy, for all its manifest shortcomings, took too much of the blame for the country's condition, considering the stupidity of the reactionary circle around the czar and the ludicrous inability of the reformers and the intelligentsia to connect with the reality of the country they were living in.

Rosen had been one of the few prominent Russians to argue against going to war in 1914. He and his colleague, Sergius Witte, had been so vocal in their pessimism that they had been accused of being pro-German, which was hardly the case. But neither man had seen what Russia stood to gain from picking a fight with Germany or Austria. Russia's future happiness and prosperity, Rosen argued, lay to the east, in the vast landscape of Siberia and Central Asia. But following the first Russian Revolution—the failed one of 1905—the czarist regime had embarked on a course of Russification of the empire's many nationalities, and as a corollary in foreign policy, it had begun to emphasize a notion that has reemerged in our own time—that Russia was the protector of all Slavs. In this way Nicholas II's government succeeded both in alienating Russia's minorities and in alarming its neighbors—notably, Austria-Hungary, home to millions of Slavs, and, by extension, Germany. Rosen argued that Russia had no natural source of conflict with either, territorial or otherwise. The hostility to the Central Powers had led Russia into an alliance with France, which badly wanted to recapture the lost provinces of Alsace and Lorraine. This alliance made perfect sense from Paris's point of view; none at all from St. Petersburg's. Second, Rosen pointed to a perhaps deeper problem, and one that dogs Russia (and its neighbors) to this day. Simply put, most Slavs—Poles, Ukrainians, Slovaks, Bulgarians—didn't want Russian protection. A great many saw Russia as a country to be resisted, not one to join in an embrace.

But Rosen was from the Baltics, and Witte was of Dutch descent, a commoner who had risen through the ranks of the state railway system and whose wife had a Jewish background, so they were easily ignored. Perhaps the only ethnic Russian close to the court who opposed the war was the mad monk, Grigori Rasputin, and even he was disregarded in the summer of 1914, when it was said that 100,000 Russians knelt in obeisance to their czar in Palace Square, expunging forever the humiliation he had suffered in the 1905 uprising.

In no sense did the baron feel any satisfaction over the disasters that visited the Russian army in 1915 and 1916. But he was not blind to the catastrophe of the war, or to the despair that it was bringing down upon the Russian people. Yet Witte had died in 1915, and Rasputin had been murdered in December of 1916, so Rosen's was a lonely voice. In the fall he was dropped from the Imperial Council, an advisory body composed of members of the nobility.

He had had two glimmers of hope that winter. The first was in December, when Germany announced that it would be prepared to enter into peace negotiations, under broadly conciliatory terms. But, as Rosen had expected, the Allies replied disdainfully that Germany wasn't serious. The Russian military argued that the great sacrifices its men had suffered up to that point—more than a million dead— required the nation to push on to total victory to redeem the loss. The government announced the call-up of another few million men who would be drawn from villages already hard-pressed because of earlier conscriptions to provide the food the nation needed. Then, in a decision that Rosen called "insane," the government announced its war aims, including the establishment of a free Poland (the part that had previously been under German and Austrian control) and the seizure of the Bosporus from the Ottoman Empire so that Russia would have access to the Mediterranean.

"That the government could have imagined for a moment that the people would be roused to any degree of enthusiasm by the prospect of having to fight for the potential conquest of Constantinople and the Straits, or the acquisition of Posen and Galicia for the benefit of Poland, merely shows how hopelessly unbridgeable is the gulf of mutual noncomprehension which in Russia separates the thin upper crust from the bulk of the nation," Rosen wrote. The announcement, he pointed out, also helped to stiffen German, Austrian and Turkish resolve against the Russians.

The German feeler went nowhere, but a second reason for hope arrived in January, when Wilson made his call for Peace Without Victory. This was exactly the solution that Rosen wanted to see, and he had good reasons for thinking it might happen, because he had seen American peacemaking before, at close hand, and was a believer.

It was twelve years earlier, in the summer of 1905, when he had been named Russian ambassador to the United States and had taken up his post not in Washington but just outside Portsmouth, New Hampshire. The Russian navy had been utterly crushed in a war with Japan—an entire fleet was lost in the Battle of Tsushima Strait. The Russian army was pushed back in China. Russian generals had derided the Japanese—they weren't white Europeans, after all—but the Japanese had whipped them.

Having made careful inquiries, President Theodore Roosevelt realized that Japan had met its war aims and had no intention of pressing onward into Russia, so he invited both sides to a peace conference. Many's the time Rosen must have thought back to that parley by the sea, in the rainy New England summer of '05. Then, thanks to the good graces of the United States—neutral, powerful and competent, above all—Russia had been brought back from the brink. President Roosevelt had been scrupulously fair (even though one of the Japanese negotiators had been a friend of TR's when they were students at Harvard together), and that was much appreciated. When representatives of the two sides met for the first time, it was on the presidential yacht, the *Mayflower*, moored in Oyster Bay by the Roosevelt summer house. They ate a stand-up buffet luncheon on board, so that there could be no argument or offense over a seating arrangement.

From there, the delegations proceeded by sea to New Hampshire, though because Sergius Witte, the co-leader of the Russian delegation, was prone to seasickness, he went ashore in Newport and took a train the rest of the way. Another Russian diplomat taking part was the prim and high-strung Konstantin Nabokov, whose nephew, Vladimir, was 6 years old and spending the summer with his parents and siblings on a family estate 50 miles south of St. Petersburg.* The actual talks took place on an island off Kittery, Maine, connected by a bridge to the mainland. Both sides lived at the Wentworth Hotel, in New Castle, New Hampshire, a grand old summer place that still stands. When they wanted to get away, the Russians would leave for Magnolia, next to Manchester, Massachusetts, where Rosen had rented a house.

---

* Konstantin Nabokov is pictured in the mural that graces the main gallery of the American Museum of Natural History, along with two Japanese delegates to Portsmouth and Theodore Roosevelt.

Roosevelt had extended the invitation to the peace talks after a quick conference with a British diplomat in St. Petersburg, an old friend of the president's, who traveled across the ocean for a one-day meeting in New York and then returned to Europe on the same ship that had brought him. Russia was ready to parley, Roosevelt heard, and that was good news for the Americans. Russia and the United States had no interests in conflict, and in fact had enjoyed good relations since at least the time of the Civil War, when, alone among the European powers, Russia backed the Union side. But America and Japan faced a difficult future, each looking for supremacy in the Pacific. The U.S. victory over the Spanish at Manila in 1898 had galvanized Tokyo. Now the huge victories of the Japanese over the Russians had Washington worried.

Japan came to the table with the upper hand militarily. But the Russians gradually won over the American press, and through it the public. Rosen finally confronted one reporter and asked if he was getting favorable coverage because he was white, to which the reporter allowed that that was probably so.

The talks lasted a little more than a month, and at the end everyone agreed that the Russians had acted far more ably at the negotiating table than they had on the battlefield. There was no explicit indemnity. Tokyo had won control of half of Sakhalin Island, and was given a free hand in Korea. That had been the Japanese war aim, and, once achieved, the negotiators from Tokyo were persuaded that there was no need to push Russia to the wall.

Rosen and Witte then made a short but happy tour of the Northeast. They stayed at the St. Regis Hotel in New York, the clangorous metropolis, just slightly older than St. Petersburg, and like the Russian capital a window of sorts to Europe, but utterly different in so many ways—boisterous, on the make, a city of action rather than protocol. They sped in a white car though Central Park, and Witte enjoyed it so much he insisted they do it again, faster. This time the cops tried to stop the party, but detectives following behind waved them off. Witte wanted to see Columbia University and the Tombs, the big jail downtown. He was surprised to find there were no political prisoners. They took J. P. Morgan's yacht, the *Corsair*, to West Point; Witte only agreed to go by boat after he was assured there were no waves on the Hudson. There (surely not by accident) they ran into the Japanese delegates again, in a brief but polite encounter. Roosevelt had them out to Oyster Bay for dinner, and it was a warm and casual evening. Because Witte didn't speak English, the president carried on the conversation all night in French.

From Oyster Bay they went directly to Washington, where they visited Mount Vernon. Then Witte returned to Russia and Rosen took up his regular duties as the new ambassador of Czar Nicholas II to the great American republic.

Rosen became a popular fixture in Washington's diplomatic and social scene, and a great admirer of American ways, though he thought they could never be translated to his own country. He was steadfast in his respect and affection for Roosevelt.

Could Wilson now pull off the same feat? Rosen had faith in America, and, with its power and wealth, he believed it could force a solution on Europe. In January, Wilson was of a very similar mind. But Rosen, who had returned to Russia in 1911, may not have realized how much the United States had changed since he had been there. There was a more aggressive spirit in the country; Roosevelt himself believed that joining the war was America's only honorable course.

As January turned to February, the Germans renewed their submarine warfare and none of the belligerent powers made any move to take up Wilson's proposal. Rosen, his mood bleak, later recalled a prophecy about the effects of the world war, made a year or so earlier by Leon Trotsky, and the old loyal diplomat saw a reflection of his own thinking in the Marxist revolutionary's phrases:

> The hammer has been wrung from the hands of the worker and
> replaced by the sword. The worker, bound hand and foot by the

apparatus of the capitalist economic system, is suddenly torn away from all this and is taught to put collective interests higher than his domestic happiness, than his very life. With the arms made by himself in his hands, the worker is placed in a situation where the political fate of the State rests directly on him. . . . The static attitude of mind gives way to the dynamic. Heavy artillery thunders the idea into his head that in cases where it is impossible to go around an obstacle, the possibility remains of smashing it. Almost the whole adult male population has been put through this school of war, fearful in its social realism, that is creating a new human type.

THE WAR HAD dragged on for thirty months, but in retrospect two-and-a-half years isn't such a long time for an entire way of life to disappear. For Baron Rosen, whose life in service to the czarist system went back to the 1860s, it must have seemed as fast as an automobile wreck. One bad turn, one moment of inattention, one neglectful oversight as to the condition of the car—and the thing was beyond repair, its passengers bloody and battered, its driver mortally injured.

The baron's lodgings, on Bolshaya Morskaya, were in a minimally ornamented classical building, in the heart of prewar St. Petersburg. A short stroll to the west, past the Astoria Hotel and the looming St. Isaac's Church, with its huge dome and interior columns of malachite, was a pink Italianate house, four stories tall, where young Vladimir Nabokov was born and raised. Russian city houses face the street lengthwise, perpendicular to the way an American rowhouse is built. In back, typically, were annexes, sheds, stables—and by the second decade of the twentieth century, occasional garages. The placement brings in plenty of light through the windows, and in the high latitudes of St. Petersburg, with the white nights of June, when it never really gets dark, there's no escaping it. But from November into February, the sun hangs low in the sky, and only briefly at that, and the uncompromising clouds coming in from the Baltic make everything even grayer and darker.

Along Bolshaya Morskaya, in the stretch between Palace Square and the Mariinsky Theater, a pedestrian in, say, 1913, the 300th anniversary of the Romanovs' ascent to the throne, would pass the Frantsiya Hotel, with its restaurant the Maly Yaroslavets; a French bakery with croissants and chaussons "the same as one would see in Paris"; Bolin's, a jewelry store with a doorman out front; a tobacconist's, "where messengers stood in their red, peaked caps"; then a factory that made bentwood furniture. Across Nevsky Prospekt sat a café; an English shop specializing in soap, fruitcakes, playing cards, smelling salts, striped blazers and talcum-white tennis balls ("all sorts of snug, mellow things"); a French florist that brought in flowers from Nice; a cigar shop; an art supply store and the Kyuba restaurant, said to be the only restaurant where a "respectable lady could go without an escort."

In 1913 the streetlamps, suspended overhead down the middle of Bolshaya Morskaya, were decorated with the illuminated monogram of the czar, and in the winter the colored lights were reflected in the snow-covered cornices. Down the avenues, brightly painted red and yellow streetcars were replacing the drab, blue-gray horse-drawn cars of the previous century. The conductor had a bell to signal the motorman, and the motorman rang a big brass clangy bell to warn pedestrians away. The open platforms were a fine place to ride in the summer.

Along the canals, young men in birch-bark shoes called *lapti* poled barges laden with firewood or bricks. Out on the choppy, silvery Neva River, boats from the far north mingled with pleasure steamers bound for the Gulf of Finland. Sometimes the royal yacht, the *Shtandart*, would be tied up on the embankment by the drafty Winter Palace, which was painted a gloomy red in those days, and was usually dark because Alexandra hated living there so much.

On Nevsky itself, there were Treumann's, a stationery shop, and three movie theaters, the Parisiana, the Soleil and the Picadilly, where the ushers wore powdered wigs. Toy shops sold "American inhabitants," in which little glass figures rode up and down in glass tubes filled with colored liquid to emulate the elevators and working life in the New World's skyscrapers. Petersburg had (and has) a height limit, making it a city of vistas, and five-story walkups. The most striking modern building on Nevsky in 1913 was the Singer Building (or Zinger, as it was known in Russian), home to the sewing machine company as well as satellite offices of the U.S. embassy, an exuberant, glassy, curvy, bronzy manifestation of the essence of Art Nouveau, a building where form trumped function.

Newsboys shouted out the latest headlines. Smoke drifted through the streets and blew across rooftops, from tiled stoves and kitchen ranges and factory chimneys and the funnels of steamships. In every home, and every office, and every railroad car, a samovar was kept stoked with wood or coal to keep water hot for tea. "Tens of thousands of horses, wafting the warmth of their bodies over passersby, strange though it may seem, made the air of the city less 'official' . . . less indifferent towards man," as one memoirist remembered.

At the great blue Mariinsky Theater, the dancer Mathilde Kschessinska, who was Nicholas's former mistress, "would fly onto the stage in diamonds." And, mirroring her in the audience, in a way, sat "rows of ladies waving fans in an attempt to make the diamonds on their deep décolletages glitter."

Society stayed out late in those years before the war; memory records that no one left the cabarets for home until three o'clock at the earliest, leaving the drivers of private sleighs to their own devices to try to keep warm on bitter cold winter nights.* A place called the

---

* One memory in particular was that of Dmitry S. Likhachev, born in 1907 and the author of *Reflections on the Russian Soul*. As a young boy, he once saw the czarevich, the hemophiliac heir to the throne, pass by on a street in St. Petersburg. He spent time in the gulag in the 1920s, and survived the Nazi siege of Leningrad, eventually becoming Russia's leading cultural historian. Toward the end of his life he was a special adviser to President Boris N. Yeltsin. I was fortunate to have the chance to interview him over the course of two days in 1998. He died in 1999 at the age of 92.

Stray Dog was a favorite. The poet Anna Akhmatova could often be found there. She and her husband, Nikolai Gumilev, were leading poets of the late "Silver Age," when Russian literature and art embraced modernist themes and there was a flowering of creativity in St. Petersburg.

IN THE COUNTRYSIDE, too, there had been so many reasons for optimism in the years before the war. Harvests were good; conscientious landowners saw themselves as stewards of the fields, villages and villagers on their often vast estates. Nabokov remembered sitting at the dining room table at his family's estate, and watching his father appear in the window once, twice, three times, horizontal, unsupported in the air, tossed high by villagers happy with some decision he had rendered. Reforms aimed to create, at some future point, a prosperous farmer class in Russia where none had ever existed.

In the woods stretching away from the fields, rainy weather would bring out that mushroom aroma "which makes a Russian's nostrils dilate—a dark, dank, satisfying blend of damp moss, rich earth, rotting leaves."

Russia's upper classes often spoke their own language badly, relying on clichés and folksy sayings they picked up from the servants. Nabokov and his brother learned to read and write in English before they did so in Russian. They were told not to become familiar with the peasants on the estate. "Through the window one could see kerchiefed peasant girls weeding a garden path on their hands and knees or gently raking the sun-mottled sand. (The happy days when they would be cleaning streets and digging canals for the State were still beyond the horizon.)"

That seeming peacetime contentment masked complex layers of disgruntlement, anger and alienation. Factory workers, most fresh from the villages, believed they were abused by overwork and low pay. The country's non-Russian minorities felt oppressed by the czar's Russification program, especially the Poles and the Jews, who suffered one pogrom after another—but also Finns and even Ukrainians. The meddlesome, intrusive mismanagement by the army of bureaucrats stifled initiative and acted as a brake on progress. Russia was painfully backward, a "rather appalling country." Radical socialists dreamed of a violent overthrow of the system, and worked diligently toward that end—though two of their most compelling thinkers, Leon Trotsky and Vladimir Lenin, were abroad, and a third, Josef Stalin, spent much of his time in internal exile in Siberia.

Nabokov's father—also Vladimir—had spent three months in solitary confinement in the still-notorious Kresty Prison in St. Petersburg because he supported the aims of the 1905 uprising. A committed liberal, he edited an influential opposition newspaper, *Rech*, and won a seat in the Duma in 1916 as a member of the Constitutional Democrats, or Kadets. He argued eloquently for the creation of a true constitutional system, a democracy, even if the only way to achieve it was through revolution. His son would chafe years later when Americans would casually remark that the czarist system was no better than the one that replaced it—there was no liberal opposition in Soviet Leningrad.

Only radicals and conservatives understood that a Russian revolution would not be a genteel affair. Baron Rosen would have agreed with Nabokov's grandmother; she could not understand why his father, "who, she knew, thoroughly appreciated all the pleasures of great wealth, could jeopardize its enjoyment by becoming a Liberal, thus helping to bring on a revolution that would, in the long run, as she correctly foresaw, leave him a pauper."

RUSSIA'S ARTISTS AND the larger number of intellectuals had welcomed the war when it came; they thought it would forge a newer, stronger country. The poet Gumilev had eagerly signed up for a cavalry regiment. His marriage with Akhmatova disintegrated soon after.

The war brought out Russia's worst characteristics: stubborn stupidity at the top; disregard for the welfare of its soldiers or its subjects; incompetence and thorough mismanagement; failure on the field of battle.

Morale drooped and sagged. Food in the cities started to become scarce, because men had been conscripted out of the farming villages and the railroads had fallen into total disarray through negligence, overuse, and lack of foresight. Petrograd—renamed in 1914 to give it a more Russian, less Germanic feel—was packed with refugees from the war zone in the Baltic provinces. Soldiers could ride for free on the now fading red and yellow trams, and they packed in so tight that it could be next to impossible to get aboard. Some passengers clung to the thick cable, the "sausage," that connected the two cars of each little pokey train. The bright colors of the city turned to gray.

Half the poets of the Silver Age fled. Gumilev had helped to organize a group called the Acmeists, including Osip Mandelstam, who may have had an affair with Akhmatova (she said it was a deep friendship). Now the Acmeists and Dadaists were eager to get away from the war, and they started to congregate in Tiflis, the capital of the province of Georgia, away down south in the Caucasus. Akhmatova stayed. She began to write less mannered verses, to craft instead a poetry that spoke for all of Russia in its trauma.

In 1916 the war was costing Russia 40 million rubles a day. More than a quarter of the country's blast furnaces had been forced to shut down because of disruptions in transportation. Mountains of coal grew where they weren't needed as the railroads approached collapse. They were short of at least 80,000 cars and 2,000 locomotives.

Liberal politicians in the Duma despaired, as Rosen did, but from a wholly different perspective. They believed not that the war was misbegotten, but that the czarist government was woefully lacking in its ability to direct the war effort. Vasily Maklakov, a member of the Kadet Party, compared Russia to a car careening down a mountain road with an incompetent driver at the wheel. Trying to seize control of the car, he said, seemed even more dangerous than passively hoping for the best. In November 1916, Pavel Milyukov, a leading liberal, delivered a lacerating speech in the Duma, cataloging Russia's setbacks and reversals in the war, and asking: Was this stupidity, or was this treason? The speech was a sensation. Even some of the Romanov grand princes lent an ear to the calls for change.

Alexander Guchkov, a conservative colleague, and others began talking indiscreetly about the need for a palace coup. They wanted to limit the czar's power, or take it from him, not to get out of the war but to push it harder. They recognized that the ranks of the army, filled with peasant conscripts, would be very unlikely to turn against their monarch. But the officer corps, filled now with former civilians who were not bound by military small-mindedness, might be willing to act for the good of the country.

But the Duma had no power. "Words are our currency," admitted Milyukov. Someone had to act. The Duma leaders declined to take the initiative. So did the grand princes. So did the leftists, who believed the time was not ripe for the kind of revolution they wanted.

"A revolutionary mood existed and people talked about it, but no one showed himself to be resolute. The conspiratorial center was little more than salon gossip," wrote one disappointed liberal, A. F. Iziumov.

"Russia was not so much war-weary," an English correspondent wrote, "as discouraged by the blind or willful stupidity of her leaders." The well-to-do hired extra servants just to stand in lines for them, at bakeries and food shops. To forestall speculation, the government prohibited the transport of food from one province to another without permission; it made the scarcity worse. Two-thirds of the cattle driven to the front to feed the troops died along the way. Scurvy became common among the soldiers.

A loaf of rye bread went from 2 kopeks to 17; potatoes from 8 to 80 per pound. Russia had stopped exporting foodstuffs—once its main source of foreign exchange—but still had little available at home. It had stopped importing coal, so firewood was diverted to use in factories, making it virtually unattainable for the stoves in Petrograd's homes and apartments. Yet as the city grew colder, and hungrier, residents couldn't help noticing that there seemed to be more luxurious motorcars on the streets than ever. Tales of profiteering were rife, if unprovable. Strikes hit one workplace after another. There was a widespread belief in the winter of 1917 that something had to give.

CHAPTER 4

"You Fellows Are In for It"

H. L. Mencken grabbed a couple of leberwursts at the officers' mess in a place called Novo Alexandrovsk, and stuffed
them in his pocket. He was outside Vilna, in Lithuania,
where he had been visiting Germany's Eastern Front. Those were
Russians on the other side of No Man's Land.

Mencken had taken a leave from his job as editor of the *Smart
Set*—which as a point of principle had published nothing about the
European conflict since its onset in 1914—so that he could go off
to be a war correspondent for his old paper, the *Baltimore Sun*. Of
German descent himself, he was entirely sympathetic to the Central
Powers. He had been to Germany twice in peacetime, and now, at the
age of 36, he wanted to see what the war looked like. It was dreary
and sobering, and he was surprised to see how run-down the country was. It was also cold, and food was scarce.

Mencken had wangled a trip to the front, hadn't seen much, was
not overly inspired to write about it, and now was heading back to
Berlin. "Dull, dismal stuff," he jotted in his diary—though he later
wrote fondly about helping German fliers down their daily ration
of French champagne and English porter, "both stolen goods, and
hence extra sweet." When not in a trench he had stayed in a log

house, built for officers by Russian prisoners. The wursts, prepared at an army slaughterhouse, were better than anything he'd likely find in the shops, and he took a few extra with him to give to others in the small corps of American correspondents.

Late on the night of January 31, Mencken got back to his room at the Adlon Hotel in Berlin, "tired, rheumatic and half-frozen." The next morning he woke and walked over to see Raymond Swing, of the *Chicago Daily News*, at his office on Unter den Linden. Mencken had borrowed a heavy overcoat and some leather leggings from Swing for his trip to Lithuania and now was bringing them back along with a leberwurst. He found Swing "hammering a typewriter." There was big news. "Pack your bags!" said Swing. "The jig is up."

Across the top of the front page of the *Tageblatt*, Mencken, though he claimed to be pretty bad at German, could see "the long-awaited, hat-in-the-ring-throwing, much-pother-through-the-world-upstirring headline: *Verkündung des uneingeschränkten U-Boot-Krieges!*" It meant: Proclamation of unrestrained U-boat war. "The adjective used to be *rücksichtlos*, which is to say, reckless. Lately it has been *vershärften*: sharpened. Now it is *uneingeschränkten*: unrestrained, unlimited, fast and loose, without benefit of clergy, knock 'em down and drag 'em out. But whatever the term used to designate it, the thing itself remains, and out of that thing itself, unless I lose my guess, a lot of trouble is about to arise."

The Germans had gone back to their pre-*Lusitania* policy, declaring that any ships in a zone along the Atlantic coasts of Britain and France, as well as a large slice of the Mediterranean, were legitimate targets for their submarines. Mencken, shaking off the fatigue of his trip to see the trenches, thought it would drag the United States into the war for sure, and sooner rather than later. "I can see no other way out," he wrote in his diary. "The day of notes, protests, promises and moral exhortations is over. There remains only a stand-up fight."

Other correspondents were less certain, some even optimistic that the German move could hasten an end to the war. Mencken won-

dered if he would end up in a civilian detention camp. He went over
to the Foreign Office, on Wilhelmstrasse, and there found the press
officer for foreign correspondents, known to everyone simply as Dr.
Roediger. He was a smooth-shaven Oxford graduate, and American
newspaper reporters banged on the door of his dingy office day in
and day out, looking for information, help with the bureaucracy,
advice and consolation.

"What do you expect?" Mencken asked him.

"Expect? We don't expect. We merely wait," Roediger replied.

THE GERMAN STRATEGY, pushed by the military leaders Paul von
Hindenburg and Erich Ludendorff, was based on a straightforward
calculation: With the British blockade imposing severe if scattered
shortages in Germany, a renewal of unrestricted submarine warfare
could starve Britain and force it to seek a truce; France and Russia
would be sure to go along. It risked war with the United States and
other neutral countries, but America had a skeleton army and not
much more of a navy, and the betting was that Britain would be out
before the Americans could make a difference. The Germans saw
it as an attack on Britain, not on the United States. They had no
particular quarrel with the Americans, and some officials said they
hoped the Americans would see it that way, too, and stay out. But the
Germans weren't blind, and understood the risk they were taking;
they just thought it was a gamble that made sense.

The Foreign Office had been opposed, but lost the argument. It
wasn't exactly a secret: As early as January 2, Lansing had passed on
to Wilson a warning about a new "reckless" U-boat campaign. Later
messages even pinpointed the timing, and by late January the idea
came up in Reichstag debates. The decision to go forward, though
unannounced at the time, was made while Mencken was at the front,
in the third week of January—that is, before Wilson had even made
his peace appeal. In New York, Bernstorff and House had had another
meeting before the announcement, and it was clear that the German

attitude was hardening. The ambassador told House that Germany would insist on peace now, or the question would have to wait until the fall. House said the Allies would be uninterested in peace talks by fall, because they would doubt that Germany could survive through another winter. Bernstorff warned him that Germany would resume its submarine campaign in the spring, but House understood that to mean that Germany would be targeting ships of the Allies, as it had been doing all along.

Still, Bernstorff had hopes that the worst could be avoided. He wrote to Arthur Zimmermann, the foreign minister, in Berlin: "If submarine warfare is now begun without further ado, the President will take this as a slap in the face and war with the United States cannot be avoided. . . . In my view the end of the war will be unforeseeable, because—despite all that can be said to the contrary—the power and resources of the United States are very great."

If, on the other hand, Germany accepted Wilson's proposal for a peace conference, and nothing came of it because of the obstinacy of the Allies, it would be hard for the United States to consider war with Germany, he said.

BERNSTORFF'S NOTE WAS received in Berlin on January 27. Three days later Zimmermann met with James Gerard, the U.S. ambassador, to inform him of the U-boat policy. The foreign office, Zimmermann said, had warned against it, but the military and naval people had argued that it was Germany's last chance—the country couldn't hold out another year.

Gerard described the conversation in a note to Lansing and added his own comments: "There is no doubt but that Germany believes that Americans are a fat, rich race without a sense of honor and ready to stand for anything in order to keep out of war. . . . The Germans think and newspapers have published that the President's peace moves are inspired by fear only."

The public announcement came on February 1. That morning, in

Washington, Colonel House went to the White House to have breakfast with Wilson. "The President was sad and depressed. . . . We had
every reason to believe that within a month the belligerents would be
talking peace. . . . The President said he felt as if the world had suddenly reversed itself. . . . The President was insistent he would not
allow it to lead to war if it could possibly be avoided. He reiterated his
belief that it would be a crime for this Government to involve itself in
the war to such an extent as to make it impossible to save Europe afterward. He spoke of Germany as 'a madman that should be curbed.' I
asked if he thought it fair to the Allies to ask them to do the curbing
without doing our share. He noticeably winced at this."

Too upset to play golf, he and House shot some pool instead. The
following day, a Friday, Lansing spoke up at a cabinet meeting and
said the best outcome would be for the Allies and the small democracies to band together and defeat German militarism. Wilson shocked
some of those at the table. "I am not so sure of that," he said. Maybe
greater justice would be done if the war ended in a draw.

TWO DAYS LATER, Wilson decided to break off relations and send
Bernstorff home. That meant Gerard would be heading back to the
United States, too, and Mencken and the other Americans had to
figure out what to do. The natural thirst to beat the competition that
newspaper reporters thrive on typically tends to diminish abroad,
and it can vanish altogether in tight situations like the one that was
likely to develop in wartime Germany. They conferred with each
other—stay, or go? If they chose to go, how? Mencken liked Berlin,
and he was sympathetic to the Germans' arguments, but he was,
after all, an American, and not a very happy one.

"The cold here is intense," he wrote on February 1. "It is positively
painful to walk down Unter den Linden. Soldiers, schoolboys, old
men, women and even girls are digging away at the frozen snow."
He trudged through the "frozen and cheerless" city, unable most of
the time to find a cab. Coal was in short supply, as were wagons,

and the authorities decided to allow Berliners to go to the railyards to collect what they could and carry it home themselves. The city, formerly "so full of gaudy nightlife, is as quiet as Blue Boston." The cafés were still open, though the food was unappetizing. In the evening he witnessed "the usual crowds, the usual stolidity, the usual grim determination to get the prescribed dose of recreation, war or no war." Elephants from the zoo were drafted to pull sledges through the streets. Elevators were shut down, though fortunately the tallest buildings had only six floors. Mencken reached for another comparison: "Berlin, once so spick and span, is as dirty as Philadelphia."

Berlin, like St. Petersburg, had been before the war a grand, imperial showcase, a city of broad boulevards, impressive squares and confident prosperity. The height limit for buildings, a characteristic it shared with the Russian capital (and Paris and Washington), gave it a uniform rooftop altitude. Apartment houses embraced courtyards, paved with cobblestones but for a central flagstoned walkway or two. In the courtyards, unadorned with architectural flourishes, was the life of the city for Berliners themselves, the critic Walter Benjamin, born there in 1892, remembered afterward. He grew up, he wrote, to the muffled rhythm of railway trains and the beating of carpets below his window.

Before the war, the great indoor food markets, with their heavy swinging doors on powerful springs, had been a place of strange magic. "Your gaze ran first to flagstones that were slimy with fish water or swill, and on which one could easily slip on carrots or lettuce leaves," Benjamin wrote. Then you noticed slow-moving vendors sitting behind wire partitions, like priestesses, "purveyors of all the fruits of the field and orchard, all edible birds, fishes and mammals—procuresses, unassailable wool-clad colossi, who communicated with one another from stall to stall, whether by a flash of their great shiny buttons, by a smack on their aprons, or by a bosomswelling sigh."

Berlin was a city of brass bands, where young lovers flirted in

"Scandal Lane" in the Tiergarten to the sound of military marches. It was a city where children had to attend a school to be given proper instruction in riding a bicycle. In Benjamin's neighborhood, which drew prosperous, assimilated Jewish families like his own, there was a canal "through which the water took its dark, slow course, as though intimate with all the sorrows of the world."

But the war, though far from Berlin, had deeply gouged the veneer. Food was strictly rationed, and it was all many people could think about. When you could get flour, you had to sift out the worms. A black market in potatoes and lard and jams flourished. (Fish were always available.) Shops sold ersatz butter, eggs, candy. "The new Germany is made up of slim people," Mencken wrote. By the spring of 1917, the city's garbage collection was faltering, the sewerage system was in decay. As in Petrograd, the trams were packed, often with soldiers home on leave, and the civilians who squeezed in next to them had to worry about the lice they brought back from the front. Fabric for clothing was made with one part wool and two parts paper. A young music student from Boston noticed people staring at her American shoes. Mencken was impressed by the stoicism of Berliners, but they were on edge, too, sudden quarrels erupting with shop clerks and tram conductors and each other.

In the name of efficiency, the authorities were trying to persuade the city's inhabitants to eat at public kitchens instead of cooking for themselves. The rationale was to make better use of the food that was available, and to free up time that Berliners spent hunting for groceries and preparing meals at home. It was a Soviet-style idea before its time. No one much cared for it. "The end will be thorough-going state socialism," Mencken thought.

Of course there were moments of small delight, all the more welcome because of the dreariness all around. One day Mencken saw an orchid on display in a shop window on Unter den Linden, and a crowd of eighteen—he counted—had gathered to gape at it. One evening he dropped by the Metropol Theater to see if he could catch a light opera, *Die Czardasfürstin*. "A packed house and gales of laughter. . . . The house was sold out when I got there, but a soldier standing in the lobby had a seat that he couldn't use, and sold it to me at a discount of one mark. An honest man. Let us hope that the shrapnel will spare him."

Mencken was struck again and again by the calm exterior. Berliners were unpanicked, unexcited, unexuberant about the prospect of war with America. "The public indeed, showed almost no interest in the crisis at all. . . . There was much more excitement among the 300 Americans in Berlin than among its 3,000,000 Germans. The latter were silent, dignified, polite to the verge of excess. I myself strolled about the city, airing my bad German and giving away my nationality with every word, yet not a soul uttered an offensive syllable in my hearing."

You never saw anyone flying a flag. There was no music in the deserted Tiergarten, because no one cared for patriotic marches anymore.

On the day following the announcement of the new submarine policy, the newspapers ran a statement by von Hindenburg plainly hinting that other nations might be joining the war against Germany. "Our front is secure on all sides," it said. "We have the necessary reserves everywhere. The morale of our troops is sound and unshaken. The general military situation is such that we can accept safely all consequences of an unrestrained U-boat war. And inasmuch as this U-boat war offers us the means of doing the maximum of damage to our foes we must begin it forthwith."

Most newspapers put the statement inside, not on page one. "Where the newspapers led, the public followed. What little talk there was at the Foreign Office ran to polite hopes, obviously insincere, that the United States would accept the new plan and stand back while England was walloped."

Mencken sought out military officers and government officials to hear from them the German argument. (All that he gathered would be published in a thirteen-part series in the *Sun*, which ran from

March 10 to March 22, at a time when anti-German feeling in America was growing especially intense. Mencken had to wait until he left Europe to file those long reports, because all transatlantic cable traffic had to pass the German censor, and then was routed by way of the Netherlands or another neutral country through London, and subject to British censorship. Correspondents in Berlin typically accepted the censorship, found couriers to take their stories by sea to America, or, for occasional big news, paid the exorbitant German rates to file by wireless.) The analysis he heard was couched in logical, rational terms; he caught little bluster, and no anger.

At noon on that first day, he dropped by the Military Bureau of the Foreign Office, to see Rittmeister Freiherr von Plettenberg, who dealt with correspondents on army matters. Plettenberg spoke perfect American-accented English, having worked for several years for the North German Lloyd shipping company at its docks in Hoboken, New Jersey.

It was too late, Plettenberg told him, for Germany to turn back. It had to take the war to the English. Yes, he said, it might draw the United States in, and that would be a pity, but there was no choice. He lit a cigarette, and poured some whisky for his guest. "Maybe the United States will see our point of view, after all. We have no desire to hurt Americans. All we ask is that they keep out of the way while we tackle England."

Other officers told Mencken the same thing. "It is difficult to define their mood precisely," he wrote. "I expected a certain amount of anxiety, for they all realize that they are at the parting of the ways, but failed to discover it. They cultivate stoicism, serenity, a dispassionate manner. The air is full of electricity, but there are no sparks."

The Foreign Office was an old, shabby barn of a building on Wilhelmstrasse, marked by "beery somnolence." Visitors had to ring a bell, and then were admitted to a stone-paved vestibule. Up a flight of steps was a dark hallway. At the far end of the hallway was a small waiting room with a porcelain stove, a "mangy sofa," and a "carafe of yellowish drinking water." Two messengers, "excessively dignified," acted as receptionists.

Mencken came to speak with Consul-General Thiel, whom he described as one of the only men in the Foreign Office who actually understood America and American ways of thinking. Thiel was packing up his things; his expertise apparently no longer needed, or wanted.

"This new submarine war," he told Mencken, "is the only way to an early peace." Germany's peace proposal the previous December was sincere and moderate, he said, and the Allies not only rejected it but responded with insults that no nation should have to bear. "We now accept the situation. It is, as they say, a fight to the finish—and we fully expect to be on our legs at that finish."

He said he would be sorry to see the United States enter the war, but there seemed no way to avoid it. "The United States, in point of fact, has been on the side of our enemies for a long while, and it has already done us more damage than most of them. To me, at least, this seems quite natural. The sympathies of nations go with their interests, and England's control of the seas makes American interests identical with her own."

Germany, he said, had no alternative but to try to inflict as much damage on England and its allies as possible. Thiel argued that America could still stay out.

"We have no quarrel with the American people, and do not want to injure them," he said. "All we ask of them is that they cease to give active aid to our chief enemy." And if the United States did decide to declare war, he said, it would take six months to prepare an effective blow against Germany, and in that time Germany could carry out its plans against England.

What then? Mencken asked. Germany would have to fight the United States, which could raise an army of 5 million.

"True," the consul-general replied, "but how will the United States get them to Europe?"

A German officer justified the U-boat policy this way: Think of it as a prize fight, he said, with the United States as referee. Every decision by the referee has gone against Germany. Now England has Germany in a chokehold, and still the referee does not call a foul, but in fact helps England. "Well, there is but one thing for us to do, and we do it. That is, we strike below the belt."

The opinion, though, was not unanimous. A naval officer told Mencken: "The trouble with this new U-boat campaign is that it promises too much. The German people probably expect a clean-up of the English merchant fleet in six months. They will be disappointed. Say 40 ships come out of a given harbor in a day. We'll be lucky if we sink one. Starving England will be a hard job—maybe, like starving Germany, a quite impossible job."

What's striking about Mencken's diary—and the material from it that was published in the *Sun* in March—is how straightforward it is. We remember Mencken today as the gleefully skewering, mean-spirited hero of 1920s journalism, the iconoclast who railed against lynching but sometimes said troubling things about blacks, and about Jews. (His parallel career as a literary critic and scholar of the English language has faded from view.) His best writing builds upon solid observation but shows off, too. He loved to play around with words, and there are moments in Mencken when he resembles no one so much as Nabokov having fun—or perhaps it's the other way around. Yet if some writers let go in their diaries, Mencken reined himself in. It's as if he wanted to be sure to get this moment right, to tell the story of Berlin, more than the story of H. L. Mencken in Berlin.

He had lunch at the Adlon with a fellow correspondent, a veteran of Berlin, the day after the United States broke off diplomatic relations. "You can easily imagine the uproar" there would be in America if the two countries' roles were reversed, the correspondent told him. In Germany, all is quiet, and will remain quiet. And it's not because the Germans are stupid. "Rather, because they have exhausted all emotion. They have lived through every imaginable surprise, every imaginable shock, every imaginable horror. They are fed up on sensations. . . . Stoicism has become a sort of national philosophy. It is regarded as bad form to show emotion."

Mencken took up the thread himself. "The strange calm of the Germans continues. There are absolutely no demonstrations against Americans. They are so polite, indeed, that one almost begins to believe that they have not heard of the break. Nothing even remotely approaching the bawling and parading reported from New York is visible. One sees no show of flags, no crowds on the streets."

Mencken's thoughts turned to one of his favorite targets. "One can well imagine the eruption of Roosevelt. The very air must be afire," he wrote. A few days later: "The papers get a lot of fun out of the news that Roosevelt has volunteered as a major-general. One of them prints a long poem this evening, describing the panic in the German Army on receipt of the news."

Americans could walk the streets, speaking in English, without attracting any attention or criticism. Certainly there were barbs in the papers, directed at Washington and Wall Street. The *Vossische Zeitung* ran a long article on "American Idealism," in which Wilson was patronizingly dismissed for having been poisoned by Emersonian platitudes. It ran another article on "Dollar Politics," alleging that Wall Street was fearful of losing the money it had lent to England. "The partiality of Mr. Wilson has been burned into the memory of the German people," wrote the *Berliner Zeitung*.

When he broke off relations, Wilson had said that no further steps were called for; Roosevelt later argued that that was the moment America should have struck out against Germany, and Mencken, though he was dismayed at the thought of war, was sure it would happen in a matter of weeks if not days. But Wilson meant it, or, in Roosevelt's eyes, he let the opportunity pass. By February 8, as it started to become apparent that the United States was not about to leap into the fray, the *Vossische Zeitung* was running a story headlined, "Wilson's Passive War."

Zimmermann, the foreign minister, had received the American correspondents on February 4 and "made a considerable show of agitation, thumped his desk, and declared that the action of Washington was a great shock to him," wrote Mencken, who hadn't been there. "Nevertheless, they all came away with the impression that it was play-acting." Zimmermann, "a large, massive fellow with a fist like a ham," thanked the correspondents and shook hands all around. A commoner, he was ousting the old Junker class from the hallways of his ministry, but Mencken didn't detect much difference in tone. Zimmermann was like his predecessors in being "marked by a gigantic ignorance of foreign ways of mind, and a gigantic indifference to foreign prejudices."

The first ten days of February were a time of uncertainty and anxiety for the Americans in Berlin. As soon as relations were broken off, Bernstorff had been unable to use a diplomatic cable to communicate with Berlin, and the Germans said they didn't know what had happened to him. Gerard, similarly, was cut off from the State Department and had no orders. There were rumors in Berlin that the Americans were seizing German property and arresting German citizens. The government was reluctant to let Gerard and his entourage leave the country—and wouldn't give them their passports—until it was sure of what was happening in the United States. At one point Gerard was told that he might be allowed to leave but the correspondents would have to remain—as hostages, essentially.

"You fellows are in for it," he told the newspapermen. "You'll all be locked up before it is over."

Gerard had free and easy sessions with the reporters, though he could barely conceal his dislike of a few of them. German journalists who occasionally dropped in to see him were put off guard by his manner. He was as informal as a diplomat could be, and he was tired of Germany. For two-and-a-half years his embassy had been looking after British interests in Germany, and the ballroom in the overcrowded embassy was stacked with cartons of British books and papers. Now they were to be turned over to the Swiss; and the Spanish would look after American affairs. Every day now, the embassy was packed with Americans trying to get their passports in order, so they could leave; they were in varying states of anger, boredom and distress. "He is a very rich man, and has moved all his life in so-called good society, but somehow his speech and mien suggest a Tammany district leader," Mencken wrote of Gerard. "Very often he drops into slang. . . . His animosity to the Germans is apparently limitless. He accuses them of all sorts of deviltries."*

As the correspondents debated what to do, Mencken had an additional problem: under the terms of his trip to the front, he was not allowed to leave Germany for eight weeks, or until March 25. "I wouldn't know a military secret if I stepped on one," he pointed out, and the Foreign Office people were sympathetic, but rules were rules.

Mencken had arrived in mid-January after an Atlantic crossing on a Danish ship that took him to Copenhagen. He had noted that the neutral Danes, fearful that they, too, might be dragged into the war, were digging trenches all the way down to the German border. Now it was impossible to go back that way; in the face of the U-boats, Denmark had called its ships back to port. He thought the idea of crossing Russia, and sailing the Pacific, was ridiculous, though other Americans were talking about it. Some correspondents thought they should stay, no matter what. But Mencken wasn't really a full-time newspaperman anymore; he ruefully called himself a "literary gent." Sticking around wouldn't be prudent.

A breakthrough finally came on February 9, when Carr Van Anda, managing editor of the *New York Times*, sent a cable to Berlin describing the situation in America and refuting the rumors that Germans were being locked up and their property taken. The German authorities were satisfied and said they would let the embassy personnel

---

* Interestingly, this description of Gerard was omitted from the series of articles published the following month in *The Sun*.

leave the next day, on a special train for Switzerland. A handful of correspondents was going, too. On the 10th, while he was at lunch, Mencken learned that the ban on his own departure had been lifted, and he quickly decided to join the traveling party. He hurried to pack his things, get his papers in order and say his goodbyes. The streets were ankle-deep in slush. At 8:10 that evening, the train pulled out of Berlin, with a few functionaries from the Foreign Office to see it off.

Through the Thuringian Forest, he could see the snow-laden fir trees, vague and ghostly in the moonlight. By morning they had reached Bavaria, in the south, passing through a series of pretty valleys, with vineyards on the hillsides. He had loved it there on previous visits, enjoyed the relaxed friendly manners of the Bavarians in contrast to the coldness of the northerners. "At Würzburg, we went gunning for some Würzburger, but the beer booths that used to stand on the station platform are gone. The war changes all things. It is a new Europe, and a much duller and sadder one. The trains pass through almost deserted stations. No more boys with trays of sandwiches. No more old women hawking postcards. No more crowds of peasants fighting for places. Soldiers everywhere—and a soldierly strictness, a soldierly hardness, a soldierly silence."

At 6:30 that evening, Mencken climbed down off the train in Zurich. "A capital dinner of *Schweinsrippen*[6] and sauerkraut—a huge and stuffing dose, now only a memory in Germany." He didn't intend to linger in Switzerland. There was just one reliable way now to get across the Atlantic, one route that stayed clear of Germany's U-boat zone. Mencken would have to get to Spain to catch his ship, and it would take him to Havana.

6   Pork ribs.

CHAPTER 5

"We Have Had to Push, and Push, and Push"

The first ship to be sunk under the new U-boat policy was German. Launched in 1890 as the *Pickhuben*, for the German Hansa Steamship Company, and later renamed the *Georgia*, it had sailed for the first decade of the twentieth century between Odessa and New York, carrying immigrants from Russia's great Black Sea port to the New World. Many if not most of its passengers on those voyages were Jewish. The ship was 331 feet long, had one funnel and a straight up-and-down bow. There was room aboard for 10 first-class passengers and 200 in steerage.

When the war broke out, its German owners directed it to seek refuge from the Royal Navy in an American port. Nine months later, in April 1915, it was sold to a group of Americans, some of whom had ties to German merchant shipping lines, for $85,000. The new owners renamed the ship the *Housatonic*, registered it under the United States flag, and put it back in service as a freighter.

On January 6, 1917, the *Housatonic* set sail from Galveston, Texas, heading first to Newport News, Virginia. Carrying 144,200 bushels of wheat, it left Virginia on January 16, bound for Great Britain, two weeks before Berlin announced its resumption of unrestricted U-boat warfare.

But the *Housatonic* was a slow old boat. It could achieve a top speed of 11 knots, which made it significantly slower than a submarine running on the surface. On February 3, after a long winter crossing of the North Atlantic, Captain Thomas A. Ensor had brought his ship to the approaches to England. Sixty miles to the northeast lay the Scilly Isles, and beyond them was Britain proper. It was a Saturday, 10:30 in the morning.

"We saw a submarine, flying no colors, about 250 yards astern," Ensor wrote in his log. (He later told reporters it had been ahead of his ship, on the port side.) "She fired two shots [from the deck gun], the second passing close to the ship and striking the water just ahead. We stopped the engines."

Ensor was ordered to bring his papers aboard the submarine for examination. The commander, he noted, spoke perfect English. His name was Lieutenant Hans Rose, and his boat was the *U-53*. Only four months earlier, Rose himself had been in the United States. He had taken his sub into the harbor at Newport, Rhode Island, in a dashing and pointed gesture. A handsome, well-mannered man with a short mustache and blue eyes, he met with reporters and asked one of them to mail a letter to Ambassador Bernstorff for him. Under the rules of naval warfare at the time, his sub could stay in a neutral port for no more than twenty-four hours, to take on essential stores or make repairs. Rose said he had no need of either; his only errand was the delivery of the letter. But his real point was to demonstrate, to the American public, that Germany's modern U-boats were capable of a transatlantic crossing—that the ocean wasn't as big and protective as it once was. He left Newport, reached international waters off Nantucket, and proceeded to sink five merchant ships—none of them American. U.S. destroyers stood by and rescued the passengers. Afterward, Wilson sent a note to Bernstorff insisting that Germany refrain from such attacks so close to the American shore.

Now he was face-to-face with Ensor. "I find the vessel is laden with grain for London," he told the American skipper. "It is my duty to sink her."

Ensor protested "vigorously." At first Rose ignored him, then said, "You are carrying foodstuffs to an enemy of my country, and though I am sorry, it is my duty to sink you."

His crew went aboard the *Housatonic*, took all the soap they could find, set explosives belowdecks, knocked off the seacocks to let the water come pouring in, and removed the hatches. The thirty-seven crew members of the freighter took to two lifeboats, and the *U-53* fired a torpedo into the ship. Rose then had his crew throw a towline to the lifeboats, and, running on the surface, he took them northward, toward England. About ninety minutes later he spotted a British patrol boat. Firing two shots from his deck gun to draw the attention of the British boat, he then slipped the towline, submerged, and vanished. Ensor and his men were picked up and put ashore at Penzance.

Americans were uncertain how to react. Hours after the *Housatonic* went to the bottom, but before news of the sinking had reached Washington, the White House had announced the breaking off of diplomatic relations with Germany. But in his statement, Wilson had declared that the United States was not going to war and would take no further steps unless Germany carried out an "overt act" of aggression against America.

The sinking of the *Housatonic* did not seem to rise to that level. No one was injured or killed. The crew was treated with courtesy and care by Lieutenant Rose. The American consul in Plymouth concluded that the load of wheat did in fact constitute contraband of war and that Rose was within his rights to sink the ship.

On February 12, an old-fashioned sailing ship, a schooner called the *Lyman M. Law*, was stopped by *U-35* off Sardinia. The American boat, captained by a salty Maine man named Stephen W. McDonough, was carrying a load of shooks—slats used to make lemon crates—to Italy, which had joined the Allies in the war against Germany and

Austria. The *U-35* captain, Lothar von Arnauld de la Perière, the most accomplished submarine skipper in the German navy, hesitated but then decided the load constituted contraband. McDonough said he proudly refused to ask the German to spare his ship. The American crew took to lifeboats and made it ashore, again without injuries, and the *Lyman M. Law*, like the *Housatonic*, was sunk.

The owners of the schooner were indignant, but Wilson himself declared that neither sinking constituted an "overt act." *The Outlook*, a magazine associated with Theodore Roosevelt, attacked Wilson for having, in effect, "condoned" the sinkings. Roosevelt, in his correspondence, insisted that American honor was being indelibly stained. Wilson, however, did not want to take the United States into the war if he could help it, and especially not over the destruction of some raggedy old tramp freighters. That would be crass and ignoble.

"He is yellow all through in the presence of danger, either physically or morally," Roosevelt wrote to Henry Cabot Lodge, the Republican senator from Massachusetts, "and will accept any insult or injury from the hands of a fighting man. I don't believe he is capable of understanding what the words 'pride of country' mean."

The muckraking journalist Ida Tarbell, touring the Midwest, wrote to Colonel House from Des Moines that she had talked to "all sorts of people" and believed they were ready to go to war if it became necessary. "There is no excitement, no disturbance, but if the time comes they will go about their fighting as simply and naturally as they are going about their daily work. It is all very impressive and very fine to me. You somehow know you can count on the country."

But even as indignation was stirring, Americans tried to figure out what to make of these sinkings. No one could be sure that other German U-boat commanders would be such gentlemen. And the attacks were threatening to severely curtail, if not shut down, transatlantic trade. Even if the U-boats couldn't possibly sink every ship on the sea, the shipping lines had trouble getting insurance. In New York, the steamships of the Holland America, Scandinavian America, Norwegian America, and American lines had all tied up, their holds filled with undelivered goods. The Swedish American line scheduled just one crossing, by the *Stockholm*. Railcars stocked with freight that had been destined for Europe idled in the yards in New York and other East Coast ports, and this contributed significantly to the car shortage that was being felt nationwide.

A British liner, the *Laconia* of the Cunard Line, left New York in mid-February, bound for Liverpool in spite of the danger. On February 25 the German boat *U-50* sent two torpedoes into its side; the ship sank and 12 people died, including an American woman and her daughter. The incident received extensive coverage in the American press, and though the *Laconia*'s British registry mitigated some of the outrage, it stoked more public pressure on Wilson to respond.

Captain McDonough had boasted that if he had had a five-pound gun on the *Lyman M. Law* he could have sunk the *U-35* "as easily as buttering a piece of bread." Now, on February 26, a day after the *Laconia* went down, Wilson asked Congress for a bill allowing him to order the arming of American merchant ships. That might just persuade the Germans to back off.

The proposal drew immediate opposition. Critics saw the arming of merchant ships as a provocative act that was likely to increase the chances of America being dragged into the war. Its consequences would be just the opposite of what Wilson intended, they said. Others clamored for its passage, and castigated their opponents as unpatriotic. Congress had just six days left in its term, so there was little time to debate before sides had to be picked. The introduction of the bill was one of those moments that sharpened and clarified the division in the country.

For some, the two sinkings seemed to be fairly minor. Wilson had shown admirable restraint when relations with Mexico had been at their hottest a year or so earlier, and that crisis, which could have broken out into a shooting war, subsided instead. What, critics asked, made this so much more important? Particularly out West, people suggested that a simple solution would be to order all American ships to steer clear of the war zone.

But others saw the attacks as an insult to America's honor, and argued that to do nothing would be to invite even more attacks. One day, they said, Americans would wake up and find the Germans in New York. The hawks despaired of Wilson, but in asking to arm the ships, he was clearly drawing away from the doves.

Behind his pointy beard, the conservative Senator Lodge could only grit his teeth. That he had no use for Wilson went beyond saying. Someday, he would get his revenge on the professor in the White House. But on March 2 he had to accept the unpalatable reality that he and the president were on the same side.

"It is awful to be obliged to meet this situation with such an instrument, but he is the only one we have because he is the President of the United States," Lodge wrote in a letter to Roosevelt.

BUT BY THE time he asked for the ship-arming bill, Wilson knew that a perhaps much more significant turning point was at hand. He was holding a closely guarded secret that could have huge implications. Two days earlier, on February 24, Ambassador Walter Hines Page had sent telegram No. 5747 from the American embassy in London, marked "Confidential for the President and the Secretary of State." He had met with Arthur Balfour, he wrote, and the British foreign secretary had handed him an intercepted telegram.

It was from Berlin, sent by way of the German embassy in Washington, containing instructions for Heinrich von Eckhardt, the German ambassador to Mexico. It had been dated January 19, and British intelligence—which was secretly decoding and reading all of Germany's wireless dispatches—knew of it at once. It contained a message that von Eckhardt was to have ready to deliver to Mexican President Venustiano Carranza. Germany had decided to resume unrestricted submarine warfare, it said—this, Wilson must have been surprised to note, was nearly two weeks before Berlin made that decision public. "We shall endeavor in spite of this to keep the United States of America neutral. In the event of this not succeeding, we make Mexico a proposal of alliance on the following basis: make war together, make peace together, generous financial support and an understanding on our part that Mexico is to reconquer the lost territory in Texas, New Mexico and Arizona."

The proposal was to be handed to Carranza "as soon as the outbreak of war with the United States of America is certain." Moreover, it suggested that Mexico could play the role of mediator between Germany and Japan—which had joined the Allies in the war—and persuade Tokyo to switch sides and attack the United States.

It was signed, "97556," the German code for Arthur Zimmermann, the foreign minister in Berlin. The Zimmermann Telegram—as it became known—concluded by directing Ambassador von Eckhardt to point out to Carranza "that the ruthless employment of our submarines now offers the prospect of compelling England in a few months to make peace."

In Page's message to Wilson and Lansing, he said he had been told that the British, early in the war, had obtained a copy of Germany's cipher code. Until this moment, they had jealously guarded the secret. It "is only divulged now to you by the British Government in view of the extraordinary circumstances and their friendly feeling towards the United States."

For four days, Wilson debated what to do. He had come to cherish the opportunity to talk things over with Edith at such moments, but her sister Annie Lee had died following an operation on the twenty-sixth and she was both understandably distracted and busy trying to care for her mother, who was distraught. Edith moved her into the White House. Other than Colonel House, and sometimes the young White House physician, Dr. Cary T. Grayson, Woodrow had few others he could confide his thoughts to in informal conversation.

He understood that the telegram was to be delivered to Carranza only in the event of an American entry into the war; Berlin was not trying to stir up a preemptive attack. Still, it was a damning revelation. And it was plausible: Going back to early 1916, federalized units of the National Guard had been deployed along the border with Mexico and had made forays into that country in fruitless pursuit of the revolutionary Pancho Villa. New York's 69th had been there for a while, and it was where Captain "Wild Bill" Donovan had gotten his first taste of reconnaissance work. The leader of the expeditionary force was a stiff-necked general who was still grieving over the deaths of his wife and daughter in a fire. His name was John J. Pershing. The Mexicans had not been pleased by the intervention, and it was only in March that the last two units, from Pennsylvania and North Carolina, were called home.

There was something else, too: It wasn't altogether a surprise. The shock that at least some American officials expressed publicly when the telegram was made public was less than sincere. On February 5, the *Washington Post* reported that American officials believed Germany was trying to enlist Mexico in its dispute with the United States. This was two days after diplomatic relations were broken off and nineteen days before Page sent the Zimmermann Telegram to Wilson.

"Germany will try to foment further trouble in Mexico, so that the United States will have not only one serious diplomatic situation, but two, according to an apparently well-authenticated report circulated yesterday among diplomatists who have been following the rapidfire developments of the last three days," the article began. It said that "secret agents" of the Justice Department had the same information.

"Evidence has been accumulating for several months," it reported, and in fact several arrests, on minor charges, had already been made. The focus of attention was the port of Tampico. If trouble broke out there, "the United States navy would be forced to send vessels there for the protection of the [resident] foreigners, as at the time of the seizure of Vera Cruz. This would divert at least part of the Atlantic Fleet from operating against German submarines and other naval craft, if open hostilities arise between the two countries."

Four days later, the *Providence Journal* reported that German officers were gathering in Mexico—some supposedly having gotten there after escaping from Russian prisoner-of-war camps and making their way to China and across the Pacific. In case of war, it said, the German officers would direct operations from Mexico against the United States.

And on February 19, a *New York Times* reporter in Washington gave more details concerning suspected German designs in Mexico.

"Information has been received here," the *Times* reported, "which some officials apparently believe is authentic, that a considerable number of German reservists have joined the Carranza forces and that a few German reservists are with the Villa army. It is reported that the number of these reservists who have joined Carranza is between 200 and 300, but this report could not be confirmed in any official quarter.

"It is understood by those who have obtained this information that if war should come between the United States and Germany the German reservists in both Carranza and Villa armies would seek to unite the two opposing forces against the United States."

Federal agents were at work in Texas, California, and within Mexico to ferret out German designs, and throughout February they sent a steady stream of confidential reports to Washington. Later events would suggest that the tales of plots were considerably overblown, but Americans could not be sure of that at the time. What readers of the newspapers did know was that responsible officials in Washington had had reason for weeks, or months, to suspect a German plot involving Mexico against the United States.

Moreover, the notion that Japan might switch sides did not seem far-fetched. American strategists had long foreseen the possibility of a conflict with Japan, and some military men thought that the logi-

cal way for Japan to attack was through Mexico, from which it could
drive up the center of the country.

At a cabinet meeting on February 23, the day before Wilson
learned of the Zimmermann Telegram, someone had raised the
idea that the U.S. Navy should convoy merchant ships across the
ocean. Josephus Daniels, the secretary of the navy, believed it
would be too dangerous. "The President said the country was not
willing that we should take any risks of war." Several members of
the cabinet pushed back, including his son-in-law, Treasury Secretary William McAdoo, and Wilson began reproaching them for
being too ready to resort to arms. "We couldn't get the idea out of
his head that we were bent on pushing the country into war," wrote
Franklin Knight Lane, the secretary of the interior. "We have had
to push, and push, and push to get him to take any forward step."
Lane wrote that Wilson had been like that earlier when it came
to domestic reforms, including the creation of the Federal Trade
Commission and the Tariff Commission. "He comes out right but
he is slower than a glacier—and things are mighty disagreeable,
whenever anything has to be done. Now he is being abused by the
Republicans for being slow, and this will probably help a bit, though
it may make him more obstinate."

That was on a Friday. By Monday, Wilson had summoned a joint
session of Congress to ask for the bill allowing him to arm the country's commercial ships if he felt it necessary. He acknowledged that
there wasn't much time before Congress adjourned, but argued that
the issue was too pressing to wait for the next Congress to be seated.

The sinkings so far, he said in his address, had not amounted to
the "overt acts" of aggression that would trigger an escalated American response. He noted that other neutral countries had not joined
the United States in breaking off relations with Germany. He said
that even the threat posed by the U-boats had been enough to curtail
most transatlantic shipping, thereby coming close to accomplishing
the German war aims. He warned that the considerate behavior of

the U-boat commanders who sank the *Housatonic* and the *Lyman M. Law* might not be repeated, and that the United States had to be prepared to act quickly if the situation deteriorated. That's why he was asking for authorization to arm ships if, and as soon as, he deemed it necessary.

"We must defend our commerce and the lives of our people in the midst of the present trying circumstances, with discretion but with clear and steadfast purpose," he said. The likely answer was in "armed neutrality."

"It is devoutly to be hoped that it will not be necessary to put armed forces anywhere into action. The American people do not desire it, and our desire is not different from theirs. . . . I am the friend of peace and mean to preserve it for America so long as I am able. I am not now proposing or contemplating war or any steps that need lead to it."

And then he took his argument to a higher plane. "It is not of material interests merely that we are thinking. It is, rather, of fundamental human rights, chief of all the right to life itself. I am thinking, not only of the rights of Americans to go and come about their proper business by way of the sea, but also of something much deeper, much more fundamental than that. I am thinking of those rights of humanity without which there is no civilization. . . . We are speaking of no selfish material rights but of rights which our hearts support and whose foundation is that righteous passion for justice upon which all law, all structures alike of family, of state, and of mankind, must rest, as upon the ultimate base of our existence and our liberty."

So this was not about ships or commerce, but about "the rights of humanity." In one deft paragraph Wilson had laid out one of the cardinal totems of American foreign policy for the century to come. A concern for human rights was to guide U.S. action—to defend them, protect them, extend them. In Paris, Georges Clemenceau, who would become prime minister later that year, was struck by Wilson's audacity in placing "human rights" at the heart of his policy. Future generations would not be able to ignore it, he said. Washington may have fallen short more often than not on that score—in 1917 and in the years that followed—but the idea that human rights should be the ultimate driver of policy, and could be the ultimate justification for whatever policy the White House pursued, was never again far from the thinking of American strategists.

Wilson had been pilloried all winter by the small but vocal faction of prowar Republicans. Now he ran into stiff resistance in the Senate from a different group—also led by Republicans—who didn't want to see the United States take any steps that might bring about its entry into the war, inadvertently or not. Senator Robert La Follette, of Wisconsin, who had competed with Theodore Roosevelt for progressive support as they each sought, in vain, the Republican presidential nomination in 1912, was determined not to let Wilson drag the nation into the war and became the leader of the antiwar faction. His aim, he wrote to his wife, was "to postpone aggressive action which would have resulted in our getting into war immediately until as I hope the crisis passes and we may in the providence of God be spared the awful catastrophe."

Roosevelt said La Follette was "an unhung traitor, and if the war should come, he ought to be hung."

Wilson didn't go that far, but he was shocked by the obstruction in the Senate. On February 28, as some of the members of Congress were complaining that the administration was trying to railroad the bill through in the closing days without any deliberation, Wilson gave the Zimmermann Telegram to the Associated Press, and it was in most of the nation's papers the next morning.

It was a sensation. "This country is on the verge of being forced into the war," ran one editorial. "We shall not be embarking upon a pleasant adventure; we shall be entering upon a serious business. And the more serious we conceive it, the better it will be in the end."

The next day, in a news story from Washington headlined "Staggered by Intrigue," the *Baltimore Sun* reported, "Men of all shades of political opinion realize today what they have appeared unaware of heretofore. They realize that to all effects and purposes the United States is now in a state of war with Germany."

It wasn't a fact, yet, though—and certainly not in Wilson's mind. Henri Bergson, the French philosopher, met with Wilson, and sent a message to his government in Paris. He warned that Wilson would not be rushed into war. Public opinion was divided, and the West was strong for peace, he wrote. Wilson was wary of England: The British seemed to be fighting primarily to maintain their commercial preponderance, "which he does not seem eager to guarantee." The president had also said he believed Germans were wearying of Prussian militarism. "I fear that I did not disabuse him of this idea."

LODGE INTUITIVELY GRASPED that Wilson was not yet ready to move toward war, but also sensed the opportunity the Zimmermann Telegram presented. "This, I think, is a great thing," he wrote Roosevelt. "We have discovered the Germans actually parceling out our country and offering our territory to Mexico as a reward for coming in. We have got Wilson in a position where he cannot deny it." Lodge was dismissive of the peace faction in the Senate and saw a chance to drive a wedge between it and the president.

"He does not mean to go to war but I think he is in the grip of events and I want to drive him forward as far as I can."

CHAPTER 6

"People Think It Will Be Very Bloody"

A mericans had never exactly flocked to Russia. It was too big, too far, too difficult. Travel within the country was daunting. Bureaucratic snares lay everywhere. Americans with the means to travel didn't feel the cultural connection that drew them, before the war, to England, France or Italy. And Russia was not only backward, in American eyes, but was in the grip of a highly unappealing autocracy. A handful of diplomats were stationed there, of course. Journalists who wrote about Russia tended to come in for short visits and leave again. A few adventurers roamed Siberia, and in the biggest cities there was always a scattering of expatriates who had found a niche and didn't want to go home. Several U.S. companies, such as Singer and the International Harvester Company, had established operations in Russia. After the war broke out, an American organization raised funds to support ambulance work in the Russian army. But the country was not a draw, to put it mildly, and had, moreover, long held visiting foreigners in suspicion. In the early months of 1917, largely cut off by the war, it was an even more daunting destination.

Americans who wanted to reach Petrograd had two choices: They could try to get to neutral Sweden, and from there cross the land border, far to the north, with Finland, then a grand duchy within the Russian Empire. Alternatively, they could sail across the Pacific to Japan, make their way to Vladivostok, or to Harbin, in China, and then take the long train ride west across Siberia. It was a week-long rail trip in the best of times. Early 1917 was anything but. Discipline was breaking down everywhere, among the men who ran the trains and the soldiers who forced their way on for free rides.

Florence MacLeod Harper, a reporter for *Leslie's Weekly*, chose what seemed the more prudent Pacific-Siberia route. Her Russian train was slow, dirty and cold. The light in her four-berth compartment was broken, so the conductor gave her and her fellow travelers a candle. The pipes in the toilet had frozen and burst, but there was another one elsewhere on the train. The cars were heated by stoves at each end, and the platforms of each car were stacked high with firewood that the passengers had to climb over, except when the firewood ran out and the temperature in the car fell to below freezing.

Riding on a train for days on end will give you an understanding of just how incomprehensibly vast Siberia is. The tracks follow its southern edge most of the way, through the most populated and most temperate zone—but it's still Siberia. In the depth of winter, when Harper traveled, temperatures of 40 below (the one point on the scale where Fahrenheit and Celsius agree) are common. Forest stretches for dozens, scores, hundreds of miles between towns. It all looks very much the same, like crossing a lonely ocean by ship. Harper, a Canadian, imagined hunters and trappers, watching from distant ridgelines as the clanking, belabored train pushed its way onward, carrying its manifest of Russians and foreigners, all jumbled together, alternately cooperating and competing for space, on their way to distant, warring Europe.

Like all Russian steam engines, the locomotive on her train burned birchwood logs, of which Siberia, and Russia, have plenty. "We were like the chosen people, guided by a cloud of smoke by day and a pillar of fire by night. We must have looked grandly infernal to any lone watcher, for millions of huge sparks trailed behind us like a comet's

tail. One lost all sense of man-crowded places and all sense of direction. It was only in the afternoon, when we rushed over white limitless
plains into the flaming sun, that we realized we were going west."

In the villages where the train stopped, the snug wooden houses
were painted pastel pinks and blues. Townsfolk would be on the platform to greet the train. Women sold butter, pails of milk, sausages,
bread, roast pork and goose. Wise passengers "bought lavishly." The
closer they got to Europe and the war, the sparser and worse the food
was. By the time the train crossed the Ural Mountains, into Europe
at last, the bread for sale was gray. A wheel bearing overheated one
night, and the train crew, using a creosote torch for light, fashioned
a patchwork fix. One day the fireman who stoked the locomotive
boiler, fed up, went on a personal strike. He walked off the job and
was never seen again. Four hours later, the trainmen found someone
willing to take his place, and the journey continued.

More than a day late, in the middle of the night, the train arrived
in Petrograd. Harper was astonished by the bustle and confusion,
the disembarking passengers laden with crocks of butter and braces
of geese, the porters who had to be argued with, the icons in the station, the soldiers and beggars and pickpockets going this way and
that. Hungry, exhausted, she and her companions hired two sleighs,
and set off for a hotel. There were no rooms—except that after serious bargaining and cajoling it turned out that there were a couple of
small rooms after all. Having had almost nothing to eat, she crawled
under "bed-clothes, traveling rugs, fur coat, sweater and all the
clothes I could pile on top of my bed to keep warm." So went her first
night in the capital.

JAMES L. HOUGHTELING, JR., took the Swedish route. He was a
33-year-old employee of the Commerce Department, the son of a
prominent Chicago banker. It was his first visit to Russia, and his
diary reveals that he set out intending to be amused by the whole
experience. But he was perceptive at the same time, and as he got to

know Russia—over a period measured only in weeks—the arch tone of his early writing gradually subsided. In the beginning, you can hear him wondering why Russia couldn't be more like America, but then the uniquely Russian events of March 1917 began to unfold, and he had the wit to see it clearly.

He entered the Russian Empire at a point fifteen miles south of the Arctic Circle. It was 20 below, Fahrenheit. He and his companions crossed a frozen river by sleigh, leaving Sweden behind, and were directed through a gate and into a small customhouse. The officer in charge spoke to them politely in English, and his men examined the luggage, slow and cursory at the same time. While drinking tea in glasses in a dirty canteen, they learned that just a few days earlier a diplomatic courier from the Russian embassy in Stockholm had come their way. Something about him aroused suspicion, and though the courier threatened to have the officer cashiered, his bag was searched and pamphlets "of a revolutionary pro-German nature addressed to the peasants of Russia" were unearthed. "The courier was, naturally, taken out and shot. What a futile errand to pay for with a man's life!"

Another sleigh ride took the American party to the train station at Tornio. "The crispness of the air and the slanting sunlight on the snow"—the sun rose only about 20 degrees above the horizon even at noon that far north—were exhilarating. On a river they passed long caravans of freight sledges being pulled by horse teams on the snow-covered ice. The train from Tornio was but two hours late.

On Friday, January 19, they arrived at the Finland Station in Petrograd. The expected car had disappeared, so they were treated to another sleigh ride. "But what an untidy town! The buildings are of such a discouraged color." His hotel had "dark walls, torn paper, drab furniture!" Its halls "smell like a third-class boarding house in Chicago." But at least, as a diplomat, he had a hotel suite waiting for him. There were so many people crowded into Petrograd that hotels were packing them into public bathrooms to spend the night.

The next day he reported to the American embassy, at No. 15 Fur-shtatskaya Street, not far from St. Ann's Church.[7] He found it "a dis-appointing two-story affair without dignity of facade, squeezed into the middle of a block with a big apartment building on one side and another modest residence on the other." The flag was at half-staff, in mourning for Admiral Dewey, the hero of the Battle of Manila Bay in 1898. The Americans had an option to buy a seventy-room palace from the Demidov family for a new embassy; its beautiful banquet halls and reception rooms, and grand conservatory, had everyone excited about its elegance. Houghteling doesn't record why the Demidovs, thought to be the second-richest family in Russia, were eager to sell. (And the upheaval that was about to descend on Russia made the idea moot, in any case. The Demidovs escaped to Finland, and the Americans even-tually opened an embassy in Moscow, the new capital.)

Houghteling began looking for an apartment; his Russian was so weak that he was afraid to get on a streetcar or flag down a sleigh. So he walked, miles and miles. He found the city to be dirty, worn-down and inconvenient. One day he passed the former German embassy on St. Isaac's Square, a heavy, protomodern stone building that to this day exudes dominance; it had been vandalized by a Russian crowd in 1914 (which included one of Nabokov's uncles) and was still an abandoned wreck when Houghteling saw it.

At lunch on January 24, he heard talk of revolution for the first time. "Some people here think it may come soon." How would it come, and how soon? How serious was the talk? That was hard to gauge. Russia was evidently troubled. But all Houghteling could do—all anyone could do in Petrograd—was to go about the normal routines of life in a wartime capital and keep a sharp lookout.

The restaurants, like the hotels, were packed, but the food was for-gettable. He went to the Mariinsky Theater, to see *Paxita*, a Spanish

7   And just a stone's throw from the apartment house where Vladimir Putin grew up in the 1950s.

ballet, which he didn't like. The sentinels at the door to the Imperial Box made a bigger impression: "They faced each other and stood like statues, a most blasé smirk on their nubbly Russian countenances."

One Friday evening he went to a supper party at 11 p.m., and danced until 3. He could sense the mood, almost giddy, of impending upheaval. The next morning, on his way to work, he passed the church of St. Panteleimon the Martyr just as its chimes began to ring. "I never heard better rag-time," he wrote, posing as the insouciant and irreverent young American. "The big bells boomed, while the little ones tinkled a syncopated anthem which showed a truly 'Rag-time Temple Bells' spirit in the heart of the bell-ringer."

He was exasperated by the poor service. "Russia is a great place in which not to do shopping. The salespeople simply don't want to wait on you, don't care whether you buy or not. . . . The best shops are manned with English, Belgians, Swedes, and Baltickers. Formerly the Germans were the great shop-keepers of Russia." The prices were prohibitive. About this same time, Florence Harper bought a pair of shoes for $14, nearly triple what she would have paid in New York.

Houghteling visited the Alexander III Museum to see the big paintings of Vasily Vereshchagin, who had gone to Central Asia in the late nineteenth century to chronicle the triumph of Russian imperialism, only to have been turned against war by the cruelty, pointlessness and cynicism he encountered. Houghteling didn't like the art.

Then one Saturday evening in February he walked out of a street called Millionaya into Palace Square, and there saw the sun setting behind the spire of the Admiralty, "and the faultless dome of St. Isaac's stood out against a sky supremely rosy and beautiful." The sky was darkening fast, and the government buildings around him, even the "grim old" Winter Palace, "were all toned down to a shadowy softness." It happens to nearly every foreigner: Discouraged and despairing of the hard ugliness of so much of Russia, Houghteling turned a corner and saw the beauty, and the country was never the same for him after that.

"THERE IS NO doubt that a revolution is coming." That was January 31. A Russian told him that "in the provinces it is regarded as certain, and that people think it will be very bloody."

Other foreigners were hearing the same thing. An excited diplomat told Harper that trouble was expected any moment. Proclamations were posted all over Petrograd warning against demonstrations. "Nobody knew what was going to happen, but everybody agreed that something was going to happen. They all said the same thing—'Wait a while!'"

The sense of anticipation was contagious. After she'd gotten her bearings in Petrograd, Harper wrote, "I do not know why, because I hadn't been in Russia long enough, but, like everybody else there, I knew that trouble was coming. In fact, I was so sure of it that I wandered around the town, up and down the Nevsky, watching and waiting for it as I would for a circus parade."

After just two weeks in Russia, Houghteling was beginning to see why. Logistics for the war effort were largely being carried out by an association called the Zemtsvo Union, self-organized by local and district governing councils. It fed and clothed the soldiers, cared for the wounded, operated tanneries, shoe shops and commissaries. It was one of the only effective bodies in Russia during the war, and as such it attracted a great deal of hostility and interference from the bureaucrats of the imperial government. Voluntary association has always been suspect in Russia—and still is. It suggests the possibility of self-government.

Business owners had put up with the interference of the bureaucracy for years because they thought it preferable to socialist revolution. Now they were turning against Nicholas's government. "Russian administration of the law is so lax and so corrupt that it frightens away capital." Employers had concluded that the system had to change. "Every one is gradually coming to see that this unfair, inefficient government must go."

The czar, lobbied by Alexandra, had appointed a reactionary named

Alexander Protopopov as chief minister. One of his first acts was to ban any meetings of any branch of the Zemstvo Union without police agents in attendance. Baron Rosen was not alone in speculating that Protopopov was mentally unbalanced. He knew a revolution was likely; rumor had it that he had said he would welcome its advent. Then he could crush the opposition, close the Duma, and put himself forever in the czar's good graces. He was arrogant, sycophantic and deluded, and he was the man the czar relied on. "The throne," wrote Houghteling, "has fewer adherents every day."

The U.S. ambassador was David Francis, a former mayor of St. Louis and governor of Missouri. Always a bit clueless in his telegrams to the State Department, he reported on the discontent in Russia that winter in a message to Wilson on February 22. "I do not anticipate any revolution or violent outbreak however in the immediate future."

Despite the is-it-treason-or-stupidity speech he had given in the fall, the liberal Duma member Pavel Milyukov had hoped to persuade the czarist government to reform itself. Up to this point he was still a monarchist. He believed that liberal politicians could act as a restraining force, that they were the only ones who could reconcile the government "with the rough raging sea of people."

But his ally Nikolai Nekrasov vowed that the Kadets would not allow themselves to be cast as suppressors of the revolution, and would instead strive to take advantage of it. Another Kadet, Alexander Kizevetter, observed that if the czarist regime chose to commit suicide "one ought to save oneself and not the suicide victim."

While Russians were distracted by their impending crisis, events tumbled onward abroad. "We have just heard the unbelievable news of Germany's submarine-zone proclamation," wrote Houghteling on February 1. "It surely means that we enter the war."

HOUGHTELING MADE TWO trips to Moscow. He was dealing with business and economic matters, and Moscow, the old capital, was still the country's mercantile center. He found the trip by train "a joy."

It was a long, slow thirteen-hour journey, but the 450 miles between the cities was traversed by a right-of-way so straight that Houghteling found it easy to sleep. The rail line's unswerving path gave rise to a typically Russian tale: In the 1840s, so it was said, when Russian engineers were planning to build the railroad, they brought a map to the czar to discuss the best route, only to have the czar grab the map from them, seize a ruler, and draw a straight line between the two cities. He nicked his thumb halfway down, and that's supposedly why, to this day, the tracks follow a slight bulge away from the straight and true near the town of Malaya Vishera.

Moscow, he learned, had half the tram cars in all of Russia. That still came to only 1,500 cars for the burgeoning city. A cross-shaped subway was being planned, he was told, which would relieve the burden and allow Moscow to join such progressive cities as London, Paris, Berlin and New York in having the latest in underground transportation.*

Near the Kremlin one day, he saw a crowd gathered at a shrine to the Virgin, lighting candles, praying, crossing themselves, kissing the icons. Men and women knelt in the snow outside the shrine, praying, the men hatless in the cold. "It was a wonderful and inspiring display of religious fervor, sincere and trustful and lacking any note of superstitious fear."

That afternoon he dined with a Russian business contact at the Praga restaurant, where the Arbat meets the Boulevard Ring. "The Russian business community regards a revolution as inevitable and favors it, since present conditions are unbearable," his companion told him. "The old order has practically no support outside the court and the bureaucracy. The people are all alienated except a few of the peasantry; the army (including many of the officers) is rank with

---

* Moscow did of course build a subway—in the 1930s, under the direction of Nikita Khrushchev, who in 1917 was a metalworker exempt from the draft, an agitator against capitalists and the war, and the father of a new baby boy.

republicanism; the merchant classes are disgusted; and most of the nobility are sick of graft and inefficiency." Everyone, the Russian sitting at the table with him said, is keen for a revolution, and they "think that it will be very bloody and destructive."

Houghteling was a young man, eager, naturally, for excitement. But days ticked by. The dam was holding. Something was in the air, but all you could do was wait. He went skiing one afternoon, during the pre-Lenten festival called Maslenitsa, in Lyubertsy, a company town outside Moscow built by the International Harvester Company, of America. He flirted at dinner parties—though he was engaged—and was bored at a "tawdry cabaret theater called Maxim's, run by an American negro."

At a charity bazaar, he met a Russian girl named Natasha who had dressed as a Gypsy. They went out to supper together, conversing in French. He liked Moscow. Walking back to his hotel one night in early March, all yet still as only Russia can be still, he passed the Rostov house of *War and Peace*, on Povarskaya Street. "It was a magnificent night, with a full moon over fluffy new snow. . . . I passed along the Mokhovaya under the Kremlin battlements, and the moonlight effect on Ivan Veliki's tower and on the church domes and palaces was stunning. It's good to be alive on such a night."

He attended a service at the Cathedral of the Redeemer, and this young traveler who only weeks earlier had been making fun of "Ragtime" church bells was moved by the experience. "I have never seen a sweeter face than that of this dear old man, his white beard streaming to his waist" he wrote of the archbishop, who led a procession while two male choirs sang. "His voice was plaintive and sweet, too, as he read the prayers from a great gold book brought with much ceremony from the sanctuary and held by a kneeling priest during the reading. Two black-bearded priests sang the responses; one with a deep thunderous voice which filled the high dome above and seemed to shake the four evangelists and serried saints on the upper walls; the other, a weak-faced man with spectacles, with a bass voice clear as a clarion."

He visited the headquarters of the Zemstvo Union. "It is a place to gladden the heart of an American," he wrote. "The atmosphere is absolutely different from that musty file-an-application-and-wait-three-weeks air which oppresses one in the huge ministry buildings in Petrograd."

One day the bread ran out at a bakery. The crowd outside caught sight of three wagonloads of flour in the courtyard behind it. They discovered that the flour was consigned to the postmaster and two other officials. "People are beginning to rebel and to cry out that there is plenty for the rich and powerful, but only bread-cards and scarcity for the poor."

He lunched with the matriarch of a rich merchant family at her home overlooking a big square, the house filled with modern Russian art. The liberal leaders of the Duma, she told him, were far too impractical to form a working government, even if they had the chance. Houghteling responded by talking about the "unworldly and kaleidoscopic idealism of the Intelligentsia." No one, she replied, "wants a change to a feeble Liberal government."

Houghteling was discovering the enigma that was Russia. The American way of looking at the world seemed to have a big blind spot where Russia was concerned, for it was a country where surface appearances were almost always misleading. Americans saw a wrecked country and asked how it could be made better. Russians saw a country at risk of becoming very much worse.

For well more than a decade, Americans had viewed Russia as a monolithic autocracy, the "prison-house of nations." This wasn't wrong. The United States had restricted trade with Russia specifically over the treatment of its Jews. When the hard-line reformer Pyotr Stolypin was assassinated at the opera house in Kiev in 1911, Rabbi Stephen Wise, a leading voice among American liberals, gave a Yom Kippur address at Carnegie Hall in which he said that Stolypin was the victim of an internal war that he himself had started, and that justice would not come to Russia as long as the czarist system remained. Stolypin,* who was ruthless, had nonetheless fallen out of favor with Nicholas because of the land reforms he was pushing; his assassin, Dmitry Bogrov, was an anarchist but also a police agent. Wise was right, but the complexity of Russia was confounding.

After the war broke out, and Russian troops captured Galicia—western Ukraine—from the Austrians, Ukrainian schools, institutions and newspapers there were shut down, and the church was persecuted. Russians suspected that Jewish populations in villages near the German front were disloyal, and most of the Jews were driven out of the region. Rabbis and the well-to-do were seized as hostages.

On March 3, in St. Paul, Minnesota, Aino Malmberg, a Finnish novelist, asked an open forum at the People's Church: "Why do you people of America keep silent at the atrocities and barbarities going on today in Russia?" The Russians, she said, were a menace to Europe. There could be no peace in Europe until the system there was overthrown.

> The English language does not contain words that will describe the life of Russian Jews. They are slaughtered by the thousand. Lithuanians are flogged, cast into prison, hanged and their property confiscated. If Finland is to progress, it must be independent of Russia.
>
> There is no hope for the awful slaughter of war to end until the United States places itself on the side of the downtrodden, small nations.

Put another way, her message was this: Imperial Russia was an obstacle to progress and self-determination, and the United States should consider it a hostile power. The way some Americans saw

---

* Stolypin believed in a strong Russia most of all, and he is one of Vladimir Putin's biggest heroes—the conservative who would have saved his country by reforming it. Putin put up a large statue of Stolypin outside the Russian White House.

it, two repellent, nondemocratic countries—Germany and Russia—
were at war with each other, and the United States had no business
siding with either. The *New Republic* warned that, far from being a
potential ally, Nicholas II was in danger of succumbing to German
pressure and switching sides in the war.

BUT NOW THERE was talk again of a coup in Petrograd. On March
5 and 6, liberal leaders of the Duma met, first at the Medved restaurant, and then at an apartment rented just for the purpose, to discuss
a coup. Even Milyukov, who had hoped to save the regime, took part,
though he argued that the politicians should avoid playing an active
role, and instead move in to take power after the dust had settled. Five
others who were there disagreed. "We could never allow the mob to
assume control," remembered Mikhail Tereshchenko. They decided
to act first, before a street revolt could break out. Nicholas was off at
the front, and their plan was to arrest him on his train. They would
make their move, they agreed, in mid-March.

RUMORS REACHED MOSCOW of a bread strike in Petrograd. Police in
Penza were said to be practicing with machine guns every evening,
just outside the city. On March 11, on his last day in Moscow, Houghteling noted in his diary: "We hear there has been some rioting in
Petrograd during the last day or so; a food store in Kamenny Ostrov
Prospekt broken into; the mob fired on, etc. Certainly all is quiet
here, although distress is evident."

CHAPTER 7

"A Twilight Zone"

The month of March, the most critical month in Washington since the Civil War, the month that set the stage for the course of the century to come, began with a mixture of indignation, perplexity and dread. Submarine warfare—Mexico—Japan—what had these to do with life in Missoula or Brockton or Raleigh or Madison?

Henry Cabot Lodge had hoped the Zimmermann Telegram would rouse the American people to war. At the very least, he hoped it would sweep aside the peace faction's objections and open the way for the country to prepare for war, as best it could, beginning with the arming of ships.

In releasing the telegram to the Associated Press, Wilson was certainly trying to achieve the second of those two possible outcomes.* He was leading a country with no army to speak of and not much of a navy. Teddy Roosevelt had been hammering away at him since 1916 over "preparedness," or, more precisely, the lack of it. Wilson had been of a mind that to raise a standing army would be to succumb to

---

* The one thing he did achieve was to infuriate the United Press, which argued that its rival, the A.P., shouldn't have been given a scoop of that magnitude.

a Prussian sort of militarism. He had to send the National Guard to chase Pancho Villa in Mexico.

Now he wanted the authority to put guns on boats.

On March 1, the House of Representatives passed the ship-arming bill, with 13 voting against. Among those in favor was the 73-year-old Representative Charles Stedman of North Carolina, a former major in the Confederate army, who let out a Rebel yell that resounded throughout the chamber. The bill went to the Senate, and, for good measure, Wilson sent a note affirming the authenticity of the Zimmermann Telegram.

But there it stalled. Senators like to ask questions. Had anyone thought through what it meant to put guns on ships? Was it to be war without a declaration of war? Or, a warlike engagement? Could an American freighter even sink a submarine? The Royal Navy hadn't had much luck so far. And what about the British blockade of Germany?

Senator Oscar Underwood of Alabama said the United States had entered "a twilight zone" between war and peace.

If the United States did nothing, American shipping across the Atlantic would most likely dwindle away to almost nothing. The nation would pull back to the safety of its own shores, going it alone, isolated from much of the world. If merchant ships were armed, on the other hand, and continued their sailings to Europe, that would be putting American citizens and American assets in harm's way. There was no splitting the difference.

On March 2, a Friday, the Senate took up the bill. The 64th Congress had three days left before it expired. Senator William Stone, a Democrat from Missouri, joined with La Follette, a Republican, to organize a filibuster. Though in the end he never had a chance to speak—the chair wouldn't recognize him—"Fighting Bob" La Follette, with his huge head of angry hair, was recognized by everyone as the intellectual force behind the opposition to the bill.

In a long article that was later printed in the *Congressional Record*, La Follette offered the speech he would have given if he had had a chance. The arming of ships was sure to entangle America in the war, he wrote, but in a one-foot-in, one-foot-out sort of way. The British were just as bad as the Germans, and if they needed American supplies so badly, let them use their own ships. The principal shipping company backing the bill, the American Line, was owned by British interests. It would essentially be British officials ordering American sailors to fire on German subs.

Germany, he argued, had not invaded the United States. There was no danger that it would invade the United States. America had no quarrel with Germany. Giving the president authority to arm ships as he saw fit would give him the authority to make war as he saw fit, destroying the legitimate war-making power of Congress. It would undermine the republic. And what, he asked in a dozen different ways, would it actually accomplish?

Congress, he said, was being stampeded into passing this bill in the hectic last days of its term, given no time to consider or consult on the issue.

"Shall we, to maintain the technical right of travel and the pursuit of commercial profits, hurl this country into the bottomless pit of the European horror?"

Again, he asked, for what? "For commercial advantage and fat profits beneficial to a limited number of our dollar-scarred patriots. . . ."

Here he was jabbing directly at Wilson. The one thing Wilson did not want to do was go to war over something as tawdry as commercial interests. Wilson believed that America had a calling, to bring peace to the world even if, as it now began to appear, that would mean imposing peace by force of arms.

La Follette was indefatigable and unmovable. He believed he had plenty of support.

"Please accept my congratulations for the heroic courage for peace you are showing at a time when such virtue is tested and tried. Many babble of peace when there is no fear of war, and preach the gospel of love and forbearance to other nations. Even if the pacifists fail, the courage and the loyalty to their ideal which they have shown, already exalted America." So wrote Rabbi Alter Abelson, of Orange, New York. La Follette, he said, was one of the "few rare pearls."

Letters against war came in from all over the country:

"You will see the people will get wise to the jingo press soon, and you will see sentiment change." J. A. Adamson, Denver.

"The plain people here are not for this war. The loud war talkers of my acquaintance are not going to the firing line. The fighting will be done by those who, at least most of them, believed in staying out of the European conflict." Emil Ahlrichs, Cullman, Alabama.

"Keep up the good fight, my dear senator, for the common people. We do not want any war. Those, that want war, are the ammunition makers, the food speculators, the demagogues and the jingo press." Pastor William Albrecht, Forreston, Illinois.

"Let us declare war if we must have it but not allow some merchantmen carrying contraband to have the power to start it." M. M. Alexander, Okmulgee, Oklahoma.

A machinist in Cleveland, Frank Allen, wrote that he and other workingmen were all against going to war, because the United States had no cause for it. He applauded La Follette's tactics. "The filibuster has always been used to the disadvantage of good legislation and in favor of the privileged," he wrote. "It now has been used as a weapon against those whom formerly it has protected."

From Chicago, J. M. Bronson wrote: "More than any other man you have educated the people to the idea that the only way to keep liberty is to have incessant vigilance. Your reward will be that proud consciousness."

A telegram from Shenandoah, Iowa: "The laboring men do not want war we have nothing to sell but our lives the enemy is not in Germany but in Wall Street." Jim Baugh.

Despite Wilson's note attesting to the authenticity of the Zimmermann Telegram, many Americans, including some in the Senate, still suspected that the whole thing was an elaborate hoax, cooked up by British intelligence. Lansing worried that it would be hard to shake that doubt, if it took hold, because the message seemed so incredible. But on Saturday, March 3, Zimmermann himself owned up to it.

"Germany expected and wished to remain on terms of friendship with the United States," he said. "but . . . prepared measures of defense in case the United States declared war against Germany. I fail to see how such a 'plot' is inspired by unfriendliness on our part. It would mean nothing but that we would use means universally admitted in war, in case the United States declared war." German intentions were entirely conditional, he said. "The whole 'plot' falls flat to the ground in case the United States does not declare war against us."

That same day Wilson promised that he would not take the United States into the war without getting a declaration from Congress first; La Follette and the others were unmoved. Wilson was feeling as moody and wretched as the early March weather. Finally, at about four-thirty, Edith couldn't stand it any longer and dragged him out for a walk. They stopped in at the Corcoran Gallery, just across Pennsylvania Avenue, and the paintings helped him clear his mind.

On Sunday, time ran out on the bill, and it died.

That evening, Wilson denounced "the little group of willful men" who had "rendered the great Government of the United States helpless and contemptible." Other governments must have gotten the impression that they "can do as they please." At a moment of extraordinary peril, "when only definite or decided action can make the nation safe or shield it from war itself by the aggression of others, action is impossible."

The leaders of the new Senate, elected the previous November but not yet sworn in, announced that they would consider a new rule, called cloture, allowing debate to be shut off if a large enough majority wished to do so, and end a filibuster such as the one against arming the ships. They were as good as their word, and the rule, though modified over the years, is still in force today.

La Follette had won but, as he expected, his victory let loose a torrent of abuse from around the country. Newspaper cartoonists compared him to Benedict Arnold. *The Chicago Journal* ran this headline above its editorials: "The Army and Navy Forever! Three Cheers for the Red, White and Blue!"

Digging out an old insult from the Civil War era, it called the senators who held up the bill "Copperheads."

It continued: "They have proved that they care more for disloyal votes at home than for the rights of Americans abroad."

An investment manager in Salem, Oregon, A. C. Bohrnstedt, wrote La Follette that "to try to thwart the will of the great majority of the American people is nothing short of being contemptible."

From Detroit, a man named John O. Brennan wrote, "If the nation can't stand as a unit in the face of the present crisis, then there is nothing to Americanism. Your stand on the question under the present circumstances deserves nothing but condemnation."

In this hour of national peril, wrote A. C. Buchanan, of Chester, Virginia, "if you favor the Kiser [*sic*] and his ilk you should go to Germany. . . . We have no room in this country for 'Benedict Arnolds.'"

A postcard from A. R. Bruce, of Bridgeport, Connecticut, read: "You miserable Rotten *Traitor.* You should be hung up by the Heels and Shot to Pieces."

But then, too, Mrs. J. H. Bryant, of Quincy, Illinois, had sent a letter on a large sheet of paper, with one short message, capitalized, in the center of the page:

GOD BLESS "THE WILLFUL MEN"

Eugene V. Debs, the socialist labor leader, telegrammed from Providence, Rhode Island: "Let the Wall Street wolves and their prostitute press howl. The people will sustain you and history will vindicate you."

The Eastern press was heavily against La Follette, but the man who was credited with driving the country into war against Spain in 1898—William Randolph Hearst—was in his corner. A signed editorial by Hearst ran in the *Chicago American*. It accused Wilson of attacking American democracy by seeking unconstitutional powers. The president's "diatribe" against the "senators who refused to surrender the powers of Congress to the executive was leveled equally at the founders of this government who endeavored to provide a system by which the powers of Congress would NOT be surrendered to the executive."

From Lakewood, New Jersey, John S. Bryant wrote: "Let the Morgans and Smoots and Roots and Lodges rage, and let the Colonel rave; I guess you can endure it, Senator."*

He did endure it, but it took a toll.

"Fought it through to the finish," he wrote home. "Feeling here intense—I must take the gaff for a time." He said he was getting about five hundred letters a day, and they were running four-to-one in support.

A synagogue in Wheeling, West Virginia, disinvited him from giving a scheduled lecture, and sent a telegram of praise to President Wilson instead. At a prowar rally at Carnegie Hall, a reference to the senators who thwarted the bill brought jeers from the audience of "Traitor!" and "Hang them!" La Follette was hanged in effigy by students at the University of Illinois.

In a personal letter to Roosevelt, Lodge wrote that "it is a melancholy business." He said 77 senators were prepared to vote in favor of the bill; another 4 were out sick; 12 were against and 3 were unsure.

* J. P. Morgan, the financier, who had significant investments in Britain, and through whom all British and French war purchases were made; Senator Reed Smoot of Utah; Elihu Root, the former secretary of war; Senator Henry Cabot Lodge of Massachusetts, and Colonel Theodore Roosevelt.

Roosevelt apparently never answered that letter, probably because he in fact disliked the ship-arming bill as far too cautious, a typical half-measure by Wilson that would make the United States an object of derision.

He considered the senators who fought the bill treasonous, "but I feel infinitely more keenly that the President is a thousand times more to blame.... The bill itself is almost worthless. Armed neutrality is nothing but timid war." The crisis of the past month had given him a certain respect for the Germans. "I think Germany has made up her mind quite rightly that Wilson, as an enemy, is hardly more redoubtable than Wilson as a friend. We shall earn the contempt of mankind if we try to wage war by dollars instead of by blood."

Roosevelt's impatience was coloring everything for him. Since his revolt against the Republican establishment in 1912, when he bolted and ran for president on the Bull Moose ticket—ensuring the victory of the Democrat Wilson and the defeat of President William Howard Taft—TR had come back to the GOP. Many of his fellow progressives in the party were dubious about entering the war or outright opposed. He was more in tune with the conservatives, like Lodge. The war, for Roosevelt, was a cause—and then some. Perhaps, despite his histrionic exploits in the Spanish-American War, he still had not quite shaken the shame he felt over his father's decision not to serve in the Union Army during the Civil War; Theodore Senior had hired a replacement instead. The war against Spain had been glorious but brief and maybe a little too easy, and it was hard to overlook the large degree of bungling and amateurishness by the U.S. Army and its volunteer regiments. Now here was a war that would determine the future of the world, pitting great powers and great systems of national identity against each other—and Americans were little more than bystanders, slack-jawed, bickering, worried about their investments, dreaming of new cars, going to the picture show. Roosevelt saw that the war could be a test of American manhood, and he had caught the fever that was to be the hallmark of the twentieth century: he believed the war would forge a new kind of American—stronger, cleaner, purer. He was thinking, in his own Bull Moose way, a little bit like Trotsky, and like that German corporal on the Western Front.

He must have known he wouldn't see another chance. His father, whom he revered in all things except the avoidance of Civil War duty, had died at the age of 46. Roosevelt was 59 in 1917. He wished to go into battle. He talked about how he would rather die than see his sons die. He hadn't fully recovered from the illness that struck him on his expedition to the Amazon after retiring from politics. He was a man driven to perform his last and greatest act of heroism.

As Congress was taking up the ship-arming bill, and Roosevelt was criticizing it for being too paltry and inadequate for a great nation, he was also making the argument that Americans should raise their sights. The war was a profound event, a clash of right and wrong, and all the United States was talking about was protecting its trading ships. They were important, yes, but hardly the main point. He was oddly in sync with Wilson on this point, but they were coming at it from much different directions.

This was when he received a long letter from Representative Irvine Lenroot, a Republican of Wisconsin, who gently tried to remind the old Rough Rider that politics, in the real world, is the art of the possible. "We must deal, as best we can, with conditions as we find them." Besides the "substantial" minority of Americans who were firmly against going to war, either out of pacifism or pro-German feeling, he wrote, an "overwhelming majority" was simply unable to see the point of getting involved.

America first needed a general revival of patriotic spirit, Lenroot argued. "You are the most influential citizen of the United States," he told Roosevelt. "For more than two years you have lost no opportunity to bring about that awakening. I feel safe in saying you must be disappointed in the result."

Maybe, Lenroot wrote, Roosevelt was correct in predicting that

America would be deeply challenged by a German victory in Europe, if not actually imperiled, but the American people didn't agree with him. Most Americans sympathized with the Allies, he wrote, but that didn't mean they were willing to join them in the war.

The goal must be to keep the country united, and this "can only be brought about by confining ourselves to maintaining our rights in such a way as will command the support of a practically united country." In other words, through measured steps designed only in response to immediate and concrete challenges—such as the arming of merchant ships in the face of the German U-boat declaration.

"In the present crisis no real American can defend Germany's action. No real American can refuse to give willing support to the Government." A decision to use the Navy to subdue the U-boats would spark a much-needed wave of patriotism and deflect arguments that the United States was out primarily to help the English and French.

"I may be wrong but, in my judgment, if we assert our rights upon the sea now, with the use of our naval forces, and make it clear that if we must act it will be only for the purpose of maintaining those rights, it will not be necessary to send a single man to engage in the land warfare of Europe."

Roosevelt remarked to Lodge that the letter was commendable, given how many Germans lived in Lenroot's district.

Lodge also saw the bill as a half-measure, but unlike Roosevelt, he was still thinking like a politician, not a crusader. It was a half-measure, yes, but in the right direction, and in fact he corroborated one of La Follette's complaints about the bill. "In my opinion for us to arm a vessel loaded with contraband, or to convoy a vessel loaded with contraband, would be an act of war," he said on the Senate floor. Another senator in favor of the bill, James A. Reed of Missouri, elaborated more fully on the point: "The proposition is to take naval guns, perhaps to take expert gunners from our warships, and put them aboard these vessels, to sail into the prohibited zone, and, if a

German periscope shows itself, to send a shot or shell through it. Of course we know the minute that is done by a vessel thus equipped it will be treated as though it were done by a war vessel of the United States; in other words, the act will be the beginning of war."

But La Follette and his allies had prevailed, at least for the present. No freighters would be armed. Now Washington could only wait—for the beginning of a new presidential term, and the seating of a new Congress. Despite the gathering crisis, one reporter wrote, "Washington is not enlivened, it is deadened; not excited, but grave and silent."

SUNDAY, MARCH 4, was cold and wet. In a room reserved for his use in the Capitol, Woodrow Wilson took the official oath of office to begin his second term as president—while in a pouring rain 400 women demonstrated outside the White House in favor of national suffrage. The police were called out to hold them back. A band played for a while; the wind whipped the women's banners around. One idea had been to circle the White House seven times, like the march of the Israelites around Jericho, but that plan was abandoned amid arguments that it was a bad tactic at a time of international tension, and possibly sacrilegious.

At the Capitol, Wilson was "mad as a hornet" at the large number of hangers-on who crowded in to watch him take the oath, administered by Chief Justice Edward Douglass White, in what was supposed to be a private ceremony. The president's daughters were not invited; Colonel House, who had come down from New York, claimed he had been asked to attend but begged off. "I never like to be conspicuously in evidence. There is enough jealousy abroad without accentuating it unnecessarily." Thousands more who had come to Washington for the inauguration spent that Sunday in nearby Baltimore, where the bars didn't close for the Sabbath.

A congressional committee ordinarily tells an incoming president that Congress has adjourned "having finished all business." But that was manifestly untrue, given the successful filibuster. So the clerk of the Senate simply told the chief justice (a Confederate veteran), "It is now 12 o'clock." Wilson stood up from his littered desk, where he had been signing bills. The clerk handed him the Bible, open to Psalm 46: "God is our refuge and strength, a very present help in trouble."

The next day, Monday, the capital held the usual public inauguration ceremony. The rain petered out, but the wind whipped across Pennsylvania Avenue. A regiment from New York, just back from duty along the Mexican border, the men's faces still deeply tanned, guarded the route. It was the first time that soldiers had protected the inauguration parade since the beginning of Lincoln's second term, in 1864. Armed police officers and detectives were posted on the rooftops along the route. The *New York Times* reported that on every block eight to ten plainclothes detectives mingled, gimlet-eyed, with the crowd. Sand had been strewn on the streets to make them less slippery following the rain, and now the wind was picking up the grains and whipping them into the faces of the participants.

President and Mrs. Wilson left the White House at 11 a.m. in an open carriage, preceded by mounted police and surrounded by cavalry. She was by his side all day, another precedent. As the House chamber began to fill with members of Congress, La Follette was one of the last to enter. Reporters could see that he was having trouble finding a seat. He headed for one but Senator Ben Tillman put his hand on it and, stony-faced, said, "Pardon me." La Follette kept wandering, and finally found a free chair between two desks. No one joined him.

The swearing-in ceremony at the Capitol was brief, as was the president's address. He had sent it over to the printer at 11 p.m. the night before. But it promised a great turn in the fortunes of his administration, and in the history of the country.

"We are provincials no longer," he said. The dramatic progressive reforms of his first term—new banking laws, a new antitrust act, a graduated income tax and an inheritance tax, aid to farmers, an end to child labor, the Federal Reserve and the Federal Trade Commission—were now in place. It was time for America to turn its attention to the great cataclysm abroad.

Wilson was not a stem-winding orator. His words had an easy flow, and in his soft and mild Southern accent his enunciation was precise. He had a way of making his listeners feel better about themselves, nobler. He displayed the easy fluency of the college professor he had once been, but also unmistakable echoes of the gentle sermons of his Presbyterian father. Now he was calling Americans to a higher moral duty, in the interest of securing the country's destiny and spreading peace throughout the world.

"We are a composite and cosmopolitan people," he said. "We are of the blood of all the nations that are at war. The currents of our thoughts as well as the currents of our trade run quick at all seasons back and forth between us and them. The war inevitably set its mark from the first alike upon our minds, our industries, our commerce, our politics and our social action. To be indifferent to it, or independent of it, was out of the question."

The United States, he said, had been "deeply wronged upon the seas," but had no wish to lash back just for the sake of retaliation.

"We have grown more and more aware, more and more certain that the part we wished to play was the part of those who mean to vindicate and fortify peace." In a sense, of course, that sounds like the insincere declaration of any belligerent leader (including a few of Wilson's more recent successors). Some Americans mocked him for sentiments like this, long afterward, but there can be no doubt that they were genuine. He believed that this was America's destiny, and that the responsibility had fallen to him to lead it there.

He wasn't unaware of the risks ahead but thought the country had little choice, and risking war wasn't the same thing as declaring it. "We may even be drawn on, by circumstances, not by our own purpose or desire, to a more active assertion of our rights as we see them and a more immediate association with the great struggle itself. But nothing will alter our thought or our purpose. They are too clear to be obscured. They are too deeply rooted in the principles of our national life to be altered. We desire neither conquest nor advantage."

Here then, he was leaving the door slightly open. Americans might find themselves in "more immediate association" with the war. Peace was Wilson's aim, but underlying it was the thought that the United States might conclude that the only way to impose peace on Europe was by force.

Toward the end, he added another thought. He denounced revolution. Specifically, he said, no nation should support a revolution in another nation. He probably had Cuba in mind, where unrest had broken out, warning the Germans away. But a great number of those who read the text of the speech glossed over the nuance and took it as a blanket rejection by the president of the United States of all revolutions, and all revolutionaries.

In the weeks leading up to the inauguration, Wilson had received pleas urging him, as a southerner, to speak out against lynching. A resident of Washington named Louis G. Gregory wrote, "You can, Mr. President, use the moral influence of your position in a most effective way. . . . The colored people of the Nation would then know that the President of the Nation is not their enemy. . . . Is it too much to ask that the humanitarian views which you so nobly feel and express for the struggling masses of Europe, be extended to millions of American citizens, who may be likewise passing through the valley of the shadow of death?"

James Shepard, president of the National Training School for the Religious, Industrial and Literary Training of the Colored Race, in Durham, North Carolina, made the same request. "Your stand for righteousness and justice for the oppressed of all nations gives me courage to present this plea to you in behalf of the Negroes of the Southland," he wrote. "I hope that you will be spared to continue your good work for a universal peace and that you may be able to lead from bondage the oppressed of all nations and races."

The president chose to say nothing.

"THERE WERE NO demonstrations, no torrents of applause, no happy, irresponsible enthusiasm. The crowd's mood reflected the feeling of the Government, and the Government is in no holiday mood," wrote the *New York Times*.

As the Wilsons rode in their carriage back to the White House, and nervous Secret Service men scanned the rooftops for bomb throwers, the procession came to an unexpected halt. Edith felt something suddenly fall into her lap; it was just a clump of flowers.

The inaugural parade that followed was the smallest in memory. For once, the crowds gave only scattered applause to the Tammany Hall contingent and the Cook County marchers. They reserved their cheers for the soldiers who took part. Bringing up the rear of the three-hour parade were the members of a colored Elks Lodge from Washington.

"It was the plainest, simplest, briefest inauguration in the history of half a century at least, and yet perhaps there has been no inauguration so full of meaning."

A buffet luncheon reception at the White House was jammed with two hundred officials and well-wishers. House complained that "I had difficulty getting something to eat since there were so many people who insisted on talking to me. I lead a retired life and avoid public functions to such an extent that the general public rarely get at me. When they do, they make full use of it."

House was staying at the Executive Mansion, and he took Lansing up to his bedroom for a quiet discussion. Half a dozen more officials came through, including the assistant secretary of the navy, Franklin D. Roosevelt.

Wilson took time during the afternoon to issue an executive order to arm the country's merchant ships, without congressional approval.

When Navy Secretary Daniels, FDR and Admiral William Benson, chief of naval operations, met later to prepare formal orders, "it was rather a solemn time," Daniels noted in his diary, "for I felt I might be signing the death warrant of young Americans and the arming of ships may bring us into war."

That evening, House joined the Wilsons in the Oval Office, to watch the fireworks. There was no inaugural ball that year. "The President and Mrs. Wilson sat by a side window, curtained off, and asked me to join them," House noted in his diary that night. "The President was holding Mrs. Wilson's hand and leaning with his face against hers."

A little after 9 p.m., Wilson suggested they go for a ride to see the illuminations. There was no Secret Service man on the car with them, though some trailed behind in another car. "We had gone no distance before we were in a jam and the people, thronging the sidewalks and streets, recognized the President and sent up cheer after cheer. It was a dangerous moment. . . . I sat with my automatic in my hand and was ready to act if the occasion arose."

Back at the White House again, Edith Wilson had one more thought for House: Why didn't he go to London, to take the place of Ambassador Page? That would be one way to get him away from Woodrow.

The weekend had a strange coda in the House of Representatives, which like the Senate went out of session on March 4. There was little rancor in the House; it had passed the bills the president wanted, and if there was a logjam, it was the Senate's fault. The members gathered for a last meeting. They were in no particular hurry, but finally, most had ambled in. Suddenly, there was a stir at the back, and the House erupted into a thunderous ovation. Miss Rankin of Montana had arrived—the first woman elected to Congress!—and she waded through the well-wishers on the floor, shaking hundreds of hands.

This was extraordinary. The 65th Congress hadn't been seated yet, and wasn't to meet until April at the earliest, but here she was, the most exciting new member, the history-making female sensation from way out West.

Representative James A. Gallivan of Massachusetts, a Democrat, jumped up onto a table. He called on Representative Frederick Britten, a Republican from Chicago, to escort Miss Rankin to the front. "My friends," she said modestly, "I prefer to make my first speech in the next House." She bowed and sat down.

The members and their families mobbed her. Then, when the greetings were over, the Congress burst into song, as was the tradition on the last day. Congressmen and friends and relatives cheered the Red, White and Blue, sang one patriotic song after another, and then, prohibition already a popular cause, they sang "How Dry I Am." The wife of a Kentucky congressman whistled "Dixie." Helen Linthicum, the wife of Representative Charles Linthicum, a Maryland Democrat, unfurled a large flag from the east gallery rail.

After the session was over, Representative Linthicum told the *Baltimore Sun* that it had been his idea to have Congress veer away from its usual practice and indulge in singing patriotic hymns, "rather than in singing 'coon' songs and popular airs," as it was accustomed to doing on the last day of a session.

No one had to ask why, with war in the air. The threat was real, and so was the patriotic gust that blew through the Capitol. But the arrival of Miss Rankin of Montana was not. It had all been a joke. Hardly any of the members had any idea what she looked like. The wife of Representative George Edmonds, a Republican from Pennsylvania, had agreed to play the part. It was an odd prank to play, a practical joke at a time of impending crisis.

The real Miss Rankin had just embarked on her monthlong speaking tour, and her hour was to strike a month later, on April 6, at 3 in the morning.

CHAPTER 8

"No, Sir, Boss"

On February 28, a constable in Hammond, Louisiana, named Fred Karleton went in search of Emma Hooper, a 45-year-old black woman who was thought to be mentally unbalanced. He had a warrant for her arrest, for "shooting and slightly wounding a negro boy." When he found her, at home, and called upon her to surrender, she pulled out a pistol and shot him in the chest. An alarm went out and the police chief, Leon Ford, rounded up a posse that surrounded her house. When he told her to give up, she leveled a shotgun at him and pulled the trigger. But it misfired, and the chief shot her in the face with his service pistol. She retreated into the house, and barred the door. Ford's men broke it down and eventually found her hiding in an armoire. She was subdued and put into Ford's car so she could be taken to the county jail. He stopped off at the police station in town, leaving her in the car, while, he said afterward, he went to get a pair of handcuffs.

Men who were to remain unidentified hauled her out of the car, took her to the edge of town, and hanged her from a tree. When they went back to her house, they said, they found a rifle, a double-barreled shotgun, a pistol and "a plentiful supply of ammunition."

Lynchings fell sharply in 1917 from the year before. It wasn't a trend. They would spike upward again in 1918. A lynching might happen anywhere, but usually it was in the South. Of the 38 lynch victims in the United States in 1917, all but two were black. It was the way by which the white South preserved the social order, especially in the rural counties where the long arm of the law was rarely long enough to interfere with a fired-up mob. That order was under strain in 1917: Newspapers in the South and elsewhere denounced lynching, and Negro leaders, North and South, spoke out against it. As well, the colored people of the South, upon whom the South's economy depended, were beginning to realize that opportunities just might be waiting for them—away from Dixie.

Not all extrajudicial killings of Negroes happened at the hands of a lynch mob. Police were quick to shoot in those days, maybe even more so than now. It's impossible to count up the numbers of black men and women gunned down by the cops, or to say how many of them were armed and how many were not. Most of them attracted little notice when they died, and their stories are long forgotten.

The same day that Emma Hooper was hanged, a young black man named Linton Clinton was released from the county chain gang in Meigs, Georgia, and promptly lynched. He had confessed, it was reported, to molesting a 6-year-old white girl.

On March 17, in Wingate, North Carolina, a police officer named Edward Williams tried to arrest Bunk Maske, a black man, for beating his wife. Maske shot the cop and fled, but a posse caught up with him and killed him in a gun battle. Maske's brother was taken to the jail in Monroe and held hostage there, "as a precaution against further trouble."

On March 12, William Sanders, suspected of robbery, was lynched in Maysville, Kentucky. Joe Nowling, accused of rape, was lynched in Pelham, Georgia, on March 28.

In Amite, Louisiana, not far from where Emma Hooper was lynched, a mob on March 25 tried to string up a black man named Joe Rout, wanted for murder and caught hiding in a corn crib after a posse had searched for him for thirty-six hours. Rout was hauled off to a large tree, terrified. Several of the more "conservative" men in the lynch mob suggested that he should first be forced to confess and name all the other Negroes involved in the crime. This slowed the crowd down, and as they deliberated, a car full of armed sheriff's deputies pulled up. For once, the lawmen said they were taking Rout with them. They needed him as a witness. The men protested, but at that point the excitement drained out of them. As the deputies led Rout away, the women in the lynch mob began jeering at their husbands, accusing them of cowardice.

On March 16, in Brookhaven, Mississippi, police arrested a white man, Alphonse Kelley. Acting on a tip, they stopped the northbound train on the New Orleans, Mobile & Chicago Railroad, and took Kelley into custody. The last two coaches of the train were filled with more than 100 colored working men, and Kelley was charged with "enticing" them to take jobs in Bloomington, Illinois. Brookhaven is in Lincoln County, and in its account of the arrest the New Orleans Times-Picayune explained that the Negro laborers were needed in the county's sawmills, and couldn't be allowed to move north in search of better work and, perhaps, the hope of a better life. The economic boom that had swept the industrial north because of the war in Europe was creating many thousands of new jobs, and with immigration from Europe cut off, employers were happy to hire African-Americans. Places like Lincoln County had to put a stop to it, or be ruined. But though they may not have quite grasped it, the white Mississippians were contending with the first stirrings of the Great Migration, which was to have such a profound effect on both the northern and the southern states and which no one could derail. Even Negro track workers on the railroad, the Times-Picayune exclaimed, were walking off their jobs; who would do the work if the blacks all left?

"The migration to the North is not merely a hunt for higher wages; it is a racial movement," a black educator, W. W. Lucas, said that spring. Oppressed by terrible schools, injustice at the hands of the law, and economic exploitation in the form of farm store credit, he said, Negroes naturally saw better opportunities in the North. That meant more self-respect, as well. Thousands had left the South by 1917. Many thousands more would follow.

In Brookhaven, though, Kelley was led off to jail, and the two coaches at the back of the Chicago-bound train were detached and put on a sidetrack. The men spent the night in them before being sent back home.

ON THE EVENING of March 7, in West Palm Beach, Florida, a police officer named H. E. Seaman walked into the kitchen of a café on Clematis Street. He was looking for a Negro cook named Joe Wideman, wanted for theft. Wideman was there, but he ran out through the front of the restaurant, past the startled patrons, with Seaman chasing behind. Wideman began running down Clematis. He was not armed. Officer Seaman had his revolver in his hand and fired what were described as two "warning shots," but Wideman kept running. The third time Seaman pulled the trigger, he plugged the cook in the back. Wideman fell dead to the sidewalk. It was 9:30 p.m. A crowd gathered, and grew restive. The police were called out in force, and managed to maintain order. The next day a jury was impaneled and immediately ruled the killing a justifiable homicide.

Clematis Street ends at Lake Worth, which isn't a lake at all but a long thin bay that separates Palm Beach, on its barrier island, from West Palm and the rest of the Florida mainland. Six blocks north on Flagler Drive lies a bridge that connects the two. The original was built for promenaders, and was sometimes called the Wheelchair Bridge, not as in conveyances for invalids but after the little two-seater buggies that young black men would push back and forth. Parallel to it was a railroad bridge, so that the millionaires coming down from New York and Philadelphia in their private cars could be deposited directly at either of the island's grand hotels—the Break-ers, or the Royal Poinciana.

Just across the water and within a few hundred yards of the spot where Joe Wideman was gunned down, the country's foremost soci-ety orchestra leader was guiding two of his bands through the winter season at the Poinciana. James Reese Europe was no stranger to the injustices and hardships America imposed on its black citizens, nor to the often self-destructive responses those insults provoked. Born in Mobile, Alabama, he had grown up in Washington and spent the past fifteen years living in Harlem. Blacks had been barred from the musicians' union, so he formed the Clef Club, a combination hir-ing hall, social organization and civil rights group. He had struggled through the rapid decline of black musical theater that started around 1910 as the movies came in, and he knew that he would always be paid less for his songs and less for his performances than his white counterparts.

Yet by early 1917 he had achieved tremendous success as a musi-cian, composer and, mostly, impresario. The first dance craze was sweeping America, and his were the leading bands. He dreamed of creating a great Negro orchestra that would play great Negro music, that would demonstrate that the finest music and musicians in the nation were African-American. He reveled in large ensembles. When he put together a Negro orchestra for a one-time performance at Carnegie Hall in 1912, it featured 14 upright pianos, 65 musicians on bandolas, guitars, violins, celli, basses, flutes, saxophones—and one bassoon. They were accompanied by a large battery of drums.

But dance music paid the bills, and the people he mostly played for were the elite of American white society. It was Jim Europe's band that helped thrust the professional dance couple, Vernon and Irene Castle, to fame. He played at private functions for the Ham-ilton Fishes, the Wanamakers, the Pinchots. He played at clubs in New York that were for whites only. (He was once turned away from a colored club in Harlem when he showed up with the Castles, who were white, in tow.) He played in Newport in the summer, and Palm Beach in the winter.

Noble Sissle, who had a long and successful career as a singer and songwriter, and was acting more or less as Europe's right-hand man, had fond memories of the Poinciana. But the musicians were never allowed to forget that they were hired help. The resort sat on five acres, a town all to itself. It had its own power plant and refrigeration plant, which produced 10 tons of ice a day. It boasted in a large ad in the *Palm Beach Post* that its 2,500 or so guests ate their way through eight barrels of flour, 30 boxes of oranges and grapefruit, 7,200 eggs, 150 pounds of coffee and 400 bottles of water every day. At a typical dinner, 1,700 squab were cooked.

The hotel went to fewer pains when it came to counting some of its workers: There were, the ad proclaimed, between 800 and 900 colored employees. "Discipline of this great hotel is strictly enforced," it assured prospective guests. The hotel's 32 assistant head waiters and 500 waiters had been recruited from all over the United States, and were looked after by Dr. Berkely C. Walker, a colored physician educated at Howard Medical School. None of its colored staff had died on the job the preceding fifteen years, the ad boasted. Nowhere was it mentioned that America's foremost band leader was in residence.

A men's clothing store attached to the hotel ran an ostensibly humorous ad featuring a colored waiter who wouldn't buy tan shoes because he had once had a pair in Philadelphia that were too tight. "No, sir, boss," the ad copy read. "Those shoes hurt me every time I put them on. They hurt me even when they were lying on the floor under the bed. No more tan shoes for me."

In the 1917 season, the Poinciana's guests included Mr. and Mrs. Payne Whitney, Mr. and Mrs. William Randolph Hearst, Mr. and Mrs. Coleman du Pont, Harold and Willie Vanderbilt, the financier Otto Kahn, and Representative Ira C. Copley, Progressive of Illinois. On February 22 they enjoyed a grand Washington's Birthday fete, with 4,000 in attendance and with appropriate musical accompaniment. The ballroom was draped with ornamental boughs of smilax, and with purple, red and green electric lights; statuary lions crouched on pedestals, holding glass balls in their paws, shedding a glow of moonlight blue. The year before, the party had been called the Neutrality Ball. Not now.

Guests enjoyed the balmy weather, as temperatures rose into the low 70s. They raised $3,000 for the American Ambulance Field Service in France at a benefit showing of a movie called *The Isle of Tomorrow*, which was about Palm Beach, "the Millionaire's Playground." It was made by Pearl White and financed by Hearst. Tickets were an unheard-of $3 apiece.

They heard a lecture by a blind sergeant-major from the King's Own Scottish Borderers who had been wounded at the Dardanelles, in Turkey. It inspired the Reverend W. J. Carpenter to write a short piece for the *Palm Beach Post*. "The Turkish grenade which exploded near his head, causing the loss of his eyes, is an illustration of the beastly and hellish character of modern warfare," he wrote. "When one hears such a recital the conviction is burned in upon one's soul that we should be profoundly grateful that up to this time our country has been kept out of war."

On a tranquil Sunday evening, March 18, guests flocked to a concert on the veranda by one of Jim Europe's two orchestras. Under the colonnade that ran out into the gardens, they listened "until a late hour, enjoying the music and the beautiful southern night."

JIM EUROPE WAS physically strong, heavy of build but graceful, shrewd, disciplined and hardworking. He could be furious when one of his musicians did something that might bring discredit on the Negro race. In the winter of 1913–14, he went on tour with the Castles, and they played 32 cities in 28 days. It would, wrote Irene Castle later, "have been a hardship without the inspiration of this splendid music." Europe, she thought, was highly intelligent and had great musical knowledge, and "his was a very commanding figure when he faced his men." She gave him credit for suggesting a slow tempo for the foxtrot, which the Castles then made famous.

He kept the black music world of New York together when it was threatening to crumble with the advent of movies, and he elevated it with his talent for music and his skill in organization. "To my mind," wrote John W. Love, a Wanamaker family servant, "Lieutenant Europe was to our people what Theodore Roosevelt was to the white people. He was a plain, simply [sic], straight gentleman."

Eubie Blake, who worked for him and became Noble Sissle's long-time songwriting partner, described him years later as the Martin Luther King of music.

The only white music Europe admired was Russian. He loved the use of balalaikas to set the rhythm, much as he used banjos and mandolins to do the same. He felt a kinship with the Russians. They, too, expressed all the suffering and emotions of an oppressed people in their compositions, he told Sissle one day. And only Negro musicians, in America, could voice "the cry of their soul's harmony." It was no use trying to play white classical music, he said—Negro musicians would never be able to do better than a "pale imitation" of it, and would earn the condescension they would receive from white critics. By the same token, only blacks could successfully master black music. "We have our own racial feeling," he once said. "The music of our race springs from the soil, and this is true today with no other race." No other nationality, he said, could manage to "reproduce the rhythm and expression [of Negro music], because it will come from the soul of those in whose blood there runs the chord of response."

In the late summer of 1916, with American entry into the war still hard to imagine, Jim Europe was enjoying perhaps the height of his commercial success. He had just finished a season at the Casino in Saratoga, and once back in New York, he was in constant demand. He had put together dance bands that were playing at cafés all over the city. Their music was "viscerally stimulating," a critic wrote. Every night, patrons wanted to see him in the flesh, so every night he and Sissle would make the rounds of all the high-society nightspots of New York. He never rested. In 1915 he had composed and copyrighted twenty songs; the year before he had copyrighted twenty-eight. But now he had something else in mind.

He burst in on Sissle one day, as summer turned to fall, and told him he had joined the 15th Regiment of the New York National Guard—that is, the Harlem regiment. And he said he had signed Sissle up, too. Sissle began sputtering about how busy they were, especially in the evenings, and it didn't make sense, and anyway Europe was 36 years old. The older man said he, too, had had all those reasons for not joining when the idea first came up, but then realized what an opportunity it was, and an obligation. It was a chance to meet and work alongside the best Negro men of the city, he said. If the regiment could be made a success, it would attract financial support and that would mean an armory, where young men could get exercise and train in athletics. "It will build up the moral and physical negro manhood of Harlem," he said.

But that would require that the best and most sincere men in the community get involved, he told Sissle. "New York cannot afford to lose this great chance for such a strong, powerful institution, for the development of the negro manhood of Harlem." It could be, he believed, a step toward asserting racial equality.

Europe, because he had been in a cadet corps in his Washington high school, was made a sergeant, and was soon promoted to lieutenant. Then, in December, the commander, Colonel Hayward, approached Europe about putting a band together. He knew it would be a good one if Europe was in charge, and he believed it could do wonders for the visibility and prestige of the fledgling regiment, which was woefully ill equipped and almost entirely ignored by the upper leadership of the state Guard. Europe resisted—he wanted to be a real soldier, if part-time. He also worried about his own reputation if the band turned out to be mediocre or worse. So he told Hayward that he would need $10,000 to make it happen, hoping it would dissuade the colonel. A few days later, he had the money, and he agreed to lead the band.

War was still a distant prospect as 1917 began, and Jim Europe was heading to Palm Beach. He put Sissle, who stayed behind in New York that year, in charge of recruiting black musicians to the regiment. (The $10,000 would go toward paying them salaries.) In the winter, when word went out, hundreds of letters of application poured in, from all across the country. But Europe knew that a military band, more so than the dance bands he had been leading, required reed players—on clarinet and saxophone—and he knew that there wouldn't be any time for training. He needed the most accomplished musicians he could find, and he didn't have confidence in African-American reed players. So he and Sissle agreed that as soon as he was done at Palm Beach, he would be heading to Puerto Rico, where they believed the finest clarinetists and saxophonists in the United States could be found.

JAMES REESE EUROPE came out of show business, and though he encouraged some improvisation by his players, he didn't encourage much. He believed in being in charge. He was a master of syncopation—which lies at the heart of ragtime, and which he believed black musicians had a natural feel for. His dance bands tended to be small, but his heart lay with symphony-sized groupings. He thought a hundred musicians would be a good number for his National Guard band.

He knew, of course, about other tides that were starting to flow in popular music. Small bands were emerging from New Orleans, bands that laced ragtime with the blues, bands that played with a certain swing, bands that took songs and ran with them on their own, this way and that. Jim Europe had heard a group he called Razz's Band, which played for a few days in New York before breaking up, a decade or so before the war. The musicians were most likely veterans of either the pioneering (and white) Razzy Dazzy Spasm Band, or a knockoff called the Razzy Dazzy Jazzy Band. Both were from New

Orleans. "The four musicians of Razz's Band had no idea at all of what they were playing," he told an interviewer. "They improvised as they went along, but such was their innate sense of rhythm that they produced something which was very taking."

At first, Americans thought this sound was too discordant. In 1915, Freddie Keppard's Creole Band appeared in New York, and flopped. In Chicago, things went a little better. A feebly humorous yet positive column appeared in the *Chicago Daily Tribune*, accompanied by a cartoon of a black man with huge white lips and big white eyes playing a sax. "Blues Is Jazz and Jazz Is Blues," was the headline.

In January 1917, while Jim Europe was in Palm Beach, Nick LaRocca, whose parents were Sicilian, led a New Orleans group to New York, and they began a run at Reisenweber's Restaurant, at Columbus Circle. They were a huge hit. They called themselves the Original Dixieland Jass Band, and in March they made the first commercial jazz recording, for Victor. In a matter of weeks, seemingly, jazz was in the air, everywhere. Later that spring, even Europe's Clef Club Orchestra would start billing itself as a jazz band, though he said he had to keep a stern lookout to make sure his musicians didn't overly "embroider" their music. That it had been a white band that successfully brought jazz to New York was an irony soon forgotten.

In March of 1917 the famous red-light district of New Orleans, known to us as Storyville but simply called the District back then, was in full swing. Soldiers returning from duty on the Mexican border were delighted with the stopover in the Crescent City on the way home. Brothels provided good opportunities to musicians to learn their trade, and to play around with ways to "jazz up" their music. Funeral parades, where the band played slow marches on the way to the cemetery and then sped up the beat on the way home, helped spread new styles. And of course Mardi Gras played a role, too.

On March 1, 1917, a city ordinance went into effect that would segregate prostitution. Black prostitutes and black customers were limited to an Uptown neighborhood adjacent to the District. But no such restriction applied to the musicians; in all of Storyville's history, wrote the historian Al Rose, fewer than half a dozen white music makers played there. As it turned out, in any case, the segregation order was to have little effect.

Readers of the *New Orleans Times-Picayune*, the city's leading (white) newspaper, would have been hard-pressed in March 1917 to find anything suggesting that jazz was happening, in Storyville or in any of the places elsewhere in the city where white musicians were playing. But that month Edward "Kid" Ory, on the trombone, was still playing in the District. There was the great piano player, Tony Jackson. A young clarinetist named Sidney Bechet had toured some, but now he was back in his hometown. So was a piano player named Ferdinand LaMothe. Better known as Jelly Roll Morton, he said he had invented jazz. He hadn't. A great trumpet player, Joe "King" Oliver, was still playing in the neighborhood of Basin Street. So was his protégé, a 15-year-old with evident and astonishing potential, Louis Armstrong.

The following November, the Navy leaned hard on the city to shut Storyville down. That helped encourage another small wave of the Great Migration, of black jazz musicians to the nightclubs of the North. By that time, though, Lieutenant Europe was getting ready for a different trip altogether, to the trenches of the Western Front.

CHAPTER 9

"A Pleasant Air of Verisimilitude"

T he day before, he had seen a Florida lighthouse way off to starboard, but now, on March 2, Morro Castle loomed close to the portside, and then the Cabaña Fort, with its dark and ancient prison, beyond it, as H. L. Mencken's ship wheezed into the harbor at Havana. It was nearly the last stop on a long, difficult and unexpected journey home. He had gone from the Eastern Front, in January, to cold and dismal and increasingly dicey Berlin, in February, and now March had brought him to the tropics, and Cuba. He basked in the sunlight, felt the warmth reaching to the tips of his shoes. He enjoyed a good smoke, and, if he had a straw hat, there can be no doubt that he put it on at a jaunty angle.

After that plate of pork chops in Zurich, in neutral Switzerland, two weeks earlier, Mencken had made his way the next day to Berne, to meet with the editor of the English translations of the works of Nietzsche. He found the city engulfed in a thick, clammy fog. It seemed "miserably small and unattractive." The Federal Building looked too pretentious for such an unimportant country. "The whole place is damp and creepy. I cough, snuffle and long for a sunstroke."

Oscar Levy, the editor, turned out to be "much delighted by certain psychological phenomena of the war: they bear out his prophecies and reinforce his philosophy. He looks for a long contest, consistently increasing in virulence. The end, he says, will be the complete bankruptcy of Christianity."

Mencken found that attitude to be honest and particularly refreshing. That same morning in Berne he ran into half a dozen Americans from the Y.M.C.A., who had also just left Germany, after working there as neutrals in prisoner-of-war camps—"typical evangelists, ingratiating, caressing, elocutional. . . . What the average prison camp needs is an American burlesque troupe—four or five good rough comedians, armed with slapsticks and seltzer siphons; a score of fat, intriguing peroxide blonds."

The city, small and clammy as it may have been, was bustling.

"Berne houses enough Hawkshaws to outfit a thousand melodramas," Mencken wrote, using what was probably even then an archaic slang word for undercover agent. "If one sends a telegram, they hear of it at once. If one lunches with a friend, they are on the job—a German to the right and a Frenchman to the left. . . . I was told in Germany that no less than 50 German secret agents were here; the number of French, English and Italian agents must be very much greater. They are disguised as porters, waiters, Americans, evangelists, bartenders, hack drivers, even as detectives."

If Mencken had stuck around for a few weeks, he could have greeted a young American diplomat who moved to Berne from the embassy in Vienna; his name was Allen Dulles, and it was while he was trying to make himself useful in the Swiss capital that the future director of Central Intelligence got into the spirit of the place and began devoting himself to gathering the fruits of espionage.

But the journalist was not in a tarrying mood, and after rejoining Ambassador Gerard's party, he left Switzerland for Paris, worried (needlessly as it turned out) what French customs agents would make of the reams of German papers he was carrying. He stayed in a vast, gloomy hotel, the Continental. On the wall of the office he saw a list of all the employees then at the front—about two hundred names. Eighteen had been killed. His passport had been stamped with a visa that allowed him to transit France but without stopping; he heard that it was not difficult to get that amended, "but as for me, I have my eye on Spain, and the good red sun."

He was surprised at the language he saw in the English newspapers. "The German papers, in the midst of their worst fulminations, always speak of the foe with decency. No opprobrious nicknames are in use. It is always *die Franzosen*, or *die Englander*, or *die Russen*. But here we are in the midst of Huns, pirates, Boches and Goths."

Mencken spent less than twelve hours in Paris, and two of those were given over to a meal he considered superb, but like any hardworking journalist, he was able to form impressions quickly and state them forthrightly. "The French, like the Germans, seem confident of victory: I encountered half a dozen in the course of the day, and all of them declared that they would see this thing through to a finish."

If he had stayed longer, he might have adjusted his opinion. An American diplomat in Paris named Arthur Hugh Frazier wrote to Colonel House in New York: "It would be idle to deny that the last few weeks have been a very severe trial for the French nation; the intense cold weather, coupled with a shortage of coal have brought the war home to the civil population as never before; there can be no doubt that they are intensely sick of the war and only the thought that a peace at the present moment would be disastrous for the future holds them together; how long they will be able to hold out I do not know but they have nearly reached the limit."

Mencken thought the war would have to go on for five or even ten more years. "Any notion that the Germans will give up, even with the United States against them, seems to me to be chimerical. They know too well that their backs are to the wall, and that they must fight the thing out. Moreover, they still regard themselves as holding the offensive, and talk of taking Odessa in the spring."*

He still expected the United States to join the war at any moment, though by this time two weeks had passed since the renewal of unrestricted submarine warfare. "Once the United States gets into the war, we shall have a staggering exhibition of money-grabbing," he wrote. "By the time we fugitives get home, the show should be on. As for me, I shall probably volunteer as a military critic. My knowledge and experience of war, true enough, are meagre, but they are still greater than Major-General Roosevelt's. He has one day of fighting behind him: I have five days.† Perhaps I better go in as a lieutenant-general."

In Bordeaux, on his way to Spain, he breakfasted with his hat on, because he'd lost his comb. In Biarritz he finally saw the "clear blue sky." Across the border, at San Sebastian, the king of Spain's private car was attached to his train, "so I came down to Madrid in state, between two rows of soldiers presenting arms."

Madrid was balmy; Mencken was bilious. He spent a day "loafing around . . . and recovering from the war." Anti-American feeling was running high, there were no good-looking women around, as far as he could tell, and the clothes seemed to burlesque Paris fashions. He saw cows and goats milked at customers' doors, little streetcars rattling along at a walking pace, and a "multitude of professional beggars, one-legged, one armed, blind, battered, mutilated."

Spain, he learned, had definitely decided not to join in Wilson's attempt to stand up for neutral rights. "They are against the 'sharpened' U-boat war, but they are even more against *los Yanquis*." A map would suggest that Spain was considerably closer to the fighting than the United States was, but in Madrid the war seemed very far away.

---

* It's worth noting that this comment, and the one that follows, were among extensive excerpts from the diary that were published in the *Sun*, in a series that ran from March 10 to March 22, even as hostility to Germany was mounting.

† A reference to Roosevelt's charge up San Juan Hill in the Spanish-American War, compared to Mencken's time in Lithuania.

The Spanish were little affected by it, except that it was good for their economy, and they showed little interest in it.

Spain wasn't the only neutral country to refuse to step forward in solidarity after Wilson broke off relations with Germany. The Dutch ambassador complained to Colonel House that month that his nation and others had been trying in vain for two years to get Wilson's cooperation. The Dutch had Germans right on their border, and thought it prudent not to provoke their big, well-armed neighbor.

Mencken bought a copy of the *Paris Herald*, the European edition of the *New York Herald*, and read that 38 women and children had been killed by police or troops ("the special atrocity squad," Mencken called them) in German-held Strasburg as civilians there were protesting over the lack of food. "Somehow I suspect that the story is full of typographical errors," he wrote. "Nevertheless, by the time I get home I may have to spit on my hands and do some of that sort of stuff myself."

After an overnight train through beautiful Galician countryside to La Coruña, in northwest Spain, Mencken boarded a steamship called the *Alfonso XIII*. Built in Scotland in 1890, it had sailed for nearly a decade between Hamburg and New York as the *Oceana*. A little over 500 feet long, it sported two funnels and an elegant, yacht-like bow. "The number 13 bemuses me," he wrote to a friend. "No doubt it will give encouragement to mines and U-boats." Mencken had separated from Ambassador Gerard's group, which included the other American correspondents who had left Germany on the special train, and was now going to be five days ahead of them in the crossing to Havana. That got his old newspaper juices flowing, because he'd be providing American readers the first uncensored reports about conditions in Germany since the break in relations.

Over eight full days at sea, he collected his notes and his thoughts and wrote about 60,000 words—200 typescript pages. He had filled notebooks in Germany, but he had not really kept a diary. Now it all poured out.

The ship stayed within 20 miles of the Spanish coast, to avoid the submarine zone, until it reached Cape Finisterre, and from there it was able to sail unmolested, southwesterly across the Atlantic. Mornings and afternoons, he hammered away on his typewriter, but that still left him time to look about the ship, enjoy its offerings, and size up his fellow passengers, about two dozen of whom were Americans. Champagne every Thursday and Sunday; red wine the rest of the week. "The ship is copiously scented; I detect garlic, onions, burning olive oil, bilge, cologne water, stale fruit, dish water and the great masses of the Iberian plain people. My room seems to be below the water line; the atmosphere down there has a jelly-like consistency and clings to the hair."

Outside his stateroom was "a hallway used by the stewards for quarreling."

On the second full day out on the ocean, the sea grew rough and a great wave of seasickness swept the ship. Children were screaming. Mencken took his typewriter and beat a retreat to the smoking room, where good Havana cigars cost 10 cents. It was a rule on the ship that passengers were not allowed to carry matches; they could only light up in the smoking room. "It goes without saying," Mencken wrote, three years before Prohibition would make the word a central part of American English, "that every American has a match *speakeasy* in his pocket."

Like generations of Americans after him, Mencken found that he soon grew accustomed to garlic, and worried that without it food wouldn't have any flavor for him anymore.

About midway through the voyage, the air started to grow warmer, and even as Mencken kept banging out the words, it began to seem that he was truly leaving the war behind. "The chill of Northern Europe is behind us and already almost forgotten. The war, too. It is hard to grasp the fact that the United States is preparing to horn in, and that the country will be running 109 degrees of fever when we land." It had been a month since he was in Lithuania, visiting a German trench, the temperature minus 12. Now: "Warmer and smoother. The sea grows blue. A few pieces of yellow seaweed floated past this morning. The wireless brings news of the sinking of the Laconia—a lamentable business. I crossed in the Laconia in 1914, just before the war."

Mencken was tidying the last of his opus, and was nearly home— or so he thought. On March 1, as the *Alfonso XIII* was threading its way through the glittery aqua seascape of the Bahamas, a wireless message was delivered to him. It was from the editor of the *Sun*, in Baltimore, who told Mencken that a revolution had broken out in Cuba. No one in the United States could make heads or tails of it, he said. Would he stay on in Havana and write about it? Mencken agreed, and sent his own wireless message to a well-informed Dane he knew in Havana, Captain Asmus Leonhard, asking for help.

THE NEXT DAY, a launch sent by Leonhard motored out to the Spanish ship as soon as it had reached its mooring in the Cuban harbor, and Mencken was taken off and whisked through customs. "The captain himself was waiting in the arcade of the Pasaje Hotel on the Prado, eating a plate of Spanish bean soup and simultaneously smoking a Romeo y Julietta cigar."

The hotel, an old favorite of Americans, was built of limestone, three stories on one side of a middle arcade, and four on the other. A row of columns along the Prado picked up the theme of that great boulevard, lined for block after block with the columns of stately, ornate buildings. Behind the hotel lay the narrow, jumbled streets of Old Havana, practically covered in awnings, where the *gritería*, the shouts of the *habaneros* from street to balcony, filled the air.

The rooms in the hotel had 20-foot ceilings, big shutters that opened out to the street or the arcade, mosquito netting on the beds, a couple of rocking chairs and marble-topped nightstands. More rocking chairs faced each other in the main parlor. The dining room featured tropical fruits: zapote, caimito, mamey and mango. Oranges, too, eaten with a fork. It wasn't Berlin's Adlon, where Mencken had stayed, but it would do.

The Dane told Mencken what was afoot.

> "The issues in the revolution," he said, tackling the business in
> hand at once, "are simple. Menocal, who calls himself a Con-
> servative, is president, and José Miguel Gomez, who used to be
> president and calls himself a Liberal, wants to make a come-
> back. That is the whole story. José Miguel says that when Meno-
> cal was re-elected last year the so-called Liberals were chased
> away from the so-called polls by the so-called army. On the
> other hand, Menocal says that José Miguel is a porch-climber
> and ought to be chased out of the island. Both are right."

Mencken recounted that disquisition twenty-four years after the
fact, in his memoir *Heathen Days*. (And he had noticed while he was
in France in 1917 an unusual—to him—"Continental" practice: a
reporter taking extensive notes during an interview.) But what Leonhard said, or was remembered to have said, or was embellished to
have said, was largely true. Mencken, looking back from the vantage point of 1941 and poking fun at himself, said he was ready to
write the story then and there, but the Dane suggested he do some
actual reporting first. And this first revolution of 1917 was, of course,
slightly more complicated than Mencken was letting on. The United
States, to boot, was hardly as innocent as that wireless message from
the editor in Baltimore had implied.

After the break with Spain in 1898, Cuba had been administered
by the United States for four years. In 1902 a Cuban constitution,
written in Washington, was adopted; it allowed the Cubans to consider themselves a sovereign people, but a provision called the Platt
Amendment gave the United States the right to control the country's finances and foreign relations and to otherwise intervene as
Washington deemed necessary. President Theodore Roosevelt took
just such a step in 1906, after an armed uprising, and for nearly
three years Cuba was once more under an American governor. Some

Cubans say that this was when corruption first entered the country's politics, or at least on a major scale. In 1908 the United States withdrew again, and Gómez, the Liberal, was elected president. A former general in the war for independence, he was believed at the time to have enriched himself considerably while chief executive.

He was succeeded in 1913 by Mario Menocal, the Conservative. The Liberal Party had split into two factions, and the anti-Gómez Liberals believed they had reached an understanding that, in return for supporting Menocal in 1913, they would have their own turn in power beginning in 1917. But Menocal decided to run for a second four-year term. That's when the trouble started.

The election was held November 1, 1916. Menocal was declared the winner. But the Liberals (who had by now reunited) cried foul and won an order in the Cuban Supreme Court to rerun the voting in a handful of districts in two provinces. Cuba had been given an electoral structure similar to that of the United States, where each of the six provinces was allotted a number of votes in an electoral college in proportion to its population, and from province to province it was a winner-take-all system. The do-overs in Santa Clara and Oriente were to be held in a sufficient number of districts to tip each province, and thus the election, to the Liberals.

The makeup dates were February 14 in Santa Clara and a week later in Oriente. The Liberals, whose candidate was Alfredo Zayas, believed they had rightfully won the vote back in November, and despite their victory in court, they feared that the Conservatives would steal the elections again in February. They appealed to the United States to step in and supervise the voting.

But their timing was decidedly unfortunate. Germany had just made its U-boat announcement, and ambassadors in Washington and Berlin were being sent packing. As February began, most of the U.S. Atlantic Fleet was divided between the American base at Guantánamo Bay and a station off Port-au-Prince, Haiti. The U.S.S. *Olympia*, Admiral Dewey's flagship at the Battle of Manila Bay in

1898, was at Santo Domingo, in what today is the Dominican Republic. Most of the battleships, too, were in the Caribbean; an exception was the nearly new U.S.S. *Arizona*, undergoing repairs at the Navy Yard in Brooklyn. In the event of war, the fleet could be bottled up by U-boats at Guantánamo, and in any case the ships would be needed in the North Atlantic. Franklin Roosevelt, the assistant secretary of the navy, had received advice from British intelligence to get the ships away from Cuba. At just the moment when the Liberals were asking for American intervention, the Navy was moving its assets out of Cuba as fast as it could. By the end of February, most of the fleet was gone.

On February 11, three days before the revote in Santa Clara, a revolt broke out, involving civilians and several dozen soldiers. Liberals defended the uprising, arguing that they couldn't just stand by and watch Menocal win again through fraud. The government responded by arresting leading Liberal Party members. Police were deployed to oversee the publication of Liberal newspapers, and Menocal's aides said they had unearthed a plot to assassinate him, or maybe kidnap him to force him to resign.

Gómez slipped out of Havana aboard his yacht and established himself as the leading figure of the revolutionaries. The Liberal strategy was simple: Create so much disruption that the United States would be forced to intervene. With fair elections, supervised by the Americans, the Liberals were sure they would win. (Even Menocal's supporters were inclined to agree that the Liberals were the more popular party.) The government in Havana confidently predicted that it would crush the rebellion in days, but it kept spreading. On February 12, the rebels captured Santiago, Cuba's second-most-important city, not far from San Juan Hill where Colonel Roosevelt had made his name nineteen years earlier.

Washington was not pleased by any of this. Secretary of State Robert Lansing issued a statement of "no small concern," instructing the Cubans to settle their dispute through the courts, not by resort to arms. The United States would be gratified by a peaceful resolution, he said, "particularly at the present time when a great portion of the world is embroiled in armed conflict." Menocal's government replied that Lansing must have been misinformed, because there was no need for worry. Then the police shut down the leading Liberal newspaper, and the next day the government asked for volunteers to serve in the army for ninety days. The homes of suspects and others on the outs with Menocal were searched throughout Havana, though there was no unrest there. A "fair sized cannon" was discovered at the house of a customs inspector. The U.S. government announced that it was selling 10,000 rifles and 5 million rounds of ammunition to Cuba—not the intervention the Liberals had been hoping for. But the War Department was also preparing a standby plan to send 5,000 to 7,000 American troops to Cuba if the need arose, and when that was reported in the New York Times, it raised Liberal hopes. Could they succeed in forcing a replay of the occupation of 1906?

On February 14, Lansing sent a formal note to the Cuban government in which he said the United States was viewing the situation with "the greatest apprehension." Then he made a pointed argument against revolution, of any kind, anywhere. The United States, he said, could not support the overthrow of governments.

"During the last four years," he said, meaning since Wilson took office, "the Government of the United States has clearly and definitely set forth its position in regard to the recognition of Governments which have come into power through revolution and other illegal methods." It wouldn't happen.

This matter of policy was clearly rooted in attempts to justify the American effort to capture the revolutionary Pancho Villa in Mexico, but within another month it would be "clearly and definitely" set aside, as another, more distant revolution flared.

THE LIBERALS LOOKED to the United States not as a protector, exactly, but more as an unbiased umpire. Their task was to demonstrate to the

United States the inability of the Menocal government to reestablish order, and a logical, if unintuitive, way to get Washington's attention was to go after American interests on the island. These consisted primarily of sugar plantations and sugar mills, fruit growers, and iron ore mines. Most of the iron ore that came to the big new steel plant at Sparrow's Point, just outside Baltimore, came from Cuba. Turned into steel rails, much of it had gone to Russia over the preceding decade to build the Trans-Siberian Railway. But there seem to have been more scare stories than actual attacks on American property, or American citizens. (One was shot and wounded when he refused to hand over some dynamite.) Some sugar cane fields were set afire; the mines were never threatened. Still, the Wilson administration was not in the mood to consider the possibility of damage to American interests; it wanted the threat to go away.

Menocal's men played to that attitude. Raoul Desvernine, a Cuban diplomat, wrote, in a letter to the editor of the *New York Times*, "Can Cuba afford to . . . embarrass the United States at this critical moment in American history? Can Cuba afford to give the impression that she is incapable of self-government? The United States has twice intervened in Cuba, and has twice returned Cuba to the Cuban people. Cannot the patience of a nation, as well as an individual, become exhausted?"

There was, too, another element at work. The Liberals were seen as the "negro" party, the one that attracted the majority of black voters. "In Cuba, the fact that a man is a negro does not draw the sharp line of racial demarcation that it does in the South," the *New York Times* noted. But it pointed out that over the years the white population in Cuba, like the white population in the South, had used various forms of "subterfuge" to dominate at the polls. It didn't point out that Wilson was a man of the South, and content with both subterfuge and Jim Crow. The paper did report two days later that Menocal's call for volunteers "was being answered by many of the better class."

Washington sent investigators to Cuba to ascertain whether German agents were behind the Liberal unrest. They couldn't find any evidence of that—it's hard to tell if their reports were received with relief, or disappointment. The postmaster general, Albert Burleson, cut off the sending of money orders from the United States to Cuba out of fear that funds could go to the rebels. An editorial on February 23 laid out another reason to support Menocal: He could be counted on not to allow any foreign naval bases to be established in Cuba, whereas if Gómez came to power, who could say?

THIS WAS THE Cuba that Mencken landed in. He wasn't on the Eastern Front any longer, nor was he in Berlin. Over there, he had witnessed the ways of industrialized mass production of death. In Cuba—brief skirmishes with few casualties, none of which he had a chance to witness because they were far from Havana and it was just about impossible to get around. The war in Europe had been a boon to Cuba, and the city Mencken walked through was prosperous as never before. Cubans later called the five years between 1913 and 1918 the "Dance of the Millions," as sugar prices tripled and tourism from the United States boomed. As one reporter put it, "Sugar, tobacco, copper, and, in short, everything which the island republic had to sell to the outside world, including the privilege to hold no-limit prizefights, horse races with wide-open betting ring, and a score of other attractions for tourists cut off from European fields, were in demand at the best of prices."

Havana was an electoral bastion for the Liberals, but the idea of open revolt didn't go over well with the business-oriented residents of the capital. "At the start there was undoubtedly a great deal of sympathy for the Liberals, on the ground that they were roughly used in the general election," Mencken wrote, "but when they took to the field and began burning sugar fields this sympathy was alienated, and today the average Havana business man is in hopes that General Menocal will soon put them down. The wish has two springs, the one commercial and the other patriotic. On the one hand, the revolution has paralyzed business on the island and caused a very large loss in money, and, on the other hand, the demand for intervention is extremely offensive to most of the more cultured and well-to-do Cubans, and they would blush to see their country reduced once more to the level of Nicaragua and Honduras."

But then, much to the surprise of both Havana and Washington, Americans *did* intervene. On his own initiative, Commander Reginald Belknap, leading a squadron of four ships that included the *Olympia*, put 400 men ashore in Santiago and issued a proclamation calling on both sides to desist. This effectively helped the rebels, who were about to come under attack by forces loyal to the government Washington recognized as the legitimate power in Cuba. Belknap was within his rights, the Navy Department said, but it put the Wilson administration in an awkward position.

Mencken continued to make his rounds in Havana, dropping in on the government spokesman, finding—with Captain Leonhard's help—Liberals still at large and trading rumors with other Americans. There weren't many facts to be had, but he gathered enough material at these stops, he wrote afterward, "to give my dispatches a pleasant air of verisimilitude, soothing to editors if not to readers."

To avoid the censor, a friend of Leonhard's smuggled his reports by boat to Key West, and from there they were telegraphed to Baltimore. It was difficult to know how large the opposing forces were or how serious the fighting. The more the government trumpeted its victories, the less Mencken thought of them. The Cubans described the battles "in terms almost applicable to so many Tannenbergs," he wrote, referring to the crushing and tactically brilliant German victory over the Russians in the opening month of the Great War.

"Colonel Colazzo's official account of the Jatibonico fight, for example, is a truly thrilling piece of writing. He tells of how he disposed of his forces, how an advance guard of volunteers 'began to feel the fire of the rebels,' how his column then advanced in echelon formation, how the action 'developed with a frightful intensity,' how the enemy attempted a cavalry charge, how he sent in two machine guns to break it up, how his reserve were kept out of action by the 'furious fire,' how a group of enemy cavalry and infantry advanced 'as a ring of iron on my front,' how he ordered a charge which kept up for 'more than a league,' and how, finally, 'there were salutes and conferences for the surrender of the enemy forces as a stratagem to secure their orderly retirement.'

"This singular battle lasted two hours and a half, and . . . resulted in the killing of one government soldier."

On March 5, Menocal wrote to Wilson saying he needed just a few days more "to radically crush the outbreak" and restore peace "within the spirit of your noble policy." On March 8 the Liberal leader Gómez was captured at Placetas, and with that the rebellion rapidly deflated. That evening Mencken joined a happy crowd outside the President's Palace, and enjoyed watching the singing and hugging and kissing and dashing about of handsome officers. "The Cubans are folks of sudden and violent passions. Their politics constantly verges upon armed assault. But they forgive just as quickly." Later, looking back, he wrote, "I observed two things especially. The first was that, for all the uproar, no one was drunk. The other was that the cops beat up no one."

This was entertainment, for Mencken and for his readers, and he gave them a portrait of emotional, foolish, strutting Latins. His writing from Germany had been uncharacteristically modulated, perhaps because there he hadn't felt superior to those he was writing about. But in Cuba, as at an American political convention, he had been eager and willing to let the barbs fly.

With Wilson's support, Menocal had defeated the Liberals, who had characteristically taken to arguing among themselves and nurturing unrealistic fantasies. Menocal, at least, was grateful, and he would keep Cuba and the important naval base at Guantánamo, guarding the approaches to the Panama Canal, on America's side. Wilson had put down a marker against revolution. Gómez went to the Cabaña fortress prison—still in use as a prison today—but was soon afterward released by a forgiving Menocal.

CHAPTER 10

"We Are Sitting on a Volcano"

The night before her appearance at Carnegie Hall in New York, Jeannette Rankin was a guest at a dinner hosted by Harriet Laidlaw at her home on East 66th Street just off Fifth Avenue. Laidlaw was a prominent longtime suffrage activist. The following day, Rankin had lunch with Carrie Chapman Catt, president of the National American Woman Suffrage Association. Rankin was wary of Catt, on several counts. Catt had enthusiastically supported Wilson's 1916 reelection campaign, while Rankin, a Republican, had been deeply skeptical of Wilson's He-kept-us-out-of-war slogan. But the Montanan also felt that Catt was too deeply embedded in the Eastern establishment, and condescended to her as a westerner.

The West had useful lessons for the East, if only the East would pay attention. Though Rankin had picked up ideas about social justice while a student in New York eight years earlier, her distaste for the "money system" had been forged back home, in the copper-mining towns of Montana, and in the way the Anaconda Copper Mining Company mistreated its mostly immigrant workers and bought off the state legislature. She didn't believe in the survival-of-the-fittest ethos and the cruelties it inflicted on those left by the wayside, but neither did she believe that structural reforms, or better regulation, would solve the country's problems. Americans needed a new way of looking at the material world, she believed, and that's one of the reasons she had devoted so much of the past decade to winning the vote for women. Men and women were fundamentally different, she believed: Men wielded "force," and women wielded "power." Force was blind to possibilities; power looked to the future. "The greatest power in the world was the emotion of an ideal," she would recall years later.

As Rankin set out on her twenty-city speaking tour, the debilities of the American system were all too evident. High prices, food shortages and overwork were fueling discontent. Workers knew the economy was booming, thanks to the war in Europe, but most of the new prosperity was going to those at the top. Legions of Americans believed they were being unfairly exploited as the railroads and manufacturers kept up the pressure to fulfill as many orders as possible. Resistance burgeoned.

Carpenters in the shipyards of Tampa threatened to walk off the job. There was a streetcar strike in St. Louis, and one in Washington. Cigar makers in Baltimore were on strike, as were molders in Schenectady. Laundry workers in Kansas City, who were protesting particularly squalid workplace conditions, walked off the job. The owners there persuaded the city to allow them to deputize and arm squads of thugs who terrorized the women workers. There was a strike on the docks in Puerto Rico, and several men were killed when police opened fire on picketing longshoremen. Soda dispensers and moving picture operators were on strike in Houston, as were ice packers in Murphysboro, Illinois. Department store employees in Pittsburgh were on the streets in a lockout. The Philadelphia Horse Hair Dressers Union was threatening a walkout, and so were workers at the American Tobacco Company in Kentucky. Neckwear workers in Boston, garment workers in Chicago, and shipyard workers in California went out on strike. Umpires inquired about affiliating with the American Federation of Labor, as did the Base Ball Players Fraternity. The vaudeville actors' union went out on strike. "Colored" waiters in Atlantic City tried to form a union. The Bayonne silk mills were closed by a strike, and the Baldwin Locomotive Works in Eddystone, Pennsylvania, laid off 1,800 workers upon the completion of a contract to make artillery shells for the Russian army.

And at the Navy yards in Norfolk and Brooklyn, draftsmen and pattern makers were angry over their working conditions and low pay, and threatening to walk out.

THROUGH THE WINTER, the connection between the labor unrest and potential American entry into the war was a dim one, at best— even after the February jolt of renewed submarine warfare. That changed abruptly in March. The filibuster organized by La Follette against arming merchant ships sharpened a divide that ran throughout the country. The issue came out into the open. Americans had to decide if they were for guns, preparedness and war, or not. Hostility on both sides mounted.

An advisory commission on defense, appointed by Wilson, received a report from Kansas City endorsing the demands of the laundry workers. Their complaints were justified, the report said, and the owners' obstinacy was bad for the city, bad for morale, and bad for unity.

Elsewhere, naturally, it was the owners who accused their workers of undermining the national purpose. And plenty of union leaders, reflecting the opinions of their members, denounced the prospect of war as a device by the capitalists to grab further control of the country—while the workers would be shedding their blood on the battlefields.

In late February, William C. Durant, the founder of General Motors Co., visited Colonel House in New York with a message that took House by surprise. Durant said he had just traveled across the country and had met only one man between California and New

York who wanted war. He told House that "we are sitting on a volcano"—and that entry into the war might cause it to erupt.

But the anger stoked by the submarine warfare, the Zimmermann Telegram and the Senate filibuster started to make itself felt around the country. Suspicion was everywhere—of German-Americans (though that would intensify later) and of the disloyal. If La Follette could be called a traitor, how many others were out there?

Schoolteachers in New York were asked to take loyalty oaths. The trustees of Columbia University, alarmed by "radical pacifism" among the students, appointed a committee to investigate charges of "unpatriotic instruction." Theodore Roosevelt took an interest in a story about an elementary school in Newark, New Jersey, where, according to the *New York Tribune*, students, most of them from German-American families, refused to sing the National Anthem. Three times the teacher raised her ruler to start the song, and three times the classroom was filled with silence. Then one of the boys began whistling "Die Wacht am Rhein," the German anthem, and the class marched out to its martial strains. The paper quoted a local suffrage advocate as saying, "We need good Americanism here." The state commissioner of education demanded an investigation, and nine days later the head of Newark's school board reported back, in a letter that was forwarded to Roosevelt, that the school mentioned in the article didn't exist, and that in other schools nearby close questioning of teachers and staff found no evidence that anything like the incident described had occurred.

Marguerite Harrison, the *Baltimore Sun* writer who had once knitted socks for Austrian soldiers, was told by her editor to start working on a series of articles that would promote preparedness. Baltimore was getting ready to put on a charity bazaar to raise money for relief aid in the Allied nations, and Harrison, who was from the right social circles, undoubtedly wrote all or most of several articles the paper ran before and during the weeklong event. (Like most stories in those days, they didn't carry a byline.) But only a mile or two from the elegant Mount Vernon neighborhood where Harrison lived and the bazaar was held, Baltimore was also dealing with quite a different issue.

Four boys at School No. 1, in South Baltimore, past the steamer wharfs and fish-oil plant that lined what was then called the Basin, refused to salute the flag. All of their mothers, when questioned, said they believed in internationalism. Then, at School No. 21, another boy, 14-year-old Simon Burgatch, also refused to salute the flag. Three of the boys, it turns out, had been born in Russia. Baltimore had a large German-American population and a large Irish-American population—two groups that, for different reasons, were generally opposed to going to war. But here the agitators were Russians, a group that also resisted the calls for war because the immigrants who came from there to the United States were implacably hostile to the czar and his anti-Semitic autocracy. All four boys at School No. 1 were members of the school's Socialist Club. Etta Gibson, the mother of the one non-Russian, said she was proud of her son Robert. She and her late husband had taught him socialism from earliest childhood, she said, and a true socialist believed in the solidarity of workers irrespective of nationality.

The boys were suspended, until two weeks later when they finally gave in. Their punishment was to stand in front of the other students at an assembly, salute the flag, and recite the words to both "The Star-Spangled Banner" and "My Country, 'Tis of Thee."

THAT PUBLIC SCHOOL No. 1 in Baltimore had a Socialist Club speaks to the American attitude toward socialism a century ago. It was not a hugely popular political strain, but it was a largely respectable one. A Socialist, Victor Berger, had been elected to Congress from Wisconsin in 1910, and another, Meyer London, won a House seat from New York in 1914. Milwaukee had several Socialist mayors. America had had a long history with communal utopias; the Shakers were an obvious early example, but it wouldn't be too much of a stretch to look back to 1620 and the landing of the Pilgrims. Modern, political socialism arrived with German refugees fleeing the Kaiser's autocracy after the failed revolution of 1848. The Socialist Labor Party was founded in New York in 1876; most of its members were German or British immigrants.

The socialists' objective was to create a political party that would represent the interests of the industrial workers of America. Their goal was to merge the labor movement with a political organization. There was some resistance to that within the existing unions, which in that era largely represented skilled workers in the various crafts. But the sense of exclusion felt by unskilled workers, whose numbers were booming as larger and larger mills and factories became mechanized, heightened socialism's appeal. It wasn't hard to imagine that America would keep moving toward greater and greater industrialization, concentrated in larger and larger economic combines—all of which would make socialism look like a viable response. The excesses of the industrialists, and the violent suppression of strikes at the Homestead Steel Works in 1892, at the Pullman Company in 1894, and among coal miners who worked for John D. Rockefeller at Ludlow, Colorado, in 1914, gave the socialists a powerful argument. True socialism, as well, would do away with Wall Street—then as now a popular target across much of the country.

But the socialists were beset by factionalism, as different socialist parties arose and divided and were superseded by others. And they struggled against the indifference of large numbers of American workers, who, unlike their European counterparts, were quite willing to pick up and move somewhere else, and try something else, whenever they became dissatisfied. Americans' physical mobility was one of socialism's biggest challenges. Socialist candidates ran regularly for president; Eugene V. Debs got more than 900,000 votes in 1912, which amounted to just a bit more than 6 percent of the total. In percentage terms, that was the movement's high tide. It was the advent of the Union of Soviet Socialist Republics—after World War I—that gave socialism a bad name in the United States, even as a very large number of democratic socialists here were horrified by what they saw as the perversion of their ideology by the Russians.

RANKIN'S SPEAKING TOUR took her to Chicago and throughout the Midwest. In Des Moines, she impressed the *Evening Tribune* with the "accuracy" of her address—less fervor than a male politician might employ, but also less "sloshing around." City after city, she stayed away from the topic of the war. Brother Wellington had insisted, and she had agreed. She hadn't always been so reticent. In 1914 she had referred to the "brutal useless . . . great economic war" that had broken out in Europe. She campaigned for Congress in 1916 on a platform that included a call for preparedness—for permanent peace. While stumping across the state that fall, "I judged the sentiment in Montana was overwhelmingly against war."

But Carrie Catt, who had spoken out against preparedness for war in early February, was changing her mind by the end of the month. She thought the suffrage movement could hurt itself badly by taking a stand against war. There was more to gain from showing its loyalty to Wilson and its readiness to back war if necessary, she argued. Rankin had her difficulties with Catt, but the older woman was, after all, one of the two or three most important women in the suffrage campaign. They almost certainly talked it about it at that luncheon back in New York. Rankin didn't like war because she saw it as something that men did when they couldn't find an alternative, but the whole point of her going to Congress was to win the vote for women. That was paramount.

By the second week of March, in any case, the entire country was about to come to a standstill—literally. The four biggest railroad unions—the brotherhoods, as they were known—had had enough of overwork and planning began for a nationwide strike. At just the moment when Americans were arguing over the most momentous question to have faced them since the Civil War, at a moment when swift mobilization of the country's resources might be called for, in a land without paved highways or, of course, air service, a catastrophic shutdown of the railroads was in the offing.

The issue was the eight-hour workday. Federal employees had enjoyed an eight-hour day for more than twenty years, but the railroad owners—and most industrialists—were adamant that they had the right to set hours, and any worker who didn't like them could find another job. In 1916, Congress had passed the Adamson Act, which established an eight-hour day for railroad workers, but the owners sued and, quite quickly, the case made its way to the Supreme Court.

The idea behind eight-hour legislation is that management, to avoid the excess payments of overtime, will hire more employees and thus create more jobs. In 1917, a year of full employment, the railroads would have been hard-pressed to find more workers, and the effects of the law would actually be felt in considerably higher pay packets for the engineers, trainmen, conductors and firemen who worked the extra hours.

Restraint of trade, the railroads said of the Adamson Act. It inserts the federal government in a place it doesn't belong, between capital and labor. The law's backers said it was about ensuring safety on the railroads, but the owners said it was really about placating the brotherhoods.

In fact, there was already a law on the books limiting railroad workers to sixteen hours a day; between 1912 and 1915, that law was violated 544,000 times. Among them, the four big unions had nearly 300,000 members. They had decided in January to wait for a ruling by the Supreme Court before moving ahead with a strike, but week after week went by without a decision. Finally the unions announced at the beginning of March that if there was no word from the Court by March 5, they would feel justified in launching "aggressive action," though because of the threat of war they promised no "radical" moves. March 5 came and went and still the Court was silent.

In Washington, the president was indisposed. Wilson had come down with what was described as a bad cold immediately after his new term began, and for ten crucial days he was out of the public eye. For ten days—nothing out of the White House. The railroad strike was on course.

The owners, led by Daniel Willard of the Baltimore & Ohio, now made a big show of their readiness to serve the country if war should come. Troop trains would get priority, they announced in newspaper ads, and they would follow Washington's directives. "The serious international situation causes every good citizen to put every thought of personal right or desire second to his duty to his country. Surely this is no time for internal industrial warfare," they said in a public statement.

The unions issued their own statement, calling the insinuations of disloyalty "absurd." It continued: "Assurances of our willingness and intention to support our country should war be declared, have been given to the president of the United States. . . . Seemingly it has been the purpose of the railroad companies to postpone settlement of this question [the eight-hour day] until either a panic or war would defeat our demands."

On March 10 a trade publication called *Railway Review* lashed out at the unions and at Congress, for doing the unions' bidding. "There is nothing now in our laws to prevent the most destructive of railway strikes—even when foreign war is impending or upon us," it fumed in an editorial. "Our country's greatest enemy just now is the labor demagogue and his subservient tools in congress."

Two weeks later: "It is greatly to be hoped that the advent of the first woman 'congressman' will be followed by droves of them. We really need a congress of real women. They would have so much more virility and gimp and spunk than the effeminate neurotics who constituted the 64th congress."

On March 9, freight handlers walked off the job at the New York Central yards on the West Side of Manhattan. They were not within the jurisdiction of the big brotherhoods, but were hoping to affiliate with the American Federation of Labor. They wanted a raise in pay, from 22 cents to 25 cents an hour. A news article in the *New York Times* referred to their leader, Antonio Corelli, as the "ringleader." The railroad brought in extra cops and one hundred "negro strike-breakers."

Two days later, the leaders of the four big unions met in Cleveland and decided to convene four regional meetings of union executives, in St. Louis, St. Paul, New York and Washington, to plot a course. They vowed not to "embarrass" the nation in the event of a crisis. No one was sure what that meant. They also said they had a compromise offer to bring to the railroads. Company executives unsurprisingly dismissed it out of hand before they knew what it might propose.

The next day, a Monday, the country waited for the Supreme Court ruling on the Adamson law. It didn't come. The Brotherhood of Locomotive Engineers denied that it had called for a strike to begin the following Saturday, March 17. But that Wednesday, as a precaution, the Baltimore & Ohio placed an embargo on all perishable freight and livestock. It wasn't going to be responsible for its shippers' losses if the trains should grind to a halt.

That day, Joseph Pulitzer's paper, the *Evening World*, ran an incendiary editorial.

TREASON

Food riots—national discord proclaimed by pro-Germanism and pusillanimity in the United States Senate—and now a threatened tie-up of the country's railroads!

What can we do next that will sound well in Berlin?

Whatever the railroad brotherhoods may promise in case of war their deliberate action at this moment in threatening to paralyze transportation and thereby embarrass the nation in its preparations for defense can be called by but one name.

The railroad employees are entitled to state and urge their

claims. But they are neither starving nor oppressed. They can offer no excuse for menacing the country with a general strike just now, save the excuse of seizing a strategic moment to fight at all costs for what they want.

The Supreme Court has not yet reached a decision on the Eight Hour Law. No further legislation is possible until Congress convenes next month. War may come. So the railroad brotherhoods push forward with demands and threats, taking advantage of a national crisis to further their special interests.

Do they call it patriotism?

Whether loyal or disloyal in case of war, any organization of American labor that chooses such a time as this to try menacing or disruptive tactics, thereby interfering with the nation's defense plans, casting doubt upon national unity and inviting the Imperial German Government to regard this country as too full of domestic trouble and dissension to be dangerous, is guilty of nothing short of treason.

The president was still sick. But William Wilson, the secretary of labor, wrote on that same Wednesday to Joseph Tumulty, Woodrow Wilson's secretary. He had learned through back channels, he said, that the unions had decided against calling a general nationwide strike, at least right away. Instead, they would strike first against lines serving Chicago, then, if their demands were not met, they would expand the strike to an eastern railroad (probably one of the smaller lines, the New Haven or the Delaware, Lackawanna & Western). And then they would keep widening the walkout in stages until, if need be, it did in fact become a national strike.

The next day, Daniel Willard of the B&O wrote to Samuel Gompers, head of the American Federation of Labor. "I believe that I am honestly a friend of labor," he wrote. But at a time of national crisis, he warned, the unions couldn't have it all their way.

Gompers didn't have much use for the railroad managers of the country. "They are not blessed with constructive or conciliatory talent in dealing with the human agents necessary to transportation," he wrote.

On Friday the 16th, President L. W. Hill of the Great Northern Railway sent a telegram to Montana Governor Sam Stewart demanding that he command the police to "preserve order and protect all property and persons" in the event of a strike.

That same day, the president of the Union Pacific, Edgar Calvin, suggested that Germany, a "shrewder and more astute power," was organizing the strike. "The brotherhood leaders have overlooked the fact that in many ways a railroad strike in this country would be worth more to our enemies than the winning of many battles," he said.

Tumulty sent a letter in to the president in his sick room. "I am afraid there will be a great deal of criticism and censure leveled at the Administration unless something is done immediately. . . . I do not think we can afford to sit down and wait for the results of a nationwide strike." Wilson told him he didn't see what more could be done. Tumulty urged the president to issue a statement calling on both sides to come to their senses. Wilson would be justified, he wrote, in calling efforts to launch a strike "acts of the highest treason."

That suggested that the unions bore the responsibility, but when Wilson stirred himself he instead wrote an appeal to the railroad management bargaining committee asking it to work out "an immediate accommodation" at a time when the peace of the nation and of the world was in peril. He cc'd the brotherhoods.

The two sides were to meet for a bargaining session over the weekend at the Biltmore Hotel in New York. Surely the Supreme Court decision would come down the following Monday, the 19th, but now the brotherhoods wanted to press their case. The White House sent four "mediators" to lean on the bargainers: Secretary of Labor Wilson (formerly of the United Mine Workers); Secretary of the Interior Franklin Lane; Willard, chief of the B&O; and Gompers, head of the

AFL. Gompers was late; no one knew where he was. An Associated Press reporter finally found him at a bar in Atlantic City.

ON MARCH 15, the newspapers reported that another American ship had been sunk by a German U-boat. It was a freighter called the *Algonquin*, and this time there had been no warning. The *U-62*, sixty-five miles west of Bishop Rock in the English Channel, had opened fire on the *Algonquin* with its deck gun, causing enough damage to sink the ship. All twenty-seven crewmen got off safely in lifeboats. This time, the submarine captain refused to give them a tow, and it took them two days to reach the English coast. "Merciless," headlined the *Atlanta Constitution* when word reached the United States. But the foodstuffs, metals and machinery the freighter had been carrying could well have been considered contraband, the American consul who handled the incident reported. And, on top of that, the ship had just recently been transferred from British to American registry. Again, it didn't look like a clear-cut case, not the "overt act" that Wilson had said would propel the United States toward a state of war.

"I am sick at heart, and burned up with fiery indignation, at Wilson's timid shuffling and hesitancy," Theodore Roosevelt wrote to an English friend. "He is as baneful to this country as an overdose of morphine to an invalid. We should have been in the war six weeks ago. He has not even been preparing. He seems impervious to every consideration of national honor and right; and he has behind him the solid alliance of the utterly base materialists, the utterly silly sentimentalists, and all that portion of the population which is at heart traitorous."

On March 16, another U-boat attacked another American ship, and this time there were no mitigating factors. But Americans wouldn't get that news for several days. Instead, they opened their papers over breakfast, or perhaps while riding the commuter train to work, to read that, as the *New York Tribune* headlined it, "Railroad Strike Called, Men Quit To-morrow."

Management had said it would abide by the Supreme Court decision, whenever it came down, even if it required them to observe an eight-hour-day rule. But the unions wanted an agreement. They announced, as William Wilson had expected, a gradual unrolling of the strike, but it was considerably less gradual than he had thought it would be. And the unions targeted big railroads from the start: First, on the seventeenth, the New York Central, the Baltimore & Ohio, and eighteen lines serving Chicago. The next day: the Chesapeake & Ohio, the Norfolk & Western, the Southern, and others. The union men said they might allow milk trains to run. The New York Central called on its retirees to come back to work.

The nation was about to be paralyzed. New Yorkers, reading the *Tribune*, learned that the city was close to running out of food. Yet even so, there was another, bigger story on the front page that day:

CZAR OF RUSSIA ABANDONS THRONE;
ARMY REVOLTS AND JOINS PEOPLE

CHAPTER II

"Cossacks, Riding Up and Down"

On March 8, a Thursday, a small group of angry women gathered beneath the winter sky on the short block in Petrograd between the Troitsky Bridge over the Neva and the Marsovo Polye, the "Field of Mars" parade ground. Behind them, police closed off the bridge. They directed pedestrians coming over from the other side onto the embankment, away from the women. There were about fifty of them, wrote the journalist Florence MacLeod Harper, who had just come out of the nearby British embassy, and they were shouting. Students appeared among them. One started to make a speech.

The women were angry, said one bystander, because they had no food. Women had been standing in breadlines from four or five every morning, in the bitter cold. When they finally reached a counter, more often than not there was nothing left. One such line formed daily across from the U.S. embassy. No one was actually starving to death in Petrograd, but the bare shops stoked an anger that had long been building. Most of the women Harper saw were textile workers from the section of the city called the Vyborg side. Police agents noticed that the factories where the women worked and the breadlines where they stood served as forums for discontent. About one-third of the women of Petrograd were employed in 1917, 130,000 of them in factories. Real earnings in the textile mills had dropped 3.4 percent since the war began, 16.4 percent in woolen mills. Now the women were agitating for a general strike. Employees at the Putilov Plant, the city's largest factory, where more than 26,000 workers turned out boilers, cannons, gun carriages, shrapnel and other machine-tool products, had walked off the job the day before. Would the action spread? March 8 was International Women's Day, and that was reason enough to rally. Some on the Field of Mars began to sing the "Marseillaise."

The crowd began to move slowly across the parade ground, while the police watched from a distance. A streetcar suddenly swung around the corner, and the women, joined now by men, rushed over to block its path. They forced the passengers to get off, then threw the motorman's control handle into a snowbank to prevent the car from moving again. Another streetcar came up behind it, and another, and another, and the crowd grew as each was disabled in turn.

Now there were maybe 500 people. Young army recruits who were out drilling—they were among the 322,000 soldiers then in Petrograd and the surrounding region—were hustled away by their officers. The crowd kept moving down Sadovaya Street, still growing, until it reached Nevsky Prospekt, Petrograd's grand thoroughfare. They turned right, as if to march on the Winter Palace itself. Ordinary policeman at their posts along Nevsky tried to stop them, but they swept past. The mood brightened. Harper heard more and more laughter. She noticed that the men tended to stick to the sidewalks, but the women marched down the center of the avenue. At the Fontanka River they met a line of mounted Cossacks and stopped. An officer shouted, "Keep moving!" A woman in the crowd shouted back, "It is easy for you to say keep moving—you're on a horse!" The crowd started laughing.

At the Catherine Canal[14] they met a line of "pharaohs"—as the

14   Today's Griboyedov Canal.

cops were called—who in tight formation blocked the bridge. The marchers split in two, flowing in both directions along the embankment. They didn't re-form, and as they drifted off home, it seemed this had been just another spontaneous demonstration, a brief eruption of protest, easily handled by the authorities.

In fact, across the river on the Vyborg side, out of sight of the diplomats and journalists who were in the center of the city, the street protests were at least as large, and more unruly. At the Neva Thread Mills, windows were smashed and the women workers surged out of the plant. They moved down a lane to the Ludwig Nobel Machinery Works. They pelted the windows with snowballs until the employees came out to join them. Then they did the same at the Bolshoi Sampsonievsky Mill No. 1. "Down with hunger!" they shouted. "Bread for the workers!" And also this: "Down with the war!"

At the Erikson Plant, workers climbed atop piles of scrap metal and discarded machinery, and called for a general strike. At the Russian Company for Aerial Navigation, a police commander drew his pistol in an effort to stop a crowd of workers approaching the main gate. The strikers grabbed his gun and beat him senseless.

An army captain, Alexander Chikolini, was surveying the unrest on the Vyborg side when he saw a group of protesters marching and chanting "Bread!" Another group came from the opposite direction, chanting "Down with the war!" The groups merged, and so did the demands.

Estimates by the police and other government agencies put the number of those going out on strike at between 78,000 and 128,000.

That evening, radical Bolsheviks gathered at the apartment of a couple named Pavlov on the Vyborg side, at 35 Serdobolsk Street. After reviewing the events of the day, they concluded that a revolution was not imminent. Across the Neva, a dinner was held at the U.S. embassy in honor of the newly arrived Japanese ambassador. It was the last such function ever to be attended by ministers of the Imperial Russian government.

Calm as it appeared to be to those in the center, the Cossacks were sent out to patrol Petrograd that night. Someone smelled trouble— or perhaps Protopopov, the interior minister, was trying to instigate a revolt so he could put it down, as his many detractors feared he would. In any case, the next day brought out crowds in even greater numbers.

"I was sure they meant business, because all traffic was stopped and the crowds formed on Nevsky," Harper wrote. "Cossacks, riding up and down, dispersed them as soon as they would form." She walked along the avenue until she came up against a squad of Cossacks riding toward her. They formed a solid wall, from one side of the street to the other. She noticed that they were smiling as they prodded people to turn back. She also noticed that they all appeared to be teenagers.

"We slid and slipped and ran, and slid again, until finally we reached the Kazan Cathedral. There the American vice-consul joined us. All around the cathedral there was a big mob. Sometimes the Cossacks used their whips, sometimes the butts of their lances, but they weren't rough. There was no violence. No one was hurt, and when they would gallop a few feet, or make a run on the people, the people would scatter and then turn around and cheer them. It was a very good-natured mob."

Overnight, bread shops were broken into and cars overturned. There was still no shooting. By Saturday morning, 300,000 workers were on strike. A huge crowd formed outside the Nikolaev railroad station—the terminus of the line to Moscow. Then the protesters began marching up Nevsky, this time smashing store windows as they went. "Young Russia is on the march!" a speaker shouted. Harper watched as a man tried to drive through the crowd in his sleigh. Angry protesters pulled him out, threw him to the ground, and beat his head in with a streetcar control handle. It was the first fatality she encountered. Later in the morning, a crowd broke into a small café and killed two men who were inside.

The numbers on the streets swelled and then diminished. Some thought the main trouble was over. But protests broke out in another part of the city, known as the Petrograd side. Fourteen thousand workers walked out of the Obukhov Factory, with red banners that read: "Down with the autocracy! Long live a democratic republic!" And in the afternoon an even bigger assembly formed again outside the Nikolaev station. Students stood on lamppost bases haranguing the crowd. Cossacks rode through from time to time, but the people just closed up behind them again, as if they were boats moving through water. A group unfurled a huge red banner, and the demonstrators set off up Nevsky again, toward the Catherine Canal.

Harper took refuge briefly in the flamboyant Singer Building, then followed the crowd up the street. A squad of cavalrymen again blocked the bridge leading over the canal. Abruptly, they dismounted, forming two rows. A volley rang out, and then another. Bodies fell to the snow-packed street, as those who had not been hit ran for safety. The shooting had begun, but it ended as quickly as it started. Elsewhere that day, mobs began to set upon lone policemen, beating them with bricks and bottles, and stealing their guns. The pharaohs began putting on soldiers' overcoats, or changing into civilian clothes, so they wouldn't be recognized.

The president of the Duma, a wealthy landowner named Mikhail Rodzianko, thought that this was the last day the regime had a chance to save itself. If new ministers had been appointed, and if the hated empress had been packed off to the czar's Crimean estate at Livadia, he later wrote, the revolution might have been contained. Neither happened. Alexandra spent the afternoon seeking solace at the grave of the monk Rasputin, murdered in December. "I felt such calm and peace at His dear grave!" she wrote Nicholas. "He died to save us." The czar, away at the front, received a telegram from Petrograd telling him of disturbances there. That evening he played dominos.

The city was quiet again that night. Somewhat astonishingly, Harper saw a play at the French Theater. Nevsky was deserted, lit up by a powerful searchlight on the Admiralty Building. The police fanned out under cover of darkness and arrested more than a hundred suspected revolutionaries. Then it all boiled over on Sunday, March 11.

Crowds again began to form. The police had set up machine-gun nests in the upper windows of buildings on the main streets. The young soldiers Harper had noticed a few days earlier were nowhere to be seen. Yet the mood was buoyant as the day began. Many families had turned out with their children in tow, to witness history in the making. Police units and groups of protesters sparred here and there; people shouted and pushed and then moved on to the next confrontation. Restaurants were open, and those who could afford one enjoyed the opportunity to eat a hot lunch.

As soon as the streets filled again in the early afternoon, the police opened fire. At Sadovaya Street, machine guns shot down scores of people in the front ranks. The mob retreated, running, trampling some of the victims, until it reached the Fontanka River, where another police line met it with a barrage of bullets. Police snipers, on rooftops, began shooting into the crowds below. Others emerged from behind palace gates, and set up a crossfire. "The dead were thick. The wounded were screaming as they were trampled down."

At the Moika Canal, soldiers from a reserve battalion of the Pavlovsky Regiment sank to one knee and opened fire on an approaching crowd. But when the news reached the regular soldiers at the Pavlovsky barracks nearby, they pushed their way out onto the street to retrieve their comrades—and to stop the shooting. At the canal, they skirmished with the police.

That evening, they assembled on the Field of Mars, defying their officers.

NICHOLAS, WHO HAD left for the front the day before the women's march, received a telegram from General Sergei Khabalov, commandant of the Petrograd garrison, downplaying the number of dead and wounded. Khabalov did mention that 240,000 workers had gone out on strike. Rodzianko, the Duma president, also telegrammed the czar that day.

"The situation is serious," he wrote. "The capital is in a state of anarchy. The government is paralyzed. Transport service and the supply of food and fuel are completely disrupted. General discontent is growing. There is wild shooting in the streets. In places troops are firing at each other. It is necessary that some person who enjoys the confidence of the country be entrusted immediately with the formation of a new government. There can be no delay. Any procrastination is tantamount to death."

Nicholas was annoyed by that telegram. His response was to order his troops to open fire on demonstrators.

This the young men of the Pavlovsky Regiment in Petrograd refused to do. When an officer tried to force them to obey, one of the men cut off his hand.

It was an act of disobedience on the unit level, a small-scale mutiny. The turning of the tide happened later that night, when platoon leaders and some of the officers of the Volynsky Guards Regiment decided to join the uprising. At 6 a.m. on March 12, 400 soldiers of the regiment lined up in parade formation. When their commanding officer appeared, the soldiers shouted *"Ura!"*—Hurrah!—instead of the usual prescribed greeting. Puzzled, the army captain began reading the czar's order. The men began banging their rifle butts on the floor. Some officers fled. The commander, Captain Lashkevich, was shot dead. Then the men, with their arms, marched out to the street, accompanied by the regimental band.

Throughout the day, one regiment after another went over to the rebellion. Now it was the army versus the police. Everyone remarked at the way the dreaded Cossacks—the mounted units recruited from the Russian borderlands, fearsome in reputation and legendary practitioners of pogroms against Jews—went through the motions of crowd control. They had become disaffected after almost three years of war and hardship. They served their emperor with considerably less zeal than their reputation warranted.

A Russian journalist spoke with soldiers of the storied Preobrazhensky Regiment—Peter the Great's favorite—who had decided to defy orders. One of their complaints had to do with the diet of lentils the army was feeding them. They told him that they had to see this through to the end; if they backed down now, they'd be shot.

The soldiers began mixing with the striking workers. A truck full of soldiers roared down Sampsonievsky Street on the Vyborg side, bristling with bayonets, all flying red flags. A mob broke into the Kresty Prison and freed the prisoners. One of them, the Bolshevik Vasily Schmidt, was shocked to see thousands of soldiers handing out arms to civilians. He grabbed a gun himself, and set out for the Duma, across the river.

The Petrograd commandant, General Khabalov, ordered a detachment under the Preobrazhensky commander, General Alexander Kutepov, to surround and subdue the rebel barracks off Liteiny Prospekt. But his men began mixing with the crowds of civilians, and melted away. Kutepov went home.

JAMES HOUGHTELING STEPPED off the overnight train from Moscow. It was 1 p.m., and there wasn't an *izvozchik*, or sleigh, for hire, in sight. The trolleys that normally clanked past the Nikolaev station weren't running. The crowds that had filled the square the day before were nowhere to be seen. "I knew instinctively that the revolution had begun," he wrote in his diary. "A workman came and explained, and then showed me by gestures, that there had been shooting."

Houghteling buttoned up his overcoat, slung the strap of a consular bag over his shoulder—he said it must have weighed 100 pounds—and set off on foot through the snow to the American embassy, more than a mile away. He heard no sounds of fighting in the eerily quiet section of the city. He did pass scattered groups of soldiers from the Semyonovsky Regiment—still nominally loyal, but some of the soldiers were giving their guns to boys on the street, and many were ignoring the noncommissioned officers who were trying to get them to form up. Soldiers from other regiments that had already turned went by in cars, and there was friendly bantering between them.

Once Houghteling reached the embassy, colleagues filled him in. One told him he had seen the Preobrazhensky Regiment in formation that morning, while an officer harangued the men about their duty to subdue the street protests. A soldier broke from the ranks and clubbed the officer unconscious with his rifle butt. Houghteling headed back out with a colleague. When they came to Liteiny Prospekt they were stopped by an eruption of shooting. A few still-loyal companies from the Semyonovsky were in a pitched battle with other soldiers. Houghteling watched as the insurgents wheeled out five field guns, but it became apparent that no one knew how to use them. Then they began sending cars against the loyalists, with riflemen lying on each fender, two more crouching in front next to the driver, and more in the *tonneau*, or rear cabin for passengers.

"We stood," he wrote, "halfway between the lines, and watched them catapult to our corner, discharge a broadside at the enemy and swing off past us into shelter, skidding beautifully on the hard snow. Crowds of citizens standing in the protection of the buildings shouted encouragement as they passed."

Houghteling saw blood on the snow but few casualties. At dusk, the loyalist soldiers gathered their things and marched back to their barracks, unmolested. Crowds streamed onto the section of Liteiny where the battle had taken place. Houghteling joined them. Down a way, he came upon the District Court Building, entirely engulfed in flames. Police dossiers dating back decades—"masses of accumulated blackmail"—were reduced to ash. When firefighters showed up, protesters told them to let the building burn. The firemen perched idly on their carts, "watching the flaming spectacle with open-mouthed admiration."

The Americans had taken over the Austrian embassy when war

broke out in 1914 and were using it as additional office and living space. Now 20 soldiers, led by an officer, arrived at the back gate. Apparently they were loyalists. The Americans couldn't figure out if they had come to guard the building, attack it, or hide in it. None of the possibilities looked auspicious, so most of the Americans there left as evening was coming on to find quarters elsewhere. Houghteling was with a group that reached Palace Square just as the Pavlovsky Regiment marched by. "They marched in perfect order singing the Marseillaise," he wrote, "and the sergeants and corporals who commanded them were equipped with swords and in some cases with the field-glasses of officers."

RODZIANKO SENT THE czar a last message: "Civil war has started and is waxing hotter and hotter. . . . Sire, do not delay. If the movement spreads to the Army, the Germans will triumph, and the ruin of Russia, and with her the dynasty, will become inevitable. . . . The hour which will decide the fate of Yourself and of the homeland has come. Tomorrow it may already be too late."

Rodzianko was a large man, over six feet tall and weighing in the neighborhood of 300 pounds. He was eloquent and had a fine speaking voice that "on a still day could be heard a *verst*," the Russians liked to say. That was about two-thirds of a mile. But Nicholas willed himself to be deaf to "that fat man."

That evening, at the Mariinsky Palace, the czar's ministers assembled. They were unable to make any decisions. They feared they were about to be arrested. They were never to meet again.

Now soldiers, strikers, protesters, and politicians began descending on the Tauride Palace, home of the Duma. The czar's prime minister, Prince Golitsyn, had several hours earlier presented a decree, signed in advance by Nicholas, dismissing the Duma. The members ignored it. At a closed meeting, they decided to form a Provisional Duma Committee, with the conservative Rodzianko at its head. He believed he had done what he could to help the old regime save itself.

Now someone had to save Russia. The committee leaders believed they needed to take control of the uprising before it got out of hand. What if the protesters, for instance, demanded an end to the war, asked Vasily Shulgin. "We could not agree to that." Alexander Kerensky, the socialist, said that when rebellious soldiers began appearing at the Tauride Palace, "we knew we had to act decisively." The Provisional Committee decided it must assume power. The coup that some of its central figures had been planning for later in the month had been overtaken by events—events that unfolded on the angry streets of the capital.

That afternoon, a group of soldiers disarmed Captain Chikolini in the street and began chasing him when he started to run. Fearing that they would kill him, he sprinted into the Tauride Palace and burst through the doors of the Duma chamber. He was immediately named to a key post in the just-formed Military Commission of the Provisional Committee.

Across the hall, radical activists decided to gather representatives of the striking factories and of the rebellious regiments. They didn't trust the "bourgeois" politicians of the Duma. They wanted the voices of the workers who had launched the uprising to be heard. They were determined to push the revolution onward. They called themselves the Petrograd Soviet of Workers' Deputies.

An armored car was sent to arrest the czar's ministers. But none of the men in the car knew what they looked like, and they slipped away. "From that moment, the government no longer existed," remembered Nikolai Nekrasov, one of the Provisional Committee members. "But we did not figure that out for more than 24 hours." One of the committee's most pressing early concerns was figuring out where to get a map of the city.

That night police roamed the streets of Petrograd, shooting any soldiers they came upon. When Houghteling got to the apartment where he was staying, he found three soldiers in the kitchen, hiding out from loyalists and police. They spent the night. "With the Duma, the entire

Petrograd garrison and the people working together," he wrote in his diary before turning in, "this should be a real revolution."

ON TUESDAY, MARCH 13, the Semyonovsky Regiment joined the revolution—known ever afterward as the February Revolution, because by the Russian calendar then in use it was just February 28 at this point. Several thousand Cossacks were seen riding out of the city, heading south. "Today begins the long-needed house-cleaning and the police are the first refuse to be swept out," Houghteling wrote.

> Many of them are resisting and meeting violent deaths. One shot a soldier on our corner this morning and was promptly bayoneted and beheaded, much to the horror of our little servant girl who chanced to be passing. They are tremendously hated, these police, for they are all husky fighting men who are needed at the front but instead stay at home and cruelly oppress the people. Now they seem to be bewildered; they hide in apartments and on roofs and take pot-shots at soldiers and have to be laboriously captured or killed outright.

The U.S. ambassador, David Francis, reported to Washington a rumor that the imperial government had decided to abandon Petrograd, cut off all access, and subjugate it by starving the residents out. That never happened; it would be left to the Germans to try that tactic against the city twenty-five years later. In fact, plentiful stores of food were found. The belief was that the food had been held back by officials in search of graft, and this only infuriated the revolutionaries even more.

By Wednesday the city was firmly in the hands of the protesters and soldiers. Cars were commandeered and cruised the streets, bristling with rifles and bayonets. This was the first revolution in history to use automobiles. Young teenage soldiers were showing off behind the wheel. Guns were everywhere, and plenty of people had them

who didn't know how to use them. When gunmen saw an army officer on the street, they would demand his sword—and shoot him if
he refused. The police by this time were on their own, still shooting
from rooftops and out of windows. An army officer named Sergei
Mstislavsky, who had joined the rebels, was dismayed by the anarchy. An attack by loyalist forces from outside the city was a very real
possibility. "If only we had one, only one division which remained
in close-knit formation," he remembered thinking. "We had neither
artillery, nor machine guns; neither commanding officers, nor field
communications."

As Houghteling watched from the street outside the Tauride Palace, prisoners began to be brought to the Duma, army officers and
policemen who had managed to avoid being killed by the mob. "It
seemed rather decent to give these hated enemies even a drum-head
court-martial," he wrote. Then came some of the czar's ministers,
including the reviled Protopopov. He had calculated that he'd be
safer as a prisoner than on the run from the revolutionaries.

Red flags, red banners, red ribbons, adorned all Petrograd. Some
members of the Provisional Committee still hoped the czar might
designate them as Russia's lawful government. But patience had run
out; even Pavel Milyukov, who had favored a constitutional monarchy, told a colleague, "It is absolutely clear to me that everything is
over for the scoundrel Nicholas." And actual power, in any case, was
in the streets.

FINALLY, PRODDED BY a telegram from Empress Alexandra, who was
with her children at the palace at Tsarskoye Selo, Nicholas decided
to return. He was in Mogilev, about 500 miles to the southwest.
His plan was to join his family at the suburban palace. But railroad
workers blocked the lines. The imperial train first headed east, to
Bologoye on the main line connecting Petrograd and Moscow. But it
was stopped nearby, at the little town of Malaya Vishera, just north
of the point where, decades before, the tracks had been laid with that

small jog said to replicate the place where Nicholas's great-grandfather, Nicholas I, had nicked his thumb while drawing the route on a map. Petrograd was beyond the czar's reach. His train headed due west again, finally coming to a halt in the city of Pskov.

NO NEWSPAPER HAD been published since the previous Friday. Most Russians still had no idea what was going on. On the Cantacuzène-Speransky estate at Bouromka in the Ukraine, where the first hints of spring were appearing; in Lyubertsy, the planned Moscow suburb built by the American International Harvester Company; on the rocky ice-bound shores of the Solovetsky Monastery archipelago in the White Sea; in Crimean palaces and on the steppes of Central Asia—all was unchanged, unknowing, affected by the years of war but unstirred by revolution.

But on March 13, the new Duma commissar for communications, Alexander Bublikov, directed that a telegram be sent to every train station in Russia. It informed the railroad men that the Duma had assumed authority in Petrograd. Now the whole empire started to stir. In Kharkov, the chief of police stood up in his carriage, doffed his hat, and shouted, "Long live the revolution! *Ura!*"

EARLY ON THE afternoon of Thursday, March 14, Baron Rosen, the former ambassador to the United States, was having lunch at his club on Bolshaya Morskaya, where he was staying. With him were three generals and a captain, all socially prominent: a former governor-general of an outlying province, a division commander, a close relative of "one of the Allied sovereigns," and a leading member of the Polish nobility. None of them, Rosen wrote later, had had any interest or involvement in politics. They were eating in an upstairs bedroom facing a courtyard; the regular dining room looked out on the street, and that was far too dangerous a place to be with all the gunfire still taking place.

Rosen finished and walked down a hallway to his bedroom. Just

then, about 20 soldiers and sailors burst into the club. They said
they had arrived to arrest the three generals, who were marched
down to the street. There a truck was waiting to take them away,
but an angry crowd had also gathered, and insisted that the "blood-
suckers" be made to walk the two or three miles from there to the
Duma, where they were to be locked up. The weather had started to
warm, and the snow had turned slushy, which made it all the harder
to navigate the streets and sidewalks. The crowd followed the generals, jeering at them all the way. Finally, they reached the Duma.
The halls were packed with people, smelled of leather and sweat and
bread, were muddy and littered. In one hallway, explosives had been
gathered, with a small No Smoking sign next to them that everyone
ignored. Alexander Guchkov, just put in charge of military matters
for the Provisional Committee, recognized the generals and immediately ordered their release.

As they began the long slog back, another group of heavily armed
soldiers stormed the club. This time the objective was loot. Boxes and
drawers were rifled, a fine pair of boots was taken, and then the men
began clubbing at a wooden trunk that had been left in the hallway.
Rosen, incautiously, summoned up the gravitas of a long career in
the diplomatic service and tried to shame them into stopping. They
told him to put his coat on; they intended to arrest him. He went
back to his bedroom but began stalling. He could hear the soldiers
arguing over what to do. One voice cried out, "For shame! This is a
political action and you behave like a lot of scoundrelly bandits!"

Then the whole group rushed into his room, and were about to
frog march him out, when a young man in a reserve officer's uniform
appeared at his door. He told the men he recognized Baron Rosen
and would vouch for him. They argued a bit longer, but the fever
went out of the mob, and the men slunk away. The "officer" turned
out to be a student at the University of Petrograd who had been given
orders by the Provisional Committee to take a car and verify that an
order directing the confiscation of privately held firearms was being

carried out properly. That order was one of the first substantive acts of the Provisional Government, an urgent measure to subdue the anarchy that had taken hold in Petrograd and get the huge numbers of guns out of the hands of those who had no business with them. The officer-student had been riding down Morskaya when he saw the crowd outside Rosen's club and went in to investigate.

That evening, yet a third group of soldiers showed up at the club. Rosen at first thought their leader was a woman, but then realized he was a high school boy, 15 years old. There were 20 of them, on a house-by-house mission to collect guns, and with nightfall they felt the safest course was to ask for lodging for the night right there. The boy explained to Rosen that there were no regular army officers to lead such missions: Some had been killed or otherwise abused by their men; many were not trusted; virtually all were despised. Schools and colleges had been asked to supply leaders for these patrols, and, strangely enough, the practice seemed to be working. The soldiers under his command addressed the boy as "*tovarish*": comrade. Rosen and his officer colleagues, who had by that time returned from the Duma, put them up in the club bowling alley for the night, and made sure they got supper.

It was a graphic illustration, Rosen thought later, of the contradictions of those early days of revolution. Soldiers and sailors had been killing their officers, often with sadistic lust, but could then turn around and meekly obey a student who had been presented to them as the one in charge. "They were still dazed and bewildered by the unexpected results they had themselves achieved, and were not yet awake to the consciousness of having entirely at their mercy the capital of the empire—nay, the empire itself—and more particularly the bitterly hated educated classes, whom they held responsible for the war and the misery of its indefinite prolongation."

IN PSKOV, ON March 15, Nicholas received two of the more conservative members of the Duma, Alexander Guchkov and Vasily Shulgin.

They had had to sneak out of Petrograd. Shulgin was mortified to be appearing before the czar unshaven, and with a crumpled collar. Guchkov, avoiding eye contact with Nicholas, began speaking. The situation was very serious, he said. There were no reliable troops, the leftists were on the ascendant and talking about a socialist republic. If the disorder reached the front, it would be a catastrophe. Guchkov urged Nicholas to abdicate.

The czar looked as though he just wanted Guchkov to finish whatever he had to say. Then, unemotionally, the emperor said he had already decided to give up the throne—not in favor of his son, Alexis, but his brother, Michael. At about midnight, he signed the manifesto—in pencil, which seemed to suggest how indifferent he was to the occasion. "This pitiful excuse for a czar could not even see fit to sign his abdication in ink like a real man," said a Moscow politician. Nicholas squared his shoulders and admitted that a great burden had been lifted from them. Now, he told his associates, he could take his family to the palace at Livadia, just outside Yalta on the Crimean peninsula, and lead a quiet life at last.

CHAPTER 12

"Happier Days for All Humanity"

From the day German soldiers first marched into Belgium, Theodore Roosevelt and his allies had been arguing that this was a war between democracy and despotism. This was the showdown that would determine the course of history. There had always been one big flaw in that argument: Russia. The czar was even more autocratic than the kaiser. The subjugation of Poles, Armenians and especially Jews was what Russia had come to stand for in the American imagination, certainly far worse than Germany's treatment of its own minority communities. Since the turn of the century one of the great migrations of history had taken place, as more than 2 million people, Jews and others, fled Russian persecution and Russian backwardness and found a haven in the New World.

The Outlook, a magazine so closely associated with Roosevelt that he kept an office at its New York headquarters, acknowledged the problem. Russia had spearheaded the drive against democracy in Europe in the nineteenth century. It was impossible for "lovers of freedom" to forget that, the magazine editorialized. "It has been impossible for them to ignore her *pogroms*, her Siberian exile system, her police espionage and censorship, her corrupt officialdom, her war on Japan, her inefficiency in government, her despotism. . . . And when the war broke out and Russia was found on the side of France and England, some of those who had distrusted her extended their distrust to include her allies. If this is, as has been claimed, a war between autocracy and democracy, how is it, they asked, that among those who are supposed to be fighting for democracy is to be found this land of the Czar?"

From time to time, someone would describe Nicholas, accurately enough, as a mild-mannered man, modest in his comportment, dedicated to his country. But that didn't make him a democrat.

William M. Sloane, a prominent historian at Columbia University who had been accused in the press of being pro-German, argued that in fact he was anti-Russian. The danger in the war, as he saw it, would be the implications of a Russian victory. "It has been very hard, with Russia in alliance with England and France, to feel that the whole of Eastern and Southeastern Europe was to be handed over to the Russian sort of government." Russia, he argued, was intolerant of diversity, hobbled by the "rascality" of its bureaucracy, held back by the doctrines of the Orthodox Church, which occupied a paramount place in the life of the country. One of the consequences was a complete absence of the idea of citizenship; the Russian people, he said, had shown that they were unwilling to care for themselves or to assume the duties and responsibilities that true citizenship requires.*

"It is this fear of Russification that has made our sympathies in this country so divided," he said. "Nine-tenths of our so-called pro-Germans have been anti-Russians only."

Others, of course, were drawn to Russia. Put politics aside: This was the land of Tchaikovsky, Dostoevsky, Chekhov. The great Siberian *taiga* fired the imagination; so, too, the icons and incense of the dark holy churches. But Russians had another hold on the American imagination, as well. These were people who conquered a wilder-

---

* Critics make precisely the same arguments today.

ness that spanned a continent, largely untouched by European pre-
tensions and sophistication. Russian and American pioneers had the
log cabin in common, adapted in both cases from the Swedes. Russia
had the natural resources that would ensure a brilliant future. Americans saw a kinship—but at the same time romanticized a distant and
exotic country of which they had no true understanding. The United
States could seem so rational and materialistic and humdrum—Russia was of a different, soulful order. America had no Tolstoy among
its writers. It had no Kandinsky or Akhmatova, either, though these
were names unknown to virtually every American in 1917.

Marguerite Harrison had left the society page of the *Baltimore Sun*
to write about music. She reviewed a concert by the Baltimore Symphony Orchestra—then a part-time collection of professional musicians who earned a living playing in dance orchestras and movie
houses—and was thrilled by its performance of Tchaikovsky's Symphony Pathétique, capturing "all the mysticism and melancholy of
the Slav." When the New York Symphony Society came to Baltimore,
she was struck by the "barbarism" in Rimsky-Korsakov's *Coq d'Or*.

"Its weird harmonies and extraordinarily fascinating rhythm
surely must have come from Asia by way of the proverbial Tartar
under the Russian skin," she wrote, referring to a saying that all you
have to do is scratch a Russian and you'll find a Tatar (not a Tartar)
within. "It has a distinctly Oriental flavor and is a fascinating bit of
audacity."

The well-bred Harrison, in her own life of audacity, would one day
be drawn to Russia more than she could have imagined in her genteel
Baltimore years; she would see a Soviet prison, from the inside, and
travel the steppes of Central Asia. But in 1917, like a great many Americans, she found the struggles of the smaller nations trying to break
free of Russia more compelling. The cause of Poland, in particular,
which had disappeared from the map of Europe when Germany, Austria and Russia divided it among themselves in the eighteenth century,
captured the imagination of the American public.

When the greatest pianist of the time, Ignacy Paderewski, played at Baltimore's Lyric Theater, with an emphasis on works by Frédéric Chopin, Harrison was deeply affected. "The concert closed," she wrote, "with the playing of the Polish National Hymn, which Paderewski played with the tears streaming down his cheeks, a never-to-be-forgotten incident of a never-to-be-forgotten evening." Days later, Paderewski met with President Wilson, to talk about the formation of a Polish regiment in the United States.

The Boston Symphony, shortly afterward, aroused strong feelings with the "intensely nationalistic" Symphony No. 1 in E minor by Sibelius, the Finnish composer. Americans were thrilled with the thought that after the war the small nations of Europe might finally be able to be free, in acts of self-determination. This would mean a carving up of the Ottoman and Austro-Hungarian empires, of course, but also of Russia. Finland, Poland, the Baltic countries, perhaps even the Ukraine—if they could throw off the Russian yoke, what progress and happiness there would be.

FOR WILSON, WHO all along had had no desire to get entangled in Europe's conflict, Russia was a stumbling block. He wanted a better world to arise from the ashes of the war, and he wanted America to help form that better world, but how could that happen if Russia won a victory by force of arms on the Eastern Front? That was one reason he pushed the Peace Without Victory idea in January. The czar's government had been peddling the idea of creating an "independent" Poland, to appeal to Americans, but Wilson and his adviser, Colonel House, saw it as a ploy to seize Danzig from the Germans and thus establish an ice-free port for Russian use.

House also worried about Russia's reliability. Might Nicholas seek a separate peace with the Germans? Over the winter, the czar had installed a thoroughly repressive cabinet of ministers, notably including Protopopov, who was in charge of the police. On January 12, House was in Washington conferring with Wilson about the war in Europe but left the White House for a luncheon where he sat next to Jules Jusserand, the engaging and popular French ambassador. They talked about Russia. "I again expressed the opinion that Russia was the danger point for the Allies, and to this he agreed. The recent changes in the Government there have alarmed him. It has now gone from reactionary to liberal and from liberal back to extreme reactionary, showing how unstable conditions in that country are."

A few days later, back in New York, House met again with Sir William Wiseman, the savvy if unofficial British representative to the administration. "One of the interesting things Wiseman told me was that Great Britain would probably try to force Russia into a constitutional monarchy when peace was made. He thought this could be done by declaring that the Western democracies would not be willing to give a warm seaport [Russia had been promised control of Constantinople] or other concessions to a government which was not responsible to the people. That it could be dangerous to democracy to take any other course. I thought the United States' active cooperation could be counted upon in this direction."

House was concerned, at the same time, that in the event of an Allied military victory, czarist Russia might then go to war with Britain over the spoils.

Or would a defeated Russia be even more dangerous? Wiseman thought Wilson had failed to understand that threat. Even as the first paving stone was about to go through the first shop window in Petrograd, on March 11, he was writing about the Americans: "It is not realized that Russia is struggling for domestic freedom at the same time that she is fighting a foreign war; that the success of the Germans would mean the success of the reactionary movement in Russia." In other words, this *was* a war for democracy—for democracy in Russia. It was not, perhaps, the most convincing argument.

Then came the revolution. In a few short days, it upended all this thinking. It was virtually over before anyone in Washington or London knew of it. It totally changed the calculus. Never mind that no one had elected the new leaders of the Provisional Government: Clearly they were democrats and Russia had become, overnight, a democracy. That's what Americans, all the way up to the White House, were telling themselves. The war had been a clash of interests, a futile, stupid, extravagantly destructive struggle, especially on the Eastern Front. In a twinkling, Russia's February Revolution had ennobled it. Now this war had a higher calling. Prominent Americans—Wilson would not have been among their number—recalled how the war to save the Union in 1861 had become a war of emancipation by 1865. It was transformed into a more profound struggle, a *better* one. It was touched with grace—and this was potentially the same. Out of deep suffering and bloodshed would arise a finer civilization. All the world's democracies had now aligned in a single cause—to smash tyranny. All the world's democracies, that is, except for one—the United States. The cause was glorious and unstoppable. If Russia—even *Russia*—could become a democracy, Germany itself couldn't be far behind. Americans had been hearing and reading that they should go to war over the demise of a handful of clapped-out steamships, or because of intrigue south of the border; now the argument was simpler, and grander. The ultimate triumph of democracy demanded action.

Two days after the czar abdicated, Colonel House wrote Wilson from New York, urging immediate recognition of the new Russian government by the United States. He wasn't swept up by the emotion of the revolution, and he was still wary of getting into the war, but he had some advice. "I think this country should aid in every way the advancement of democracy in Russia for it will end the peril which a possible alliance between Germany, Russia and Japan might hold for us," he wrote.

"You will come out of this war as its central figure, and largely because you stand easily to the fore as the great liberal of modern times." Wilson, House assured him, had already "accelerated democracy throughout the world, and I am not too sure that the present outcome in Russia is not due largely to your influence."

Robert Lansing, the secretary of state, had been the hawk in Wilson's cabinet for some time, trying to push the president toward entry into the war. That Wilson didn't care for Lansing, and didn't value his advice, was a problem, but the nation's top diplomat tried to shake it off and persevere regardless. On March 19 he tried again to argue for war.

"It would encourage and strengthen the new democratic government of Russia, which we ought to encourage and with which we ought to sympathize. If we delay, conditions may change and the opportune moment when our friendship would be useful may be lost. I believe that the Russian Government founded on its hatred of absolutism and therefore of the German Government would be materially benefitted by feeling that this Republic was arrayed against the same enemy of liberalism."

ON MARCH 22, 12,000 people came to Madison Square Garden for a "patriotic mass meeting," to cheer for war, Roosevelt and Russia. Charles S. Fairchild, the former secretary of the treasury, said: "What an hour would be that, when a great division of patriot soldiers from our land marched up to the long battle line in France, under the Stars and Stripes, greeted by 'Britannia' and 'The Marseillaise,' answering with 'America' and 'The Star-Spangled Banner,' led by that ex-President of ours whose name you know so well!

"Such another would be when, from over the Pacific, another great division marched to the front in Russia, sent by the oldest to the youngest democracy to help save both from the dreadful foe of all democracies."

On March 25, a "mass meeting to celebrate the success of the Russian revolution," drew 1,500 people to the Manhattan Opera House on West 34th Street. A telegram from Prince Georgy Lvov, the head of the new Provisional Government, was read out: "We ask our American friends to rejoice with us in a free and happy Russia."

Roosevelt wasn't there, but he sent a message: "I rejoice from my soul that Russia, the hereditary friend of this country, has ranged herself on the side of orderly liberty, of enlightened freedom, and for the full performance of duty by free nations throughout the world. . . . This wonderful change in Russia marches with and is part of the mighty and, I believe, irresistible movement of the whole world to substitute democracy for autocracy in human government and to build up the structure of justice and liberty, of right and duty and service from the bottom instead of accepting them from human superiors. No earthly power can reverse or stop that movement. . . . Russia must go on. She will go on, and the hopes and prayers of all liberty-loving people of America will go with her."

Roosevelt was still hoping to organize his division of volunteers if the United States should enter the war, and now a lawyer from Raleigh, North Carolina, wrote him with a suggestion. The Russians are united and enthusiastic, wrote James H. Pou, but they need help before dissension is sown among them. "I believe if you were to go to Russia, with even a small American force, you could exert an influence of transcendent importance upon the war and render an inestimable service to the Russian people."

Another lawyer, W. W. Symmes of Cincinnati, had the same idea. "The Russian front is the proper place to fly our flag," he wrote. "The moral effect on the Russian people would be one of the wonderful events of all time. It would tend to spread the beneficent influence of the spirit of 'Liberty,' as nothing else could."

Headlines reflected the excitement that Americans felt. On March 19, the *Evening Ledger* in Philadelphia proclaimed:

RUSSIA FREES JEWS; ANCIENT PALE SMASHED
GREAT REJOICING REIGNS AS AGE-LONG
PERSECUTION ENDS

"Petrograd is astir with enthusiasm," the front-page article began. Newspapers and other publications found experts to explain what it all meant; most of them discerned a natural democratic tendency in Russian culture, which may have come as a surprise to many.

"I should like to say very emphatically that I was deeply impressed by the character of the Russian people and by the tremendous growth of democracy among them," a missionary named Fred Haggard, just returned from Russia, told a *New York Times* reporter. "It is a stupendous spectacle to see 160,000,000 people, most of whom are thoroughgoing democrats, under the domination of a Government that is not in the least disposed that way."

Haggard said he had been told in considerable detail the previous November how the revolution, when it came, would proceed, and he said it happened just as forecast. Among the signs of deep democratic feeling that he pointed to were the mingling of the social classes in church, where rich women knelt down beside paupers, and, oddly, the Russian practice of using patronymics, which he argued gave all men and women, from the czar to the lowliest peasant, the same standing.

"It is impossible to think of Russia, with her vast millions of people, with common language, ideas and ideals, and her unlimited resources and awakening democracy, and imagine for a moment that she is not going to become a great power in the world. And not an evil power either," Haggard said. "The future of Russia is bright."

Norman Hapgood, who had been editor at *Harper's* and was a leading proponent of a league of nations to ensure peace after the war, wrote from London: "This, the most significant political change the world has seen in many hundred years, is actually not as vast an overturning of institutions as it first appears. Russian democracy is in reality already created, for Russia has been in essence for years a democratic nation, except at the very top." When his essay was published in the *Baltimore Sun*, the deck under the main headline ended with the phrase, *"Happier Days for All Humanity."*

George Kennan, who had traveled through Siberia in 1885 and

written the seminal book *Siberia and the Exile System*,* declared the revolution "the complete triumph of democracy" and "an almost unmixed blessing" to the welfare of the entire world. Preceding his article in *The Outlook* was an unsigned editorial that congratulated the Russians for throwing out the "Prussianism" of the czarist system. "The Jews and the Poles the world over need no longer fear lest a victory of the free peoples of France and England may lead to a disaster for those Jews and Poles within Russia who are seeking to be free," it said. "The people of the United States, in particular, will find at this crisis, when they are on the brink of war with Germany, a new cause for thankfulness that circumstance, indeed their very destiny, is placing them side by side with the free peoples of Europe—the people of Italy, and France, and England, and now Russia."

On March 20, 10,000 people squeezed into the old Madison Square Garden for an event organized by the Jewish Socialist Federation of America. A thousand more stood on the sidewalks outside. The throng "shouted themselves hoarse cheering for the new government of Russia." A large band played both "The Marseillaise" and "The Star-Spangled Banner," and each provoked loud cheers. One of the speakers, a Socialist named Joseph Cannon, said the "house of Rockefeller and the house of Morgan will fall as has the house of Romanov."†

That same week, the editor of the *American Hebrew*, Herman Bernstein, said that the great Russian Empire, "fettered and tortured, kept in darkness and in bondage, has suddenly been set free. . . . The wild orgies and debauchery of the forces of darkness are ended. The spirit

---

* A cousin of Kennan's, who was named for him, became one of America's premier diplomats, devoting most of his long career to Russian affairs. He wrote the famous "Long Telegram" of 1947 arguing for a policy of containment against the Soviet Union. In 1917 he was 13 years old.

† Cannon had run unsuccessfully for the Senate from New York in 1916. He was not to be confused with "Uncle Joe" Cannon of Illinois, the former Speaker of the House of Representatives.

of democracy is awakening, the spirit of justice may follow. The spirit of America is spreading abroad." Rabbi Stephen Wise told a reporter that "a war started as a conspiracy of kings against the people will end in a triumph of the people."

Oscar Straus, who had been America's first Jewish cabinet member when he served as Roosevelt's secretary of commerce and labor, predicted that the "magnificent uprising" in Russia would ensure a shift toward nearly unanimous support for the Allies among American Jews. David Philipson, a leading Reform rabbi in Cincinnati, said that the revolution would mean the end of Zionism, since Zionism was the product of the anti-Semitism of the old czarist regime.

In late March, Wilson wrote of the Jews of Russia in a letter to Julius Rosenwald, the Chicago businessman and philanthropist. "The Russian revolution has opened the door of freedom to an oppressed people, but unless they are given life and strength and courage, the opportunity of centuries will avail them little."

THE PREVAILING EXPLANATION for the Russian Revolution was what might be called the German Theory. The idea, often publicly stated in Petrograd, and even in the Duma, was that Nicholas's government had been infected by German influence, starting with Empress Alexandra, herself a German. The Russian people, according to those in the capital, blamed German conspirators for the sorry performance of the Russian army and the breakdown in food distribution at home. Russians were growing more and more angry at the government because of its apparent German sympathies. Russians were said to be outraged at the prospect of a peace settlement with Germany after so many lives had been lost.

"It was freely asserted that the failure of the army administration and the shortage of food in Petrograd and Moscow, which had become acute, were part of a treasonable scheme to induce the masses of the people to demand that the Government make a separate peace with Germany," Lansing later wrote. "Whether these charges were true or

In early March 1917, residents of New York's Lower East Side protest food shortages and high prices.

These paperboys in Oklahoma City are ready to spread the news from Europe and around the country. This photo, by Lewis Hine, shows (left to right) Jack Ryan, 6, Jesse Ryan, 10, and Onem Smith, 12.

James Reese Europe, at the piano with his Clef Club Orchestra, was at the height of his popularity in 1917.

Rep. Jeannette Rankin of Montana, the first woman elected to the United States Congress, wanted to fight for women's issues but was immediately confronted with the question of war and peace.

Two National Service School campers enjoy a light-hearted moment outside their tent. They were taking part in a program that taught young women skills that could be useful in the event of war.

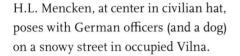

H.L. Mencken, at center in civilian hat, poses with German officers (and a dog) on a snowy street in occupied Vilna.

Teddy Roosevelt, America's foremost advocate for war, headed to Florida in March to hunt manta rays. Here he poses with his guide, Russell Coles. Overweight and 58 years old, TR was itching to take a division to France and get into the fight.

Franklin Roosevelt, the assistant Navy secretary, takes time out from his Washington duties to visit a firing range in Maryland as the United States prepares for war.

A Russian farm family tries to stay warm by a fire next to the remains of their house, wrecked in the war. This German postcard blamed Cossacks for the destruction.

Revolutionary Russian soldiers man a barricade on Liteiny Prospekt in Petrograd, in front of a tea shop.

Revolutionary soldiers take up position on a car as they prepare to set off on a mission in Petrograd. The car appears to be a pre-war Benz saloon, imported from Germany.

Alexander Kerensky, a Socialist who took part in the revolution and later headed the Provisional Government, was determined to keep the war against Germany going, in the face of increasing unpopularity and the disintegration of much of the Russian army.

A banner hailing the Soviet of Workers' and Soldiers' Deputies is raised above a revolutionary crowd in Petrograd.

Clifford K. Berryman, political cartoonist for the *Washington Evening Star*, captured the prevailing sentiment in regard to the Russian revolution: that it was driven by popular outrage against supposed pro-German circles close to Czar Nicholas II.

Another Berryman cartoon reflects the fight for control of an almost evenly divided House of Representatives.

Antiwar protesters begin to gather for a demonstration on the steps of the Capitol, in Washington.

Some African-Americans said they had no reason to fight on behalf of a Jim Crow country. But others believed that joining the war effort offered them a chance to advance their cause. These soldiers are carrying out KP duty at a training camp in the spring of 1917.

The Civarro family, at home in their tenement apartment on Second Avenue in New York City, assembling patriotic pins, for which they earned three cents per gross.

Uncle Sam and Columbia appear together at a patriotic rally in 1917.

false makes no difference, the important fact was that the belief was general that they were true, and it was this belief which influenced the people to revolt."

John Reed, the fiery journalist, concurred, up to a point. The treachery of the autocracy, and its scarcely concealed desire for a separate peace, had turned the middle class, and even business interests, against the czar, he wrote. "This is a middle class revolution, led by business men, publishers, and the progressive country nobles. The army is with them, because they are in favor of continuing the war against Germany; the Duma, because they stand for untrammeled representative government; the workingmen, peasant and Jews, because they have proclaimed the most democratic program since the French Revolution."

The Provisional Government did in fact vow to pursue the war with new determination, and few doubts were heard in the American press or halls of government. This reflected a long-standing habit of American journalists and diplomats stationed in Russia: They talked mostly to those cultivated Russians who were at ease conversing with foreigners. In other words, their sources of information tended (and still tend) to be well-educated urban liberals, cosmopolitans, who don't always have the best sense of true Russian feeling.* So *The Outlook*, for instance, could write that the Russians would now turn to the task of beating the Germans "with renewed confidence and vigor." Kennan pointed out that the impending spring thaw would make roads impassable for weeks, and that would give the Russians time to regroup and prepare themselves for the renewal of fighting once the mud had dried. "That there will be some friction and lack of coordination at first is probable; but ultimately the war will be carried on with greatly increased vigor and effectiveness."

On March 16, the day after Nicholas abdicated, Lansing passed on to Wilson a telegram from a Russia expert at the University of Chi-

---

* I was often guilty of this myself in my years as a correspondent in Moscow.

cago. The aim of the revolution, it said, is "to create conditions that will make it possible for Russia to bring into force all her strength." It will mean, therefore, "more effective prosecution of war and war until victory."

But Wilson was still sick, still out of sight, practically unheard from. It wasn't clear to anyone what his thinking was at that time. A clue, though, emerged the following week, when he sent a note to Waldo Lincoln Cook, the chief editorial writer of the *Springfield Republican*, a Massachusetts paper he had long admired, praising the good sense and eloquence of its arguments on international affairs. Wilson apparently had the Russian question in mind, among others. The paper's interpretation of events in Russia is instructive.

It called the revolution "the most portentous event of the war"— but not necessarily a welcome one. It was not at all clear where the revolution would lead. Germany was sure to try to take advantage of it, and even if the Provisional Government did intend to pursue the war, the disruption of the revolution was bound to cause some amount of chaos. Moreover, the paper wrote, Russia had been a badly run, dysfunctional country for many years; new leadership, however well intentioned, wasn't going to cure that overnight.

> In normal times revolution in Russia, beginning with the forced abdication of the czar and the assumption of power by a committee of safety would be a sufficiently great and terrible event, with wide implications for world history; coming as it does in the midst of an unprecedented world war, while it less excites imaginations already stupefied by events, its consequences are even more ominous than if it had occurred in peace.

Two days later, the paper returned to the theme. "It is much too soon for confidence that there will be no split between the moderates and the proletariat radicals, the danger of which is abundantly shown in the history of revolutions." If the Provisional Government can escape that threat, and myriad others, it will be "little short of a miracle."

The editorial then goes on to suggest that the revolution created an ideal opportunity to end the war in Europe. If Russia were to let its subject peoples form their own new countries, Austria-Hungary would surely be forced to follow, it argued. It was czarist Russia's mobilization in 1914, its intrigues in the Balkans, and its desire to take Constantinople that had been so central to the outbreak and prolongation of the war; now, all those factors had disappeared. This was a moment to seize, the newspaper said. And that was surely an argument that spoke directly to Wilson's own desires.

Theodore Roosevelt got a letter from an old English friend, a former member of Parliament named Moreton Frewen. "Petrograd you know more about than we here do," Frewen wrote, "but I much mistake if the news is not worse before it is better. It is not possible that a Revolution so 'man-sized' can be already complete."

In New York, hours after word came that the czar had stepped down, a reporter stopped by St. Mark's Place and the offices of *Novy Mir* to see what "Leo" Trotsky, the professional revolutionary, made of the events. Trotsky said the committee that was to become the Provisional Government did not represent the interests or aims of the revolutionaries. It would probably be replaced soon by "men who would be more sure to carry forward the democratization of Russia."

Trotsky told the reporter that "the cause of the revolution was the unrest of the mass of the people who were tired of war, and that the real object of the revolutionists was to end the war not only in Russia but throughout Europe." He said, though, that Russia would not make a separate peace with Germany. "They do not favor Germany, they do not wish to see Germany win," Trotsky said. "But they are tired of war and they wish to stop fighting."

CHAPTER 13

"Nothing to Lose but Their Miserable Lives"

Butte, as usual, was seething. Anger just came naturally there. More than 15,000 miners worked more than 150 copper mines, cutting their way through the Montana granite to get to the ore. Butte is at an elevation above 5,000 feet; one mine was said to be a mile high and a mile deep. There were hot spots in the mines, where the men had to pour the sweat out of their boots. The largest group of miners consisted of Irish immigrants, but there were also Serbs, Italians, Swedes, and Chinese. Montana had one of the highest proportions of immigrants of any of the states, and a good number of them were in Butte. The city, on a steep hill—"the richest hill in the world"—produced 10 percent of the world's copper. It had a population of 91,000 in 1917, with eight newspapers, 238 saloons, one spaghetti manufacturer and one tamale maker. It was a one-company town by 1917, that company being the Anaconda Copper Mining Company (also known as the Amalgamated Copper Mining Company), in turn controlled by Standard Oil—and that meant the Rockefellers. The city had a history of labor violence, often punctuated by dynamite.

Back in 1903, one of the last independent mine owners had tried to take on Anaconda, and nearly succeeded. F. Augustus Heinze, flamboyant and popular with the men, won a lawsuit against his giant competitor; Anaconda responded by buying up the Montana state legislature and changing the law. Heinze held a rally in Granite Square, and he told the crowd:

"If they crush me today they will crush you tomorrow. They will cut your wages and raise the tariff in the company stores on every bite you eat and every rag you wear. They will force you to dwell in Standard Oil houses while you live and they will bury you in Standard Oil coffins when you die."

Heinze lost, though he made a tidy sum, more than $10 million, selling out. The miners weren't so lucky.

The union in Butte was called the Western Federation of Miners. It was one of the most radical unions in the United States, certainly among those that had won recognition from employers. (In the 1920s it would have close ties to the Communist Party.) Yet it was too conservative for a leftist faction among the miners, and in June of 1914 insurgents had disrupted a union parade and tossed the mayor of Butte, a Socialist named Lewis Duncan, out of a second-story window. He wasn't too badly hurt. Then they dynamited the union hall. On July 3, an enraged Finn stabbed the mayor in City Hall; Duncan, though wounded, shot him dead. The company took advantage of the infighting and declared an open shop, tearing up the union contract.

That was how things were when Jeannette Rankin campaigned in Butte in 1916. The value of copper, essential to wiring, had soared after the introduction of electric power in the 1880s, and the demands of the war had doubled it again. The miners, who in those years made about $4.50 a day, didn't believe they were getting their fair share of the profits. Prices were high and living conditions were terrible. In 1912, one-third of all deaths in Butte were linked to tuberculosis.

The Irish there, like Irish immigrants throughout the country, were particularly hostile to Great Britain, and Rankin was sympathetic to the Irish cause. But the American West in general was a stronghold of antiwar feeling. In the immense spaces of Montana, Europe seemed especially far away. And for a population that felt abused by eastern banks, eastern railroads and eastern industrialists, suspicion of the forces driving the country toward war was naturally high.

How much longer, the wife of an insurance agent asked Rankin, could the nation endure, "98% slave and but 2% free?"

The miners hated what was called the "rustling card." A man couldn't get a day's work from the company unless he qualified for one. A mine organizer in Butte described it to her this way:

> The applicants are lined up outside of the building by a gunman, regardless of weather conditions, and are compelled in many instances to stand for hours at the time and then in many cases to meet with a refusal.
>
> Those that are permitted to enter are handed an application blank by another gunman on which blank are printed many questions. . . . It is then taken by a clerk who refers to many books and is then passed on to another clerk who is higher in authority who places his official O.K. if the applicant is desirable, and on the other hand if the applicant is not desirable his name is called out and he enters another room and is told by the clerk in attendance (who by the way has two gunmen with him) that there are no more cards for him, the Company does not want them to work for them anymore.

New men were required to provide job references going back four years. It could take weeks or months to hear back.

"You must remember that when they do receive a card, they do not have employment. It is only a permit to seek employment. . . . This card is a blacklist of the most degrading type."

Its principle object, the letter said, "is to remove from the path of the A.C.M. Copper Mining Co. any of their political enemies or men who through their influence may induce others to ask for a reasonable wage or better conditions in or about the mines."

A Rankin ally in Butte told her that the easiest way to get around the rustling card system was to run up a big debt with one of the members of Butte's Merchants Association, who might then vouch for the deadbeat customer in hopes of recouping some of the money he owed.

THE MINERS, WHO sweated and died with pickaxes in their hands and dynamite at the ready, deeply resented the craft unions of the American Federation of Labor. Samuel Gompers' AFL was reserved for skilled workers—lathe operators, machinists, cigar makers. Ditch diggers and copper miners could go elsewhere. As far as the men and women of Butte were concerned, Gompers, who wanted to make unionism respectable and responsible, was in league with their exploiters.

In February, after the resumption of unrestricted submarine warfare, Gompers had written to a labor movement colleague in Germany asking if there was a way they could work together to keep the two countries from going to war. But by March his mood had changed: He felt that German militarism and autocracy really were anathema to a democratic world.

Sam Gompers, whose parents were Dutch Jews, was born in England in 1850 and grew up in the East End of London. When he was 13, his father moved the family to New York; they arrived right after the draft riots of 1863 had been put down by Union soldiers. Solomon Gompers was a cigar maker and Sam followed him into the trade, and into the cigar makers' craft union. He was drawn to Marxism and socialism in the 1870s, and was a stalwart union man. He was five feet four, truculent, manipulative, bigoted and hard-working. Though he later turned against socialism, he was happy to have socialist workers help organize and agitate for the AFL after its founding in 1886, and he was adept at speaking in socialist turns of phrase long after he decided that labor and capital should get along. He never lost his Marxist belief that industrial concentration was inevitable and welcome. And being a conservative in the labor movement in his era didn't mean what it might mean today: He supported compulsory education, an eight-hour law, workers' compensation, municipal ownership of utilities and transit lines, and nationalization of the telephone system, the country's railroads, and its mines.

After steering the Federation clear of politics in its early years—he had no desire to get mixed up with an American version of a Labor Party—he had wholeheartedly backed Wilson's reelection bid in 1916, as payment, in part, for the passage of the Clayton Antitrust Act of 1914. In early 1917 the Federation had 2.4 million members, more than ever before, even as the I.W.W. and the Socialists denounced it for being too cozy with the bosses, too discriminatory against blacks and women, and too hostile to immigrants. Now, if it turned out that Wilson decided on war, Gompers wasn't going to protest. He was a loyal supporter, and he also wanted to be sure that in an America at war, labor would have a say. He was worried about a crackdown on the gains the labor movement had made if the United States went on a war footing, and he thought the best way to defend the movement was from the inside, and not in opposition.

On February 28, he wrote in a memo, "There is an immediate critical problem that the labor movement must meet. The world is afire and there is imminent danger that at any time the United States might be involved in the conflagration. The organized labor movement cannot stand idly waiting until some dire catastrophe shall happen before formulating a definite constructive policy of ideals, rights, freedom and justice, and deciding upon the part labor must take to maintain them."

On March 12, he called a meeting of the AFL's executive council at which it adopted a resolution pledging its support to the government in the event of war. Many in the unions took this to mean a no-strike pledge, which Gompers went to considerable pains to deny. But most of the uproar that ensued stemmed from anger over the idea of going into battle at all.

"I do not want to see the yoke of militarism thrust upon the neck of the toilers of this country as it can only lead to war," wrote George Woodson, an organizer in Memphis for the retail clerks union, who noted that his father had been wounded serving in the Union army in the Civil War.

A streetcar union organizer in Pottsville, Pennsylvania, wrote a letter to Gompers that started with considerable respect and praise for his past efforts, though expressing surprise at the resolution. It continued: "We cannot conceive how any individual or organization, holding inviolate the traditional principles of unionism, can sanction, by word or act, the calling to arms by any nation, irrespective of the causes inducing such action; and we cannot understand, furthermore . . . how the ideals of the American workman could be construed to give the Government the interpretation, and even assurance, that we Unionists will lend our loyal support."

The letter writer referred to the war as "the wholesale slaughter of international workingmen" and suggested that any union man who endorsed it should be "strung up."

It concluded:

With best wishes, I am,
Yours fraternally,
Thomas V. McGovern

In Dayton, Ohio, the International Brotherhood of Electrical Workers adopted a resolution against the war. It called the war a "slaughter caused primarily by the capitalist system of production encouraged and intensified by the militarist and armaments interests." It accused the ruling class of trying to "saddle upon the nation" a militarism that the working class emphatically rejected, "recognizing as it does that the workers of all countries are its brothers and the capitalists and the ruling class in general are its natural enemies." The signers of the resolution pledged themselves to work toward the day when "this cannibalistic system shall cease to work its curse upon mankind, and when a higher civilization shall be ushered in."

Locals in Cleveland and Pittsburgh joined the criticism. The head of the Typographical Union local in Indianapolis told Gompers he had "no confidence whatsoever in your integrity."

"Working men have NEVER profited by WARS," wrote the members of a Machinists Union local in Dubuque, Iowa. "They are all fought for and at the behest of CAPITAL. Working men do the fighting the paying suffering and dying, solely for the benefit of CAPITAL."

But in Texas, a union local backed the AFL resolution, endorsing "our great President Woodrow Wilson." A group of machinists in Brooklyn came closest to catching Gompers' way of thinking, even before the resolution was adopted. In a letter, they urged labor to figure out before war came how the unions could best cooperate with the government to ensure their continuing influence. The task, they said, was to "raise, in a time of madness like this, that status . . . which American labor has attained through years of fighting for recognition."

COAL MINERS IN Red Lodge, Montana, sent a telegram to their new congresswoman. "Some three hundred members of the working class having nothing to lose but their miserable lives have sent a few words of praise to Senator La Follette commending his stand on jingo armed ship bill. Earnestly urge you to use the greatest opportunity ever afforded a woman to do a great deed for humanity by taking a stand against war."

Travelers—a salesman in the East, a couple who had gone the length of California, a Methodist preacher from Scobey, Montana—wrote her saying they heard widespread opposition to war everywhere they went.

The overwhelming desire in northern Montana is for peace, wrote the Methodist. He asked Rankin to do her best to "preserve us from the fierce waste and destruction, which the graft and greed of some of our wealthy eastern citizens would thrust upon us."

THAT THE WEST, and Montana, were strongly inclined against going to war, no one doubted. That the feeling was unanimous wasn't true. A group of engineers in the town of Anaconda wrote to Rankin saying they saw no alternative to war, given German aggression.

Harvey Coit, a rancher in Big Timber who knew Rankin, said that if Germany didn't respect international law its representatives in America should be arrested and executed.

Evelyn Cameron was a widow in Prairie County, near the Dakota line, a 49-year-old English immigrant who had become a talented photographer of western life. "Try not to worry too much over this unspeakable war," she wrote to a friend back in England in 1916. "Remember, we have gone astray, luxury, greed, and all the vices that follow in their train have been our undoing. We are mere puppets, a higher power is pulling the strings and in the end humanity must be cleansed and purified— ready for the millennium. . . . I believe ability and strength will be given to those in authority to bring the war to a successful issue."

Her winter was consumed by chores on the ranch, visits with neighbors, dealing with the cold, wondering why the local train on the Northern Pacific always ran so late. She confided to her diary that she had developed a pain in her left breast; it came and went and she thought it had to do with carrying a nine-pound Graflex camera, strapped to her side, while on horseback over the past fifteen years. She didn't trust the local doctors and thought she'd try to get to the Mayo Clinic, in Minnesota, "only," as she put it, 26 hours away by train. Rail fare would be $18.50. She figured an operation would cost $200 to $300. She had $324.50 in the bank.

Sunday, January 7—Chores. Read Bible. Killed colony mice. Victrola.

Tuesday, January 23—Store filled with Germans. Roesler family, Koesel, Nies, Kranzler, etc.

Wednesday, February 7—[A neighbor asked her to shoot his horse.] I got the bullet in the right spot.

Sunday, February 18—Bright afternoon, East wind. Night 12° below. . . . Let Fluffy out in night. Out 9:20. Milked, got about 1½ pint enough for my wants especially as I drink only hot water now. Watered, fed young stock. In 10:30. . . . Read XXXVII Psalm, appropriate for this time of war. Read World of 7th, An Am. Visitor to Germany, says they are very hard up for food. Chores 4:00 to 5:50.

Sunday, March 18. Lovely. First day of semi thaw. . . . Read President Inaugural address very short on blustery cold day. That wretch La Follette is catching it from his constituents for opposal to Armed Neutrality bill. At 5:00 out to chores, fed all stock, calves, heifers & cows in barn & corral. . . .

Saturday, March 24. Czar abdicated! Letters Hilda, Ralph, railroad land deed. 4 eggs. . . .

Theodore Roosevelt's great love for the West didn't blind him to the antimilitarist feeling that was so strong out that way. By February, Roosevelt had hatched his plan to raise a division of volunteers for service on the Western Front, and that month he sent his old Springfield rifle to Abercrombie & Fitch (then on 36th Street, just off Fifth Avenue) to get a new gunsight mounted and a crack in the stock repaired. Now he asked an old friend for help.

"The West has been slower than the East in realizing the need of preparedness," said Frederick Russell Burnham as he stopped off at the Rocky Mountain Club, at 65 West 44th Street in Manhattan. He was the only American up to that time to have held a commission in the British army without losing his citizenship. Major Burnham, D.S.O., born on a Lakota Sioux reservation in Minnesota, had fought Apaches out West as a U.S. Army scout but then made his way to South Africa, where he took up arms against Zulus and Boers on behalf of Queen Victoria and her son, Edward VII. His admirers styled him the King of Scouts, or He-who-sees-in-the-dark. In Rhodesia he befriended Robert Baden-Powell, who later founded the Boy Scout movement. When he came back to the United States, Burnham helped start the American Boy Scouts. He had blond hair, a British officer's mustache, and a thoroughly derring-do outlook on life.

The major, by then 55 years old, could hardly have been a more old-fashioned figure, or a more ridiculous one. The war then raging in Europe did not require gallant horsemen or adventurous Indian scouts; it was a war of machine guns, heavy artillery, aerial bombardments, submarine attacks, poison gas, rat-filled trenches and daily casualties that could mount up into the tens of thousands. But Burnham gladly took on the task Roosevelt asked of him.

He left New York for California, stopping in Arkansas and Arizona, seeking only the very best men, as Roosevelt wanted. He divided the West into "districts," and out of each district he planned to raise a regiment of "minute men." He said he had received more than a hundred answers to telegrams he had sent out to potential volunteers, announcing their "hearty cooperation." His right-hand man in Phoenix was J. H. Lightfoot, "one of the best known old time cowpunchers in the state." He did warn a reporter that, because of the circles he moved in, most of the men he anticipated recruiting would be middle-aged.

His public backers in this venture—besides the former president—were David Goodrich, one of the heirs to the B. F. Goodrich tire fortune; J. Parke Channing, a highly successful copper mining engineer; and John Hays Hammond, who had made a fortune in mining ventures in South Africa and the West. All were members of the Rocky Mountain Club on West 44th Street, and none would have been particularly welcome in the miners' saloons of Butte.

THE INDUSTRIAL WORKERS of the World, known as the Wobblies, had their eye on Butte. Their organization had been founded in 1905 by a group that included "Big Bill" Haywood, whose remains today lie in the wall of the Kremlin, and Eugene V. Debs, who had run for president and would run again on the American Socialist ticket. The I.W.W. advocated "One Big Union." It rejected the craft union structure of the AFL; its members believed that all workers should join together to speed the coming triumph over the capitalists. Based in Chicago, the Wobblies were particularly strong out West, among farmworkers, lumbermen and miners. John Reed (also buried in the Kremlin wall) was a supporter. Peak membership of about 150,000 was to come in August 1917. Butte would play a large role that summer in swelling that number, but sympathy with the ideals of the I.W.W. was already strong there by March. The Wobblies were unalterably against the war. Their emblem was a black cat, because black cats take orders from no one.

"Dear Comrade," reads the telegram from Butte Local Number One to the Hon. Jeannette Rankin, "We emphatically urge you to work and vote against this country's entering the war. The working class of this country will necessarily have to do the fighting and they have nothing to gain by shedding their blood and that of their brothers."

Local No. 241 of the American Federation of Musicians, in Butte, asked Rankin to keep the country out of "the horrible European war." In Bonner, Montana, closer to Missoula, a public meeting adopted a resolution stating that "modern war serves to enrich the capitalist class and to strengthen their hold upon the government," and asked the state's congressional delegation to oppose entry into the war.

To all of these entreaties, Rankin's assistant, Belle Fliegelman, sent a form letter in reply.

At first, in early March, Fliegelman simply acknowledged that the sender's letter had been received, adding, "I earnestly appreciate your attitude in this question and thank you for calling my attention to your wishes." As the month went on, and the mail continued to run strongly against the war—by 16-to-1, Rankin said—the tone of her reply changed slightly. After thanking the sender, the letter continued: "I feel sure we are all anxious to avoid war, and I shall give your suggestion my earnest consideration."

CHAPTER 14

"The Great Liberal Leader of the World"

On Friday, March 16, Wilson finally got out of his sickbed and returned to work. "The President has had a bad cold and a sore throat," an aide, Thomas W. Brahany, wrote in his diary. He was not seriously ill, Brahany wrote, yet the president's doctor, Cary T. Grayson, had insisted he get complete bed rest. He had been out of circulation for ten days, though Edith had been reading him some of the long memoranda that the attorney general and secretary of state sent in to him. On the eleventh, when he was feeling a little better, he and his brother-in-law Randolph Bolling had taken out a Ouija board. Edith reported that none other than the specter of Lord Nelson, of Trafalgar fame, appeared, to talk about submarine warfare. (It isn't clear what his opinion was.) But when William McAdoo, the secretary of the treasury who was also Wilson's son-in-law, had paid a visit to him on the fourteenth, Wilson was visibly displeased, Brahany noted. McAdoo "stayed too long and talked too much."

The White House barber told Brahany that after McAdoo left, Wilson erupted. "Dammit, he makes me tired. He's got too much nerve. . . . I'm getting damn sick of it."

But now the president was feeling better. He dispatched the mediators to New York to seek a settlement of the railroad dispute, and took care of other routine business. The next day, St. Patrick's Day, Lansing sent him a long memo marked "Personal and Confidential" outlining the possibility that a peace settlement could be sought through dealings with Austria, Germany's weak and crumbling ally and a country with which the United States had no argument. "It is my belief," Lansing wrote, "that the Austrian Government is almost as fearful of its powerful ally as it is of its enemies."

John Redmond, the Irish nationalist leader, sent sprigs of shamrock to all the White House staff, and the president put one into his lapel. The Irish posed a particularly thorny problem. It was just under a year since the Easter uprising in Dublin, which the British had ferociously put down, and ill will toward the English was still strong—and naturally strongest among the most vocal and committed Irish nationalists then in America. Irish-Americans held most of the political power in such Democratic strongholds as New York, Boston, Cleveland and Chicago. Liam Mellows, who led the Galway brigade in the Easter rebellion, was in Boston in March denouncing the English, arguing that they wanted the United States to join the war so that they could bring it back under British dominion. Theodore Roosevelt received a fascinating long letter at this time from a British officer who had been in Dublin the year before, recounting with evident pain the ways in which the British had completely mishandled the rising. It had had a significant effect on American opinion toward England. But Roosevelt wanted to ally with Britain, and he was continuously denouncing hyphenated Americans. A true American, he said, would love America more than he hated England. That evening, at the dinner of the St. Patrick's Society of Brooklyn, a boisterous crowd fell silent, out of disapproval, when his name was mentioned. But the assembled partiers cheered and toasted Wilson, and joined together to sing "The Star-Spangled Banner."

Indeed, the leader of the Irish Party in the British Parliament, Joseph Devlin, saw an omen in the Russian Revolution. "The Irish party," he said, "regards the Russian revolution—striking, noble, dramatic, well-nigh bloodless—as a message of hope to all oppressed peoples and all the freedom-loving nations. But it is something more. It is also a warning and a portent of doom to autocracies and tyrannies everywhere.

"We might draw a moral therefrom, but we do not desire to avail ourselves of the opportunity, preferring to let the voice of Ireland join in the united harmony of rejoicing at Russia's emancipation."

WILSON WAS BUOYED by good news that day. After all-night negotiations at the Biltmore Hotel in New York, the railroad brotherhoods had agreed to postpone their strike by forty-eight hours. Word was that the owners were giving in. A reporter stopped Daniel Willard, of the Baltimore & Ohio, as the negotiators emerged, exhausted, from their talks. It was evident that, despite the unions' fears and taunts, management had no stomach for a strike. When the president of the United States was putting pressure on you to find a solution, at what everyone realized was a critical moment for the nation, and the War Department talked about the possible need to seize the railroads, it wasn't hard to guess where the blame might fall if the trains stopped running. The railroads, after all, were enjoying their greatest prosperity ever. "Look at those faces and judge for yourself," Willard said, and the reporter could see that the tension had eased all around.

But the Supreme Court had still not issued its ruling on the Adamson law requiring an eight-hour workday for railroad employees, and no one outside the court knew when it might come. A lot could happen in forty-eight hours. Willard had been on the scene at the Biltmore, leading the management committee, but other members might go back to the powerful owners—the Vanderbilts of the New York Central, the Hills of the Great Northern, and others—and find a more intransigent mood. One minority owner would probably not be in a position to object: The deposed Nicholas II, the *Evening Ledger* of Philadelphia reported, apparently owned $50 million worth of stock in the Pennsylvania Railroad. Nonetheless, the weekend would be crucial.

COLONEL HOUSE WAS at home in New York, and on that Saturday his thoughts were far removed from the mundane developments in the railroad dispute, paralyze the nation though it might. He was thinking about himself, and found it an occasion for congratulation. A visitor from Washington, House confided to his diary, "was good enough to say that he considered me the financial expert of the Administration." An English caller, the critic Sydney Brooks, "stated that I was the only American he knew who had a European mind."

Brooks complimented House for persuading Wilson to denounce the Senate filibusterers when he did, and to have done so in such a timely fashion. If the president had waited to speak out, it would have been nowhere near as effective, Brooks thought. House despaired of Wilson's inertia in general, but he made a show of pushing back. "I told him there were two sides to that question. Oftentimes the man who delays is the one who is successful, and the man who acts quickly often regrets it. He agreed to this in a general way, but thought in political and military affairs it was quick action that got the best results." You can imagine House smiling now. "In this I agree with him."

Someone from the State Department dropped by and mentioned that over at the Navy most of the personnel wanted to see the assistant secretary, Franklin Roosevelt, take over from Secretary Josephus Daniels, the slow-to-move southerner who, unlike FDR, was firmly opposed to entering the war.

House, who once said he always slept well because he never worried about anything, had been digesting the news from Russia for two days by this point and was starting to come to some conclusions. After he wrote to Wilson urging U.S. recognition of the new government as a means of promoting democracy globally, he expanded on the theme in his diary. "I have been fearful lest bureaucratic Russia and autocratic Germany would link fortunes and make trouble for the democracies of the world. Now that Russia bids fair to be free, one sees more hope for democracy and human liberty than ever before."

But he was hardly an idealist, and he tempered that optimism. "I foresee a long and bloody road down which the world must go for freedom," he wrote. And then he looked back at the road already traveled.

"My whole life work has been directed toward the unfortunate many without equal opportunity, and their bitter struggle for existence. . . . I stood back of every liberal movement, both in Texas and in the Nation, which seemed rational and headed in the right direction. Sometimes I have feared that other zealous friends of progress might go too fast and cause a reaction which would be difficult to overcome. I have advised moderation, but have always pushed in the one direction."

Perhaps, he wrote, the most valuable work he had done had been in pushing Wilson, even before the White House years. "At every turn, I have stirred his ambition to become the great liberal leader of the world." The events in Petrograd now presented that opportunity; it would be up to Wilson himself to seize it. House believed that with Russia finally free, there would be less need on his part to keep pushing the president. Wilson's moment was at hand.

HERE IS WHAT no one in America knew that weekend.

On Friday, March 16, an American freighter called the *Vigilancia* was in the North Atlantic, about 150 miles west of Bishop's Light. The twenty-five-year-old ship was owned by a New York firm called Gaston, Williams & Wigmore, which had profited greatly during the war, chiefly by shipping trucks and automobiles to the Allies. A heavy swell lifted the 4,115-ton steamship, bound from New York for the French port of Le Havre with a load of general cargo aboard. It had been at sea for seventeen days. At 10 a.m. the officer of the watch and a lookout both spotted a streak in the water, off to starboard. It was a torpedo, but it passed harmlessly under the stern. A minute later, another torpedo found its target, exploding as it hit the *Vigilancia* nearly amidships.

The damage was fatal. As the ship began to heel over, the crew lowered all four lifeboats and climbed into them. But momentum was still carrying the Vigilancia forward through the water, and before the lifeboats could be cleared away, two had capsized, plunging the men into the frigid ocean. Eleven members of the crew on Third Officer Niels North's boat drowned, as did four from Captain Frank Middleton's boat. Middleton himself, like most of the men who were with him, was pulled to safety on one of the two remaining lifeboats.

The ship went down, and the wind and large rolling waves pushed the boats away from the spot. The lone survivor from North's boat, Assistant Engineer Walter Scott, was in the water. He wriggled out of his overcoat and managed to swim a mile until he caught up with one of the lifeboats. He was among the thirty survivors.

The victims included six Americans, one of whom was a Puerto Rican, along with five Spaniards, two Greeks, a Peruvian and a Venezuelan.

Two open boats, on the wintry sea. Fortunately, they were equipped with masts and sails, and the men headed east, toward land. They had biscuits and drinking water, but no way to stay warm. On the first night—as President Wilson was rising from his sickbed and the railroad negotiators were sitting face-to-face at the Biltmore—the two boats lit emergency flares while crewmen held them aloft in the bitterly cold air. What they saw in the dark chilled them even further—a submarine, probably the *U-70*, the one that had torpedoed them, was tracking on the surface behind. It was, in all likelihood, waiting for a rescue ship to appear, which could then also be sent to the bottom.

But no ship came, and after another day and night had passed, the sailors landed, exhausted and suffering badly from exposure, on the Scilly Islands in the English Channel. It was Sunday the eighteenth.

The American consul in Plymouth, Joseph G. Stephens, interviewed the survivors and wired a brief account to the State Department late that same day.

MONDAY, MARCH 19, was a tumultuous day. In the morning, word came back from the railroads: Management would indeed relent, and had agreed to allow a board appointed by the president to set the terms for working conditions. The railroads had decided to abide by the spirit of the Adamson Act no matter how the Supreme Court ruled. It meant a victory for the brotherhoods, because with federal intervention the eight-hour day was established. Mondays, as it happens, are when Supreme Court decisions are handed down, and later that same day the court released its ruling on the challenge to the Adamson law: It was constitutional, the justices said. The federal government had the power to intervene in a labor dispute. Union leaders grumbled that the law also gave the government power to forbid a strike, but the ruling was in fact nearly a total victory in labor's struggle against management. The powers of the executive branch—so long used to suppress striking union workers—were now to be wielded on behalf of the employees, not the employers. The eight-hour day achieved its foothold in the private sector. And given the stakes and the moment in American history, the railroad companies acquiesced without a further fight. The trains kept running.

The newspapers, of course, were also headlining the sinking of the *Vigilancia*. For the first time, a U-boat attack on an American ship had taken lives. News came that two other commercial ships, the *City of Memphis* and the *Illinois*, had also been sunk, and it would be several days before confirmation came that no one from either ship had died. Both were empty of cargo, and heading westbound, which seemed to highlight Germany's disregard for even its own stated policy. Wilson hated the U-boat issue; he thought it made America look small and self-interested to use it as an excuse for war. Yet he had drawn a very public red line, in February, when he broke off diplomatic relations with Germany. He had said there would be no further consequences, barring an "overt act." What, his critics and many of his allies asked now, could be more "overt" than the deadly sinking of the *Vigilancia* on the high seas?

"It is simply war," wrote Senator Lodge to Theodore Roosevelt. "Germany is making war on us and we are doing nothing. Wilson ought at once to call Congress and declare war, which is now a mere form. I do not think that he will. He is casting about evidently for some hole to creep out of so that he may avoid getting Congress here before the 16th of April. No words can do justice to his conduct."

Wilson in fact began the day by playing a round of golf with Dr. Grayson. His aide, Thomas Brahany, said he "did not seem to be greatly perturbed." Wilson, ever thrifty, always paid the prescribed fee to his caddy, but never added a tip. That's why, Brahany said, there was never a rush to carry his bag when he showed up to play a round.

After golf, Wilson met with Secretary of State Lansing and told him the U-boat attacks hadn't changed the equation, and did not constitute a reason to declare war. Lansing replied that war was inevitable, that he had felt that way for months, and "that the sooner we openly admitted the fact so much stronger our position would be with our own people and before the world." Lansing said that this was the "psychological moment," especially because of the Russian Revolution. Wilson said he was reluctant to call Congress into session because of the danger that any course he chose to follow would get bogged down. Overall, Lansing couldn't gauge Wilson's reaction, but thought the president resented being compelled to abandon the neutrality that he had striven so hard to maintain.

As soon as he left the White House, Lansing dashed off a letter to House in New York. "If you agree with me that we should act now," he wrote, "will you not please put your shoulder to the wheel?"

Wilson saw Secretary of the Navy Josephus Daniels next. He told Daniels he had been urged to call Congress to declare war—Lansing had done the urging. "He still hoped to avoid it," Daniels wrote in his diary.

Newspaper reporters filled the outer office at the Executive Mansion. They were hoping for, and expecting, the president to make some statement about the loss of the three ships, to ascertain whether this meant war. They were disappointed; Wilson and the White House were silent all that day.

In the evening, Lansing went to a dinner at the Japanese embassy, and afterward, at home, he sat down and wrote a long letter to Wilson. He knew Wilson didn't have a great deal of respect for him, and generally didn't heed his advice on foreign affairs, but now he was going to make the effort to be heard. Or, more precisely, read—Wilson, he knew, preferred written statements, which he could mull over, to the back-and-forth of a conversation when he hadn't made up his own mind.

Germany, Lansing wrote, was certain to continue perpetrating hostile acts against American shipping until eventually the United States would have to recognize that war was being waged against it. "I firmly believe that war will come within a short time whatever we may do," he wrote. Now that the United States was arming its merchant vessels on Wilson's order, it was inevitable that a shooting confrontation would take place, and probably soon. And then, Lansing wrote, "I do not think we can successfully maintain the fiction that peace exists."

Lansing wrote that he had struggled against reaching the conclusion that war would come, and had only accepted it with the greatest reluctance. (This was a polite fib; Lansing had been hawkish for quite some time.) The only question, he wrote, was whether it was better to act right away or wait for the next incident. Waiting, he conceded, had one potential advantage: A battle at sea might cause Germany to declare war on the United States, which would make it much easier for Wilson and the American cause in general. But he pointed out that Germany, even after a shooting incident, would have no real reason to declare war, because it was already pursuing hostilities against the United States without the bother of a declaration.

Better, Lansing counseled, to take the initiative and declare war. "It is for the welfare of mankind and for the establishment of peace in the world that Democracy should succeed," he wrote. It would not only be an encouragement to the new Russia, but it would also "put heart into the democratic element of Germany." He said the American people were getting restless, and "bitterly critical of what they believe to be an attempt to avoid the unavoidable." Lastly, he wrote, "our future influence in world affairs, in which we can no longer refuse to play our part, will be materially increased by prompt, vigorous and definite action in favor of Democracy and against Absolutism. . . . The longer we delay in declaring against the military absolutism which menaces the rule of liberty and justice in our world, so much the less will be our influence in the days when Germany will need a merciful and unselfish foe."

Lansing may not have had Wilson's esteem, but he knew the president and knew how to talk to him. He did not dwell on the U-boat campaign except as a spark that must ignite the fire of war at some point; he played all the right notes to appeal to the man who considered himself a visionary—the defense of democracy, the encouragement of good over evil, the opportunity for America to lead the world to a more peaceful era. One argument alone would have irritated Wilson, and that was the reference to critical public opinion—not the way to sway a man who believed he had a noble calling.

WILSON COULD BE immensely charming in private. He loved to sit by the fire reading to Edith or his daughters. He doted on his granddaughter. Colonel House was devoted to him, just as the students at Princeton had been devoted to him when as university president he clashed with the trustees, barely a decade earlier. When speaking in public, he could move his supporters with his easy eloquence. He would call his audiences to a higher purpose in ways that struck many as genuine and deeply felt. His detractors fumed at his righteousness and what men like Lodge believed to be his fecklessness. He had double-crossed the political bosses who put him in the New Jersey governor's seat by unexpectedly backing a set of clean government measures. And he had won reelection in 1916 after helping millions of Americans—and yes, blacks as well as whites, economically—with sweeping reforms. There was the war, too: Wilson, so his admirers thought, had steered a wise and careful course that had kept the nation out of the European catastrophe.

Wilson thought things through, sifting them, bringing his years of academic study of effective government to bear on them. He didn't like to be rushed or lobbied. He admired parliamentary systems, where parties in power can take action without the give and take that saturates American politics. Once he had made up his mind, after due consideration, he had no patience for counterarguments. As soon as he had jumped off the fence, those still sitting on it struck him as fools or worse.

Wilson, characteristically, was keeping his own counsel. He sent word around to his cabinet: They would be convening at the White House the next day, March 20.

THEY MET AT 2:30—all ten cabinet secretaries. Flocks of reporters were in the hallways outside, bombarding any official they saw with questions, but getting no answers. Three minutes after they assembled, Wilson walked into the room. He shook hands with each secretary in turn, but with a genial smile. He was not a man who got excited; if he had shown any agitation on this occasion, it would have alarmed those who had served under him. Wilson began by congratulating Interior Secretary Franklin Lane and Labor Secretary William Wilson for their efforts to resolve the railroad dispute. Then he turned to Germany and reviewed the events of the past two months. He said he had two questions on which he was seeking advice from the cabinet: Should he summon Congress to meet earlier than April

16, for which he had already issued a call? And what should he propose to Congress when it did meet?

He brought up Russia and its revolution, which had changed conditions, but he did not think that in and of itself justified an American entry into the war. He mentioned reports that dissent was growing in Germany. He talked about the "indignation and bitterness" in the eastern United States, and the apathy in the Midwest.

William McAdoo, his son-in-law and treasury secretary, spoke first. He could see no reason for delay, he said. Americans might as well face the issue squarely. The German government represented "every evil in history," and it would be a humiliation to have to be prodded into war. He said the best assistance the United States could give to the Allies would be financial backing; he doubted that the Americans could send a significant army to France.

David Houston, the secretary of agriculture, spoke next. He thought Wilson should summon the Congress at once because a state of war already existed. The Navy would have a role to play, he said, but raising and equipping an army would simply interfere with the material help the Allies were depending on.

It was time to bring the kaiser to his knees, said William Redfield, secretary of commerce.

Newton Baker, the secretary of war, spoke next. He made an eloquent appeal for an immediate declaration of war. It was clear, he said, that the Germans "did not intend to modify in the least degree their policy of inhumanity and lawlessness." He disagreed with the others on one point: He thought it essential that the United States train an army and be prepared to send it across the Atlantic. The Allies had lost millions of men, as had the Central Powers, and reinforcements were going to be vital. Just knowing that the Yanks were coming could cause Germany and its allies to understand their cause was hopeless.

Then it was Lansing's turn. An actual state of war already existed, he said, but it wasn't in the president's power to declare that fact or act upon it. He would have to summon Congress, and it would have to adopt a declaration of war. Lansing said "that the revolution in Russia, which appeared to be successful, had removed the one objection to affirming that the European War was a war between Democracy and Absolutism." Silence at this point would be interpreted abroad as weakness, and at home as indecision, he said. The government could not act as if it was afraid to perform its duty. Lansing was warming to his subject, and his voice was rising. Finally, Wilson had to tell him to lower the volume, lest the reporters in the hall outside hear what he was saying.

William Wilson, who had resolutely opposed going to war, spoke slowly. We must recognize, he said, that Germany has made war upon this country. In reply, "I do not believe that we should employ half measures or do it half-heartedly."

Attorney General Thomas Gregory, who was extremely hard of hearing and had probably been unable to catch most of the discussion, said Congress should be called at once. Postmaster General Albert Burleson—Wilson's largely ineffective liaison with Congress, a quick-tempered, domineering and stingy man—said he was in favor of declaring war and then pursuing that war to the bitter end. Up to that moment he had been the strongest critic of Britain's conduct of any of the cabinet members. Now he said the United States had to throw all its weight into the fight, "so that those Prussians will realize that, when they made war on this country, they woke up a giant which will surely defeat them."

Then it was the turn of Josephus Daniels, a follower of William Jennings Bryan who had been staunchly opposed to war all along. Tears filled his eyes. His voice trembled with emotion. There was now no alternative to war, he said. If Germany prevailed over Britain and France, he said, the United States would be forced to become a military nation. War, now, would be preferable to that.

The last to speak was Franklin Lane. He brought up public opinion, which was sure to annoy Wilson. "I could almost feel the President stiffen as if to resist and see his powerful jaw set as Lane spoke," Lansing wrote that same day.

"I do not care for popular demand," Wilson said. "I want to do right, whether popular or not."

The conversation continued a little longer. "Well, gentlemen," Wilson said as he closed the meeting, at a little past 4 p.m., "I think there is no doubt as to what your advice is. I thank you."

He gave no sign as to what course he would follow. He did ask Burleson and Lansing as the others were leaving when might be the best time to call Congress, if he were to do so. They agreed on April 2, and Lansing asked if there would be a proclamation that afternoon. Wilson said he would sleep on it.

First, though, he went to see the vaudeville show at Keith's, just a block away in the Riggs Building at 15th and G streets. As the president sat in the dark that evening, on stage the Rials juggled flying rings and hats; Frank Parish and Peru did their tumbling act while playing concertinas; Max Cooper and Irene Ricardo put on a nonsense routine. The main feature was an amusing playlet by Dion Titheradge, "Peg for Short," and then the evening closed, with "The Dancing Girl of Delhi."

CHAPTER 15

"It Might Be All Right for You to Have Your Little Pocket Gun"

A t 4 p.m. on March 20, just about the time Wilson's cabinet meeting was breaking up, Theodore Roosevelt strode into the Flower Show at the Grand Central Palace, an exhibition hall that was just north of the New York Central Railroad terminal. With him was James W. Gerard, the just-returned U.S. ambassador to Germany whose years in Berlin had made him believe that the only thing Germans respected was force. A large crowd was drawn to the former president as he bustled through the floral displays to a Red Cross tea garden. At the entrance he stopped, delighted, before a large blue and white sign that read, "My Country 'Tis of Thee." TR doffed his hat in salute.

"That's the stuff—no fifty-fifty there!" he exclaimed. The crowd cheered. The house orchestra played "The Star-Spangled Banner." Roosevelt gave an impromptu speech. America had been blind for two-and-a-half years, he said, and in that time it had become clear, to those who could see, that "evil forces" could not be thwarted by platitudes. A nation, he said, that prides itself on its manliness had to be ready to step up and prove itself.

A boy walked up to him, shook his hand, and told him, "I wish you were president."

THAT MORNING, THE newspapers had carried a statement that Roosevelt had hurriedly written out the day before at his house on Sagamore Hill. The news of the sinking of the three ships proved, he said, "that words are wasted upon Germany." America should "hit hard" in response.

"What we need is effective and thorough-going action," he wrote. "It is well to remember that during the last two years the Germans have killed as many, or almost as many, Americans as were slain at Lexington and Bunker Hill." Any American who was still pro-German was as much a traitor as the Tories were in the Revolution. The pacifists were no better than the Copperheads who assailed Lincoln during the Civil War. And in the seven weeks since Berlin resumed submarine warfare, the United States had done nothing, he wrote. "Armed neutrality is only another name for timid war; and Germany despises timidity as she despises all other forms of feebleness. She does not wage timid war herself, and she neither respects nor understands it in others."

He touched, not for the first time, on the national humiliation that came with American dependence on the British navy for its defense. "We have done nothing to help ourselves. We have done nothing to secure our own safety or to vindicate our own honor. . . . Let us dare to use our own strength in our own defense and strike hard for our national interest and honor. There is no question about 'going to war.' Germany is already at war with us. The only question for us is to decide whether we shall make war nobly or ignobly. Let us . . . wage war on Germany with all our energy and courage, and regain the right to look the whole world in the eyes without flinching."

AFTER AN HOUR at the flower show, Roosevelt hurried over to West 39th Street, where the American Geographical Society presented him with the David Livingston Centenary Medal for his explorations in Brazil. "No man can go into the wilderness who thinks all achievement should be avoided if there is risk connected with it," Roosevelt said. And then this: "A man who won't bear arms in a republic is not fit to vote in a republic." The several hundred members of the society burst into cheers and gave him a standing ovation, while he "bowed delightedly."

From there he rushed back down 39th Street to Fifth Avenue, where the Union League Club then stood. He had been blackballed when he first applied for membership in the club, back in 1881, perhaps because his mother was a southerner and had had brothers who fought for the Confederacy. After she died in 1884—on the same day as TR's first wife, Alice—the members relented and he was accepted. But in 1912 he made himself unwelcome again by running on the Bull Moose ticket for president, in opposition to the Republican, William Howard Taft. Now, on the evening of the vernal equinox, the front door opened for him once more.

Roosevelt swept inside, through rooms designed by Louis Tiffany and John La Farge, past statuary by Augustus Saint-Gaudens. The Gorham silver shone in the soft light. Here, in 1890, the 70-year-old William Tecumseh Sherman had been feted. The club embodied the height of Beaux Arts sumptuousness, and already, in 1917, it was starting to look a little dowdy. Roosevelt joined 600 other Republican Party leaders to plot a course of action in the impending crisis. The meeting, at the elite club, was ostensibly private, but the *New York Times* ran a full account of the major speeches the next day.

The main argument was that Germany was at war with the United States, declaration or no declaration. Members recalled that the Union League had been founded to generate support for Lincoln and the Northern cause during the Civil War, at a time when Copperhead sentiment for a truce was widespread in New York. That effort had been a great success, and now, they said, it was time for the club to arouse public opinion again.

"This city is not half awake to the perils that encompass it," said Joseph H. Choate, one of the leading attorneys of his day, who forty-five years earlier had helped to break up the Tammany Ring and who later served as U.S. ambassador to the United Kingdom. "Go up and down the streets and avenues of this city, and by day and by night you will see people devoted to pleasure, to their ordinary pursuits, to enjoyment and luxury without limit. They have got to find out what is the matter."

Americans had sold a great deal of goods to the Allies, at excellent prices, and lent a great deal of money at considerable interest rates, he said. Now it was time for Americans to give a little, or more than a little, to pay the Allies back for fighting on behalf of democracy.

It had been two months, he said, since Wilson declared that the country was on the brink of war. "Well, we can't stay on the brink forever—we have tumbled in, that is what has happened, we have fallen in. The president may still be on the brink, but the rest of the people are not."

Elihu Root, who was secretary of state under Roosevelt and secretary of war under Taft, said there was no going back to the way things were in 1914. "We are passing into a new world, with new duties and new dangers, and we must confront our future," he said. "Germany is making war on us, and we are all waiting to see whether we are to take it lying down. . . .

"If it is understood that we are a weak, flabby, divided and indefinite people, who can be insulted and assaulted and abused with impunity, then the tide flows over us and we are gone. Our union is gone. Our liberty is gone."

He noted that no action could be taken except through the White House. "My diagnosis of the situation is that the president wants to hear from the people. Let us answer to his want and tell him that the American people do not want him to discuss, not to plan, not to talk about what is going to be done, but to act."

Then it was Colonel Roosevelt's turn to speak. Germany, he said, had established a partial blockade of the Port of New York. It had sought to dismember the United States with the help of Mexico and Japan. It had carried out on the high seas a campaign of murder—

yes, he said, the word "murder" describes with "scientific accuracy" what the U-boats were doing.

"If you go to war, hit hard. We are in war now," he said.

He said being an American meant giving up your ties to the country your forebears had left behind. "The American who loves Germany more than America is not a good American. The American who hates England more than he loves America is not a good American, he is a bad American." German lovers should go back to Germany, he said. Haters of England should go—anywhere but here. Just go.

America, he continued, had to do more than fight a "dollar war." Yes, it was the great supplier of Allied matériel, but it had to put its manhood on the line. "We want to prepare at once a great army, I should hope an army of a couple of million men, so that if the war lasts for a year we will be able to be the decisive and controlling element in it.

"But do not wait for that great army. We can perfectly well send an expeditionary force abroad now to fight in the trenches or fight in the Balkan peninsula, wherever it is desired. We can get that expeditionary force, if we choose to, within four or five months into the trenches, and it will mean everything for the morale of France, of Belgium, of the Allies generally, to have an American force under an American flag training in France and moving forward into the trenches to take its place beside the other armies which . . . are fighting our battles at this moment."

It would have been clear to every single man in the audience who Colonel Roosevelt thought should be leading that expeditionary force. A band erupted into "The Marseillaise." The club adopted a resolution setting up a committee to express to Wilson the Union League's desire to aid and support the government at this time of crisis. And with that the evening drew to a close.

In Washington, Henry Cabot Lodge wrote to Roosevelt to express his disgust with the "fatuous cry of 'Stand by the President.'" He called it a "general and sloppy" sentiment.

Lodge boasted that he stood against Wilson when he thought the president was being too accommodating to the Germans, and stood by him only at moments when he thought that by doing so he could "force his hand and push him forward along the path he does not want to follow."

"IT IS NOT our war," wrote John Reed that month. "I know what war means. . . . I have seen men die, and go mad, and lie in hospitals suffering hell; but there is a worse thing than that. War means an ugly mobmadness, crucifying the truth-tellers, choking the artists, side-tracking reforms. . . . Already in America those citizens who oppose the entrance of their country into the European melée are called 'traitors,' and those who protest against the curtailing of our meager rights of free speech are spoken of as 'dangerous lunatics.' . . . The press is howling for war. The church is howling for war. Lawyers, politicians, stock-brokers, social leaders are all howling for war."

An antiwar movement had been growing in the country ever since February. Thousands of individual Americans took the trouble to write to Robert La Follette, Samuel Gompers, Jeannette Rankin and other leaders to speak out against entering the war, but there was organized opposition as well. The American Union Against Militarism, the Emergency Anti-War Committee, the Friends National Peace Committee, and the Emergency Peace Federation were among the groups that worked to head off U.S. intervention in Europe.

In mid-February, a peace rally organized by the Emergency Anti-War Committee had filled the 12,000-seat Chicago Coliseum, a barn of a building on the near South Side, featuring a crenelated stone wall that had been moved in pieces from a Civil War prison in Richmond. The rent was $1,000. The result was a resolution, addressed to Wilson, urging him to warn Americans and American ships to stay out of the war zone, to avoid conflict. If the United States joined the world war, the resolution said, "our opportunity in the establishment of an international organization for the preservation of world peace

will be jeopardized." It further demanded that no action toward war
be taken without first holding a national referendum.

A group called the Congress of Forums invited Theodore Roosevelt to debate William Jennings Bryan over the question of war
at Madison Square Garden, on a date of his choosing. Roosevelt
contemptuously declined. And he made sure the press got a copy
of his refusal:

"I cannot accept your proposal . . . because I regard it as a waste of
time to debate nondebatable subjects." Holding a debate with Bryan
would, he said, "be precisely on a par with debating the undesirabil-
ity of monogamous marriage or the morality of abolishing patriotism or the advantage of the reintroduction of slavery or the right of
judges to accept bribes from suitors or the duty of submission to the
divine right of kings, or the propriety of action such as that of Benedict Arnold."

To drive that last comparison home, he added, "American pacifism, throughout these years, has been the timid apologist and potent
ally of the ruthless brutality of German militarism."*

That brought a sharp rebuke from the man who extended the invitation, Percy Stickney Grant, rector of the Church of the Ascension.
"America's hesitation to go to war is neither cowardice nor enerva-
tion, but is rather a profound aversion to war as an instrument of
progress," he wrote. "Cannot Colonel Roosevelt see and respect the
seriousness of the nation's mood? Can he not understand the profound nobility of a republic pondering how it may stop or prevent
war without adding to the fuel of war? The country has taken a great
stride spiritually in the last twenty years, since he was Assistant Secretary of the Navy, and refuses to be stampeded into war. . . . That
he no longer understands the soul of America, or even its body, is
deplorable."

---

* George Orwell would make the same argument about British pacifism twenty-five
years later.

By March, groups were circulating postcard-sized ballots that could be marked for or against war (the idea being that most people who took part would vote against). On March 5, a large peace gathering was held in Quincy, Illinois, at the Labor Temple. A Catholic priest and two Lutheran ministers inveighed against war. The chief speaker, a lawyer named John Wall, hit hard at the war advocates. "The favored class, backed by a subsidized press, seeks to inculcate a war spirit among the people," he said. "What care they for the horrors, the sufferings, the miseries of the poor who must bear the brunt of the fight, if fight there be? The golden gains they will reap is the thing in which they are interested."

Americans would take their time deciding on going to war, he predicted. "As for me, I shall not be stampeded into war, nor will I keep step with the drum beats of Wall Street."

At an antiwar gathering at Carnegie Hall on March 9, the full house erupted into cheers when one of the speakers mentioned Senator La Follette. Two days later, on a Sunday afternoon, a peace meeting in Lincoln, Nebraska, drew about 500 people. When someone praised La Follette, "it called forth a storm of applause."

In Chicago, the Emergency Anti-War Committee took out ads in five local newspapers—the *Examiner*, the *Daily News*, the *Evening Post*, and the *Herald*, as well as the German-language *Staats-Zeitung*, which charged the group $6.40.

The Quakers placed large ads in major newspapers, arguing that war is futile. "The alternative to war is not inactivity and cowardice. It is the irresistible and constructive power of good-will," one read. "The peoples of every land are longing for the time when love shall conquer hate, when cooperation shall replace conflict, when war shall be no more. This time will come only when the people of some great nation dare to abandon the outworn traditions of international dealing and to stake all upon persistent good-will.

"We are the nation and now is the time. This is America's supreme opportunity.

"Unflinching good-will, no less than war, demands courage, patriotism and self-sacrifice."

ON MARCH 21, David Starr Jordan, the former president of Stanford University, tried Roosevelt again. Like some of his progressive
allies, Jordan was a eugenicist, and opposed war because he thought
it killed off the best people. He had organized an unofficial commission to look at ways to solve the crisis with Germany without resort
to arms, and he invited Roosevelt to meet with its members—one of
whom was an officer of the virulently antiwar Western Federation of
Miners—so they could hear his "frank opinion." Roosevelt declined,
comparing the U-boat campaign to the firing on Fort Sumter. It was
too late to think of peace, he said. "The action you now propose to
take is action against this country and humanity, and in the interest of German militarism, at the expense of this country, and at the
expense of humanity."

The war posed an excruciating challenge to progressives and cut
right through the heart of the movement. La Follette and Roosevelt
had been bitter rivals within the Republican Party, but they were
both progressives. So, too, was Wilson. All three men had starkly different attitudes toward joining the war. There were progressives who
opposed war on principle. But there were also progressives who genuinely felt that German militarism posed a global threat to democracy
and liberalism. There weren't many progressives who agreed with
Roosevelt that America had to prove its manliness on the battlefield,
but there were more than a few, like Gompers, who thought that
support for whatever course the White House and Congress pursued
could be parlayed into political gains later on.

One of the roles Colonel House had assumed was as the administration's informal and off-the-record contact for the press, especially
the progressive publications. He met weekly with Walter Lippmann
and others from the *New Republic*, advising them on what to write,
and often trying to rein them in, because the fledgling magazine

was hot for war. "I am finding it difficult to keep them in line," he confided to his diary on March 9.

Two weeks later, House met with a group of prominent pacifists. "I think I satisfied them that the president knew more about the situation than they did, and was quite anxious to keep out of war."

An issue that was beginning to take form in March was the question of conscription. If war came, should a draft come with it? Legions of ordinary young men, and plenty of their mothers, took a dim view of a draft, and said so in torrents of mail to Congress. Progressives who feared a militarized state—American Prussianism—opposed a draft. But others thought that a draft would be more equitable, and ensure that the well off as well as the poor would serve in uniform.

As in Europe in 1914, even Socialists were of two minds. John Reed and his colleagues at *The Masses* denounced the war as industrialized slaughter for the benefit of the few. But when Leon Trotsky and Louis Fraina showed up at a meeting of the New York County Socialist Party at the Lenox Casino, a dance hall on 116th Street that later became a mosque (and was firebombed following the assassination of Malcolm X), their proposal that Socialists should encourage strikes and resist recruitment in the event of war was soundly defeated. "We should be asses," said Morris Hillquit, "to tell members of Local New York that they must risk death and imprisonment rather than join the army!"

One of the most fascinating, if slightly maddening, figures against the war was a prominent New York attorney named Amos Pinchot. His brother, Gifford, had been appointed by then-President Roosevelt as the first chief of the U.S. Forest Service and was still on good terms with Roosevelt in 1917. (He sent a letter to his old boss applauding one of TR's ideas—federal highway building to improve national defense.) Amos was not quite the outdoorsman that Gifford was, though he had worked for Roosevelt in the 1912 Bull Moose campaign. His wife, Gertrude, was active in progressive causes, and supported James Reese Europe's plan for a music school in Harlem.

Pinchot wrote excruciatingly long letters, which he apparently relied on as a way of thinking his way through a problem. He had a gift for asking questions to which the answers seemed obvious on the surface, but then not so much as he slowly unraveled them. One of his shorter efforts—more declarative than most and probably edited for length—appeared in the old *New York Evening Post.*

Germany was clearly in the wrong, he wrote. The United States was well within its legal rights to respond militarily to German attacks. But maybe, he suggested, stopping the war was more important than rights or national honor. "I have tried to look at this peace and war question from every angle. I have been puzzled and doubtful at all times of my own mental processes in regard to it. . . . I feel we cannot square our national rights with the universal wrongs that have arisen out of the war."

The cataclysm in Europe had created its own virulent reality, like an epidemic, he wrote, and for the sake of humanity some nation had to be both brave and humble enough to find an end to it. The warring powers had long since lost track of what they were fighting for, except to outlast their opponents. Pinchot couldn't imagine that either side would give up, and he predicted that American involvement would maintain the stalemate and prolong the war.

"Heaven knows we have every legal excuse for going to war. . . . America has a higher duty than that of maintaining its national rights and privileges. It is not a duty of self-conscious example or hypocritical moral aloofness—God knows our commercial profits in the war have taken from us all right to preach—but one of humble and practical service, a duty to stay out of the war and to bring the contestants to some understanding, impossible as this may now seem."

He envisioned an American-sponsored peace conference. He knew the odds were long.

"Today, as in every similar crisis, the calm opinion of the nation is unfortunately drowned by the voices of war-shouters. The center of the stage is held by fear-mongers, accredited servants of privilege, and well-meaning, but unmeaning, enthusiasts. They are playing upon the fears of the public. They are trying to persuade our people that the country is in imminent danger; they say democracy all over the world is menaced by German militarism, and that the only way to save democracy is for us to join the Allies in crushing this militarism."

He praised Wilson for keeping the country out of war as long as he had. He seemed to recognize, though, that public opinion was now driving the country toward war, that there were limits to what a president could do—or not do.

The problem, he wrote, was that German militarism would not be crushed by an American victory. Militarism "is a psychological condition that can only be destroyed from within by the democratic impulses of the people themselves."

Then he warned: "Fight this war out to a finish—to a 'dictated peace'; leave the Central Powers with an undying grudge against their conquerors, and you have sown the seed for a period of intrigue, international alliance, and militarism, that will bear fruit in our children's time, in another disaster perhaps more terrible than the present war."

ON THE EVENING of March 22, there was another rally for war in New York, this time at Madison Square Garden, the vaguely Moorish arena designed by Stanford White that stood on the east side of the square. But Roosevelt wasn't there, despite a last-minute plea from Franklin Roosevelt's law partner. The old Rough Rider was packing that evening, readying for another adventure.

The next day, a Friday, Theodore Roosevelt strode through the pink granite hall of the magnificent six-year-old Pennsylvania Station, a few reporters trailing after him. A long-held ambition was to go spearfishing for manta rays, and all winter long he had been planning this trip to the Florida Gulf Coast to do just that.

"I am going away because at the moment there is nothing for me to do," he said as he paused at the gate to the platform below. "I have made all arrangements in regard to raising my division which, without governmental action, I can make."

Then he headed down into the gloom and found his way to car K-56 of the Atlantic Coast Line Railroad's train No. 187. A porter took his things and directed him to Drawing Room A, a private bedroom on the Pullman car. At 2:12 p.m., the train slipped out of the station, hurtled through the still-new tunnels under the Hudson River, and turned south for Jacksonville.

That evening, in Richmond, Roosevelt was joined by Russell J. Coles, a tobacco leaf dealer from Danville, Virginia. Coles made a living off tobacco, but his real passion was fish. He was an amateur ichthyologist and an early sport fisherman. A big man, he liked to go hunting for sharks off the North Carolina coast, and in Florida had speared the largest manta ray, or devilfish, as they were often called then, ever brought to shore up to that time. Measuring 18 feet 2 inches from tip to tip, it was a prized possession of the American Museum of Natural History, the institution so closely associated with Roosevelt himself. TR had arranged with Coles to organize the expedition.

All winter, Coles had been sending him updates on the planning. He had hired a crew of North Carolina fishermen who would build a camp for them ahead of time at Captiva. He reported on a cold wave that citrus farmers feared would damage their crops, and, if it persisted, might keep the rays away. But then a warm spell came to the rescue. The onions were so sweet you could eat them raw and not worry about your breath afterward.

Nearing 60, Roosevelt was not the image of vigor he had once been, though especially now that he was trying to raise a division to serve in France, he was loath to admit it. He hadn't fully recovered from illnesses he brought home from his 1914 Amazon expedition. Coles had laid in some Mexican hats, blousy shirts and four pairs of pants for the ex-president; the waistlines were 44 inches. But Roosevelt wasn't going to let this chance slip by. Manta rays were "the most dangerous game of the sea," and he was going to best one. Coles assured him, in letter after letter, that he was certain to make a kill.

When word of the trip leaked out, some of the papers made fun of Roosevelt, wondering if he'd try to catch himself a U-boat. But Coles was worried the Germans might attempt to kidnap him. What did a U-boat look like, he had asked Roosevelt in one letter. Could you puncture the hull with an ax if one came alongside? Roosevelt said he didn't know.

But Coles thought of just about everything. He made sure to subscribe to two Tampa newspapers, which would be delivered to camp a day late. He shipped down binoculars, three cameras, some books. Also, a supply of harpoons and lances. He sent ahead a .38 Colt revolver, a .405 Winchester, a .32 self-loading Winchester, a .22 Winchester and a shotgun. Roosevelt didn't need to bring his own rifle—that Springfield that had just been overhauled by Abercrombie & Fitch—because it would only get rusty in the salt air. Coles told the former president to ship his heavy revolver. And he added one other thought: They would have a long layover in Jacksonville while waiting for the connecting train to the Gulf Coast. "It might be all right for you to have your little pocket gun while traveling."

As the train sped south from Richmond, through the night and most of the next day, Roosevelt and Coles talked of many things, including Roosevelt's plans for a volunteer division. He was getting letters from all over the country from men wishing to join, some addressed, "Dear Comrade." They came from old troopers from the San Juan Hill days, cowboys, ranchers, middle-aged businessmen hoping for a commission and a ratification of self-worth. Roosevelt had been conducting a long correspondence with Newton Baker, the secretary of war—Roosevelt's letters full of enthusiasm, laying out details, this many infantry regiments, this many cavalry, naming officers of the regular Army he'd like to have serve with him. Baker was deferential, polite, noncommittal. On March 19, Roosevelt had telegrammed:

"I again earnestly ask permission to be allowed to raise a division for immediate service at the front. My purpose would be after some six weeks preliminary training here to take it direct to France for intensive training so that it could be sent to the front in the shortest possible time." He proposed assembling the division at Fort Sill, Oklahoma.

Inasmuch as the United States was not at war, Baker replied, any raising of troops would require an act of Congress. If war did come, he added, the country would be looking for a much larger force than Roosevelt envisioned, and it would be led by serving generals.

Exasperated, Roosevelt had sent off another telegram just before boarding the train to Florida. Of course, he said, the United States would need to build up a large army, but *in the meantime* he wanted to organize a small preliminary force that could go to the front right away and show the American flag. As to Baker's comment about putting only regular Army generals in charge—he reminded the secretary of war that he had previously served as commander-in-chief of the United States.

Coles wholeheartedly approved. America needed a man of action at a time like this, and Roosevelt was the man.

IN JACKSONVILLE, THE reception was friendly. Roosevelt didn't need to wield his gun. A band playing "Dixie" was at the station to welcome the train. "I would like to hear that tune against von Hindenburg's line in France," Roosevelt remarked. Then came the long ride down and across Florida; they arrived in Punta Gorda at midday on March 25, a Sunday. They took a fish company steamboat down to Captiva. There were seven men, all told, and they'd be living on a scow that was equipped with a cramped bunkhouse, moored in the bay behind the barrier island. It enabled them to stay away from the tourists.

EARLY THE NEXT morning, all but the cook set out on a 30-foot launch that wound its way past bright green banks, past palmettos and coconut palms, their fronds swaying enticingly in the warm tropical breeze. Herons and egrets perched in trees, or swooped across ahead of the boat. Shore birds darted about on the beach; ungainly pelicans glided through the air, their wings unmoving. Oysters grew on mangrove roots, and when, from time to time, the men passed citrus orchards, the fragrance of their blossoms hung heavy in the air. Roosevelt spotted sapodilla, pawpaw, rough lemons.

The skipper brought the boat out through Blind Pass into the Gulf. New York—argumentative, dingy, clamorous, avaricious, mid-March-beset—was now far behind.

The boat hopped pleasingly through the waves, the morning sun burned bright white. Roosevelt had only his big-brimmed soft hat, made from cabbage palm fronds, to shield his eyes. The men admired the schools of fish below them in the limpid water, and the pompano skimming along the surface. Then, abruptly, a ray came swimming toward them. Roosevelt stood in the bow, made sure his foot wasn't tangled in the rope from the harpoon, and tensed—but the ray was coming too fast, he hurried his throw, and the ray swam unmolested beneath the launch.

Before long another was sighted, and this time Roosevelt didn't miss. It thrashed in the water but his boat mates quickly dispatched it with their lances, and hauled it on board. Teddy was pleased, but it was small and had hardly been a challenge. His blood was up. A puny ray wasn't enough. And then they saw it—a big brute, a monster basking in the sun. Its wide black back lay just at the surface. Roosevelt's eyes gleamed. He focused on its horns. Again, to the bow. The boat approached, and still the huge fish drifted unsuspectingly. He braced his left foot hard against the stem of the boat. The ray didn't move. They came up to it. He should have used both hands but instead he raised the harpoon high in his right hand, above his ear. He torqued his hips, and summoning the strength and will and manliness of a much younger hunter, he thrust the harpoon down, deep and hard into the back of the devilfish, two feet down through skin and gristle and muscle. The ray swept its great wings up, dousing Roosevelt with water, swam to the stern of the boat and nearly lifted it from the water. The men sank lances into the big fish, and then it took off swimming, away from land, out into the Gulf, pulling the launch behind it by the rope of the harpoon, like a great stabbed whale towing a crew out of Nantucket in the old days. Roosevelt hung on, salty, drenched, his teeth flashing in the light glinting off the sea, the wind pushing back the wide floppy brim of his hat. For a mile the devilfish pulled them, and then another mile, all along leaving a dark wide trail of blood in the water.

Finally the ray, slowed, turned, made one last convulsive shudder. The men with Roosevelt dispatched it with their lances.

CHAPTER 16

"Like a River at Flood"

Very early on the morning of March 16, a Duma delegation went to meet with Grand Duke Michael, brother of Nicholas and now the occupant of the Russian throne. He was staying in an elegantly furnished apartment at No. 12 Millionaya Street in Petrograd. It was guarded by hussars. Mikhail Rodzianko, who as president of the Duma had tried to save the Romanov dynasty, now believed uncompromisingly that Michael should abdicate. So did most of the men who were with him. They were, by this time, "dirty and unwashed, with creased faces, eyes red and bloodshot from sleepless nights, uncombed hair and wrinkled collars." The liberal politician Pavel Milyukov stood almost alone; he delivered a half-hour predawn lecture to the grand duke and the others explaining why Michael should keep the throne as a figurehead. It was obvious to Alexander Kerensky that Michael could barely tolerate Milyukov's exegesis. He was clearly anxious. Kerensky then spoke forcefully for an abdication. "By assuming the throne you will not save Russia," Kerensky said. "I cannot vouch for your safety, Your Excellency." Michael asked to speak privately with Rodzianko and Prince Georgy Lvov. When they finished, Michael told the others that he agreed: He would refuse the throne for the good of the country.

Vladimir Nabokov helped to draw up the proclamation. Michael insisted he was not abdicating, but declining to accept the throne in deference to the Duma Provisional Committee. Thus was conferred legitimacy on what now became, as of that instant, the Provisional Government. This was a huge relief to Rodzianko and other conservatives who had been deeply worried about the legality of what they were doing. Now they saw themselves as the unencumbered authorities of Russia. But the leaders of the Petrograd Soviet had other ideas.

A BLACK SNOWSTORM of burned police dossiers filled the air along an entire block near the American embassy. It lifted James Houghteling's spirits. How could he not be an optimist, now that Russia's revolution had finally come? And how could he not be enjoying the excitement of rebellion? He and a colleague were walking to the telegraph office— the streetcars still weren't running—to see if any messages had come in for the embassy. At St. Isaac's Square, they stopped to inspect the ransacked Astoria Hotel, where a few days earlier British officers in residence had directed the smashing of the entire contents of the wine cellar to keep the alcohol out of the mob's hands. Houghteling walked into a room and to his surprise found an elegantly framed portrait of the czar and czarina still hanging on a wall.

No telegrams for the Americans had arrived, but the telegraph clerk was remarkably friendly and promised the diplomats they could send telegrams out any time they needed to, in code if they wanted, and no one would interfere. This, Houghteling thought, showed that a new era was at hand.

A few commandeered cars were speeding along the snow-covered avenues. A civilian stepped out onto the street and signaled a private car to stop; he had a few words with the driver, a lieutenant, who got out unhappily, and the civilian drove away. Houghteling was especially impressed by the cars full of eager soldiers with their rifles leveled, often with a machine gun mounted in the back.

Next they walked to a telephone office, guarded by a squad of soldiers. "They were commanded by a blond, scared-looking officer-boy, who, when he heard we were from the American Embassy, drew us aside and asked in French, very earnestly and pathetically, 'Do you think you could get me the necessary papers to go to America?'" They asked him why he wanted to go. He was worried, he replied, that things in Petrograd were bad and going to be getting worse. "Poor youngster," thought Houghteling, "he is probably the scion of some unpopular noble family, just clinging to the revolution by his eyelids and knowing that a single misstep will end him."

The young Chicagoan did note that on Friday, March 16, householders were informed by the Petrograd government that they were free to shoot intruders. In a city with no police, no courts and no laws, burglary had become an epidemic. "The emptying of all the jails has not helped the orderliness of the situation," he wrote in his diary, then quickly added, "which, however, is wonderfully good under the circumstances."

That Sunday a holiday mood engulfed the city. Crowds turned out, the barricades came down. A lone airplane buzzed up and down the Neva. Houghteling and a friend went over to the burned-out courthouse, hoping to snag a trophy. But others, more energetic, had beaten them to it. He ran into an acquaintance who told him how she had picked out a czarist emblem from the debris of a police station, only to be stopped by a soldier pointing his rifle at her. "I want to take this back to America as a souvenir of the Great Revolution," she told the soldier, "to show it to my grandchildren and my great-grandchildren when I tell them that I was there when Russia was freed." The soldier grinned and found someone to help her carry the iron shield.

SOVIET IS AN ordinary Russian word that can mean either "advice" or "council." The Petrograd Soviet was neither advisory nor statutory. A small group of white-collar radicals called for its creation and asked workplaces to send delegates. It was based on a similar body at the time of the 1905 revolution. Before it could properly meet, the organizers elected themselves its leaders. But they attracted support.

Groups of workers who had been out on the streets wanted to gather to discuss what to do next. The Duma was widely considered to be representative of Russia's exceedingly thin middle class. The men and women who began showing up to take part in the Soviet's deliberations ranged from skeptical to violently hostile in their attitudes toward the Duma. Until Michael renounced the throne, there had been deep suspicions that the Duma would acquiesce to a continuation of the monarchy.

Bedlam seemed to have taken over the Tauride Palace, as new delegations from factories around the city continued to arrive, and seemingly everyone tried to speak at once. As Leon Trotsky later described it, "The meeting flows on without order, without shores, like a river at flood. The Soviet chokes in its own enthusiasm. The revolution is mighty but still naïve." At first the soldiers had leaned toward creating a separate Soldiers' Soviet, but then they joined with the workers in one unruly body. Alexander Kerensky, "thin as a candle," was one of its early leaders. Nikolai Chkheidze, a Menshevik from Georgia, was another. They were socialists but they were not Bolsheviks. At this formative moment, they chose not to challenge the Provisional Government. For one thing, Marxist theory held that there must be a period of bourgeois rule before the final victory of the proletariat. Another, and perhaps more pertinent reason, was that the Soviet's leaders didn't want to take responsibility for what might very well turn out to be extremely unpopular moves. Leaders of both the Provisional Government and the Soviet agreed, for instance, that the lawlessness on the streets of the capital had to be brought under control, and that the troops had to return to their units. But the Soviet didn't want to take the blame for that. The idea, its leaders said, was that it would keep a wary and vigilant eye on the Provisional Government. The army officer Sergei Mstislavsky was not impressed: "The members of the Provisional Committee and the Executive Committee [of the Soviet], in the overwhelming majority of cases, were united from the first hours of the revolution by one single characteristic which determined all else: this was their fear of the masses."

The Provisional Government had to accept the arrangement, in any case, because it had very little ability to assert its authority. Kerensky and one other member of the Soviet did, after much debate, agree to join the government, he as justice minister.

Houghteling visited the Tauride Palace, where he found exhaustingly endless debates and the drafting of all sorts of proclamations. Men stood on staircases giving speeches. People worried about betrayal of the revolution, or a counterrevolution, or a German attack. He was hustled in to see a bone-weary Guchkov, the new minister of war, because his aides thought the American had brought an important message from Wilson. Guchkov, who spoke English, was good-natured about the interruption. Houghteling began to notice that Russia's new leaders were spending a lot more time talking than acting.

The most famous—or notorious—move in the early going was the issuance in the name of the Soviet of a general order, Prikaz No. 1, that was aimed at the officer corps. The Soviet never actually considered the order. On March 14 it had set up a commission on military organization, and late that night its members gathered around a long table covered with green cloth. Nikolai Sokolov, a famous defense lawyer, wrote out the order as soldiers dictated it to him. When they couldn't agree on something, they'd repair to a window and watch the snow falling gently through the night air. Then they'd go back to arguing. Finally they completed the document, amid much delight, and rather than return to the Soviet with it, they had it published in the March 15 issue of *Izvestia*, the newly founded Soviet newspaper.

The order called on all military units to elect committees that would be responsible for all "political action." Soldiers were instructed to obey their officers on strictly "military" matters, except where they conflicted with political directives. Discipline was to be relaxed, especially for soldiers off duty. Officers were not to be given arms. Sokolov said that the intent was actually to bring the army back to a state of order—that the enlisted men would have to take care of that themselves since so many officers had left their posts.

Members of the Provisional Government didn't see it that way, but the order underscored just how powerless they were. This was the moment, Sokolov said, when the leaders of the Soviet realized it was "a real factor." Once they read the order, soldiers around Petrograd in many cases decided to take it a step further, and began to insist on electing their officers.

In practice, a significant number of officers remained in their posts. Unpopular ones were hounded out, imprisoned, or killed. Even in the most cohesive units, though, the order had the effect of undermining discipline. Soldiers, who had been treated like cattle before the revolution, now came to believe they could obey or disobey orders as they pleased.

Kerensky called Order No. 1 "the greatest crime" and an "absurdity." It encouraged soldiers to follow "their base instincts," he said. "It was the height of irresponsibility and thoughtlessness."

Leon Trotsky, who was still in New York when the order was proclaimed, later called it "the single worthy document of the February revolution."

It encouraged the radicals in the Soviet and on the streets to turn up the pressure on the Provisional Government. Speakers denounced the leaders of the government as bourgeois parasites who were trying to steal the revolution from the people. The hostility took its toll; Kerensky said the government got most of its work done between midnight and 6 a.m., when the flow of delegations to the Tauride Palace slowed to a trickle. Sleep—there was no time for sleep. They feared a leftist uprising. They feared a rightest counterattack. They feared a German invasion. They feared anarchy and disintegration.

Houghteling persuaded himself that the army would remain intact. Regiments began parading around Petrograd, and he liked the look of them. The pessimists he ran into started to seem like cranks. When an American, whom Houghteling didn't name, met with the embassy staff and outlined what he saw as the dangers that the army would fall apart, no one—including the ambassador, David Francis—was inclined to take him seriously. News from the navy, which might have changed a few minds, was slow to make itself felt among the representatives of the United States in Petrograd.

AMBASSADOR FRANCIS MET informally with the new foreign minister, Pavel Milyukov, on the eighteenth. He left the conversation convinced that the "right-thinking, sincere and determined Russians" now running the country "would prosecute the war fearlessly regardless of its cost in blood and treasure." That evening he sent a cable to Washington asking permission to extend U.S. recognition to the new government. If the United States acted quickly, it would be the first nation to do so, which would "have a stupendous moral effect."

The next day Francis called, again informally, on the new war minister, Guchkov. The weary and nervous Russian told him that American recognition would be enormously helpful to the Provisional Government, and asked how quickly it could happen. Three or four days at the earliest, Francis replied. "With much agitation he expressed doubt as to whether the provisional government could survive until that time."

The Americans had faith that Kerensky, now serving as justice minister, would be a moderating influence on the radical leftists in the Soviet—and, indeed, Guchkov's fears proved to be unwarranted.

On March 22, with the all-clear from Washington, Francis set off in his sleigh, driven by a coachman in full livery, for the Mariinsky Palace, where the Provisional Government had taken up quarters. Behind him, in another sleigh, were the counselor, the four secretaries, various civilian attachés—all in formal diplomatic attire—and the military and naval attachés, each in full dress uniform. As anachronistic as the military outfits were—the officers would have looked as though they had stepped out of a Gilbert and Sullivan operetta—Francis wanted this to be an impressive and formal ceremony. The Russian ministers, in rumpled business suits, were pleased to welcome them. The United States was the first nation to recognize the new government, and thus, in American eyes, the United States made itself the first and most significant ally of the new Russian democracy.

STREETCAR SERVICE RESUMED, and that was a welcome sign. During the uprising, the trolleys had been easily disabled with the removal of the operators' steel controllers, the handles by which they regulated the motors. Some people threw them into snow drifts, others kept them as clubs. The city appealed for anyone who had taken possession of a controller to turn it in, and enough people did so that service was finally restored. The first car to go into action crossed the Troitsky Bridge, with a band on board and a big red banner that said Land and the Will of the People.

To Houghteling, it was emblematic of Russia's recovery. Everything looked normal. The new recruits he saw being drilled on the streets seemed to suggest that discipline was as intact as ever. He stopped to have tea with an acquaintance, and a "timorous American" joined them. This annoying person had heard a fresh crop of pessimistic rumors: that the workers were refusing to go back to their jobs at the munitions plants, that soldiers were locking up their officers, that socialists were demanding the death penalty for their prisoners, and that there had been some sort of bloody revolt at the Kronstadt naval base. "Poor Russia, if one believes some of these faint-hearts, she is about done for," Houghteling wrote in his diary. "We think that she is just beginning."

The Menshevik newspaper, *Rabochaya Gazeta*, warned that the political revolution had to be completed before the country could move on to resolving socioeconomic problems. But workers began agitating for an eight-hour day. And women, who had been promised the vote, took to the streets when they began to fear that the promise wouldn't be fulfilled.

Trotsky called the struggle for the eight-hour day the "great test of strength." Both the Provisional Government and the Executive Committee of the Soviet were calling on workers to return to their jobs. But the workers' point was, this was the moment to secure a positive change in their lives. The Mensheviks who ran the Soviet thought the proletariat was not equipped to conduct a struggle on two fronts at once—that is, against counterrevolution, and against the capitalists. So they wanted to postpone measures that would alleviate conditions for the workers but might antagonize the business owners and their liberal friends. As it happened, at a number of workplaces, in piecemeal fashion, employees reached agreements with the owners to reduce their hours without a cut in pay. "The industrialists were more far-seeing," Trotsky observed, "than the democratic strategists of the Soviet."

Leon Trotsky wrote his *History of the Russian Revolution* in 1930, while living in exile in Istanbul. It's a work to read skeptically, because he inevitably devoted a fair amount of his attention to the settling of old scores, against liberals, monarchists, Mensheviks and especially some of his fellow Bolsheviks. He wasn't there to witness the revolution.[20] Yet he knew the principal characters and was no stranger to the currents of thought and grievance and ideology that were coursing through his native land. The decision by the leaders of the Soviet to hand over power to the Provisional Government failed to stabilize the state, he argued, but instead sowed chaos, bitterness and collapse. At a time, as he put it, when the past and the future were engaged in gun battles on the streets of Petrograd, the socialists should have seized the opportunity to make the future theirs. The leaders of the Provisional Government pretended to cheer the revolution, but they knew that they were captives of much larger, hostile forces that were sweeping them along. The Soviet, said Trotsky, shouldn't have been so meek, and so afraid of real revolution. Workers who looked to the Soviet for

20   But then again neither was I.

leadership ran the post and telegraph offices, all the train stations, the printing houses. The Soviet had power it was unwilling to use.

The Socialists, he pointed out, still characterized the bourgeoisie as their enemy, but at the same time insisted the bourgeoisie agree to accept the gift of power. It was reminiscent, he said, of the way the Slavic tribes of the ninth century appealed to the Scandinavian princes to come rule over them.

The leaders of the Soviet kept insisting that they would support the government "in so far as" it pursued palatable policies (in Russian, *postolku poskolku*). Trotsky was not the only one who mocked that formulation. It bestowed on the Provisional Government what he called "semi-contraband sovereignty."

On March 21 workers on the Vyborg side demanded the overthrow of the Provisional Government, but the Soviet leadership refused to budge. "Such was the Executive Committee," Trotsky wrote, "with a staff of leaders who were incapable of passing from word to deed, [having] arrived at the head of revolution called to break the fetters of a century and lay the foundations of a new society." Their compromises with the liberals "became one long chain of painful contradictions exhausting the masses and leading to the convulsions of civil war."

HOUGHTELING LEARNED THAT foreign newspaper correspondents in Petrograd were now allowed to send their dispatches uncensored, except for military information that might be useful to the Germans. Yet the censor, who was still looking them over, said that most of the newspapermen were sending home "the worst slush imaginable."

On March 25, for instance, Harold Williams filed a dispatch to the *London Daily Chronicle*, picked up by the *New York Times* and featured on the front page. "Movement, effort and strain are the outstanding features of the new life of Russia," he began. "Everything is in motion, but the strongest current of all is in one direction, the direction of establishing genuine liberty and creating a very free and powerful Russia secure against attack from within and without."

He continued, "It is a great and splendid struggle. With deep joy at the heart of it and a constant feeling that now at last work and effort are worthwhile. . . . The forces of good and evil now have a clear field, and the forces of good are steadily gaining the upper hand." He noted that the "change from the long delays and procrastination of the old regime is startling, yet it is less surprising to residents here than it will probably appear to outsiders. Modern, intelligent Russia was here all of the time, full of ideas, full of the best impulses, but chafing and fretting under a humiliating bondage which constantly checked initiative. Now it has its opportunity."

News stories like this one, as they filtered back to Russia over the weeks that followed, bewildered Russians and foreigners alike, who found themselves increasingly unable to recognize the country the correspondents were describing.

On March 22, Nicholas Romanov joined his family at the palace at Tsarskoe Selo. He was escorted on a train from the army headquarters at Mogilev. The troops at the garrison there, who had formerly protected him, now had an ambiguous role to play. They were both jailers and bodyguards.

"Lord, what a difference," Nicholas wrote in his diary, "on the streets and around the palace, in the park are guards, and inside, in the hall some kind of ensigns!" He was allowed to stroll in the garden, "but no further!" His daughter, the 17-year-old Grand Duchess Maria, had the measles.

The next day, leaders of the Petrograd Soviet caught wind of a plan by the Provisional Government to allow Nicholas and his family to flee by train to the port of Archangel, and from there to take a British warship to England. It looked like a scheme to keep him safe until such time as the monarchists could arrange a restoration. Even the cautious leaders of the Soviet knew they couldn't allow that. The fury that would erupt on the streets of Petrograd if the czar were to be escorted into exile was all too imaginable.

Reluctantly, the Executive Committee agreed that the Soviet would have to assume control of the royal family from the Provisional Government, and immediately. The loyalties of the garrison at Tsarskoe Selo were not clear. Now Sergei Mstislavsky, an army officer but also a Socialist revolutionary, was ordered to take a detachment from the reliable Semyonovsky Regiment and assume command at the suburban palace.*

The soldiers left almost immediately for the little train station that served the short line out to Tsarskoe Selo. They formed up on the platform, then began hefting the heavy machine guns of that era onto the train. Guards kept bystanders away, but then a reporter slipped through and began shouting questions from the platform. "Where are you going?" A soldier replied, "Drop dead!" The train started with a jolt, and for a while the lithe reporter ran alongside it on the platform. "Tell them that the Semyonovtsy are paying a visit to the czar," shouted one of the troopers.

But the mood on the train quickly turned somber. The soldiers didn't know what to expect, they didn't have much ammunition—and their objective was, after all, the man who just a week earlier had been the autocrat of all the Russias.

Before long the train pulled into the station at Tsarskoe Selo. The soldiers crossed themselves and fixed bayonets. They rolled the machine guns out onto the asphalt platform.

Two officers from the garrison were there to meet Mstislavsky. They refused to recognize his orders. He bluffed and threatened. It was clear they weren't sure of their own standing. Finally they reached an agreement: Mstislavsky would leave his troops at the station, and, taking a single aide, proceed by himself to the palace. If he wasn't back in an hour, his soldiers would come get him.

At the palace he was met by the commandant, a Captain Kotsuba. The detachment was under orders from the legal government not

---

* Mstislavsky, in his book *Five Days Which Transformed Russia*, said this happened on March 22, but it was almost certainly the 23rd.

to allow anyone to pass further into the palace grounds, the captain told him. Mstislavsky showed him the orders from the Soviet. But the Soviet recognizes the authority of the Provisional Government, Kotsuba countered. The real issue, Mstislavsky replied, "is where the actual power lies."

Kotsuba considered, and grudgingly relented. They walked through a series of passageways and into a larger room full of soldiers. "Greetings, Comrades!" shouted Mstislavsky. "Best wishes from the Petrograd Garrison and the Soldiers' Soviet!" The men leaped up in their enthusiasm. The game, thought Mstislavsky, is ours.

It turned out that the troops were from the 2nd Infantry, not the Imperial Guards, and after a lengthy parley Mstislavsky was convinced they would not allow Nicholas to leave the palace for exile. But he insisted on seeing the former czar. This act of "abasement," as he called it, was necessary. The czar must be inspected the way any prisoner is inspected. And Mstislavksy knew it would be better to report back to the Soviet that he had laid eyes on citizen Romanov.

It was arranged. Mstislavsky traipsed through the royal rooms. He hadn't changed his clothes since the revolt broke out three weeks earlier. His sheepskin coat had pieces of straw sticking to it. His hair was uncombed. The handle of his automatic pistol was sticking out of his pocket.

He and his escorts stopped. A door opened, and there came the sound of quick footsteps, spurs jingling. Nicholas appeared, bareheaded. He was wearing a khaki tunic, and rubbing his hands together.

"His face was puffy and red, his swollen eyelids forming a heavy frame for his dull, bloodshot eyes. For a moment he stood there, indecisively, then slowly, he came toward us. It seemed as though he was about to speak. Our eyes locked; he drew ever closer, step by step. A dead silence hung over the room. The still yellow gaze of the Emperor, so like that of a tired, hunted wolf, suddenly flickered with a flame which broke the surface of its leaden indifference. It was a spark of deadly malice. I felt the shudder which passed through the officers standing behind me. Nicholas paused, shifted from foot to foot, and sharply turned around, walking rapidly away, twitching his shoulders, and limping."

CHAPTER 17

"To Scold an Earthquake"

Official Washington was close to panic, Frank Polk believed. If Wilson didn't do *something*, he feared the entire executive branch of the government would declare itself on strike against the president. Polk, the State Department counselor, was in New York on March 22, pouring out his frustrations to Colonel House. Secretary of War Baker had finally come around to the belligerents' side, he said, but the Army was of course still in woeful shape.

But Wilson was moving. He had promised Lansing and Baker, after the cabinet meeting two days before, that he would sleep on a decision. Late in the morning of the next day, he formally summoned Congress to meet in a special session to begin on April 2, two weeks earlier than scheduled. (House thought it was a mistake—that there was too much spadework still to be done before the issue got tangled up on Capitol Hill.) The White House did not reveal what Wilson intended to ask of Congress, and even cabinet secretaries could only guess at his intentions. Would he make one last bid at convening a peace conference? Would he seek a more militant "armed neutrality"? Or, if he accepted that Germany was at war with the United States, what would he propose? Matériel and financial support to the

Allies? A naval campaign? Or the deployment of a heretofore nonexistent army overseas? What about conscription? What about taxation?

Wilson didn't make himself available, and made little headway through the towering stack of papers that he needed to sign and that had been building up since he took to his sickbed right after the inauguration. "Apparently he is not in a working mood these days," White House aide Thomas Brahany wrote in his diary. "He spends nearly all his time with Mrs. Wilson, reading, playing pool or visiting. The newspapermen are in the air as to what line they should take." Another aide suggested the president should hold a press conference, but Wilson declined. He said the papers should "conjecture nothing."

They did anyway.

The lead news story in Philadelphia's *Evening Ledger* began: "President Wilson has decided to meet Germany's high seas affronts with sweeping action. War today seemed just ahead."

A few paragraphs later: "If the president does not seek a war declaration, Congress will demand it." Wilson's decision to convene Congress "was based on a tremendous appeal from the country for revenge for Germany's killing of American citizens and destruction of American property in contravention of all international law and the ideals upon which the United States was founded and exists today."

THOMAS GREGORY, THE attorney general, met with his friend and ally House in New York on March 22. "He thinks the president had no idea of calling Congress together earlier than the 16th but was persuaded to call it on the 2nd of April because of the unanimous opinion of the Cabinet that he should do so."

That evening, Gregory and House went together to the Lyceum Theatre, which still stands on West 45th Street. Texans both, they were there to see a revival of *The Great Divide*, an enormously popular play that touched on feminism, sexuality, and the sharp cultural and social differences between the eastern states and the American West.

House enjoyed going to the theater. In January, he had seen a play called *Turn to the Right*, and the producer, John Golden, had taken him backstage during the show. House was fascinated by the conversations he had with the actors while they were awaiting their cues. Golden, who had rewritten much of the script, talked about the effects he was trying for with certain of his lines. A few weeks later, on the day Wilson decided to break off diplomatic relations with Germany, it occurred to House that a great government crisis involves quite a lot of stagecraft. The public has little sense of the actors waiting their turn, in the wings or behind the drops. And how much waiting there is until the denouement. And how important it is to get the lines right.

WHILE TR WAS preparing for his Florida adventure, more than 12,000 people jammed the old Madison Square Garden on the night of March 22. Many more were turned away. A group called the Junior Patriots of America assembled a Boy Scout troop and a company of the Junior Naval Reserve on Fifth Avenue. They were told at first that no minors were allowed in, but then the committee that organized the rally relented, and the boys, led by a band, marched across the park and into the Garden, where they took seats in the upper gallery. Down on the floor, John Philip Sousa's band played patriotic songs while the exuberant throngs pushed in, cheering and jostling and arguing over seats. Thousands were carrying American flags.

There wasn't much new to say, but what was said came with fervor. Elihu Root warned that America would be at the mercy of Germany if the Allies were defeated. What would stop Germany from establishing a naval base in the Caribbean to block the Panama Canal, he asked. And once Germany had a foothold in the Western Hemisphere, he warned, there would be no defending against it. Far better, he declared, to fight the enemy over there, than to fight them at home.

"All history teaches us that the rich and defenseless peoples, the

people who are too luxurious, too fond of their comfort, their prosperity, their wealth, their ease, to make sacrifice for their liberty,
surely fall a prey to the aggressor," he warned. "Every American,
every true American heart should respond with joy, amid its sorrow,
to the feeling that if we enter this war to do our part toward bringing about the victory that is so important to us, we shall be fighting
over again the battle of the American democracy. The democracy
of England, the democracy of France, and now, God be praised, the
great democracy of Russia."

Suddenly came a shout from the audience: "Lie!" one man yelled.
"We want peace!" called out another. While the crowd looked on,
men in olive khaki uniforms, wearing yellow armbands and swinging nightsticks, subdued the hecklers and tossed them out. The uni-
formed men were from a new organization, called the Home Defense
League, established in conjunction with the New York police. There
were 500 HDL volunteers prowling the Garden that night, looking
for trouble. And more was to come.

But first John Grier Hibben, who had succeeded Wilson as president of Princeton, spoke. "I am here tonight as a pacifist," he declared,
and that brought the crowd to an uneasy hush. He paused. "I believe
in peace at any price, and the price at the present time is war." Cheers
of relief filled the hall.

Then Charles S. Fairchild, former treasury secretary, told the rally
that "no cause, religious, civil or social, has ever gone on without a
call, without a leader."

A chorus rose from the gallery. "We want Teddy! We want Teddy!"
The band played a march; pandemonium beckoned, as a fever set
in. (Teddy was at home, packing for his trip to Florida the next day.)
Finally a semblance of order was restored.

Now it was time for the mayor of New York, John Purroy Mitchel.
Though a Catholic, he was the grandson and namesake of a great
Protestant Irish nationalist. Just 37, Mitchel was called the Boy Mayor.

He had hardly gotten more than four words out when an Irish

immigrant in the crowd shouted out, "What about your grandfather?" The implication was, how could the descendant of a famous
nationalist support going to war alongside England? The men in
khaki and armbands put the man out. The mayor pretended to take
no notice.

"There has been a question raised by some as to the attitude of the
people of the country," he said. "Let the expression of these people
who have come here freely be the answer to that question."

Another shout from the floor. "How about the Irish Republic?"

This time, as the volunteers moved in again, the mayor responded.
"Today, first of all we are discussing the protection of the American
Republic." The crowd cheered. "When the nation is in a situation like
this on a question of loyalty to the country . . . men and women may
divide into but two classes, Americans and traitors."

Then a third cry. "What would your grandfather say?"

Now the mayor was shouting, too. "My grandfather was a good
citizen of the United States, and he'd say precisely the same thing."*

TWO NIGHTS LATER, on March 24, Madison Square Garden was
filled to the rafters yet again, this time for a rally organized by the
Emergency Peace Federation. Three fights broke out. David Starr
Jordan, who had asked Roosevelt if he'd debate Bryan, was in the
middle of his speech when he mentioned both Roosevelt and Elihu
Root. The hall erupted in boos and hisses, but a young man at the
back began to cheer. In moments, there was a general uproar, a
bench tipped over, a dozen people were knocked to the floor. Jordan called for quiet, then the band struck up a tune to distract the
crowd. Finally, after all had fallen silent again, he suggested that
anyone who was feeling especially bellicose should come up to the

---

* The elder John Mitchel had spent twenty years in the United States, where he
defended slavery as preferable to the capitalism he saw in the North. He supported
the Confederacy during the Civil War.

stage, and arrangements would be made for him to enlist immediately in the U.S. Army. Then a man shouted out, "To hell with
America!"

More bedlam. The organizers had recruited just 20 security
guards—wearing white armbands—but they were burly men and
were able to restore order.

Jordan said that a victory for German militarism would be a calamity, but that that was no reason for the United States to enter the war.
Then the rhetoric heated up.

An angry Benjamin C. Marsh, a social reformer and city planning
pioneer, denounced Roosevelt, Root and Mitchel as "Wall Street's
traitorous tools." He called Roosevelt "the greatest moral coward
in the country." All this was in the prepared text of his speech, but
catching the spirit of the crowd he began to ad lib. "Let's pray for the
death of Root and Roosevelt!" he said.

He mocked Root for having brought up the Founding Fathers in
an earlier speech. "Everyone knows," he said, "the Revolutionary
fathers would have shot Root at sight as a horse thief."

Rabbi Judah L. Magnes, a prominent Reform leader who had
been raising funds for the Jewish community in Palestine, decried
munitions makers and "bloodthirsty ex-presidents" who were whipping up public opinion. "The war spirit is too much abroad," he
exclaimed.

A loud shout from the gallery. "Thank God!" The security guards
hustled after the heckler. And so the raucous meeting continued.
Speakers asked for financial pledges to support the antiwar fight.
Professor H. W. L. Dana of Columbia University pledged $30. (He
was fired six months later for being a pacifist.) Mark Twain's daughter Clara, married to the Russian pianist Ossip Gabrilowitsch, promised to contribute $25, Marsh announced. Minnie Untermyer, whose
husband Samuel was a wealthy civic leader and attorney, pledged
$1,000. The evening ended with the assembled participants voting
for a resolution that demanded a national referendum on the ques-

tion of entering the war. The police said afterward that despite the brawling no one had to be hospitalized.

THAT SAME EVENING, Jeannette Rankin was in Indianapolis, at the Claypool Hotel, and though the end of her tour was now in sight, she had a tough schedule still to go. She had kept her word; she hadn't talked about the war, even as both sides were whipping up their supporters. When letters or telegrams caught up with her, they were running heavily—but not unanimously—against going to war. Now, as she traveled, she had to decide: Was opposition to war good for the women's movement, or would it isolate and undercut the cause? It was a utilitarian question, but it was the question that mattered. Most of her thinking had to be done on trains. She had appearances in Indianapolis on the 24th, Chattanooga on the 26th, Dayton on the 27th, Minneapolis on the 29th, Des Moines on the 30th. At each city, there'd be a reception, interviews with local reporters, requests for appearances, the main lecture. Then it was on to the next city, always on an overnight train. Her manager, Lee Keedick, had had to scramble when Wilson called Congress to meet on April 2. He was able to squeeze in Minneapolis. Kansas City had to be canceled.

She was in Minneapolis just three days before Congress was to convene. She spoke in favor of suffrage, and against corporate ownership of natural resources. "Wages may be high in dollars and cents, but they are low in food and shelter," she said. "The life of our laborer is not valued highly, with the result [that] social problems are increasing. Our prisons are filled; everywhere we find delinquents, defectives and vagrants. To offend against property is considered a greater offense than to offend against human happiness." Still, she said nothing about the war.

It's clear where her heart lay. On February 3, she had sent a telegram to the state chairman of the Montana Good Government State Central Committee, Eleanor Coit of Big Timber. "What do you think," Rankin asked, "of telegraphing County Chairmen to wire

Wilson their attitude towards war and your telegraphing Wilson for the organization that we wish everything possible done to avert war."

Coit declined that same day. "We cannot be a free nation if we submit longer to violation of the rights of our individual citizens," she replied. "This German order challenges civilization."

Jane Addams, the veteran social-work activist, had also organized a February letter-writing campaign by women to protest against going to war, but by March she was in Florida, recuperating from an illness. Rankin sent word from her speaking tour, through an intermediary, that she hoped to have a chance to consult with Addams on "the most valuable work she could do for peace during the coming extra session."

The suffrage movement and established peace organizations, such as the Woman's Peace Party, largely overlapped. But Eleanor Coit out in Big Timber, Montana, wasn't the only one to break ranks on the question of war. Just days after Germany announced its resumption of the U-boat campaign, Carrie Chapman Catt, head of the National Woman Suffrage Association, pledged its support for Wilson in the event of war. An ally, Vira Whitehouse, made a similar pledge to Governor Charles Whitman of New York. It caused a deep and bitter split within the movement.

"I never heard of anything so bumptious, so undemocratic, as what Mrs. Whitehouse did," said Margaret Lane, a leading pacifist. "It was a miserable political crawl, that's what it was—trying to get favor for our suffrage bill in the legislature by promising that we'll turn in and help the war. I wouldn't take the vote on such terms, and I am a good suffragist." The members of the Woman's Peace Party, she said, "including the large number who are in the suffrage organizations, have no intention of rolling bandages. If war comes we shall be busy fighting unjust censorship and other infringements of our liberty that war brings."

But Catt sensed an opportunity. She wanted federal action on suffrage, rather than leaving the decision to the individual states. In January, when North Carolina passed a partial suffrage bill, she had suggested that the time was ripe for Wilson to endorse a federal voting law, but nothing came of it. Now, she recognized that war would mean a hugely increased role for the federal government in the life of Americans, perhaps including male conscription, and she thought it would be unacceptably hypocritical, in the midst of a national mobilization, to continue denying women the vote. If, that is, women could prove their worth to the nation, and to the president, by pitching in. And if war was going to come anyway, what could be gained by taking a futile public stand against it?

Some women wanted to be prepared to show what women could do—what women *must* do—if war should come. Beginning in 1916, the Women's Section of the Navy League had begun sponsoring a series of encampments, called National Service Schools, at which over a three-week period several thousand young women, in khaki uniforms, had been learning everything from first aid to hygiene to dietetics to semaphore signaling to radio telegraphy. Wilson himself had helped open the first camp, in Washington; Franklin D. Roosevelt was also there. Subsequent sessions had been held in San Francisco; Lake Geneva, Wisconsin; and Narragansett Pier, Rhode Island. They were run in military fashion, including reveille at 6:30, calisthenics, inspection, drill, and classwork. Now two more encampments were announced, for April and May, both to be held in Washington. "Attention! Women of America! Here is Your Chance!" proclaimed one recruiting poster. "Enlist for Training in War Service."

The brainchild of the sisters Vylla Poe Wilson and Elisabeth E. Poe, the latter a newspaper writer in New York, the Women's Section of the Navy League required its members to sign a pledge "to think, talk and work for patriotism, Americanism and sufficient national defenses to keep the horrors of war far from America's homes and shores."

The *Washington Post* ran a long story that was almost entirely cribbed from a National Service School press release. It was headlined: "When Washington's Debutantes Prepare for War."

On March 21, a member of the Women's Section named Loretta Walsh was sworn in as a petty officer in the U.S. Navy. She was the first woman to serve in the U.S. armed forces in any role but that of a nurse. Secretary Daniels had ordered the Navy to admit women just two days earlier; the idea was to use them in clerical jobs, freeing up men for duty at sea. Walsh, 20, from Olyphant, Pennsylvania, went to work as a recruiting officer in Philadelphia. It was left to her to design the uniform that, within the span of 18 months, 13,000 other women yeomen would wear.

ROSE PASTOR STOKES was a prominent feminist and socialist who had been born in a *shtetl* in the Russian Empire. Now she decided to resign from the Woman's Peace Party. "I love peace, but I am not a pacifist," she wrote. The war, she argued, was an outcome of the worldwide competitive system, evidence that human civilization, in its long ascent, had still not achieved the best that it was capable of. To inveigh at this point against violent struggle, she wrote, "seems to me as futile and unscientific . . . as it would be to scold an earthquake."

FROM GREAT FALLS, Montana, a letter arrived for Rankin. "It was the vote of the women in the West who gave this territory to President Wilson and the women voted for him on that false campaign slogan 'He Kept Us Out of War,' and let us now, at this time, compel him to live up to that reputation."

In Missoula, a branch of the Women's Section of the Navy League was formed and immediately expressed "our hearty support and cooperation" in any action Wilson or Congress might deem necessary.

Nina Swinnerton sent a wire: "Jeannette, dear, don't sell us out as Mrs. Catt and all the rest of them have done. We count on you to vote for peace."

A public gathering in Kalispell, Montana, endorsed a resolution supporting the president. A similar meeting in Bonner voted overwhelmingly against war.

Rankin heard from other states, as well.

Cornelia Welles, of Schenectady, New York, sent her a letter on March 26. "In spite of the spectacular military drilling of a few women, the great mass of women are Christian and do not approve of entering the European War, nor of militarizing our nation," she wrote. "The honor of our country is upheld better by righteousness than by barbarism."

Grace Woods, of Pittsburgh, wrote, "The women of Pennsylvania appeal to you to use all your Woman's Intelligence, Wit and Magnetism" to keep the country out of the war. "It is horrible to think of our young men being sacrificed to the commercial war now being waged in Europe—and their bodies feeding either the birds or the soil of a foreign country."

From Rogers, Arkansas, came this letter, handwritten in pencil, signed by Mrs. George E. Wilson. "I am the mother of an only son who is dearer to me than my own life. The thought of him being plunged into this European inferno-war turns me sick."

JIM EUROPE HAD lost weight. He tired easily, and there were great circles around his eyes. A physician staying at the Poinciana Hotel in Palm Beach had noticed his condition and invited Europe to his guest suite for a checkup. He diagnosed an exophthalmic goiter, growing inward toward his esophagus, and recommended a specialist the bandleader should see as soon as he got back to New York. It could potentially become very serious, the doctor told him.

But Europe had no time for that. He was on the threshold of what would be his "biggest contribution to the race and country." He had to get that band together for the regiment, so the day after he arrived in the city, he was off again to Puerto Rico to find reed players. He had been wearing evening clothes throughout the Palm Beach season, but now he put on his lieutenant's khaki. Rushed, harried, ill, he bustled downtown to the steamship that would take him back south. Noble Sissle, who had been managing the band's affairs, was in tow; he would stay in New York and continue to round up musicians.

Europe swore him to secrecy about the goiter. They were late—the gangplank was up. One last load of luggage remained to be hauled up from the pier in a net. So they threw Europe's trunk in with the others, then he scrambled after it and sat on top while a derrick lifted the whole load to the deck. Europe stepped out of the net and stood by the rail as the ship eased away, limp and perspiring, weakly waving his campaign hat.

Sissle, with the benefit of hindsight, later mocked Wilson's reluctance to go to war. "Germany was sinking our boats right and left. The president had written 'Notes' till there was a shortage of diplomatic letter heads in Washington, and every time he wrote a note, one of the Kaiser's Undersea Dogs would apologize by sinking a larger ship." Sissle and Europe were fully prepared to get into the fight. But as war talk grew louder and louder throughout the country, any number of musicians who had been eager to join Europe's band over the winter suddenly found all sorts of excuses to stay away.

The prospect of war was pulling African-Americans in sharply different directions. Loyalty to the land of their birth contended with outrage over Jim Crow. Some, like Europe, believed the race could occupy its rightful place in society by joining in the fight against Germany. Others saw this as an opportune moment to make demands first, and serve second.

White southerners were spreading stories about German agents plotting with "Negroes" to foment a racial uprising. Two men were arrested in Birmingham, Alabama, on suspicion of doing just that. Black leaders saw these tales as a fiction designed to keep them down. As early as October 1914, W. E. B. Du Bois, of the National Association for the Advancement of Colored People, had responded angrily to a German letter writer after a group of German scientists signed a statement insulting "Mongrels and Niggers."

"I believe Germany is responsible for the war," Du Bois wrote. "I sincerely hope that your country will be thoroughly whipped." The principal of Hampton Institute, Hollis B. Frissell, said, "The negro has always been loyal." Forty students, he said, had applied to attend officer training camps for black regiments. In Durham, North Carolina, the head of a "colored" insurance company said Germany should know "that we stand for a principle and cannot be bought." In Tuskegee, Alabama, the white chairman of the Tuskegee Board of Trustees, William Willcox, who was also chairman of the Republican National Committee, said, "In this great crisis, the negro race will not be found wanting."

The Crisis, the NAACP publication edited by Du Bois, accused whites in the South of trying to portray African-Americans as a menace so that martial law could be declared and migration to the North be halted. "They are playing with fire! The negro is far more loyal to this country and its ideals than the white Southern American. He never has been a disloyal rebel."

Just as Russians had secured their freedom when all seemed lost, the magazine suggested, so too might American Negroes achieve their goals as a consequence of the war. "So some day a black woman will ride down the world, crying, 'Disfranchisement is done! "Jim-Crow" cars are gone! Segregation is past! I am an American!'"

The *Louisville Courier-Journal* marveled that a Negro, universally held to be from an inferior race, could be as eloquent as Roscoe Conkling Simmons, the nephew of Booker T. Washington, had been. The paper used his example to shame white pacifists.

"Grievances I have against this people, against this government," Simmons said. "Injustice to me there is, bad laws there are upon the statute books, but in this hour of peril I forget—and you must forget—all thoughts of self, or race, or creed or politics or color. That, boys, is loyalty."

The white authorities weren't making it easy. New York's 15th Regiment relied on private donations to equip itself and was constantly in danger of failing inspection. A colored real estate agent who said he had once served Teddy Roosevelt as a porter at the

Hoboken railroad station wrote the former president, complaining that Negroes were barred from National Guard armories, and this made it impossible to train properly. Though Roosevelt wanted to recruit black troops to his division, he was not a pioneer on race relations. As president, he had ordered the dishonorable discharge of 167 black soldiers following a violent altercation with white civilians in Brownsville, Texas, in 1906, as a group punishment. Evidence had been planted against them. (Richard Nixon pardoned the men in 1972.) There is no record that Roosevelt replied to the letter about the color ban at the armories.

Charles W. Anderson, director of the Colored Advisory Committee to the Republican National Committee, worried that blacks weren't seeing anything to inspire them. "There is widespread apathy among the colored people of this city," he wrote to Roosevelt. "Something should be done at once to arouse them. It fills me with abhorrence to hear them ask, 'What have we to fight for?'"

The *New York Age*, a Harlem newspaper, suggested in a March 29 editorial that the problem was Wilson. For decades, it said, black Americans had felt that the federal government was on their side, that, especially in the South, federal buildings were sanctuaries from both the brutal and the petty discriminations of Jim Crow. But Wilson "and his administration of Negro baiters" had changed all that, ordering the segregation of the federal government. For the past four years, "the colored American citizen has been avowedly Jim Crowed" by Wilson. That's why the black men of 1917 weren't sure they wanted to be targets for German bullets.

Joel Spingarn, a Jewish cofounder of the NAACP, was pilloried by the *Age* for proposing officer training camps for black candidates. The newspaper's opinion was that blacks should have nothing to do with the Army or the war. Spingarn wrote a somewhat sheepish letter to Du Bois, saying he supposed he should be glad that he had sparked a full and open debate. But he pointed out that if war came, and most likely conscription, there would be plenty of black men serving as draftees. Wouldn't it be better, he asked, to have black officers, too?

The Reverend Adam Clayton Powell, pastor of the Abyssinian Baptist Church in Harlem (and the father of the longtime U.S. congressman), said the crisis was exactly the right time to demand that white America act on Negro complaints. Pointing to the Easter Rising of 1916, he said the Irish understood that progress comes out of a crisis, that demands are met in times of stress. And hundreds of thousands of railroad workers in America had threatened to strike as war loomed, and they won what they were seeking. Likewise, the Russians had overthrown the autocracy thanks to the strain of war.

"The ten million colored people of this country were never so badly needed as now," he said. They were needed in factories, on farms—and in the Army. "This is the psychological moment to say to the American white government from every pulpit and platform and through every newspaper, 'Yes, we are loyal and patriotic. . . . While we love our flag and country, we do not believe in fighting for protection of commerce on the high seas until the powers that be give us at least some verbal assurance that the property and lives of the members of our race are going to be protected on land from Maine to Mississippi.'

"If this kind of talk is not loyalty, then I am disloyal; if this is not patriotic, then I am unpatriotic; if this is treason, then I am a traitor. . . . It is infinitely more disgraceful and outrageous to hang and burn colored men, boys and women without a trial in the days of peace than it is for Germans in time of war to blow up ships loaded with mules and molasses."

IN PUERTO RICO, Jim Europe signed up fourteen musicians. He had hoped to get more, but he had to cut his recruiting trip short. Word came that the 15th Regiment was about to get mustered into federal service, where it would be renumbered the 369th Infantry. It was also heading off to begin serious training, at a camp near Peekskill, New York. The fourteen reed players (joining the scores of other bandsmen Sissle had recruited) would have to do. Most of the Puerto Ricans would learn English only after becoming soldiers in the U.S. Army. Europe could worry about his goiter later.

CHAPTER 18

"Reeked with Patriotism"

Detectives at the Frankford Police Station in Philadelphia were on the lookout. Someone had been stealing copper telephone wire that was strung along the tracks of the Pennsylvania Railroad. The company's communications system had been completely disrupted twice, and dispatchers said this put the lives of thousands of passengers traveling between Philadelphia and New York at risk. Between 25 and 30 miles of copper wire had been stolen altogether, even as railroad and city police had been keeping watch. Clearly, the police said, these were shrewd thieves, masters of their craft.

On the evening of March 10, Detectives McColgan and Dougherty were on duty near the Wissinoming Station, in northeast Philadelphia. Down the tracks, in the gloom, they spied two men fumbling with something. They shouted at them to stop, but the men instead turned and began running down the line, carefully spacing their strides so as not to stumble on the crossties. Cops don't enjoy giving chase, so it's likely that when the shooting began it was one of the detectives who first pulled a trigger. One of the men turned and fired back at the officers, missing. Now McColgan and Dougherty began running, along the mainline of the New York Division of the Pennsylvania Railroad,[23] firing their service revolvers in the dark. From time to time one of the suspects would stop, turn and shoot back. The chase went on for a mile or more. At an opportune spot, the desperados saw their chance and ran down off the railroad embankment. But a police bullet caught one of them in the leg. The wounded man was able to crawl away in the dark, but his companion—scared or winded or simply shocked by the shooting—stopped in his tracks and was subdued by the huffing officers of the law.

Their worst suspicions were confirmed. He gave his name as Andreas Kormbach. He was a former steward on a German ship. The man who got away, he told the police, was Emil Bostlein, a marine engineer. Between them the men had been carrying about 150 pounds of copper wire, the police said, which may account for the detectives' success in running them down. When the police searched the house the two men shared, they found more coils of wire. It was a shocking plot, said the police, intended to paralyze the railroad. And at least as far as the press was concerned, no one seems to have considered that, with copper prices going sky-high, Kormbach and Bostlein may have been ordinary metal scavengers. A juicy German plot was a much more exciting prospect.

Americans were beginning to see danger in all sorts of places, and it spoke with a German accent.

Police in Hoboken, New Jersey, had arrested Richard Kalb on March 5 and charged him with the 1916 "Black Tom" explosion that had destroyed a Kingsland, New Jersey, factory making munitions for Russia.

A German man had been arrested March 13 while standing under a Pennsylvania Railroad bridge in Philadelphia—the arresting officer said he looked like he meant trouble. Two men were blown to pieces by a bomb in a courthouse lavatory in Boston on March 16. A man suspected of being a German spy was caught on March 27 with

---

23   Today part of Amtrak's Northeast Corridor.

wireless equipment in a suburb west of Oak Park, Illinois. Another man, named Karl Rank, was arrested the next day in Albany, New York, in possession of chemicals; he told police he was an inventor.

So the Wilmington & Philadelphia Traction Company, an interurban streetcar line, asked for police guards at its power plants because of fears of German saboteurs. Retired firefighters in New York were canvassed to see if they'd be able to return to work once an expected epidemic of arsons hit the city. (It never did.) The state militia was assigned to patrol the riverfront in New Orleans for the first time in history. Mayor Martin Behrman issued a proclamation assuring residents that all public utilities were being guarded—in some cases by citizen volunteers—and he urged them "to neither heed nor circulate unfounded and disquieting rumors nor to give way to any unnecessary excitement."

A man in New Orleans named Louis Kuntz was packed off to jail for twenty-nine days for calling the flag of the United States a "dirty rag." On March 23, federal officers arrested three Germans in Atlanta who had been on a hiking trip. They said they were trying to walk around the globe. They were booked for espionage.

That evening, Colonel House had dinner at the Plaza Hotel with Elihu Root and several others. All Root wanted to talk about was the suspect loyalty of German-Americans. He proposed "hanging them from lampposts" at the slightest provocation.

A group called the National Security League began holding patriotic rallies. "Every red-blooded American man and woman in New Orleans should attend," said the announcement there. "Be present yourself and urge your friends to attend. . . . *The women of Louisiana are specially urged to help this movement which is basically intended to defend the nation and improve the race.*"

The Episcopal bishop coadjutor for Ohio, Frank Du Moulin, visited Baltimore and predicted that America would be "born again" in war. The United States, he said, "had waxed prosperous on the blood and sufferings of the people of Europe; its chivalry and manhood had declined." Since it had chosen while at peace not to undertake its destiny as a nation, or to pursue the development of its people's character, or to spread the kingdom of Christ throughout the world, "God would offer it the alternative" of doing so through battle.

YET FOR ALL the histrionic anxieties and chest-thumping, Americans had yet to digest the news that had come upon them over the preceding half-dozen weeks. The United States as they knew it was not a central player on the world stage, nor did it have the military tools to be one. The war against Spain, and the various occupations in the Caribbean and the Philippines, had been carried out by a relative handful of volunteers. Wilson and Roosevelt and most of the other men running the country had been boys when the Civil War ended; they had family lore, and the resentments and pride that went with it, but no personal experience of national mobilization, or existential threat. The senior officers in the Army had earned their spurs fighting Indians.

When spring training camps for ballplayers opened in early March, in Florida and elsewhere in the South, some of the teams began ostentatiously to practice drilling in the outfield, with bats on shoulders in place of rifles. The owners made sure to publicize this: Their boys were doing their part for God and country. But others thought the whole thing was a gimmick, and a stupid one. "Under Military Regulations for Ball Players, Must Base Runners Stop to Salute Officers?" asked a *New Orleans Times-Picayune* headline.

Once the Philadelphia Phillies had settled in at Coffee Pot Bayou Park, in St. Petersburg, Manager Pat "Whisky Face" Moran declared that his players weren't going to be taking part in any military antics. He didn't want Grover Cleveland Alexander, Eppa Rixey, or his other pitchers to hurt their valuable arms throwing pretend hand grenades. And he wanted the position players to prepare for the baseball season. The Phillies thought they had a chance to go all the way that year, behind strong pitching, and that meant no time for nonsense.

Moran disparagingly allowed that "if the other players have a desire to shoulder the musket and try soldiering on the square after the daily practices," Robert Maxwell, the self-styled "war correspondent" of the *Evening Ledger* wrote, "they can go as far as they like."

The prospect of war was something of a lark to these young athletes. On the steamship that brought them down from New York, there had been plenty of joking about U-boats, and maybe even a little disappointment that they didn't see one. On March 13, the players were in an especially giddy mood after outfielder Dode Paskert nearly burned down the ballpark. He had decided that the outfield grass was too high and that the best way to handle it was to burn it off. Naturally the outfield fence also caught fire and it was all the players could do to put it out without calling the St. Petersburg fire department. Oscar Dugey, an infielder and sometime volunteer fireman from Texas, led the effort. And then that afternoon, just as the Phillies were heading to the showers, came the sensational news that Germany had declared war on the United States, as reported by the local newspaper. Plenty of wisecracking ensued. "Pat Moran, Standing on Home Plate with Cap on Bosom, Declares War on Germany," read a subhead in the Philadelphia paper the next day.

Having a laugh, the players decided that now, they really should start drilling (with baseball bats). "As soon as the men are acquainted with this weapon, they will be promoted to muskets," Maxwell wrote. "Target practice will follow in a week or so, when the men get better acquainted and won't shoot at each other." They elected two former soldiers on the team, Gary Fortune and Gavvy Cravath, as drill sergeants.

The report of war, of course, was wrong. The next day, they were back to worrying about infield drill and avoiding sunburn. Alexander, trying to lose weight, tied a rubber belt fashioned from an old tire around his stomach. There were three holdouts that year—players who had refused to report in hopes of getting more money—and by that time they had "the same social standing as a German in Petrograd."

But as March drew to a close, and the regular season beckoned, the owners began to realize that American entry into the war was becoming a serious possibility, and that led them to worry about what it would do to their business. On March 24, the same day that Philadelphia announced plans for a huge loyalty rally, to be held in Independence Square, baseball supremo Ban Johnson announced that the season would open on schedule, war or no war. On the sports page of the *Ledger*, an unsigned column lit into the owners, accusing them of wrapping themselves in the flag with a show of phony war preparedness, not out of love for the nation but in a play for publicity. The stepped-up pseudo-training in the baseball camps had been "an amusing burlesque," but it amounted to "an attempt to advertise the game by capitalizing on a grave international crisis," the column said. "The owners simply reeked with patriotism."

THE REALITY OF the war was anything but glorious. By 1917, British soldiers' lives revolved around rats, dysentery, putrefying bodies, lung-searing gas attacks and artillery barrages. The war, for George Wear, a British soldier who was at Ypres in 1917, was epitomized by the death of his lieutenant: "He was literally blown to pieces by a shell on the battery position, bits of flesh besmearing one of the gunpits and covering the gun in blood. The remains were collected in a sandbag and buried."

There were, he wrote after the war was over, "no trees, no houses, no countryside, no sun. Wet, grey sky hung over the blasted land. . . . there was no longer any sustaining feeling that all this slaughter was leading us to anything. No one could see any purpose in it."

"What chance was there for anyone in that war of guns and mathematics?" asked Private E. N. Gladden.

At Ypres, more than 50,000 British soldiers were missing in action—which really meant that they had been vaporized by artillery or buried beneath tons of mud by that same artillery. The Germans lost more men at Verdun in 1916 than they did at Stalingrad twenty-seven years later. The French army, in March 1917, was a few months away from the mutiny that threatened to knock it out of the war.

Yet there was remarkably little discussion in America about the horrors of the war—about what American soldiers would be getting into. By the same token, no one, including Teddy Roosevelt, was making any false promises about a quick easy victory. Perhaps because hardly anyone in the United States knew any actual soldiers in the month of March, no one thought too hard about the physical or psychological consequences of their going to the fight. People understood there would be casualties, but the words later decades would attach to the war—futile, stupid, immoral, pointless—barely entered into the conversation, except among dedicated socialist revolutionaries who happily expected the war to speed the end of capitalism.

Broadly speaking, Americans understood that the Western Front was like nothing ever seen before, though strict Allied censorship kept the details hidden. Sobering reports came back, even if not from the front. H. L. Mencken met a jumpy, insomniac American on the train from Paris to Spain. "The whole of Europe is that way now, skittish, under pressure, constantly fatigued," he wrote. "These warring peoples . . . send out disturbing vibrations. They are full of care, strain, eagerness, malicious animal magnetism. One cannot sit among them and talk to them without borrowing their mood."

The *Baltimore Sun* published a revealing letter from Switzerland, written by Flora M. Pfoutz, a former clerk for the Baltimore school superintendent.

"Through Switzerland, the trains are running in every direction carrying . . . the incurably wounded or sick soldiers to their respective homelands. One car in a train will be filled with the maimed (those who have lost one or more limbs): another is filled with the blind: a third with the insane, in strait-jackets, while another contains those who are suffering with tuberculosis."

She met a 21-year-old—she didn't say from which army—who told her how he had proudly gone off to war. He had come back with his teeth and "the front of his face" torn away. "A month in the trenches, and we don't care what happens. We envy the dead and dying. One frightful shower of shrapnel from unseen guns, and we grovel in the dust, helpless and hopeless," he told her. "Many of us hoped to win laurels by our bravery and fill the hearts of those at home with pride. . . . But most of us come to this."

W. J. Patterson, the commander-in-chief of the Grand Army of the Republic, the organization of Union Army veterans, said of the war in Europe: "With its gas bombs and similar devices, it is not a test of courage. . . . The European struggle is not war—it is wholesale murder."

But he was an old man, of course, by that time, and whenever objections like his were raised, they were generally met with the same nonresponse. "We must have a stake in the game," was the way Granville Fortescue, a dashing former Rough Rider and cousin of Theodore Roosevelt's, put it in the *Washington Post*. "Our men must face the ordeal by battle. To act otherwise would be to invite to our country the stigma of cowardice."

Months before he joined New York's 69th Regiment, the poet Joyce Kilmer wrote an appreciation of a French sculptor, Henri Gaudier-Brzeska, who had died on the Western Front. The war kills "arrogance, self-esteem, pride," the Frenchman had written. The atmosphere of "blood and smoke," Kilmer elaborated, was healthier than that of pre-war Bohemian cafés and studios. "The aesthete was becoming human." War allowed Gaudier-Brzeska to escape the dreary, grubby life of peacetime. The insanity of war, Kilmer wrote, was knocking some sanity into his art—until a German bullet laid him low.

Clarity, purification, recovered humanity, humility—anything could be read into a distant war when you weren't actually fighting in it.

MARGUERITE HARRISON, THE Baltimore reporter, was from the sort of society family that made ocean crossings, and felt at ease in Europe. She had knitted socks for the Austrians early on. "I thought of all the gentle, kindly Germans I had known, peace loving, sentimental—rather commonplace." Yet after the sinking of the *Lusitania* in 1915, a passenger liner she could all too well imagine herself having taken, her sympathies had turned toward the Allies, and now she came to believe strongly in their cause.

But, as she later wrote, "the average man in the United States read the reports from Europe as gruesome but absorbing entertainment, without a sense of reality."

From serving on the Maryland board of film censors, she had been exposed to propaganda movies from both sides. The British films were subtle and effective. "Much of the German stuff was so clumsy and so obviously created for effect that it was palpably false."

As in other states, the Maryland board had been set up to regulate everything from the allowable length of a kiss—measured by feet of film, not seconds—to storylines in which people who committed sins must by the end pay for them. Yet by 1917, portrayals of the war were at least as sensitive as domestic sex and morality—and, in reality, more so.

"The only real service performed by our board during my incumbency was the controlling of German and pacifist propaganda in the months immediately preceding and following our entry into the war," Harrison wrote. "All through 1916 and particularly toward the close of that year, the German propaganda service in America managed to inject a great deal of pro-German and anti-Ally material into the films."

That made them vigilant. And the board suppressed one film altogether. It had what she conceded was an exceedingly powerful and effectively presented antiwar message. The board censored it on the theory that watching it would only lead to anguish among mothers and wives and sweethearts when their men were inevitably called away to fight.

"I began vaguely to grasp the fact that propaganda was as much an arm of warfare as were big guns and high explosives." And as March drew to a close, Harrison realized "how appallingly unprepared America was for such an undertaking, how strong was the undercurrent of opposition to our part in the war, how carefully the public mind would have to be educated to accept the principle of conscription and how essentially unmilitary we were as a nation despite the contagion of war fever."

With the enthusiastic support of her editor, Frank Kent, she launched into a project that would result in a series of articles, all designed to encourage enlistment in the U.S. Army. She kept her seat on the film board at the same time. And of course the overwhelming majority of movies that passed before the eyes of the censors had nothing to do with propaganda or ideology. They were designed to entertain and to make money. If there was a threat of impending war, you wouldn't have known it from most of the films in production that March.

For 21-year-old Buster Keaton, who had been in vaudeville with his parents since he was 5, the month marked the beginning of his film career. In a New York studio owned by the screen star Norma Talmadge, the comedian Fatty Arbuckle began shooting *The Butcher Boy*, the first of a series of comedies he would make with Keaton. It was a two-reeler that ran a little over twenty minutes, featuring a hatful of molasses, a flour fight, Arbuckle in drag, a checker player who looked like Robert E. Lee, a headmistress with a pistol, a hardworking dog named Luke, and Keaton, wearing impossibly long, pointy shoes and, of course, his deadpan face.

The Butcher Boy was all hokum and slapstick (and sticky molasses). The humorless headmistress of the girls' school wears a dress that looks about three decades out of date. On her wall are portraits of George Washington and Abraham Lincoln. Do they belong in the same film as a very fat man who tries to pass as a girl so he can sneak into the dorm to be with his sweetheart? As long as the villains lose in the end—which they do—it was all right with Harrison and her colleagues on the film board.

ONE DAY TOWARD the end of March, a young businessman in Chicago named Donald Ryerson had an idea. Americans needed to be enlightened—or perhaps "encouraged" would be a better word—on the subject of the war, and what their role in it should be, he believed. And it occurred to him that there was a perfect venue for that—the movie theaters that in just the past couple of years had become so ubiquitous. There was a four-minute gap between the showings of films, as the projectionist changed reels, and that was four minutes during which Ryerson would have a captive audience. So he recruited some like-minded men, and they spread out through the city to give patriotic and uplifting lectures every time the screen went dark. They were an instant success. Their lectures were always positive, always about reasons to be proud of America.

In Washington, a veteran newspaperman and Wilson backer named George Creel was putting together the ideas that would land him a position as head of the official Committee on Public Information. Creel wanted to try something never done in this country before—to counteract hostile propaganda with inspiring messages, to pour out so much good news about America and its ideals and intentions that, with the cooperation of willing newspaper editors (and they *were* willing), there wouldn't be much space left for the other side. In early April, just as Congress was convening, Ryerson took a train to Washington, found Creel, and sold him on his idea. From Chicago, the phenomenon of the Four Minute Men spread across the country. Lectures were distributed from Washington and delivered in person on such topics as the Red Cross, Food Conservation, Carrying the Message, the Shipbuilder, The Danger to Democracy, Fire Prevention, Where Did You Get Your Facts? and so forth. There were also Four Minute Singing interludes.

There were Yiddish Four Minute Men, Sioux Four Minute Men, Italians and Lithuanians.

But Walter Hines Page, the U.S. ambassador in England, argued for a publicity campaign to whip up feelings against Germany. James Gerard, until February the ambassador to Germany, told a New York audience that he expected Americans of German descent to be loyal, but if they were not, "we know where to festoon them." The War Department and the Navy Department began working on censorship regulations—which, as long as they were confined strictly to military matters, were uncontroversial. But critics of the administration sensed that they would be much broader.

H. L. Mencken, himself of German descent, and inordinately proud of it, had hoped to turn his Berlin Diary into a book. But even though vast excerpts had been published in the *Sun* at the beginning of the month, by late March, finally back in the United States, he realized he'd never find a publisher.

He worked instead on an article for *The Atlantic* about Erich Ludendorff, the German military chief. He was "astute," a "serpent," a "genius." He had become enormously popular, Mencken wrote, and Germans thought he could save the day. "He has reached out for the wires of civil administration," Mencken wrote, "and now he has a good many of them firmly in his hand and is delicately fingering a good many more." In occupied Belgium and northern France, "hordes of frockcoated and bespatted *Beamten* [officials] pour in; an inextricable complex of bureaux is established; the blessings of *Kultur* are ladled out scientifically and by experts." But in the Russian lands that had fallen to the Germans, "the army is the source of all law, of all privileges, even of all livelihood. And the army is Ludendorff."

Another Mencken project was *A Book of Prefaces*, which would be published by Knopf later that year. In a long essay entitled "Puritanism as a Literary Force," Mencken took direct aim at American righteousness (without bringing up the war). Americans see their republic as "an international expert in morals, and the mentor and exemplar of the more backward nations," he wrote. "Within, as well as without, the eternal rapping of knuckles and proclaiming of new austerities goes on. The American . . . casts all ponderable values . . . in terms of right and wrong. He is beyond all things else, a judge and a policeman."

American puritanism at least began with a certain humility, rooted as it was in the hardscrabble lives of the early New England settlers, he wrote. But "Puritanism has become bellicose and tyrannical by becoming rich." After the Civil War the "American became a sort of braggart playboy of the western world, enormously sure of himself and ludicrously contemptuous of all other men. . . . The American Puritan, by now, was not content with the rescue of his own soul; he felt an irresistible impulse to hand salvation on, to disperse and multiply it, to ram it down reluctant throats, to make it free, universal and compulsory. He had the men, he had the guns and he had the money too."

THE LAST WEEK of March found Theodore Roosevelt in a state of tropical serenity. He who had campaigned so hard for preparedness, who had despaired of Wilson's fecklessness, who had denounced pacifists and laid his own plans for a hard-hitting foray to the Western Front—the bellicose Rough Rider was taking it easy under the Florida sun. He had landed that big devilfish. Coles said it was the second-largest ever caught—second only to the one Coles had sent off to the American Museum of Natural History. And now there were no more heroics. Just as passion over the war began to grip Americans from one end of the country to the other, Roosevelt was on what Coles called a weeklong picnic. One day when they were out on the water off Captiva, one of the men had spotted a burrow on shore, tucked behind mangroves. They beached the boat and he pulled out a large Florida land turtle. Roosevelt had never seen one before, and took special note of the shape of its shell, and how it differed from northern turtles. Then they cooked it and ate it, with great pleasure.

Of all the things TR's detractors accused him of, single-mindedness was not one of them. For the past few months he had fended off attempts to recruit him for other causes, among them penal reform and a push to build a memorial to Buffalo Bill, on the grounds that the war demanded all his energy. But in February he had nonetheless corresponded with the assistant director of the New York Botanical Garden on the subject of mushrooms. On March 23, just before heading to the train for Florida, he dashed off a note about birds to a scientist in Brazil.

In another, discursive letter that touched on the birds of Alaska, the mammals of temperate America and the bears of the Adirondacks, Roosevelt turned to the subject of writing. He lamented that the only way a writer could be sure of making a living in America was through newspaper and magazine work, and that the result was that the country had legions of very good second-rate writers. Real value—serious books—didn't pay. In his own writings, he said, he had noticed that the fees he got were in inverse proportion to the value of his work. Writers in science and history who could be great architects were content to push wheelbarrows loaded with bricks, he said, and he included himself among that number. "But it would be a very evil thing if, with smug self-satisfaction, we think there is no need of the big men, to deal in a big way, with the big problems."

He wrote admiringly about the contributions German immigrants had made to America. He respected Germany itself as an errant but competent power. He protested "emphatically" against the use of the word "Huns" to describe Germans. It was abusive, he said, and in his mind, certainly, it diminished the speaker more than the subject.

He wrote an inscription that month in a book of Rules for Children. "Do the small duties, the humdrum daily duties, well, for they make the foundation of life; and yet keep something high and gallant in your souls, so that if the great days come, you may face them greatly daring, and treat life as a great adventure, with a fine disdain of cowardice, folly and weakness of spirit."

CHAPTER 19

"A Mending of Their Troubles"

On March 27, Leon Trotsky and his wife and two sons sailed
from New York on a Norwegian ship, the *Kristianiafjord*.
They had been seen off at the pier with bouquets of flowers
and hopeful, fiery speeches, for they were heading to the country of
the revolution. But at Halifax, Nova Scotia, British authorities took
them and other Russian travelers off the ship. Officers began asking questions of Trotsky, and about Trotsky, and concluded he was a
dangerous socialist. They sent him away to a prisoner-of-war camp in
Amherst, Nova Scotia. His wife and children were put under house
arrest in Halifax.

The camp commandant, a Colonel Morris, told Trotsky that he
posed a danger to the new Russian government. Trotsky replied that
he had received a visa from that government while he was in New York.
Morris answered back, "You are dangerous to the Allies in general."

The camp had been set up in an abandoned iron foundry. Trotsky
calculated that there were about 800 prisoners there, most of them
Germans. He set right in to speechmaking, and boasted that he had
most of the German working-class prisoners on his side by the time
he was released a month later.

He had managed to get a message back to *Novy Mir*, the Russian newspaper in New York. The paper cabled a letter to Alexander Kerensky, the justice minister in Petrograd, and after he intervened, the British let Trotsky continue on his way, back to Russia and the revolution.

THE INTREPID CANADIAN Florence Harper, writing for *Leslie's Weekly*, along with photographer Donald Thompson, wangled a ride from Petrograd out to Kronstadt, the huge Russian naval base on an island in the Gulf of Finland. They were among the first foreigners to visit the base following the revolution, and Harper, not entirely sympathetic to the rebellion, was shaken by what they learned there. The sailors of the Baltic Fleet had a reputation for radicalism, and it was well earned in 1917. They had seized the commanding admiral and 68 officers when news of the revolt in Petrograd first reached Kronstadt, and began conducting a late-night trial, but grew bored and killed them all, Harper was told. Then the sailors began hunting for other officers. Some barricaded themselves in their homes, which the sailors bombarded with naval guns. Those who were caught were mutilated, tortured and killed. Others tried to escape across the ice, but were shot down as they fled. Survivors were stripped of their clothing—sailors had a particular dislike for epaulettes—and incarcerated in the freezing hold of a ship.

Bolshevik radicals had assumed control in Kronstadt by the time Harper and Thompson visited. The Kronstadt sailors had become an important source of Bolshevik influence in the Petrograd Soviet. They took the two visitors on a tour of the base, pointing out with malicious delight the houses of officers that had been reduced to rubble. They told the Canadian that their goal was to relieve the bourgeoisie of its holdings. She thought they looked like cutthroats.

THE STREETCARS WERE jammed with soldiers. Because they could ride for free, they could do what they wanted. They had little else to keep them occupied. Most were conscripts from peasant villages and had never ridden a streetcar or seen a big city before. They clung to the outside of the cars, rode on the couplings, stood on the steps. Houghteling was lucky to be able to walk to most of the places he needed to go, though a big snowstorm on March 17, followed by the beginnings of the spring thaw, made getting around a chore. Toward the end of the month, his Commerce Department duties took him once more to Moscow.

The train was packed with soldiers. They could ride the rails for free, too. At stations along the way, soldiers crowded the platforms, restless, waiting for a train to take them home, or to the next town, or just anywhere.

Arrived safe and sound, Houghteling saw a circus troupe just off Red Square, parading a camel and an elephant bedecked with revolutionary banners. He was surprised to learn that Kerensky was also visiting Moscow. The Americans in Petrograd saw him as the great hope of the revolution—a socialist you could do business with, who would rally the Russian left and keep the extremists out of power. Before the revolution, he had been echoing Wilson's call for a settlement of the war based on a peace without victory, but now he was foursquare in favor of continuing the armed struggle against German autocracy. Houghteling thought he was the most influential man in the government.

"The responsibilities of office have toned him down and he has become very constructive. He works desperately hard," he wrote. But there was another side to him. "Kerensky is a great egotist and talks much about I-did-this and I-did-that; he addressed the Faculty of Laws while he was here and quite disgusted the lawyers by his self-glorification. Still, he needs infinite confidence to carry out the role that has been thrust upon him."

The young American made the rounds of the city. The people on the streets seemed happy. The people he talked to, less so.

Residents of apartment houses were organizing against burglars, because here, too, there were no police and crime was soaring. One of Houghteling's coworkers said there was word of peasant uprisings, and revolts by soldiers in the countryside, with the looting and burning of country houses. "The soldiers believe that the lands of the nobles are to be divided at once, and thousands of them have left the trenches without permission and are raising disorder in the provinces."

FAR AWAY TO the south, in the rural districts of the Ukraine, news of the revolution gradually filtered in, first as rumor and hearsay, then in more plausible reports. There was little distress among the czar's peasant subjects. He and his court had been unimaginably distant. The local authorities, his representatives, had been one of the God-given tribulations of existence, a burden of evil to be skirted whenever possible. For those who lived and worked on the Cantacuzène-Speransky estate at Bouromka, life revolved around village and family. Julia Speransky-Grant, as she called herself, had come to doubt since moving there from America that most of the peasants had any real concept of Russia, except that it was because of Russia and the war that their sons had been taken away to the army.

The revolution promised hope and progress—the peasants believed it meant no more conscription and no more war. Enlightened gentry, like Julia and Mikhail Speransky, welcomed what they saw as Russia's long-overdue step into the modern world. "When the revolution came, every woman rejoiced," she wrote.

She was down in the Crimea when she got the news, enjoying the southern climate. Mikhail was military commandant in Kiev, and popular with his men. Among those serving under him was an army doctor named Mikhail Bulgakov, who besides being addicted to morphine was on his way to becoming one of the outstanding Russian writers of the twentieth century.

Then as now, the Crimean port of Sevastopol was home to Russia's Black Sea Fleet. Then (as now) it was of limited strategic importance, but it carried tremendous symbolic weight, as both a totem of Russia's eighteenth-century expansion against the Muslim Ottomans and an emblem of Russia's aspirations to gain control of the

Bosporus, the outlet to the Mediterranean, and become a genuine naval power.

The recently appointed admiral in charge of the fleet was Alexander Kolchak, just 42 years old. When rumors of the uprising in Petrograd first began to circulate in Sevastopol, Kolchak had a proclamation printed on the front page of the local newspaper. He laid out the rumors, said he had no confirmation of them, and promised to provide whatever further information he received. He called on his men and the townsfolk to remain calm and continue to go about their duties—which they did, Speransky-Grant reported. "Kolchak's sailors were too perfectly disciplined to think of rebellion," she wrote.

Within a few days, confirmation of the czar's abdication was received. Kolchak joined his men in swearing an oath of allegiance to the Provisional Government. The routines of port life continued, until a delegation of agitators arrived from Kronstadt. Soon enough, Speransky-Grant wrote, a committee of revolutionary sailors demanded that Kolchak meet with them. When he did, they announced that they were in charge, and demanded his sword. All Russian officers carried swords. Ineffectual though they were against machine-gun bullets and mustard gas, they were seen as potent symbols of authority. Kolchak replied that he had received his sword in recognition of his heroic services during the disastrous Russo-Japanese War a decade earlier, and rather than give it to the sailors' committee, he flung it overboard. That was the end of his navy career; he departed the base unmolested.

AT BOUROMKA, AS at estates throughout the Ukraine and Russia, "travelers" had been passing through all winter, reading radical newspapers to the village folk, talking about the corruption and treachery in Petrograd. So when the news of Nicholas's abdication reached these farming districts, it wasn't entirely a surprise. "In Bouromka the people took it very quietly, and felt at first no difference, only they hoped to see a mending of their troubles." The peasants elected a committee to govern themselves, and debated whether they should divide up the estate. But how to do it fairly? Who would get the rich croplands, and who the forest? Would the spendthrift receive as much as his industrious neighbor? Would they have to share their own private plots? Rumors reached them that farmers from the poorer lands to the north would have to be accommodated with shares of the Bouromka estate.

Nearby, in Poltava Province, a peasant and former soldier named Nikifor Tatianenko sent a complaint to *Izvestia*. In his village of Belogorenka, he wrote: "There is a committee, but they elected its members from those people who do not care about the people, but only about their own pocket: the priest and the [district] elder who even before used to say that we would live better when the Germans conquered us. . . . The peasants gather for meetings, but they don't decide anything or resolve any problems, because they don't know and no one has explained to them what a democratic republic or a nation means . . . and even if someone started to explain it, they still wouldn't understand. Comrade soldiers and workers, send a newspaper here so that we could at least take issues from the newspapers and tell people what's going on in Petrograd."

Mensheviks in the army appealed to peasants not to burn the landlords' hay or grain, or to kill livestock, or to tear down barns. It hurts all of us, the appeal said.

Outside agitators appeared. Certainly, said Princess Cantacuzène, the Countess Speransky, née Grant, these were German agents. Within weeks, the Ukraine was crumbling. The seeds were sown then for the confiscation and destruction of the estate, the burning of the house and barns, the slaughter of the cattle, the ruination of the village. "Remaining alive meant making oneself as small as possible on all occasions."

ONE OF THE first Americans to arrive in Petrograd after the revolution was Pauline Crosley, who accompanied her husband, assigned as naval attaché, on the long trip across the Pacific and the Trans-Siberian Railway. Having missed the inspiring excitement of mid-March, she was less than enthusiastic about its consequences. She wrote home to her sister, telling her not to believe anything in the newspapers suggesting Russia was going to keep fighting.

She wrote her son: "Please do not decide that I am a pessimist; I am anything but that; however, I see and learn so much that convinces me of the *unreliability*, to put it mildly, of the Russian masses.

"I am told of the disorders and of the murder of officers all along the Russian fronts; of the murder of officers in the Black Sea Fleet; of the most unusual and unnecessary steps taken by the revolutionists outside of Petrograd to cause suffering; of the excesses at Kronstadt; of the failure of well-meaning Russian politicians now in the government to control the vindictive lower classes, and I cannot see anything bright in Russia's future at present."

The tragedy, she wrote, was that since the outbreak of the revolution more Russians had been killed by other Russians than by Germans. She saw people driven by revenge and spite. She was appalled by "those whose single aim seems to be to make everybody unhappy but themselves."

After watching Russians for several months, she wrote: "This is certainly a peculiar people; everything is happening yet nothing happens!"

BY LATE MARCH, 100,000 political convicts were heading home from the mines and settlements of Siberian exile. Fifty thousand sledges, reported the *Washington Post*, were speeding their way "in an endless chain across the snows of North Asia toward the nearest points on the Trans-Siberian Railway." On one of them was riding Josef Stalin, who when he arrived in Petrograd assumed the editorship of the Bolsheviks' newspaper, *Pravda*.

And in Zurich, Vladimir Lenin was negotiating with the Germans to arrange passage on the famous "sealed train" that would take him back across enemy territory to Russia after a decade in exile.

A worker and army deserter in the Kuban region, named A. Zem-skov, wrote to Kerensky. He accused the socialist of mouthing the same old lie, the lie that had suppressed ordinary people since the time of the ancient Greeks—the lie of freedom. "Aren't you singing the praises of new chains that are only going by the name of free-dom?" Russians hadn't had freedom "for a single second," Zemskov wrote. As soon as the autocratic yoke was lifted, the "horse collar" of the new order was fitted onto people's necks.

A PECULIAR ARTICLE appeared, without a byline, in the *New York Times* on March 21, on page 4. It was just four short paragraphs. It said that Baron Roman Rosen, the well-regarded former Russian ambassador in Washington, was "jubilant" over the revolution, believing that the new government constituted "the flower of the nation," and that the Allies could now abandon all doubt concern-ing Russia's earnest prosecution of the war against Germany. It was peculiar because so much of it was untrue. Though Rosen didn't mourn the regime he had served for so many years, he was hardly jubilant. He admired some of the men in the new govern-ment, though he was painfully aware they had no experience in governing—and he detested Kerensky. And he understood per-fectly well that the Russians weren't going to keep fighting.

The soldiers of the Russian army were not of one mind when the czar's rule crumbled. There were units on the front that were so used to fighting Germans that they couldn't imagine not doing so. Some of the soldiers who flocked to the Petrograd Soviet worried that the Germans would sponsor a counterrevolution. On March 20, the Soviet approved this resolution: "The Russian Revolution will not allow itself to be crushed by the bayonets of foreign aggression."

A few days later, newly elected delegates of the 8th Siberian Rifle Division appealed to the workers and soldiers of Russia: "The free Russian people must not dishonor themselves with a shameful peace. Their freedom, their entire future, will be decided by this war."

But the 61st Siberian Rifle Division sent a letter to the Soviet complaining that the men were still being treated in the old way by their officers, with arrogant contempt.

And in the bigger scheme of things, Rosen knew, the Russian army had been demobilizing itself ever since late 1916. By the time of the revolution, there were probably at least 1.5 million deserters out of the 4 million soldiers who were supposed to be at the front. A top official in the ministry of war calculated that there were an additional 1 million "hidden deserters"—that is, shirkers who were avoiding the front. The army had suffered 3.5 million casualties by that time, and 2 million had been taken prisoner. The leaders of the Provisional Government, in telling Americans and Allies that Russia would pursue the war with renewed vigor, might have been sincere, Rosen thought, but blind to "the manifest unwillingness of the people to stay any longer in the fight." And Rosen blamed the Allies directly for not understanding that the Russian government was a government in name only. The only government that could hope to establish its writ across the whole country would be one that could give the people what they most wanted—peace.

In the weeks following the revolution, Russia was like the *Vigilancia* after it was torpedoed—inertia kept it going for a while even as it took on water, the bureaucracy still functioned, the ordinary routines continued; but the forward motion upset the lifeboats of those trying to save themselves even as the vessel began to slip beneath the waves.

The snow and mud of the spring thaw kept the Germans from attacking, and as the reality of their position sank in, Russia's soldiers experienced a sharp turn in mood. In the first days of the revolution, desertion rates had actually declined, but now they were rising again. A soldier in the trenches sensed that peace was at hand, and if there was going to be peace tomorrow, I'd rather not die today.

Pacifism among the troops was like a contagion, said Matvei Skobelev, a Menshevik. There was no other way to put it, he thought: The army was relaxing as if it were in a warm bath.

Looked at another way, the army, as Trotsky wrote, was a copy of the society it served, except that the social differences within the army were concentrated and exaggerated. And Russian society, as Maxim Gorky wrote, was "splitting all along its seams and falling apart like an old barge in a flood."

THE REVOLUTION, ROSEN believed, created an ideal opportunity, particularly for the United States. Now, precisely now, was the moment to push Wilson's January call for Peace Without Victory. With Russia tumbling out of the war, America was perfectly situated to bring both sides, the Allies and the Central Powers, to their senses, and to stop the fighting.

The Americans had done it in 1905, when they engineered the end of the war between Russia and Japan, to the satisfaction of both sides. He had been there, at Portsmouth; he had taken part. He had seen Americans at their best—engaged, helpful, skillful, driven by goodwill and their own enlightened self-interest. Most of all, they had demonstrated a generosity of spirit. Teddy Roosevelt had won the Nobel Peace Prize because of his role in ending the war. Now— Rosen believed, he dreamed, he wished—Americans could do it again. They could save Europe. They could save Russia.

But the United States wasn't the same country it had been in 1905, and of course the war wasn't the same kind of war. A great deal had changed even since January, when Wilson made his proposal to the belligerent powers, and Rosen, in Petrograd, would not have had a feel for that. Roosevelt himself was pushing harder for war than anyone, and Wilson was caught in the tide of events. American attitudes were changing, and emotion was a powerful driver. Americans didn't want talk. They wanted action.

"OUR MOST MERCILESS enemy is our past," the playwright and essayist Maxim Gorky wrote in the days following the revolution. The old regime had dedicated itself to suppressing the human spirit and thwarting intellectual development, and to a frightening extent it had succeeded, he wrote. Then came the war, which destroyed villages, men, women, forests, the fertile Russian topsoil itself—an act of continental suicide. "Dreamy, spineless Russia," endowed with "our stupidity, our cruelty, and all that chaos of dark, anarchistic feelings, that chaos which has been cultivated in our souls by the monarchy's shameless oppression, by its cynical cruelty"—this is the country that has inherited the revolution. The Russian disease runs deep. "The most dreadful enemy of freedom and justice is within us."

ON APRIL 3, from his apartment in Petrograd, James Houghteling began his journey back to America. His temporary assignment in Russia was done. He made a round of calls to say goodbye, then crossed the Neva on the ice to fetch his things. He got an *izvozchik*, a sleigh for hire, to take him to the Nikolaev Station halfway down Nevsky Prospekt, known today as the Moskovsky Terminal. The square in front, the bustle, the antic swirl, were familiar to him now after his trips by train to Moscow, but still fascinating. He made sure to give himself time, because everything became hectic in the last moments before a Russian rail trip. "So I surrendered my last hour of Petrograd to the interesting confusion of the Nikolaev station," he wrote in his diary, "which no revolution can make less interesting or less confused."

CHAPTER 20

"The Lid Is Kept Screwed Down"

On March 26, Rear Admiral William Sims, of Newport, Rhode Island, took an urgent phone call. Come to Washington immediately, he was told. We need you to undertake a secret mission.

Sims, 58, was a career Navy man, a graduate of Annapolis. He was a modernizer. He had won a fight to introduce target practice for Navy gunners in the first decade of the century, over objections by his superiors that there was no point to it. He had written directly to President Roosevelt with his idea, and earned a quick promotion from the White House as a result. He had served, briefly, as naval attaché at the U.S. embassy in St. Petersburg before the war.

Since February, Admiral Sims had been head of the Naval War College, after a yearlong stint as the first captain of the U.S.S. *Nevada*, the nation's largest and most modern battleship. He was the right man for this secret mission—although the orders he got, once he arrived in Washington, were delivered to him orally, and afterward no one could quite agree on what his assignment actually *was*. But it meant his going, under cover, to England, and meeting with the top men of the Royal Navy. Was he supposed to be gathering information to send back to Washington? Was he supposed to be reporting to the British on the state of the U.S. Navy? Or was he expected to coordinate with the English on the expectation that the United States would enter the war? The chief of naval operations, Admiral William Benson, told him not to let his hosts pull the wool over his eyes. If the United States entered the war, it wasn't to rescue the British. "We'd as soon fight them as the Germans," Benson said.

The plan had apparently been cooked up by the assistant secretary, Franklin Roosevelt, who raised the idea with Secretary Daniels a week earlier.

Sims raced back to Newport, packed a bag—not including any uniforms—and sailed from Manhattan on the steamer *New York* with an aide, Commander John Vincent Babcock, on March 31. They went under assumed names, pretending to be commercial travelers, but a cabin steward noticed handkerchiefs with their real initials embroidered on them, and suspected they might be German spies. The captain of the *New York*, who knew of the secret, put the steward's mind at ease. Babcock was so outspoken at meals on the subject of the war, however, that other passengers began to assume he was on a government mission.

Sims, naturally, was conscious of the risk of a U-boat attack and wrote a farewell letter to his wife in which he acknowledged that he might not come back. Nothing untoward happened, though, until, at the entrance to Liverpool harbor, the ship struck a mine. The passengers were safely lowered away in lifeboats and picked up by a steamboat coming in from the Isle of Man. Sims took with him a strongbox containing his papers, but he left it behind in the lifeboat.

Sims and Babcock were to learn that the U-boat campaign was taking a much greater toll on British shipping than had been reported, and that the English were closer to the edge than Washington realized. But their Atlantic crossing had taken a long eight days, and by the time they stepped ashore in Liverpool, they no longer had to pretend to be civilians.

ON MARCH 28 the British Parliament had cleared the way for women to get the vote. American suffrage supporters were elated. They were sure this would open the door for them—especially as it appeared that Britain was about to become an ally in arms. Russia had already announced it would extend the vote to women, just days after the revolution.

"With the governments of England, France, Russia and Holland taking direct steps toward the enfranchisement of their women, even though in the midst of war; with five provinces of Canada completely enfranchising their women since war began, and with Denmark, on the brink of war, completely enfranchising Danish women, there is every reason to hope that President Wilson and the administration leaders at Washington will now be ready to give their support for political liberty for American women," said Alice Paul, head of the National Woman's Party.

Giving women the vote would contribute, she said, to national unity and solidarity, all the more pressing because of the threat of war.

"We are profiting by England's mistakes and belated remedies in all other things," she said. "Let us by all means profit by England's mistake and England's apparently belated remedy in the matter of suffrage to all citizens."

Enfranchisement would be one of the greatest steps toward preparedness the country could take, she said.

"We women, when war breaks upon us, will be called on for duty in the machine shops and for dangerous duty in the munition factories. We have shown this in the way we women have responded to the call for woman navy recruits. We will do more, and we won't be behind the men in any sacrifice for the country we are loyal to."

The vote isn't properly a privilege of one class, but a right for all classes, including women, said Ruth White, of the National American

Woman Suffrage Association. "If Russia can recognize this, America and the American Congress surely will without further delay."

Suffrage advocates, including Carrie Chapman Catt, head of NAWSA, went to Washington to begin lobbying at once for suffrage. The day of the British decision, Jeannette Rankin was on a train, traveling from Dayton, Ohio, to Minneapolis. Five days later she would be taking her seat in Congress. Her allies announced for her that her first act as the lady from Montana would be to introduce a resolution putting Congress on record as favoring what its supporters called the Susan B. Anthony Amendment to the U.S. Constitution.

IN THE REICHSTAG, in Berlin, opposition leaders began to raise questions about the wisdom of provoking the United States. Eduard Bernstein, a prominent Socialist, voted against a budget bill on March 29, saying he couldn't support a government that had managed to convert America into an enemy.

"Germany never had the slightest intention of attacking the United States and does not have such intention now," replied Imperial Chancellor Theobald von Bethmann-Hollweg. "It never desired war against the United States and does not desire it today."

Arthur Zimmermann, the foreign secretary, defended his notorious telegram proposing an alliance with Mexico against the United States, after an antiwar Socialist, Hugo Haase, suggested that it had needlessly angered the Americans. "I declared expressly," Zimmermann said, "that, despite the submarine war, we hoped that America would maintain neutrality. . . . Herr Haase says that it caused great indignation in America. Of course, in the first instance, the affair was employed as an incitement against us. But the storm abated slowly and the calm and sensible politicians, and also the great mass of the American people, saw that there was nothing to object to."

A Social Democrat, Gustav Noske, called for an immediate peace with Russia. The chancellor promised that Germany would not meddle in Russia's internal affairs. A Conservative, Count Kuno von Westarp, told the Reichstag, "Many believe that with Russia's entrance into the ranks of democratically ruled states Germany will have to follow. All arguments, however, are against comparison of our country with enemy countries." Germany had proven its superiority over its foes, he said, which was a sign that a "strong and vigorous monarchy" was the correct form of government. He added, "We wish to obtain as soon as possible peace which will permit us to live in agreement with the new Russia."

The next day, James O'Donnell Bennett, a correspondent in Berlin for the *Chicago Tribune*, filed a dispatch quoting an unnamed German authority: "We are watching with interest and mingled wonder the way war fever is being engendered in America, but it still seems to us an extremely artificial excitement. We have not felt President Wilson has been working for war but has been allowing himself to drift with the current created by the newspapers and Wall Street. Whatever the true conditions, we will take no step back. If America is going to get excited it can be sure Germany will not lose its head."

A few days later, a *Times* correspondent in the Netherlands passed on reports he had gathered from "Dutch circles" to the effect that "the influence of events in Russia and America is beginning to be felt in a manner highly disconcerting to the feudal aristocracy" of Germany. The dispatch quoted the *Frankfurter Zeitung* as saying "We are surrounded by democracies and must make democratic our own state institutions if we do not want to be left out of the running."

AS LATE AS March 24, the *Philadelphia Evening Ledger*, which was an eminently readable newspaper that had ambitions to be a great national voice for Progressivism, could run a cartoon, called "The First Signs of Spring," depicting a golf ball labeled "Peace" trying to out-distance an artillery round. The sports page continued to mock the baseball owners for wrapping their teams in the flag. (Maybe that was easier because the Phillies were one club that didn't.) But in the last week of the month, the newspaper began fervently promoting a huge loyalty rally to be held in front of Independence Hall. It got results. The headline on March 31:

NATION-LOVING MULTITUDE
MAKES LIBERTY SHRINE RING
CHEERING LOYALTY ADDRESSES

The first sentence of the article described "the most wonderful patriotic meeting ever held." The paper estimated the turnout to be as high as 200,000. "It was a meeting of superlatives. The crowds were bigger, the spirit finer, the hope higher than at any meeting before, and for a dynamic expression of patriotism there was never anything like it. . . . No partisanship, only Americanism. That was the high point."

It was published in what was labeled the newspaper's "Patriotic Edition." A cartoon across four columns at the top of the front page depicted Liberty blowing a bugle, with William Penn and soldiers from all of America's previous wars heeding the call. There was an American flag waving in the breeze, the spire of Independence Hall, and, behind all, the big word LOYALTY.

A front-page sidebar was headlined "France Hails Patriotic Meeting in Philadelphia as World Event."

THOSE OPPOSED TO war weren't giving up yet. The Emergency Peace Federation organized a "patriotic meeting" to protest against war, in Philadelphia's South Broad Street Theater, on April 1. On March 29, the organization had run a half-page ad in the *New York Tribune* and other papers that asked: "Mothers, Daughters and Wives of Men— Have you no hearts? Have you no eyes? Have you no voice? We are being rushed to the brink of war—AND YOU DO NOT WANT WAR." It argued that there was no real cause for war, that women didn't want war, and that the Midwest and West didn't want war but didn't realize how close the country was to joining in. It sought

$200,000 in contributions within the next twelve hours to arouse the nation. "If the people are heard from there will be no war." The ad was signed by Helen Villard, the daughter of the abolitionist William Lloyd Garrison. She had helped found the NAACP and was the widow of Henry Villard, a railroad tycoon and onetime owner of the *New York Post*. (That same day, Elihu Root and his allies took out a smaller ad, addressed to Wilson: "A great nation . . . anxiously awaits your address. . . . Let us not fight sparingly and grudgingly.")

The federation began organizing a "March on Washington" to take place on April 2, when Congress was to convene. Special trains were chartered from New York, Philadelphia ($3.06 each way) and other cities. The Philadelphia branch ran an ad in the *Evening Ledger* arguing that there were honorable alternatives to war—a joint high commission, or a peace appeal by the president, or at least a national referendum on war. "There is no call to rush into war with its horror and sorrow," the ad read. "It is the solemn duty of every loyal American to raise his voice against war. We are not fighting a lost cause. If you are silent now there will be war."

One of the organizers, Louis Lochner of New York, sent word to the White House asking if a representative committee of marchers could meet with Wilson. But Thomas Brahany, the White House aide, noted that "the president has reached a point where he has little patience with the peace at any price propagandists."

LETTERS CONTINUED TO pour in to Senator La Follette's office. "If the people of this country were awake to the realization of what such a calamity means they would arise en masse and demand peace, but unfortunately, they are asleep, or mad," wrote R. C. Akin, of Waterloo, Iowa. "IN GOD'S NAME, SENATOR, I BESEECH YOU IN CLARION TONES. Halt, by any means within your power, this insane, diabolic blood lust that has seized our ruling class," wrote Morton Alexander, of Santa Cruz, California.

"We shall be made a cats-paw for European diplomats," wrote

Brent Allinson, president of the Harvard International Polity Club. "Neutrality is an historic American policy and in abandoning it we need some assurance that something higher will take its place."

From Scranton, Pennsylvania: "I cannot see any reason why after 30 months of waiting etc. we should plunge into war in 30 minutes," wrote William Bartley. "Use all your power in an endeavor to prevent the *sending of our men to the disease-infested trenches of Europe*," wrote Franklin Boothe of Philadelphia.

From John E. Broshar, in Lebanon, Indiana (with his original spelling): "You are certanly all right, I have bin talking with some of the Boys that fought under the flag from 61 to 65 and I find a large number of thim that is aganst War one thim said that if the Preachers wood quit preaching War and there was a call for Men that there will be less than a Brigade enlist.

"It took all of the Preachers hear with the help of the Editors three Days to get Four Boys to enlist in Boone Co."

Earl Browder, who was later to lead the Communist Party in this country, wrote from Olathe, Kansas, urging La Follette to keep up the fight.

"No white man should be compelled to wear a British yoke," telegrammed Frank Brunswick from Chicago. "You have your backbone with you on all occasions," wrote Alice Stone Blackwell, editor-in-chief of the *Woman's Journal*. From Portland, Oregon, a Democratic national committeeman sent a telegram of support to the Republican senator.

"I fear before this Administration has run its course we will have an autocracy instead of a democracy," wrote Harold Child, of Ocean View, Virginia. "The traitors of the country are those men who are striving to turn the President into a dictator, and secure imperialism through militarism."

"One czar has been deposed another rises in the land of the free," wrote Thomas Claffy of Detroit. "One man speaks and all must say yes or be termed traitors."

"I have a beautiful young son, just nineteen," wrote Anne Throop Craig, of the Woman's Peace Party in New York. She hoped he would not have to awaken to "the knowledge that war is murder, with the needed ecstasy of criminal madness."

GERTRUDE CAMPBELL, OF the Woman's Christian Temperance Union of Indiana, wrote to La Follette to say she still hoped the United States would stay out of the war, but if war came—and with it conscription—she had a proposal. Conscript wealth to pay for it.

"The middle classes are growing tired of being exploited for the benefit of the immensely rich," she wrote.

Edward Filene, the Boston department store magnate, had suggested the same thing as early as March 10. "If we have war its expense should be borne by the people with big incomes," he told Navy Secretary Daniels. He suggested an income tax of at least 50 percent on the well-to-do—perhaps 100 percent would be better.

Amos Pinchot, the peace activist, went to work on that. On April 1 he announced the formation of a new American Committee on War Finance. He argued that a powerful, coordinated nationwide demand that well-to-do-people pay for the war was the best way to prevent war. And "if we go to war we must go to war in a decent way," he said. "There is a feeling today, largely justified, I believe, that selfish interests have been working for war." Americans, he said, should feel confident that if war came it would be for the good of the country, not those special interests. "Our committee is frankly against war. We have tried to prevent war. We are still trying. But if there is war we want it the kind of a war that no American citizen will regret or feel ashamed of."

LA FOLLETTE, STUCK in Washington, waiting for the special session, wrote a long letter to his son Philip, 19, who was back in Wisconsin. He gave him suggestions on what crops—alfalfa and hay, mostly— to plant on the family farm, and asked him to send several suits of clothing. But of course the war crisis was uppermost on his mind.

"Whatever the cost of my course—never have I been in a better position to render so great a service," he wrote. "It may not prevent war. It did stop its coming for the time being but more important if possible than that—it prevented the surrender to the President of the war making power.—That was a real service to democracy—to constitutional liberty."

He hoped, he wrote, to prolong debate as long as possible, "on every phase of the war issue—thus giving time for more rational and well-considered action."

He continued: "No one knows just what the President will ask Congress to do.

"He may . . . ask for authority to use the 'armed forces of the U.S.'— which include both army & navy to enforce our 'rights' upon the sea.

"He may ask for a resolution declaring that a state of war exists and then ask for either a declaration of war or for authority to use the armed forces of the U.S.

"The lid is kept screwed down and no one knows what form of action will be proposed. He may spring some new sensation—as in the Zimmermann letter. . . . But all I can do is to be as nearly ready as possible to *serve the real interests of our own country with all my might as the call comes.*"

La Follette was not alone. The members of Wilson's cabinet were equally in the dark as to what the president intended to say on April 2. At a cabinet meeting on March 30, during which he had started doing calisthenics, he told them only that he didn't plan to put any emotion into his message—just the facts. He declined an invitation to speak at a graduation ceremony at Annapolis. He was concerned that anything he might say would be misinterpreted. Navy Secretary Daniels went instead. "I could go as I could speak without saying anything," the garrulous North Carolinian noted in his diary.

On Saturday, March 31, the United States took possession of the Virgin Islands from Denmark, for $25 million. The neutral Danes had been eager to sell, afraid of a German attack as part of a move by

Berlin to close off or even conquer the Panama Canal. Daniels, back from Annapolis, oversaw the transition.

After a morning round of golf with Edith, Woodrow Wilson sent a short note of appreciation to Senator Joseph France of Maryland, who had urged him in a letter several days earlier to pursue an "aggressive" armed neutrality. He also wrote Senator Gilbert Hitchcock of Nebraska, who had argued that armed neutrality had never been given a try, that conditions had not materially changed in four weeks in a way that made war necessary, and that the business interests who were pushing for war over the objections of the American people were ready to "lick their chops."

He wished, Wilson replied, he could agree with Hitchcock's arguments. "My own mind has been forced to the acceptance of a different policy for reasons which I hope I shall be able to state with something like convincing force when I address the Congress."

Now it was time to turn his hand to the message he would deliver on April 2. As always, he had sketched out the first draft in shorthand, then corrected it in a combination of shorthand and longhand. For the final version, he worked in an upstairs room of the residential part of the White House, striking the keys of his small Hammond typewriter slowly but precisely. He was in a bad mood. Edith left to call on friends. The staff tiptoed around. "If the president is writing as he feels, Germany is going to get hell in the address to Congress," the chief usher, Ike Hoover, remarked to Thomas Brahany. "I never knew him to be more peevish. He's out of sorts, doesn't feel well and has a headache."

CHAPTER 21

"When the Man-World Is Mad for War"

Thirty-one days that wrenched America toward a new course: That was March 1917. When it began, Wilson was still determined to keep the United States out of the war. Labor disputes and food shortages at home preoccupied millions. The promised German U-boat campaign was shocking, outrageous even—but hardly tangible for a shore-bound population. Shipping was a *business* for America, it wasn't a necessity the way it was for England. As the month unfolded, activists for and against war argued loudly. Americans, characteristically, only half paid attention. But beginning with the astounding news of the Zimmermann Telegram, followed immediately by the Senate filibuster thwarting the president's determination to arm U.S. merchant ships, the people of the country more and more were unable to avoid taking sides. Ships were torpedoed. Russia erupted—a step forward for democracy, surely, but in the short term, if America didn't act, would this tip the balance of the war toward Germany? Newspapers, especially on the East Coast, weighed in strongly for war, and were more than willing to whip up fears of German plots on this side of the Atlantic. Even as some Americans were bewildered by the sudden and seeming inevitability of conflict, more and more were gripped by the passion of the moment.

Wilson had held out, and when the month ended, almost no one knew what course he would propose. Antiwar activists believed they still had a chance to mobilize public opinion against jumping into the conflict. But huge "loyalty" rallies, like the one in Philadelphia, showed how slim their chances were. The peace groups wanted Americans to pay attention, to think about what the country was doing and where it was heading—but by now enthusiasm was outrunning calm reflection.

Intervention in Europe—for the 140 years since its founding, the United States had never contemplated such a deeply transformative act. Once in, could it ever fully retreat again to its own side of the Atlantic?

The first week of April would decide the question. Members of Congress knew that, in the end, the burden would fall on them. A large number of them wished the problem would go away—they didn't want war, they didn't want to be responsible for refusing war. For Jeannette Rankin, the lady from Montana, the dilemma was especially acute. Her one aim was to secure the vote for women. Did she desire suffrage more than she loathed war? For her it was to be a week of tears, and a week that would mark her for the rest of her long life.

She finally arrived in Washington on April 1, at about noon. Her last appearance had been in Des Moines, Iowa, two days earlier. "All in black—black coat and skirt, that is, and wide-brimmed black sailor hat, with white shirtwaist and a bunch of violets making the only touch of color—she looked singularly fresh and unruffled after five nights in a sleeping car," the *Philadelphia Evening Ledger* noted.

She was besieged by reporters at Union Station, and she was polite but didn't give them any thoughts on war or peace. She talked about suffrage, prohibition and welfare for women and children. She promised to keep her "mouth shut and her eyes open" for a while.

She stopped by her new office at the Capitol, a spare room unadorned with feminine flourishes, as the *New York Times* commented, though her two secretaries had already been at work there a week. The House of Representatives was just about evenly divided: 213 Democrats and 215 Republicans, with 3 Progressives, 1 Socialist and 1 Prohibition Party member. It wasn't clear whether Champ Clark, the Democrat from Missouri, or James Mann, the Republican from Illinois, would be elected speaker, though Clark seemed to have the edge. Democrats had been suggesting that Rankin would vote for Clark, but now, in her office and meeting again with reporters, she said she had been elected on the Republican ticket and would stick with Mann.

She was nervous. A reporter asked her about the threat of war. Quietly, she replied, "The president is, I believe, about to make certain recommendations upon which he will ask Congress to take action. As I shall have to participate in that action I prefer not indicating in advance what I shall do."

HER MOTHER HAD come to Washington along with the two staff members, and all four women would be living together in an apartment. Jeannette's brother Wellington had accompanied her on her trip from Des Moines, to be present for her swearing in.

Early the next morning, Wilson sent the transcript of his speech off to the printer. It was still a closely kept secret.

Rankin was running late. She and Florence Leech, one of her secretaries, took a cab to the old Shoreham Hotel, at 15th and H streets, for an appearance at a women's breakfast meeting in her honor. When they got to the hotel, fifteen minutes behind schedule, they went unnoticed and had to elbow their way through the crowd in the hotel lobby.

Finally, in the restaurant, with its rose-colored carpets and wallhangings, new and old friends gave her an ovation. Rankin was wearing, the *Philadelphia Evening Ledger* reported, "a stunning black satin and georgette crepe dress, trimmed with white, cut low enough to expose a gracefully rounded throat." Sitting on one side of her was

Carrie Chapman Catt; on the other, Alice Paul. They were allies and rivals at the same time in the suffrage movement. One of the other women in attendance was Champ Clark's wife. Rankin rose to speak, but not for long. "There will be many times when I will make mistakes," she told them. "And I need your encouragement and support. I know I will get it. I promise—I promise—"

Her lips trembling just slightly, she sat down.

From there she went to a reception in her honor, and then to the Capitol, where she took refuge in the Speaker's room, though it was still occupied by the Democrat Clark, who had held the post in the previous Congress. At five minutes before noon, Clark himself escorted her to a seat on the Republican side of the House chamber.

In the galleries, and on the floor itself, men and women yelled and clapped for her. This time it wasn't a hoax—it was the real Miss Rankin from Montana—and she was mobbed by well-wishers. Eighty-year-old "Uncle Joe" Cannon, the Illinois Republican, told her, "If you are looking for a grandfather, you might adopt me."

The roll was called, with the usual confusion and inattention and boisterous conversation. But then the clerk got to Montana, and rapped his desk for attention. Finally, the House grew still, and he called out Miss Rankin's name. The members burst out cheering, she blushed and smiled, and finally she stood up and bowed, first to the Republicans, then to the Democrats.

The first order of business was to elect a Speaker and organize the House officers. Both sides declared that this was no time for partisanship. Representative Thomas Schall, a Progressive from Minnesota who was blind, shouted out, "There should be but one party, the American party." He was so enthusiastic about the sentiment that he forgot he was supposed to be nominating Clark for the speakership. The House clerk reminded him; Republicans laughed derisively.

Clark won, with 217 votes. But now Mann began demanding roll calls on every single procedural matter and vote for House officer.

The afternoon dragged on. The House expected to be done by 3 p.m., then 4 p.m., then 5 p.m. The president was just going to have to wait to make his speech.

WILSON HAD BREAKFAST that morning with Colonel House, who had arrived by the overnight train from New York. House, alone, knew what direction the speech would take. He and Wilson had conferred on March 27th and again on the 28th, during his previous visit to Washington. Wilson had begun on the first day by asking House if he should seek a declaration of war, or simply say that a state of war exists, and ask for the means to pursue it. House advised the latter, because he was afraid of a war resolution spurring an acrimonious, and unpredictable, debate in Congress. He told Wilson that the crisis was unlike any other he had faced as president, and he wasn't sure that Wilson was "well fitted" for this one. Wilson agreed. House "thought he was too refined, too civilized, too intellectual, too cultivated not to see the incongruity and absurdity of war." The country, he wrote that evening, "needed a man of coarser fiber." Wilson, he thought, had taken a gamble that there would be no war, and had lost. Now, his only option was to prosecute it fully.

That evening, Wilson had written down his thoughts, and the next day, the twenty-eighth, they had discussed the war again. The president had, House, believed, adopted a number of his ideas. "Unless he changes his mind, he will have a message which could not please me better had I written it myself." They agreed he should address the German people, to differentiate them from their kaiser and government.

The next four days would have weighed on Wilson's shoulders as no crisis in his life had before. House knew his thinking, but the president still hadn't committed himself. There was war, on an unimaginable scale. War made sense. War made no sense. The Civil War had been inevitable and a disaster for the South. Was this war inevitable? Wilson as a young man had studied law, in his beautiful native Virginia. Now could he send millions of other young men into battle? Wilson recoiled from the ugliness of politics. The people in the peace movement exasperated him. He had been for peace, but how could you still be for peace, at any price? Germany had made it clear it was unwilling to be moved. The kaiser was challenging the president. The president embodies the will of the American people, and the American people were aroused.

And consistency of vision: From this war he would foster a better world, and that was still the objective. The only question was means. Appeals to conscience had been tried. Now, maybe guns were the answer. Lansing and the others were going on about Russia and the revolution. It was only starting, and no one should expect that there wouldn't be unforeseen consequences. And yet, and yet—the overthrow of the autocracy was an altogether good thing, a democratic moment was at hand, it could spread to Germany. Was this precisely the democratic arrival of which he had been the prophet? Could a democratic Russia survive autocratic Germany's hostility? Could it survive American indifference? What would the world look like if Germany took advantage of Russian weakness and won the war? What would the standing of the United States be then, with France and England crushed? Or what would it look like if Germany crumbled, and Britain and France, the two great imperial powers, should triumph while America watched from afar? Neither outcome was palatable. Could the United States go to war and be defeated? There was a simple answer to that. America was the richest, most powerful country in the world. The answer was no.

Wilson was caged in the White House, and felt it. His cousin Helen Bones once said he reminded her "of a splendid Bengal tiger she had once seen—never still, moving, restless, resentful of his bars that shut out the larger life God had made for him."

NOW THE DAY had arrived. Wilson went out to play some golf. House went for a car ride with Frank Polk, the state department counselor. Polk told him that neither his boss, Lansing, nor any other cabinet member knew what was coming. When he got back to the White House, McAdoo, Wilson's son-in-law and treasury secretary, phoned House to try to wheedle something out of him. House told him only that he expected the message "to meet all expectations."

Wilson came back from golf, and then had nothing to do but wait. He was nervous. First he told House he wouldn't speak after 3 p.m., if it took the House of Representatives that long to get organized, because he didn't want to leave the impression that he was pressing too hard. The speech could wait a day. House talked him out of it.

Messages went back and forth between the Executive Mansion and the Capitol. Still they waited. House asked Wilson why he hadn't shared his address with the members of the cabinet. "He replied that if he had, every man in it would have had some suggestion to make and it would have been picked to pieces if he had heeded their criticisms. He said he preferred to keep it to himself and take the responsibility. I feel that he does the cabinet an injustice. He should not humiliate them to such an extent."

They had dinner at 6:30. Then, finally, word came from the other end of Pennsylvania Avenue. Congress would be able to receive the president at 8 o'clock.

More than a thousand protesters had gathered on the grounds in front of the Capitol. They tried to occupy the steps that Wilson would have to use when he arrived, but the police kept them away. Eventually, a combined force of police officers, treasury agents and postal inspectors cleared the approaches to the building as well.

Earlier that day, a small group of peace activists from Massachusetts had called upon their senator, Henry Cabot Lodge, to ask him to reconsider his support for war. Lodge said he had been considering for three years and wasn't going to consider anymore. The conversation, in a corridor, grew heated, and one of the visitors, Alexander Bannwart, observed that cowards were the ones supporting war. Lodge replied that if Bannwart were calling him a coward, "he was a damned liar." Then one man or the other struck the first blow. In the ensuing melee they both took punches, but Bannwart, a former minor league baseball player and executive, was bloodied and subdued by a passing Western Union messenger boy, and arrested. Lodge, who was 66, felt he had acquitted himself capitally. "At my age there is a certain aspect of folly about the whole thing," he wrote in a letter to Roosevelt, "and yet I am glad that I hit him. The Senators all appeared to be perfectly delighted."

At a little before 8:30, Lodge, a welt on his face still visible, joined his Senate colleagues as they walked over to the House side. Slowly they filed in, most of them clutching small American flags. Wilson, accompanied by Edith and his physician, Dr. Cary Grayson, had left the White House about 8:15. Several hundred people were at the northeast gate, singing patriotic songs. They cheered when the president's car drove by. Crowds had gathered on Pennsylvania Avenue, but as a precaution, the small party drove out New York Avenue instead, and then took New Jersey Avenue to the Capitol. For the first time, the newly installed exterior lights were turned on, and the building stood out "white and majestic" in the night. At 8:32, Wilson entered the House chamber.

The first half of his address was met with respectful silence. The president touched on the German attacks on shipping as evidence of the kind of callous power the United States was facing. But he didn't dwell on the details. "Property can be paid for. The lives of peaceful and innocent people cannot be," he said.

"We must put excited feeling away. Our motive will not be revenge." He said the submarines were operating outside the law, and he had come to realize that his previous efforts at "armed neutrality"—putting gun crews on merchant ships—was not the right approach. "It is practically certain to draw us into the war without either the rights or the effectiveness of belligerents."

Being reactive, in other words, would offer the worst of both worlds: It would drag America into the conflict, but in a way that would not give the United States the standing to shape the future. The submarine attacks themselves weren't so much the real and sufficient cause for war, but they demonstrated that Germany was too obstinate to be dealt with except through force.

He therefore asked Congress for a declaration of war, and called on the country "to exert all its power and employ all its resources to bring the government of the German Empire to terms and end the war."

He declared that his thinking had not changed since January (when he called for Peace Without Victory). He was still intent on establishing peace and a "league of honor" that would link the democratic nations, and enforce that peace. But, he said, "neutrality is no longer feasible or desirable where the peace of the world is involved and the freedom of its peoples."

Wilson then called for universal conscription, an army of half a million at least, and a far more powerful navy. This was when Congress started cheering. He called on the lawmakers to raise taxes to pay for all this, so that the government could avoid ruinous borrowing.

And then he talked about Russia.

> Does not every American feel that assurance has been added to our hope for the future peace of the world by the wonderful and heartening things that have been happening within the last few weeks in Russia? Russia was known by those who knew it best to have been always in fact democratic at heart, in all the vital habits of her thought, in all the intimate relationships of her people that spoke their natural instinct, their habitual attitude towards life. The autocracy that crowned the summit of her political structure, long as it had stood and terrible as was the reality of its power, was not in fact Russian in origin, character, or purpose; and now it has been shaken off and the great, generous Russian people have been added in all their naive maj-

esty and might to the forces that are fighting for freedom in the world, for justice, and for peace. Here is a fit partner for a League of Honor.

"The world must be made safe for democracy," he said. That line created no stir at first, but Senator John Sharp Williams, a Democrat from Mississippi, picked up its implication, and began to offer his solemn applause, which soon spread throughout the chamber. "We have no selfish ends to serve. We desire no conquest, no dominion," the president said. "We are but one of the champions of the rights of mankind. We shall be satisfied when those rights have been made as secure as the faith and the freedom of nations can make them."

Finally he drew close to his conclusion: "There are, it may be, many months of fiery trial and sacrifice ahead of us. It is a fearful thing to lead this great peaceful people into war, into the most terrible and disastrous of all wars, civilization itself seeming to be in the balance. But right is more precious than peace."

He spoke for thirty-six minutes, and finished at 9:11 p.m. Nearly everyone cheered wildly, waving those little American flags. A *New York Times* reporter spotted La Follette, standing motionless "with his arms folded tight and high on his chest, so that nobody could have any excuse for mistaking his attitude; and there he stood, chewing gum with a sardonic smile."

Lodge approached Wilson and warmly grasped his hand. But on his way back to the White House, the president was shaken and quite pale.

A legend has grown up about that evening at the White House, from an account that Wilson's chief aide, Joseph Tumulty, gave more than a decade later. He said that the president, who had tried so hard to keep America out of the war and find a way to sponsor a general peace, broke down in tears over what he had just proposed. Scholars doubt that legend. By the late 1920s, the war didn't look so glorious, and Tumulty may have been trying to buff Wilson's battered image.

House, in his diary, wrote that he joined the Wilsons and Woodrow's daughter Margaret in the oval Blue Room that evening. They "talked it over as families are prone to do after some eventful occasion." House told Wilson that he thought he was embarking on a course no other statesman had ever followed. The president was surprised to hear that. "It seemed to me that he did not have a true conception of the path he was blazing," House wrote. The wily colonel left at 10:30 for the night train back to New York. "I could see that the president was relieved that the tension was over and the die cast. I knew this would happen."

AT THE METROPOLITAN Opera House in New York, late editions of the evening papers began circulating during the third intermission of an opera called *The Canterbury Pilgrims*. They carried news of Wilson's speech, and a great cheer went up. The orchestra broke into "The Star-Spangled Banner." James Gerard, until recently the ambassador to Berlin, called for three cheers for the president, and three more for the Allies, and three more for the Army and the Navy. Margaret Ober, a German contralto, fainted on stage, and had to be carried off, "with some difficulty."

Movie theaters flashed the news on their screens, to more cheering and more renditions of "The Star-Spangled Banner." At the Midnight Frolic on the New Amsterdam Roof, the comedian Will Rogers "drew a great shout when he said he was glad to get back into vaudeville at the present time because in a year or two the vaudeville stage would be overcrowded with Kaisers, Czars, Kings and their relatives."

"YOU HAVE DONE a great thing nobly!" Wilson's son-in-law, William McAdoo, wrote the next day in his vigorous round hand. "I firmly believe that it is God's will that America should do this transcendent service for humanity throughout the world and that you are his chosen instrument."

In New York, Walter Lippmann wrote a column for the *New Republic* lavishly praising the president for seeing the war as a struggle between autocracy and democracy. "For having seen this," he wrote, "for having selected the moment when the issue was so clear, for having done so much through the winter to make the issue clear, our debt and the world's debt to Woodrow Wilson is immeasurable. . . . Only a statesman who will be called great could have made America's intervention mean so much to the generous forces of the world, could have lifted the inevitable horror of war into a deed so full of meaning."

In Rome, a joint statement signed by sixty-eight members of the Chamber of Deputies read: "Your message is not addressed to the United States alone but to all humanity and awakens noblest instincts among free nations. Your message is the hymn of freedom."

Raymond Poincaré, the president of France, sent Wilson a warm and heartfelt message. "This war," he wrote, "would not have had its full significance if the United States had not been drawn into it."

But as the Senate began to consider the war resolution, La Follette used procedural rules to hold up the proceedings. In the House, Speaker Champ Clark decided to wait for the Senate to act first.

And still, letters against war kept pouring in. La Follette figured he got about 10,000 in all. An acquaintance in Chicago, for instance, wrote that when he went to the movies that week, and La Follette's image was projected on the screen, the applause outshone the hisses.

The head of the Emergency Anti-War Committee in Chicago, Grace Abbott, sent news that an antiwar Socialist, John Kennedy, had been elected to the Board of Aldermen from the 27th Ward on April 3, even though every newspaper in the city was against him on "patriotic grounds."

Elsewhere in Illinois, J. Ogden Armour told the 50,000 employees of his meatpacking company "to show their loyalty and patriotism in every way." An indignant Arthur Hummer wrote La Follette, "How long has Armour & Co. been loyal observers of the law of this country?"

On April 4, Theodore Roosevelt arrived in Washington from Florida and impulsively stopped by the White House to see Wilson. The two had never met. But Wilson was in a cabinet meeting and TR had a train to catch, so the former president contented himself with a pleasant chat with Ike Hoover, the White House usher, and then was on his way.

At the Capitol, the Senate began thirteen hours of debate. La Follette made a long and carefully argued speech. He pointed out that Wilson had completely reversed himself on the arming of merchant vessels— calling his opponents a "little band of willful men" at the beginning of March, but conceding in his war message, implicitly, that La Follette had been right. The move invited war without providing any benefit to the United States. La Follette also suggested that the removal of the czar had no bearing on American entry into the war, and that proponents of war were insincere in citing Russia as a reason to get involved.

And, he asked, how could this be a war for democracy if one of America's chief allies would be a country with a hereditary ruler, a House of Lords, and "grinding industrial conditions for all the wage-workers"? Wilson, he said, "has not suggested we make our support of Great Britain conditional to her granting home rule to Ireland, or Egypt, or India." And if the United States had actually been neutral since 1914, he said, instead of favoring the Allies, it would not now be facing war with Germany.

He knew he wasn't going to prevail, but he wanted to make his point before the entire nation. Another antiwar senator, George W. Norris of Nebraska, said, "I feel we are about to put the dollar sign on the American flag." He was accused of treason on the floor of the Senate by John Sharp Williams. That evening, the war resolution was adopted. Besides La Follette and Norris, four other senators voted no. Of the six voting against, three were Republicans, three Democrats.

ON APRIL 5, the House took up the resolution. Jeannette Rankin had been getting plenty of mail, too. Catherine Smith, president of the Washington Suffrage League in Seattle, took strong exception to Carrie Catt's support for Wilson and war. The cause of woman suffrage was on trial before the world, she wrote Rankin on April 4, and she wanted Rankin to know she would have support in her ordeal.

"You are our hope when the man-world is mad for war," wrote Mrs. George Schuettinger of Brooklyn on April 2.

"We are persuaded that a declaration of war will militate against the best interests of Montana both materially and spiritually and trust you will use your utmost endeavor to preserve us from the fierce waste and destruction, which the graft and greed of some our wealthy eastern citizens would thrust upon us," wrote the Reverend R.T. Cookingham, pastor of the Methodist church in Scobey, Montana.

"Prompted by patriotic American motives, I protest against nation participating in European war," read a telegram from Kurt Vonnegut of Indianapolis, whose son would one day write *Slaughterhouse Five*, about another war.

Laura Booth Hall, the superintendent of schools in Carter County, in the southeast corner of Montana, wrote to say she assumed Rankin was against the war, though the congresswoman had still not talked about it. Take La Follette for your guide, Hall wrote.

Rankin composed a form letter in reply. "I shall strive to do what is right," she wrote.

SHE STAYED HOME most of that day, a Thursday. Alice Paul and Hazel Hunkins, a suffrage activist from Billings, Montana, went to see her. Rankin told them about the heavy pressure she was feeling from suffrage leaders to vote for war, so she wouldn't set the movement back. When she had been at that dinner in New York before her speaking tour, at Harriet Laidlaw's house, she said, there was no form of pressure that Laidlaw *didn't* bring to bear on her. Her brother Wellington was urging her to vote for war, though he was personally against it, so as not to throw her career away.

Paul told her that there was room in the suffrage movement for pro- and antiwar feeling, and that the National Woman's Party she headed had taken no position on the question. But then she and Hunkins spoke as individuals, and told her they thought it would be a tragedy for the first woman elected to Congress to vote for war. Women, they said, constituted the peace-loving half of the world, and giving political power to women was a way of diminishing the possibilities of war.

Finally, in the evening, as the debate dragged on, she showed up. Representative Claude Kitchin of North Carolina, the Democratic floor leader, opposed the war resolution, declaring he wanted to keep America as "the last hope of peace on earth, good will toward men." He began to weep. At one point Rankin left her seat and went up into the gallery to confer again with Paul and Hunkins. April 5 became April 6, and still there was no action. At last, at nearly 3 a.m., voting began. When the clerk called Rankin's name, she was silent. He called her name again, more loudly. Most of the members of the House turned to see her. "Miss Rankin was evidently under great mental distress. Her appearance was that of a woman on the verge of a breakdown. She clutched at her throat repeatedly. Now and then she brushed back her hair, looked upward at the stained-glass ceiling, and rubbed her eyes and cheeks nervously. She clasped and unclasped her hands."

"Uncle Joe" Cannon went over to her and urged her to vote her conscience. "You represent the womanhood of the country," he said. She remained silent, as had others, and the clerk moved on.

Then the House clerk called the roll again, as was the custom, to pick up any absentees who might have come back to the floor. "Miss Rankin," the clerk called, and then he called it again.

She stood, and started to sway. She grabbed the back of the chair in front of her. She steadied herself. "I want to stand by my country— but I cannot vote for war," she said.

This was extraordinary in itself. House members didn't explain their votes. A few pacifists in the gallery applauded. Then some congressmen began shouting out at her: "Vote! Vote! Vote!"

The clerk and the Speaker didn't know what to make of it. "Did you intend to vote No?" the clerk inquired.

She nodded and sank back into her seat. It was reported the next day, and for many years afterward, that she had then begun to sob. She usually denied it: she said that she had been weeping for three days straight, and by April 6 she had no tears left. She pointed out that Claude Kitchin was unabashed about weeping in public. "It takes neither moral nor physical courage to declare a war for others to fight," he said during the debate.

Forty-eight others joined them in opposition, but the resolution carried easily, early on the morning of Good Friday, and the nation was at war.

CHAPTER 22

"History Will Count You Right"

"I remember as if it had been yesterday the hush, followed by a burst of cheers, as the flash announcing the declaration of war by the Congress of the United States came over the wires at *The Sun* office," wrote Marguerite Harrison as she looked back at 1917.

Enthusiasm swept the country. The United States was about to enter a conflict more deadly than any in history, deadlocked for nearly three years on the Western Front. Yet the response was ecstatic. Four Minute Men cropped up from coast to coast. War, at the very least, offered an exciting distraction from the tiresome labor troubles and dreary routines of peacetime.

Wilson signed the war resolution shortly after 1 p.m. on April 6. He didn't allow reporters or photographers in to record the moment, because, he said, that would be undignified.

Carrie Chapman Catt and other suffrage leaders said they understood that Jeannette Rankin had to vote the way she did to be true to her principles. "While I should have liked for her to vote differently," said Harriet Laidlaw, who had also been in the gallery when the vote was taken, "she did her duty as she saw it after one of the most terrible mental struggles any woman ever had."

But Catt was seething in private. "By the way, our Congress Lady is a sure enough joker," she wrote to a friend on April 8. "Whatever she has done or will do is wrong to somebody, and every time she answers a roll call she loses us a million votes."

Rankin continued to get letters of support, though, including one from Roger Baldwin, an attorney in St. Louis. "History will count you right," he predicted.

Baldwin, who continued to oppose the war, was alarmed by two of the first pieces of legislation taken up by the new Congress. The Espionage Act of 1917 (which is still in force) and a law creating conscription inspired him to found what was to become the American Civil Liberties Union.

THE DRAFT ENABLED the United States to confound virtually every expectation and send two million soldiers to France within eighteen months. More than 53,000 were killed in action in the war, and another 63,000 died of other causes. More than 204,000 Americans were wounded. (Russia, by comparison, suffered more than 3 million dead, and more than 4 million wounded.) When it was over, the dead of many nations were piled up all over Europe, the world did not seem especially safe and democracy was not ascendant. The United States spent $20 billion on the war (more than $330 billion in today's money), not counting veterans' benefits, interest payments on bonds, or assistance to allies.

In the disillusioned years following the Armistice, the timing of the Russian Revolution and its influence on the United States received relatively little attention. Yet its role was much more central in American thinking, in March of 1917, than was remembered later. The revolution opened the door to U.S. involvement. It suggested, to impressionable Americans, that democracy's historic global moment was at hand. That those same Americans chose later not to remember the Russian factor in their thinking is not surprising. Russia did *not* stay in the war, as Americans thought it would. Russia did *not* become a democracy. Russia in fact became an outcast, a self-described font of revolution, which it hoped to export to the capitalist West. Naturally, in retrospect, those who supported the war didn't dwell on the extent to which they had misread Russia. But in March 1917 very few people understood where Russia was going—the conservative Rosen and the revolutionary Trotsky had the clearest vision. Did Wilson share the doubts expressed in the *Springfield Republican* editorial that he praised? He never explicitly said so. Many, on all sides of the question, thought he was being swept along by an irresistible tide of public feeling by the end of the month, that the matter was no longer in his hands. The Russian Revolution made it, in any case, easier to talk about a war for democracy. It removed an obvious objection of hypocrisy.

American blindness to Russian reality in 1917 took several forms. Americans discerned deep democratic traditions and then loaded them with great expectations. They asked the wrong questions and made irrelevant predictions. They patronized the Russians, and projected their own sunny optimism onto that burdened population. In 1991, with the collapse of the Soviet Union, they did so again.

COLONEL HOUSE ONCE remarked on Wilson's inability to get along with Republicans, but in May the president asked Elihu Root, who had spoken so stirringly about joining arm-in-arm with Russia's new democrats, to lead a mission of experts to Petrograd to assess Russia's needs and ways in which the United States could lend its valuable expertise. It was, as the younger George Kennan later pointed out, an assignment that could not have been more perfectly designed to irritate both countries. Russia was in desperate straits and now had to engage with a large group of ill-informed, advice-giving Americans. Root's team was there for about a month. The former secretary of state met with Baron Rosen, and received a chatty letter from Julia Speransky-Grant, who had known Root from her father's Republican Party activities in New York. She was still in the Crimea and regretted that they couldn't meet. She hoped he would get a good impres-

sion of the real Russia, but feared that Petrograd was not the place
to do so. Kerensky had emerged as leader of the government by the
time Root got there; the American mission left just before an abor-
tive Bolshevik uprising in July.

Although the introduction to the report prepared by the Root commission played up an optimistic view of Russia's intent to reform and
stay in the war, anyone who read as far as the individual subject-area
sections could sense a profound disillusionment.

SHORTLY AFTER THE United States entered the war, the federal government took control of American railroads, created a War Industries Board (under "Industry Czar" Bernard Baruch), and established
a Committee on Public Information, under George Creel. It was as
close to socialism as the United States had ever been.

But there were different shades of socialism, some more acceptable than others. One of the two white men who were lynched in
the United States in 1917 was Frank Little, an organizer for the
Industrial Workers of the World who arrived in Butte, Montana, that
summer. Dozens of miners had been killed in an underground fire,
trapped when escape doors wouldn't open, and that sparked a bitter
strike against Anaconda. Miners flocked to join the I.W.W., which
reached its peak membership that summer. Little was pulled out of
his boarding house one night by men assumed to be cops, dragged
for a mile or more behind their car, then strung up on a bridge.
The strike continued for another six months, and ended in defeat for
the union. Dashiell Hammett worked for Anaconda that year as a
Pinkerton man; he later wrote a novel about Butte, titled *Red Harvest*,
in which he called the town Poisonville.

American attitudes began to shift profoundly in November 1917.
After months of unrest, the Bolsheviks in Petrograd tried again, and
this time seized power from the dysfunctional, distracted and disliked Provisional Government. Americans suspected a German plot,
and were convinced that the radicals would in short order be swept

from the scene. They weren't, and Russia soon signed a separate, punitive peace with the Germans.

Russia's new leaders ushered in a system of central state communism and an ideology of world revolution. Root's report became utterly beside the point. Under the provisions of the treaty signed with Berlin, the Ukraine—including the Speransky estate at Bouromka—fell under German occupation. After the Germans left in late 1918, Ukrainian nationalists, Russian Whites and Russian Reds vied for control, with devastating consequences. The Reds eventually prevailed.

HYSTERIA OVER ALL things German, already evident in March, exploded after the United States went to war. German-American families Anglicized their names, German-language newspapers shut down. H. L. Mencken's hometown of Baltimore renamed German Street, calling it Redwood Street after the first Baltimore officer to die in the war, Lieutenant George Redwood. Sauerkraut, memorably, was rechristened Liberty Cabbage. Prohibitionists exploited anti-German feeling in denouncing the country's big breweries.

TEDDY ROOSEVELT NEVER got permission to raise his expeditionary force. Secretary of War Newton Baker's correspondence with him became terser and terser. The army's top generals thought the proposal was foolish, disruptive, amateurish and potentially disastrous. In May, TR gave up. He had said he would rather be killed in battle than see his sons die. On Bastille Day of 1918, his youngest son, Quentin, was killed at the age of 20 in a dogfight over France. The former president never got over it, and died at Sagamore Hill six months later, on January 6, 1919, not long after his 60th birthday.

Joyce Kilmer, the poet who had so admired the effect of the war on art, rose to the rank of sergeant in the Fighting 69th before he was shot dead by a sniper during the Second Battle of the Marne, on July 30, 1918.

Buster Keaton served in France; he suffered a permanent hearing loss. Grover Cleveland Alexander was in the artillery and had a bad time of it; he returned to the pitcher's mound after the war but suffered fits and had taken to heavy drinking.

When James Reese Europe and the Harlem regiment got to France, the Army was unwilling to have them fight alongside white regiments, so they were assigned to the French Fourth Army instead. The French, who had had plenty of experience with colonial troops, took to them immediately. The men from New York, who became known as the Harlem Hellfighters, got into several ferocious fights with the Germans. Europe, back with his machine-gun squad, was gassed, but survived.

Germany, in the end, couldn't subdue Britain with its U-boats, couldn't exploit Russia's withdrawal from the war, and couldn't sustain the battle against the fresh American troops flooding into Europe. American factories and shipyards poured out immense quantities of equipment and matériel for the war effort. On November 11, 1918, an armistice brought the war to an end.

JIM EUROPE'S BAND toured France in the months that followed, drawing huge crowds everywhere. It was a potent and pioneering example of American culture's irresistible drawing power in the battered countries of the Old World. His band was often credited with introducing jazz to the continent. When it was time to ship home, the Army issued orders to the MPs on the docks to give the black soldiers an especially rough time, to knock any pride out of them, deserved or not. The idea was to remind them of their place back in America.

As soon as he returned to New York, after a triumphant parade up Fifth Avenue, Europe launched a successful tour with his big band, and he might well have sent American jazz in a dramatically different direction from the one it took. But in 1919, in Boston, he got into a backstage argument with one of his drummers, who pulled out a knife and stabbed him to death. His funeral, in Harlem, drew huge crowds.

The summer of 1919 saw Jim Europe's dreams for African-Americans reduced, in many places literally, to ashes. Race riots erupted across the country, driven by resentment among whites—against blacks who had left the South and against black aspirations for civil rights. In Washington, 15 people were killed; in Chicago, 38. The Ku Klux Klan entered its heyday in the 1920s. Progress wouldn't start to come until decades later.

MENCKEN, WHO HAD to step back from journalism during the war because of his German sympathies, used the time to write his classic study *The American Language*. He regained his journalistic voice once the war had ended, with new acidity, and depth. The break may have done him good, which he acknowledged. He became one of the leading journalists of the 1920s, delighting in the failings of politicians and notoriously skewering William Jennings Bryan while covering the Scopes Monkey Trial in 1925. He had nothing good to say for either Colonel Roosevelt or Woodrow Wilson.

When the war ended, Communists seamlessly replaced Germans as the objects of American blind fear and hatred, and in 1919 Wilson's new attorney general, A. Mitchell Palmer, launched a series of notorious raids against "Reds."

JULIA SPERANSKY-GRANT, WITH her family, fled the German occupation of the Ukraine and made her way to Petrograd. But with the Bolsheviks in control, she sewed the family jewels into her clothing, and they escaped through Finland to the United States. She wrote several books about idyllic prerevolutionary Russia, and consistently blamed the revolution on the Germans.

Wilson stopped hailing the Russian Revolution after the Bolsheviks took power, and eventually American troops were in Murmansk and Vladivostok. Those in Murmansk found themselves in 1919

halfheartedly fighting against Russian soldiers—who were under
the command of Leon Trotsky. The Americans soon left, and Trotsky
led the Red Army to victory in Russia's phenomenally brutal and
unforgiving civil war. He proved that Russians still had plenty of
fight in them, just not in concert with the Western Allies. One of
Trotsky's chief antagonists was Admiral Kolchak, who had thrown
his sword off his ship; he led a White army in Siberia against the
Reds until his capture and execution in 1920.

Baron Rosen managed to escape from Russia with his wife. He
arrived in New York with $300 in his pocket. He made a living as
a translator, then gained some financial security with a forty-part
series in the *Saturday Evening Post* about his experiences. One day
in 1922, perhaps distracted by thoughts of home, he stepped into
traffic on Sixth Avenue and was struck by a cab. He died eleven
days later.

James Houghteling, fresh from Russia, left the Commerce Department for the Army and fought in the Argonne Forest in 1918. Then
he went back to Chicago, where he worked as a business executive
for the *Chicago Daily News* and then the *Chicago Daily Times*, later
returning to Washington as commissioner of the Immigration and
Naturalization Service.

Marguerite Harrison spent the war years in Baltimore, writing
feature stories about the home front. She worked in a steel mill
and as a trolley conductor so she could tell her readers what it was
like as a woman to do so. She never lost her enthusiasm for the war
effort. When the fighting ended, she signed up with Army intelligence and went to Germany under cover as a reporter. Soon she
was in Soviet Russia, and in jail. One of Maryland's senators went
over to Moscow and secured her release. Several years later she
returned to Russia, for *Cosmopolitan*—and was jailed again. While
there, she helped Merian Cooper, an American who had been a
pilot in the Polish Air Force and was captured during a short war
against the Russians. They struck up a friendship and together

made one of the seminal film documentaries of the 1920s, "Grass," about nomads in the Caspian Sea region. Cooper eventually made his way to Hollywood, where he would produce *King Kong*. Harrison, barred from the Explorer's Club because she was a woman, founded the Society of Woman Geographers.

NEARLY ALL THE arguments about the war turned out to be wrong. It did not make the world safe for democracy, or usher in a new world order, as Wilson had hoped. Roosevelt was wrong in predicting it would smash German militarism. Jim Europe was wrong in expecting it to improve the standing of African-Americans. Mencken was wrong in predicting that it would take years to win on the battlefield. Trotsky was wrong in his forecast of a world revolution. House was wrong in thinking that the United States couldn't get an army overseas in time to make a difference. La Follette was wrong in thinking that the U-boat menace couldn't be defeated. Speransky-Grant was, for the most part, wrong in thinking that the Russian revolution was carried out by German agents. James Houghteling, like Wilson and Roosevelt, was spectacularly wrong about Russian democracy.

Perhaps only Baron Rosen was right about the war. But he was wrong to imagine that the United States, as it teetered in 1917, might still play the generous, disinterested role it had performed back in 1905.

In 1936, a committee headed by Senator Gerald Nye, an isolationist Republican from North Dakota, attempted to prove that J. P. Morgan and his allies on Wall Street had pushed the United States into the war. The committee gathered evidence showing that American financiers had lent $2.3 billion to England and France, money that would have been at risk if the Allies were defeated. Leading bankers and others were well aware of that risk at the time—Ambassador Page's telegram from London on March 5 makes that clear. The hearings, however, failed to demonstrate Morgan's ability to steer the Wilson administration into the war.

The president thought he was acting on a nobler impulse. He was carried along, whether he willed it or not, on a mounting wave of national passion.

THE STORY OF Woodrow Wilson is a familiar one—how he brooked no opposition to the war once he made up his mind to get into it; how he laid out his vision for a democratic future with his famous Fourteen Points in 1918, raising the hopes of millions across Europe, and winning their sincere gratitude; how the French and English checked him at the Versailles Peace Conference, imposing a harsh peace on Germany and expanding their reach through the Middle East, all in return for agreeing to his cherished League of Nations; and how Senate Republicans, led by Henry Cabot Lodge, then kept America out of the League.

Wilson pushed Edward House out of his inner circle after the war came; perhaps if he had stuck with his old strategist, he could have found a way to secure his vision. But he was stubborn, righteous and intolerant. Stymied in the Senate, he was sure he could rouse the nation to demand membership in the League, and he went on a coast-to-coast whistle-stop tour. In Pueblo, Colorado, for what would be his last public address, Wilson moved his audience to tears. He said the League of Nations offered the only hope that the young boys of 1919 would not have to go off to war as soldiers in the years to come. And then he collapsed.

His train took him directly back to Washington, where he suffered a massive stroke. Edith kept the press, members of the cabinet, and most of Wilson's aides away. He was paralyzed on the left side; she effectively took on the role of chief of staff, deciding what papers he should sign. Even then, he thought of running for a third term in 1920. But it was impossible. The Republican Warren Harding, calling for a "return to normalcy" in the wake of the war, the hysteria over alleged sedition, the bitter disputes, won the White House. Wilson, who in his final years enjoyed being taken for rides in his Pierce-Arrow motor car, died in Washington in 1924.

THE WAR SET both the United States and Russia on the paths they would follow for the next century. It changed both countries, utterly. In America, the normalcy of the 1920s looked like nothing that had come before. The United States that emerged from World War I was far and away the wealthiest and most economically powerful nation on the planet. Women won the vote. The war ended mass European immigration and launched the Great Migration of African-Americans from the South to the cities of the North. Jazz spread around the world, and the Harlem Renaissance took American art and literature in new, non-white directions. Hollywood blossomed and became a potent exporter of American culture. A great number of Americans imagined that the country could retreat from the world's cares and quarrels after the war, but ultimately that was not possible, as December 7, 1941, was to show.

The British Army seized Baghdad and then Mosul from the Ottoman Turks in March 1917, and the world is still living with some of the consequences of those imperial victories. The war inserted the British and the French into the Middle East, setting the stage for the violent and fanatical conflicts of today. But Britain and France could not maintain their empires, wracked as they were by the First World War and its sequel. So the United States took upon itself the responsibility of maintaining Western influence in the region. Zionism, of course, did not die in 1917, as the Cincinnati rabbi predicted, and thirty years later the state of Israel was born.

Two million Americans, many of whom had never seen a big city until they were drafted into the Army, came home from Europe when the war was over. The country they returned to was about to undergo a giddy upheaval—a loosening of morals, a shortening of hemlines, a fondness for drink (despite Prohibition) and a predilection toward violent organized crime (because of Prohibition). The war made America more urban, more modern, more devoted to pleasure, licit and illicit. And Americans had the means to pursue it. George Creel remarked later that the U.S. government had created what was in effect the world's largest advertising agency to sell the war, and the lessons learned then still shape aspects of marketing today. The American of the 1910s is a remote figure, living a different life from ours. The American of the 1920s is recognizably one of *us*.

THE COURSE OF Russian history, for the next century and beyond, flows as well from March 1917. The end of the old regime, the haplessness of the liberals who tried to assert their vision of a modern country on a chaotic and disintegrating empire, and the rise of the Petrograd Soviet all point to March as the seminal moment. Russia was to have a violent future; suspicion was to be its approach to all concerns. In March, Russians turned the destructive force of the First World War in upon themselves. This was when the peculiarly Russian trauma took hold. The Bolshevik coup in November, establishing Soviet rule, was only a confirmation—a consummation, in Trotsky's view—of the changes wrought eight months earlier. The example of March taught the Soviets that nothing was more dangerous to those in authority than spontaneous action from below. It wouldn't, they vowed, happen again. They and their successors in the Kremlin made the repression of civil action a foundation of the state. Russian power and Russian weakness have roots from centuries back, but both carry the mark of 1917 even today.

JEANNETTE RANKIN SERVED in Congress until 1919 and devoted the rest of her life to the cause of peace. She thought consistency required it. In 1940 she made a comeback and won a second term in the House. On December 8, 1941, she was the only member of either chamber to vote against war with Japan. She had to hide in a Capitol phone booth afterward. She never regretted either vote, she said.

She moved to a dirt-floor house in Georgia, kept up her love for cars, always made sure to dress well, and in later years wore an ash-

blond wig. In 1968, at the age of 87, she led a march of several thousand women on Washington to protest the war in Vietnam. They
called themselves the Jeannette Rankin Brigade.

"We've done all the damage we can possibly do in Vietnam," she
told the *New York Times*. "You can't settle disputes by shooting nice
young men."

But by that time Wilson's crusading spirit had become deeply
woven into the American fabric. Americans had told themselves,
with considerable justification, that it was their entry that tipped the
balance against the Germans in 1918, and that it was that victory that
led to the principle of self-determination and the creation of new
nation-states in Central and Eastern Europe, as well as the Middle
East, out of the wreckage of empires. Americans had felt for the first
time since 1812 that a foreign power had threatened the nation, that
there were malevolent actors across the sea who wished harm upon
the United States—and World War I gave rise to the idea that it was
better to fight the enemy abroad than wait for him to attack at home.
The lesson of 1917 seemed to be that America had an obligation to set
things right beyond its borders, and a noble responsibility to defend
democratic values wherever they were threatened. That Americans
tended to ignore this lesson during the distracting years of the Great
Depression, and so found themselves thrust into the Second World
War, served only, it seemed, to underscore its importance, and con-
firm its essential truth for all the decades to follow. Indeed, after the
disillusionment and cynicism of the 1920s and 1930s, World War
II restored some of the idealistic shine to American memories of
the First World War, however misguided. Every war since then—in
Korea, Vietnam, the Persian Gulf, Iraq and Afghanistan—has been
shaped and justified and exalted by Wilsonian arguments that arose
in 1917. They won't die.

ACKNOWLEDGMENTS

Francis McLaughlin, twenty-one, of the 15th Ward of Philadelphia, registered for the draft on June 8, 1917. He was of medium height and slender build, with brown eyes and dark hair. He had a job making artillery shells at the Baldwin Locomotive Works, near where he was living on Francis Street—work he had undoubtedly secured through his father, Patrick, an Irish immigrant who had been a blacksmith at Baldwin for decades. The munitions job didn't exempt him from the draft, and by 1918 both he and his older brother James were in uniform, and Francis was on the Western Front.

Their sister Isabella was my grandmother. I don't know much more about James or Francis than that, because while my great-grandfather Patrick didn't object to his two sons joining a war effort that allied their country with the detested English, he would not stand for the marriage his daughter made with a Swedish Protestant. She was cut out of the family. The wounds of the Irish were fresh and their ferocity was deep a century ago.

A German gas attack seared Francis's lungs, and I always heard growing up that he had come back to Philadelphia to die. Yet a census taker in 1930 found him alive, if not well, living with several of his siblings, unmarried, working not in a factory job but as a clerk in the Philadelphia tax collector's office. In the column marked "veteran" were the letters "ww," for World War. I don't know what became of him after that.

So here let me acknowledge Francis McLaughlin and James and the two million other men and women, so many nearly forgotten now, who did their duty as they saw it and propelled the United States into the forefront of the century to follow, sometimes at great cost to themselves. The lives of Americans today were shaped to no small degree by what they accomplished.

THE IDEA FOR this book evolved considerably over quite a few years, in fits and starts—more of the former than the latter. I am grateful to the editors of the *Baltimore Sun* for sending my wife Kathy and me to Moscow as correspondents, not once but twice, and to the editors of the *Washington Post* for sending us yet again. At *National Journal*, editors Charlie Green and Steve Gettinger enabled me to learn something about the ways of Washington and about presidential history as I covered the White House for two and a half formative years, at the end of George W. Bush's last term and the beginning of Barack Obama's first.

Yelena Ilingina helped me understand a Russian way of thinking, in her sharp-witted and indefatigable way. When we were working together and she saw me holding back from a foreigner's uncertainty, she pushed forward. She despaired of my floundering in the Russians' beautiful language, but she never gave up on me. Together we traveled far and wide. The late Dmitri Likhachev told me what it was like growing up in St. Petersburg and then surviving in Leningrad. Natasha Abbakumova encouraged me no end on this project and was a sure source of Russian perspective. Volodya Alexandrov helped enormously with logistics. A steady guide to Russian reality was the eccentric and marvelous Andrei Mironov, who until he was killed in the fighting in Ukraine in 2014 was the indispensable friend. One of the Soviet Union's last political prisoners, he had a keen sense of history and of farce. He was honest and ever unafraid.

SO MUCH IS available online now that we hardly remark on it anymore, but it's worth tipping the hat to a few sites in particular. Chronicling America, a joint project of the Library of Congress and the National Endowment for the Humanities, has digitized many dozens of newspaper archives, from 1836 to 1922, in searchable form. Eleven million pages are available. HathiTrust and Internet Archive have posted millions of books now in the public domain, also searchable. Of particular use to me as well were the diary of Edward House, posted online by the Yale University Library, and the Josephus Daniels diary, online courtesy of the University of North Carolina.

Still, live librarians are hard to beat. I found welcome assistance at Princeton University, at New York's Schomburg Center for Research in Black Culture, at the West Palm Beach Public Library, and in the manuscript room of the Library of Congress—an institution that always makes me feel a little more patriotic every time I visit. The staff at the National Archives II in College Park, Maryland, guided me cheerfully through State Department records even though I had failed to give them adequate notice of my visit. I want to thank especially Wendy Chmielewski of the Swarthmore College Peace Collection, Elizabeth Shortt of the Woodrow Wilson Presidential Library in Staunton, Virginia, and Vince Fitzpatrick, who made it possible for me to consult the original copy of H. L. Mencken's Berlin diary at the Enoch Pratt Free Library in Baltimore.

The archivists of the Montana Historical Society, in Helena, were unflagging and creative in their assistance. Anita Huslin, a former *Post* reporter, and Larry Abramson, onetime NPR correspondent who is now dean of the journalism school at the University of Montana, graciously put me up in their mountainside home when I visited Missoula, Jeannette Rankin's hometown. I had a fruitful conversation with Betsy Mulligan-Dague, executive director of the Jeannette Rankin Peace Center in Missoula, and an eye-opening visit to the Butte Labor History Center. James Lopach and Jean Luckowski kindly shared with me their thoughts about Rankin's motivations.

EARLY ON, ANDREW Stuart patiently taught me something about the book trade. Steve Luxenberg offered research advice, Robert Ruby reminded me to focus on the main thing, David Brown asked flatteringly detailed questions, and Scott Shane gave me the benefit of his authorial experience. Stephen Hunter gave me a tutorial on vintage guns. Brian Thomas, of Collegeville, Pennsylvania, was generous with his time. Dianne Donovan was always willing to lend me an ear and on more than one occasion gently talked me out of pursuing an unworkable approach. She knows books, and she knows writing, and she was constant in her support. Linda Cullen, Colleen Jordan, Brian Murphy, Michael Kimball, and Anna Fifield reassured me when I needed it. My agent, Gail Ross, is the sort of no-nonsense person every writer needs. John Glusman, my editor at W. W. Norton, grasped the idea of the book instantly, and kept me—sometimes sternly, but always smartly—on course. His assistants, Alexa Pugh and Lydia Brents, dealt with my many first-timer questions with patience and aplomb. The copyediting, by Fred Wiemer, was exacting, precise, and impressive, and saved me from more embarrassing mistakes than I care to admit.

Molly Englund, my daughter, helped me more than she knows with her interest, insights, and encouragement. Her sister Kate has an especially keen eye for the visual, which is no surprise for someone who works at Getty Images. Kate's husband, the photographer David Rothenberg, offered trenchant advice as well, and he sparked my interest in early twentieth-century Berlin, where his family lived. (At least one of his forebears also fought in the war, on the German side.)

Who helped the most? Well of course it was Kathy Lally, my wife and partner in journalism for decades. She knew when I was ready to write and pushed me to do it; she kept me out of the deep weeds of research (railroad statistics from 1916 come to mind); she endured my thoughtful (I hope) silences at the dinner table. I told her that if she caught me wearing a stiff detachable collar, she'd know I'd dived in too far. That, fortunately, never happened. She read every word I wrote and made astonishingly clear suggestions for improving the manuscript. I owe her.

NOTES

CHAPTER I. "GO! GO! GO!"

4 **"My only profession in New York"**: Leon Trotsky, *My Life: An Attempt at Autobiography* (New York: Charles Scribner's Sons, 1930), 272.

4 **"I left a Europe wallowing"**: Ibid., 273.

5 **Total U.S. exports**: *Statistical Abstract of the United States 1917* (Washington: U.S. Government Printing Office, 1918), 353.

5 **A war psychosis**: Roman Rosen, "Forty Years of a Diplomat's Life, Part 40," *Saturday Evening Post*, Feb. 26, 1921, 30.

6 **"this madness of multiform energy"**: Sinclair Lewis, *The Job* (New York: Harper & Brothers, 1917).

7 **Nine-year-old Seryozha**: Trotsky, *My Life*, 278.

9 **"The Commissioner grabbed his hat and coat"**: "Perkins Asks Rich to Halt Food Waste," *New York American*, March 4, 1917.

10 **"our local pitching Croesus"**: "Phillies Leave for Heat Belt," *Philadelphia Evening Ledger*, March 6, 1917.

10 **women's section of the Queens County Jail**: "Mrs. Sanger Flays Miss Davis's Plans," *New York Times*, March 7, 1917.

11 **"the self-bamboozled Presbyterian"**: H. L. Mencken, *Prejudices: Second Series* (New York: Alfred A. Knopf, 1920), 102.

12 **"I don't think it too much to say"**: "Negro Composer on Race's Music," *New York Tribune*, Nov. 22, 1914.

15 **"I grew up knowing"**: Interview with Malca Chall, Aug. 17, 1972; Regional Oral History Office, Bancroft Library, University of California, Berkeley.

15 **Her first-quarter marks:** *Record Book of Examinations: Grammar Department*, 52–53, Fort Missoula History Museum.

15 **"Go! Go! Go!":** Joan Hoff Wilson, "Jeannette Rankin and American Foreign Policy: The Origins of her Pacifism," *Montana the Magazine of Western History*, Winter 1980, 31. Rankin's youthful diaries have apparently been lost or are in private hands. In her 1972 interview she said she couldn't remember writing this.

15 **From New York she embarked:** Lisetta Noukom, "Our First Congresswoman Is Dainty Bit of Femininity," *Los Angeles Sunday Times*, Nov. 26, 1916.

15 **"She neither begged for support":** "Suffrage Bill Gains Support," *Helena Independent*, Feb. 2, 1911.

17 **"Doesn't it make you feel dizzy":** Atwater to Rankin, Nov. 11, 1916, Jeannette Rankin Papers, MC 147, Box 2, Folder 11, Montana Historical Society Research Center, Archives.

17 **"might classify her as a freak":** Warder to Rankin, Nov. 16, 1916, Rankin Papers.

17 **"Of course I am excited":** Rankin to Mrs. S. H. Souders, Feb. 24, 1917, Rankin Papers.

18 **"Her white chiffon dress fluttered":** "Jeannette Rankin Cheered by 3,000 for Speech Here," *New York Tribune*, March 3, 1917.

19 **She once told a friend:** James Lopach and Jean Luckowski, *Jeannette Rankin: A Political Woman* (Boulder: University Press of Colorado, 2005), 49.

20 **"She was dressed in distinctly feminine style":** "The Human Miss Rankin," *Daily Gate City and Constitution-Democrat*, March 23, 1917.

20 **"must be won by hitting":** "Roosevelt Wants US to Send Army," *New York Times*, March 2, 1917.

20 **"The entire pacifist movement in this country":** Theodore Roosevelt to John Price Jones, Feb. 27, 1917, Theodore Roosevelt Papers, Manuscript Division, Library of Congress, Washington, D.C.

20 **"I don't even know if she's a pacifist":** Marguerite Mooers Marshall, "First Congresswoman in U.S. Is Good Cook and Knows How to Make Own Clothes; Won't Commit Herself on War Question," *New York Evening World*, Feb. 26, 1917.

21 **"wickedly false":** Joseph Bucklin Bishop, *Theodore Roosevelt and His Time Shown in His Own Letters* (New York: Charles Scribner's Sons, 1920), 2:417.

21 **"earned for this nation":** "Seize German Ships, Colonel's Advice," *New York Times*, Feb. 1, 1917.

21 **"helpless spoil of any alien":** Ibid.

22 **"A *New York Times* reporter":** "Connecticut's Military Census Stimulates Others," *New York Times*, March 18, 1917.

23 **"Great events are ahead of us":** Jules Jusserand to Roosevelt, Feb. 23, 1917, Papers of Theodore Roosevelt.

23 **"I am sick at heart":** Roosevelt to Robert Ferguson, Feb. 27, 1917, Papers of Theodore Roosevelt.

CHAPTER 2. "A CRIME AGAINST CIVILIZATION"

24 **"I cannot express to you"**: As quoted in Alexander L. George and Juliette L. George, *Woodrow Wilson and Colonel House* (New York: J. Day Co., 1956), 25.

24 **"love [was] always law"**: Stockton Axson, "A Sketch of the President's Private Life," *New York Times*, Oct. 8, 1916.

26 **"We sat there and we couldn't believe it"**: Chall interview with Rankin, 80.

26 **In 1914, 4,883 were exported**: *Yearbook of the Department of Agriculture*, 1917, 721.

27 **Exports of condensed milk**: Ibid., 768–769.

27 **American railroads employed 285,000:**, "Railway Trainmen's Earnings—1916," *Railway Review*, March 17, 1917, 383–384.

27 **Between 1915 and 1916**: http://www2.census.gov/library/publications/1960/compendia/ hist_stats_colonial-1957/hist_stats_colonial-1957-chQ.pdf.

27 **Orders for new locomotives**: "Locomotives," *Railway Review*, Jan. 6, 1917, 41.

27 **The Baltimore & Ohio Railroad**: "New Curtis Bay Coal Pier of the Baltimore & Ohio R.R., at Baltimore," *Railway Review*, March 27, 1917, 409.

27 **In early 1917 the French government**: "Locomotives," *Railway Review*, 43–44.

27 **Besides locomotives, Baldwin**: "More Shells Turned Out," *Wall Street Journal*, March 31, 1917.

27 **American wire companies**: "U.S. Government Placing Steel Product Orders," *Wall Street Journal*, March 20, 1917.

31 **German propagandists**: Marguerite Harrison, *There's Always Tomorrow* (New York: Farrar & Rinehart, 1935), 82.

31 **"The more one observes their method"**: H. L. Mencken, "'The Diary of a Retreat': Americans Near Panic," *Baltimore Sun*, March 12, 1917.

31 **"She is wholly delightful"**: Wilson to Mrs. Edward Elliott, Sept. 26, 1915, Woodrow Wilson Collection, Department of Rare Books and Special Collections, Princeton University Libraries.

31 **"splendid, fearless eyes"**: Edith Bolling Wilson, *My Memoir* (Indianapolis and New York: Bobbs-Merrill Co., 1938–1939), 60.

31 **On November 22, House complained**: George and George, *Woodrow Wilson and Colonel House*, 184.

31 **"starving for the bread"**: Edith B. Wilson, *My Memoir*, 58.

32 **"and found many things in common"**: Ibid.

33 **"that he had been more and more"**: Lansing Memorandum, Feb. 4, 1917, Robert Lansing Papers, Public Policy Papers, Department of Rare Books and Special Collections, Princeton University Libraries.

34 **Spring Rice, who once screamed**: "Memorandum of an interview with the British Ambassador," Jan. 18, 1917, Robert Lansing Papers.

34 **the shipment of gold bullion**: Page to Lansing, March 9, 1917, State Department Records, M580/118, National Archive II, College Park, Md.

34 **"France and England must have"**: Page to Lansing and Wilson, March 5, 1917, State Department Records, M580/118, National Archive II.

34 **The British, for their part**: Diary of Edward Mandell House, Jan. 2, 1917, Edward Mandell House Papers, Manuscripts and Archives, Yale University Library.

34 **"thinks he is for peace"**: Ibid.

34 **"as usual it was late"**: Ibid., Jan. 3, 1917.

36 **"a vacuum"**: Ibid., Jan. 4, 1917.

36 **"Strangely enough, the train"**: Ibid., Jan. 11, 1917.

36 **"the president at last seems"**: Ibid., Jan. 12, 1917.

37 **"jaunty, carefree, man of the world"**: Lansing Memorandum, Feb. 4, 1917.

37 **"I told him we were not afraid"**: House diary, Jan. 30, 1917.

37 **she read it aloud to him**: Edith B. Wilson, 127.

38 **House told Wiseman**: Wiseman to Balfour, Jan. 26, 1917, Arthur Link, ed., *The Papers of Woodrow Wilson* (Princeton University Press, 1983), 41:26–27.

38 **"brave and timely appeal"**: "The President to the Powers," *The Commoner* (Lincoln, Nebr.), Feb. 1917, 7.

38 **"If Germany really wants peace"**: Wilson to House, Jan. 24, 1917, *The Papers of Woodrow Wilson*, 41:3.

38 **Then the British sent word**: House to Wilson, Jan. 25, 1917, *The Papers of Woodrow Wilson*, 41:17.

CHAPTER 3. "RICH EARTH, ROTTING LEAVES"

40 **"Gossip and bitterness"**: Princess Cantacuzène, *My Life Here and There* (New York: Charles Scribner's Sons, 1921), 226.

40 **"Amusing, interesting"**: Ibid., 169.

41 **"I recall suddenly being waked"**: Ibid., 11.

44 **Rosen called "insane"**: Roman Rosen, "Forty Years of a Diplomat's Life, Part 37," *Saturday Evening Post*, Oct. 30, 1920, 138.

44 **It was twelve years earlier**: This account draws heavily on Baron Rosen, *Forty Years of Diplomacy* (New York: Alfred A. Knopf, 1922), 253–273.

47 **"The hammer has been wrung"**: Roman Rosen, "Forty Years of a Diplomat's Life, Part 40," *Saturday Evening Post*, Feb. 26, 1921, 22.

49 **"the same as one would see"**: Dmitry S. Likhachev, *Reflections on the Russian Soul* (Budapest: Central European University Press, 2000), 25.

49 **"all sorts of snug, mellow things"**: Vladimir Nabokov, *Speak, Memory* (New York: Vintage International, 1989), 79.

49 **"respectable lady"**: Likhachev, *Reflections on the Russian Soul*, 25.

50 **"Tens of thousands of horses"**: Ibid., 27.

50 **"would fly onto the stage"**: Ibid., 14.

51 **"which makes a Russian's nostrils dilate"**: Nabokov, *Speak, Memory*, 43.

51 **"Through the window"**: Ibid., 80.

52 **"rather appalling country"**: Ibid., 116.

52 **"who, she knew, thoroughly appreciated"**: Ibid., 155.

53 the **"sausage"**: Likhachev, *Reflections on the Russian Soul*, 22.

53 **In 1916 the war was costing Russia**: E. N. Burdzhalov, *Russia's Second Revolution*, trans. Donald J. Raleigh (Bloomington: Indiana University Press, 1987), 71.

54 **compared Russia to a car careening**: Ibid., 43.

54 **Was this stupidity**: Ibid., 57.

54 **"A revolutionary mood existed"**: Ibid., 70.

54 **"Russia was not so much war-weary"**: Robert Wilton, *Russia's Agony* (New York: E. P. Dutton & Co., 1919), 61.

CHAPTER 4. "YOU FELLOWS ARE IN FOR IT"

56 **had published nothing about the European**: Thomas Quinn Curtiss, *The Smart Set: George Jean Nathan and H. L. Mencken* (New York: Applause Books, 1998), 116.

56 **"Dull, dismal stuff"**: H. L. Mencken, "Berlin 1917 Diary" (unpublished manuscript), Feb. 2, 1917, Enoch Pratt Free Library, Baltimore.

56 **"both stolen goods"**: H. L. Mencken, "Reminiscence," *Baltimore Evening Sun*, June 21, 1937.

57 **"tired, rheumatic and half-frozen"**: Mencken diary, Feb. 1, 1917.

58 **Lansing had passed on to Wilson**: State Department Records, M367/31, National Archives II.

59 **The ambassador told House**: House to Wilson, Jan. 26, 1917, *The Papers of Woodrow Wilson*, 41:24–26.

59 **"If submarine warfare"**: Bernstorff to Zimmermann, Jan. 27, 1917, *The Papers of Woodrow Wilson*, 41:52.

59 **"There is no doubt"**: Gerard to Lansing, Jan. 31, 1917, State Department Records, M567/141, National Archive II.

60 **"The President was sad and depressed"**: House diary, Feb. 1, 1917.

60 **"I am not so sure of that"**: Lansing Memorandum, Feb. 4, 1917.

60 **"The cold here is intense"**: Mencken diary, Feb. 1, 1917.

60 **"frozen and cheerless"**: Ibid., Feb. 2, 1917.

61 **"the usual crowds"**: "Henry Mencken Cables Story of 'Ticklish Moments' in Berlin," *Baltimore Sun*, March 6, 1917.

61 **"Berlin, once so spick and span"**: Mencken diary, Feb. 10, 1917.

61 **the muffled rhythm of railway trains**: Walter Benjamin, *Berlin Childhood Around 1900* (Cambridge, Mass.: Belknap Press, 2006), 39.

61 **"Your gaze ran first to flagstones"**: Ibid., 70–71.

61 **Berlin was a city of brass bands:** Ibid., 117 and 83.

62 **"through which the water":** Ibid., 106.

62 **Food was strictly rationed:** Josephine Therese [pseud.], *With Old Glory in Berlin* (Boston: Page Company, 1918), 92–110.

62 **"The new Germany":** Mencken diary, Feb. 26, 1917.

62 **A young music student from Boston:** Therese, *With Old Glory in Berlin*, 61.

62 **"The end will be thorough-going":** Mencken diary, Feb. 26, 1917.

63 **"A packed house and gales of laughter":** Mencken diary, Feb. 2, 1917.

63 **"The public indeed":** "Henry Mencken Cables Story of 'Ticklish Moments' in Berlin."

63 **You never saw anyone flying a flag:** Therese, *With Old Glory in Berlin*, 78.

63 **"Our front is secure":** on all sides Mencken diary, Feb. 1, 1917.

63 **"Where the newspapers led":** "Henry Mencken Cables Story of 'Ticklish Moments' in Berlin."

64 **"Maybe the United States":** Mencken diary, Feb. 1, 1917.

64 **"beery somnolence":** Ibid., Feb. 4, 1917.

65 **"This new submarine war":** Ibid., Feb. 1, 1917.

66 **"Well, there is but one thing":** Ibid., Feb. 8, 1917.

66 **"The trouble with this new:** Ibid., Feb. 1, 1917.

66 **"You can easily imagine":** Ibid., Feb. 4, 1917.

67 **"The strange calm of the Germans":** Ibid., Feb. 6.

67 **"One can well imagine the eruption":** Ibid., Feb. 3, 1917.

67 **"The papers get a lot of fun":** Ibid., Feb. 7, 1917.

67 **"American Idealism":** Ibid., Feb. 2, 1917.

67 **"Dollar Politics":** Ibid., Feb. 6, 1917.

67 **"The partiality of Mr. Wilson":** Ibid.

67 **Roosevelt later argued:** Roosevelt to A. L. Key, March 5, 1917, Theodore Roosevelt Papers.

68 **"made a considerable show of agitation":** Mencken diary, Feb. 4, 1917.

68 **"You fellows are in for it":** "Henry Mencken Cables Story of 'Ticklish Moments' in Berlin."

69 **"He is a very rich man":** Mencken diary, Feb. 4, 1917.

69 **"I wouldn't know a military secret":** Ibid., Feb. 7, 1917.

69 **"literary gent":** Ibid., Feb. 6, 1917.

70 **"At Würzburg, we went gunning":** Ibid., Feb. 11, 1917.

70 **"A capital dinner of *Schweinsrippen*":** Ibid.

CHAPTER 5. "WE HAVE HAD TO PUSH, AND PUSH, AND PUSH"

71 **Launched in 1890:** Rodney Carlisle, "The Attacks on U.S. Shipping that Precipitated American Entry into World War I," *Northern Mariner* (Ottawa), July 2007, 43–44.

72 **(He later told reporters):** "Captain Says U-53 Sank Housatonic," *New York Times*, Feb. 21, 1917.

73 **On February 12, an old-fashioned:** Carlisle, "The Attacks on U.S. Shipping," 49–53.

74 **McDonough said he proudly refused:** "Lyman Law's Skipper Wished for 5-Pounder," *New York Times*, Feb. 19, 1917.

74 **"He is yellow all through":** Roosevelt to Lodge, Feb. 20, 1917, Theodore Roosevelt Papers.

74 **"There is no excitement":** Tarbell to House, Feb. 8, 1917, Woodrow Wilson Papers, the Library of Congress.

74 **In New York, the steamships:** "Railway Congestion," *Railway Review*, Feb. 17, 1917, 240.

75 **"as easily as buttering":** "Lyman Law's Skipper Wished for 5-Pounder."

76 **"It is awful to be obliged":** Lodge to Roosevelt, March 2, Theodore Roosevelt Papers.

76 **"Confidential for the President":** Page to Lansing and Wilson, Feb. 24, State Department Records, M336/55, National Archives II.

78 **"Germany will try to foment":** "Plots in Mexico Seen," *Washington Post*, Feb. 5, 1917.

79 **the *Providence Journal* reported:** "German Blow from Mexico," *New York Times*, Feb. 9, 1917.

79 **"Information has been received here":** "See German Activity in Cuba and Mexico," *New York Times*, Feb. 19, 1917.

80 **"The President said the country":** *The Letters of Franklin K. Lane*, ed. Anne Wintermute Lane and Louise Herrick Wall (Boston and New York: Houghton Mifflin Co., 1922) 239–241.

81 **"We must defend our commerce":** Address to a joint session of Congress, Feb. 26, 1917, *Journal of the Senate of the United States of America* (Washington: U.S. Government Printing Office, 1917), 194–195.

81 **In Paris, Georges Clemenceau:** Frazier to House, February 16, 1917, Woodrow Wilson Papers, Library of Congress.

82 **"to postpone aggressive action":** Robert La Follette to Belle La Follette, March 5, 1917, La Follette Family Papers, Manuscript Division, Library of Congress.

82 **"an unhung traitor":** Roosevelt to Lodge, Feb. 20, Theodore Roosevelt Papers.

82 **"This country is on the verge":** "A Serious Business in Prospect," *Baltimore Sun*, March 1, 1917.

82 **"Men of all shades of political opinion":** "Staggered by Intrigue," *Baltimore Sun*, March 2, 1917.

83 **"which he does not seem eager":** Jean Jules Jusserand to Aristide Briand, March 3, 1917, *The Papers of Woodrow Wilson*, 41:316.

83 **"This, I think, is a great thing":** Lodge to Roosevelt, March 2, 1917, Theodore Roosevelt Papers.

CHAPTER 6. "PEOPLE THINK IT WILL BE VERY BLOODY"

85 **"We were like the chosen people":** Florence MacLeod Harper, *Runaway Russia* (New York: Century Co., 1918), 10.

86 "bought lavishly": Ibid., 16.

86 "bed-clothes, traveling rugs": Ibid., 19.

87 "The courier was, naturally, taken out": James L. Houghteling, Jr., *A Diary of the Russian Revolution* (New York: Dodd, Mead & Co., 1918), 3.

87 "The crispness of the air": Ibid.

87 "But what an untidy town!": Ibid., 4.

88 "a disappointing two-story affair": Ibid., 5.

88 "Some people here think": Ibid., 10.

89 "I never heard better rag-time": Ibid., 12.

89 "and the faultless dome of St. Isaac's": Ibid., 20.

90 "There is no doubt that a revolution": Ibid, 18.

90 "Nobody knew what was going to happen": Harper, *Runaway Russia*, 21.

90 "I do not know why": Ibid., 24.

90 "Russian administration of the law": Houghteling, 22.

91 "The throne": Ibid., 19.

91 "with the rough raging sea": Burdzhalov, *Russia's Second Revolution*, 98.

91 "one ought to save oneself": Ibid.

91 "a joy": Houghteling, 25.

92 "It was a wonderful and inspiring display": Ibid., 28.

92 "The Russian business community": Ibid., 29.

93 "tawdry cabaret theater": Ibid., 30.

93 "It was a magnificent night": Ibid., 54–55.

93 "I have never seen a sweeter face": Ibid., 59–60.

94 "It is a place to gladden the heart": Ibid., 44.

94 "People are beginning to rebel": Ibid., 52.

94 "unworldly and kaleidoscopic idealism": Ibid., 47–48.

95 "Why do you people of America": "Russia Is Menace to Europe's Peace, Open Forum Told," *St. Paul Dispatch*, March 4, 1917.

96 The *New Republic* warned: "If Germany Ruled the Sea," *Washington Post*, March 15, 1917.

96 "We could never allow the mob": Mikhail Tereshchenko, oral interview, June 7, 1917, in Semion Lyandres, *The Fall of Tsarism* (Oxford: Oxford University Press, 2013), 252.

96 "We hear there has been": Houghteling, 61.

CHAPTER 7. "A TWILIGHT ZONE"

98 "a twilight zone": "Staggered by Intrigue," *Baltimore Sun*, March 2, 1917.

99 The arming of ships: *La Follette's Magazine*, March 29, 1917, as reprinted in the *Congressional Record*, April 11, 1917.

99 **"Please accept my congratulations"**: This and the letters that follow are all in the La Follette Family Papers.

101 **"Germany expected and wished"**: "Zimmermann Defends Act," *New York Times*, March 4, 1917.

101 **"the little group of willful men"**: *The European War* (New York: New York Times, 1917) 11:52.

102 **"The Army and Navy Forever!"**: *Chicago Journal*, March 6, 1917.

102 **"to try to thwart the will"**: This and the letters that follow are in the La Follette Family Papers.

103 **"senators who refused to surrender"**: "The Right Way for the President to Proceed Is to Protect the Rights of Congress and the Privileges of the People," *Chicago American*, March 6, 1917.

103 **"Fought it through to the finish"**: Robert to Belle La Follette, March 5, La Follette Family Papers.

103 **"Traitor!"**: "Filibusterers Rouse Anger of the Nation," *Philadelphia Evening Ledger*, March 6, 1917.

103 **"it is a melancholy business"**: Lodge to Roosevelt, March 6, 1917, Theodore Roosevelt Papers.

104 **"but I feel infinitely more keenly"**: Roosevelt to J. C. O'Laughlin, March 8, 1917, Theodore Roosevelt Papers.

104 **"I think Germany has made"**: Roosevelt to Henry White, March 7, 1917, Theodore Roosevelt Papers.

105 **"We must deal, as best we can"**: Lenroot to Roosevelt, March 12, 1917, Theodore Roosevelt Papers.

106 **"In my opinion for us to arm"**: Extension of remarks of Hon. John M. Nelson, *Congressional Record*, April 11, 1917, 3.

107 **"Washington is not enlivened"**: "Await Inaugural in Solemn Mood," *New York Times*, March 4, 1917.

107 **"mad as a hornet"**: Diary of Thomas W. Brahany, March 4, 1917, National Archives and Records Service, Franklin D. Roosevelt Library, Hyde Park, N.Y.

107 **"I never like to be conspicuously"**: House diary, March 4, 1917.

108 **"It is now 12 o'clock"**: Edith B. Wilson, *My Memoir*, 130.

108 **"Pardon me"**: "50,000 See Inauguration," *New York Times*, March 6, 1917.

108 **"We are provincials no longer"**: Inaugural address, March 5, 1917.

110 **"You can, Mr. President"**: Louis Gregory to Wilson, Jan. 15, 1917, Race and Segregation, Woodrow Wilson Presidential Library, Staunton, Va.

110 **"Your stand for righteousness"**: James Shepherd to Wilson, Jan. 23, 1917, Race and Segregation, Woodrow Wilson Presidential Library, Staunton, Va.

111 **"There were no demonstrations"**: "50,000 See Inauguration."

111 **"It was the plainest, simplest"**: Ibid.

111   **"I had difficulty getting something"**: House diary, March 5, 1917.

112   **"it was rather a solemn time"**: Diary of Josephus Daniels, March 5, 1917, Josephus Daniels Papers, Southern Historical Collection, Wilson Library, University of North Carolina at Chapel Hill.

112   **"The President and Mrs. Wilson"**: House diary, March 5, 1917.

113   **"I prefer to make my first speech"**: *Baltimore Sun*, March 5, 1917.

CHAPTER 8. "NO, SIR, BOSS"

114   **"shooting and slightly wounding"**: "Officer Wounded by Negro Woman, Lynching Follows," *New Orleans Times-Picayune*, March 1, 1917.

114   **Lynchings fell sharply in 1917**: "Lynchings: By Year and Race," http://law2.umkc.edu/faculty/projects/ftrials/shipp/lynchingyear.html, retrieved Dec. 11, 2015.

115   **a young black man named Linton Clinton**: "Out of Chain Gang; Lynched," *Baltimore Sun*, March 2, 1917.

115   **"as a precaution against further trouble"**: "Negro Killed Fighting Posse," *New Orleans Times-Picayune*, March 18, 1917.

115   **"a black man named Joe Rout"**: "Joe Rout Caught by a Posse Near Scene of Murder," *New Orleans Times-Picayune*, March 26, 1917.

116   **On March 16, in Brookhaven, Mississippi**: "Man with Negroes Held in Brookhaven," *New Orleans Times-Picayune*, March 17, 1917.

116   **"The migration to the North"**: "Negroes' Side of Migration," *Christian Science Monitor*, May 12, 1917.

117   **"On the evening of March 7"**: "Negro Shot Dead While Attempting to Escape Arrest," *Palm Beach Post*, March 8, 1917.

118   **When he put together a Negro orchestra**: David Mannes, *Music Is My Faith* (New York: W. W. Norton & Co., 1938), 218.

118   **(He was once turned away)**: Lawrence T. Carter, *Eubie Blake: Keys of Memory* (Detroit: Balamp Publishing, 1979), 75.

119   **It boasted in a large ad**: "The Great Royal Poinciana Hotel," advertisement in the *Palm Beach Post*, March 17, 1917.

119   **A men's clothing store**: Palm Beach Post, March 3, 1917.

119   **a grand Washington's Birthday fete**: "4,000 at Birthday Fete in Palm Beach," *New York Times*, Feb. 23, 1917.

120   *The Isle of Tomorrow*: "At the Movies," *Palm Beach Post*, March 13, 1917.

120   **"The Turkish grenade"**: Rev. W. J. Carpenter, "Blinded Hero of Dardanelles Lectures on Meaning of War," *Palm Beach Post*, March 9, 1917.

120   **"until a late hour"**: "Social Notes," *Palm Beach Post*, March 19, 1917.

120   **"have been a hardship"**: Irene Castle McLaughlin, "Jim Europe—A Reminiscence," *Opportunity*, March, 1935, p. 90.

121 **"To my mind"**: Love to Noble Sissle, Jan. 28, 1920, James Reese Europe collection, Schomburg Center for Research in Black Culture, New York Public Library.

121 **"the cry of their soul's harmony"**: Noble Sissle, "Jim Europe—A Memoir" (unpublished manuscript), 27, James Reese Europe collection.

121 **"We have our own racial feeling"**: Grenville Vernon, "That Mysterious 'Jazz,'" *New York Tribune*, March 30, 1919.

121 **"reproduce the rhythm and expression"**: Sissle, "Jim Europe—A Memoir," 27.

121 **"viscerally stimulating"**: Gunther Schuller, *Early Jazz: Its Roots and Musical Development* (New York: Oxford University Press, 1968), 248.

122 **"It will build up the moral"**: Sissle, "Jim Europe—A Memoir," 36.

124 **"The four musicians of Razz's band"**: "That Mysterious 'Jazz.'"

124 **Freddie Keppard's Creole Band**: Schuller, *Early Jazz*, 250.

124 **"Blues Is Jazz and Jazz Is Blues"**: *Chicago Daily Tribune*, July 11, 1915.

124 **"embroider" their music**: "That Mysterious 'Jazz.'"

125 **Al Rose, fewer than half a dozen**: Al Rose, *Storyville, New Orleans: Being an Authentic Account of the Notorious Red-Light District* (Tuscaloosa: University of Alabama Press, 1974), 84.

CHAPTER 9. "A PLEASANT AIR OF VERISIMILITUDE"

126 **"miserably small and unattractive"**: H. L. Mencken, "Berlin 1917 Diary," Feb. 13, 1917.

128 **"but as for me"**: Ibid., Feb. 15, 1917.

128 **"The German papers"**: Ibid., Feb. 12, 1917.

128 **"The French, like the Germans"**: Ibid., Feb. 15, 1917.

128 **"It would be idle to deny"**: Frazier to House, Feb. 16, 1917, Woodrow Wilson Papers, Library of Congress.

129 **"Once the United States"**: Mencken diary, March 2, 1917.

129 **"By the time we fugitives"**: H. L. Mencken, "'The Diary of a Retreat'; Headed for Sunny Spain," *Baltimore Sun*, March 19, 1917. The word "fugitives" was added when the *Sun* published excerpts of Mencken's diary.

129 **"clear blue sky"**: Mencken to Ernest Boyd, Feb. 19, 1917, from Carl Bode, ed., *The New Mencken Letters* (New York: Dial Press, 1977), 70.

129 **"loafing around"**: Mencken diary, Feb. 17, 1917.

129 **"They are against the 'sharpened'"**: Ibid., Feb. 18, 1917.

130 **The Dutch ambassador complained**: House to Wilson, Feb. 10, 1917, Woodrow Wilson papers, Library of Congress.

130 **The Dutch had Germans**: Langhorne to Lansing, Feb. 4, 1917, State Department Records, M367/31, National Archives II.

130 **"the special atrocity squad"**: H. L. Mencken, "'The Diary of a Retreat'; Steaming Toward Home," *Baltimore Sun*, March 21, 1917. The sentence about doing the same

sort of propaganda work was added when the *Sun* published excerpts of Mencken's diary.

130 **"The number 13 bemuses me"**: Mencken to Boyd, Feb. 19, 1917, *The New Mencken Letters*.

131 **"The ship is copiously scented"**: Mencken diary, Feb. 21, 1917.

131 **"a hallway used by the stewards"**: Ibid., Feb. 24, 1917.

131 **"It goes without saying"**: Ibid., Feb. 23, 1917.

131 **"The chill of Northern Europe"**: Ibid., Feb. 24, 1917.

131 **"Warmer and smoother"**: H. L. Mencken, "'The Diary of a Retreat' Brought to a Conclusion," *Baltimore Sun*, March 22, 1917. The phrase "a lamentable business" to describe the sinking of the *Laconia* was added when the *Sun* published this excerpt.

132 **"The captain himself"**: H. L. Mencken, *Heathen Days* (New York: Alfred A. Knopf, 1975), 164.

132 **The rooms in the hotel**: Albert James Norton, *Norton's Complete Handbook of Havana and Cuba* (Chicago and New York: Rand, McNally & Co., 1900), 167.

134 **most of the U.S. Atlantic Fleet**: "Bulk of Our Fleet Is in West Indies," *New York Times*, Feb. 3, 1917.

135 **advice from British intelligence**: House to Wilson, Feb. 13, Woodrow Wilson papers, Library of Congress.

135 **"no small concern"**: "Lansing Warns Cuba on Revolt," *New York Times*, Feb. 13, 1917.

136 **"fair sized cannon"**: "Call Volunteers to Quell Revolt in Interior Cuba," *New York Times*, Feb. 14, 1917.

136 **"the greatest apprehension"**: "Wilson Will Uphold Integrity of Cuba," *New York Times*, Feb. 15, 1917.

137 **"Can Cuba afford"**: Raoul E. Desvernine, "Cuba's Future," *New York Times*, Feb. 21, 1917.

137 **"In Cuba, the fact that a man"**: "Wilson Will Uphold Integrity of Cuba."

137 **"was being answered by many"**: "Watching Cuba Closely," *New York Times*, Feb. 17, 1917.

138 **He could be counted on**: "Menocal and Gomez," *New York Times*, Feb. 23, 1917.

138 **"Dance of the Millions"**: Claudia Lightfoot, *Havana: A Cultural and Literary Companion*, (Brooklyn, N.Y., and Northampton, Mass.: Interlink Book, 2002), 42.

138 **"Sugar, tobacco, copper"**: "Cuban Rebels Want American Intervention," *New York Times*, Feb. 25, 1917.

138 **"At the start there was undoubtedly"**: H. L. Mencken, "Intervention Issue in Cuba," *Baltimore Sun*, March 12, 1917.

139 **"to give my dispatches a pleasant air"**: Mencken, *Heathen Days*, 171.

139 **"in terms almost applicable"**: H. L. Mencken, "Blow Dealt Cuban Rebels," *Baltimore Sun*, March 13, 1917.

140 **"to radically crush the outbreak"**: Menocal to Wilson, March 5, 1917, Woodrow Wilson papers, Library of Congress.

140 **"I observed two things especially"**: Mencken, *Heathen Days*, 174.

CHAPTER 10. "WE ARE SITTING ON A VOLCANO"

141 **The night before her appearance:** "Dinner to Miss Jeannette Rankin," *New York Times*, Feb. 28, 1917.

141 **Rankin was wary of Catt:** Joan Hoff Wilson, "Jeannette Rankin and American Foreign Policy: The Origins of her Pacifism," *Montana the Magazine of Western History*, Winter 1980, 33.

142 **"The greatest power in the world":** Ibid.

142 **Carpenters in the shipyards:** American Federation of Labor Records, Manuscript Division, Library of Congress.

144 **"we are sitting on a volcano":** House diary, Feb. 24, 1917.

144 **The trustees of Columbia University:** *Philadelphia Evening Ledger*, "Student Pacifism Alarms Columbia Faculty," March 6, 1917.

144 **"We need good Americanism here":** "Pupils Strike When Called on to Honor Flag," *New York Tribune*, March 8, 1917.

144 **to Roosevelt, that the school mentioned:** A. B. Poland to Calvin Kendall, March 17, 1917, Theodore Roosevelt Papers.

145 **Etta Gibson, the mother:** *Baltimore Sun*, "Another Won't Salute," March 10, 1917.

147 **In Des Moines, she impressed:** "A Woman Congressman," undated, Woman's Peace Party Records, Swarthmore College Peace Collection.

147 **"brutal useless":** Wilson, "Jeannette Rankin and American Foreign Policy," 37.

147 **I judged the sentiment in Montana:** "Our Busy 'Congresswoman,'" *Literary Digest*, Aug. 11, 1917, 43.

148 **that law was violated 544,000 times:** Samuel Gompers to Fred Fuillet, Feb. 3, 1917, AFL Records.

148 **Finally the unions announced:** "Brotherhoods Declare Supreme Court's Delay Will Be Overt Act," *Railway Review*, March 3, 1917, 287.

149 **"The serious international situation":** "The Threatened Strike," *Railway Review*, March 17, 1917, 376.

149 **"There is nothing now in our laws":** Untitled, *Railway Review*, March 10, 1917, 336.

149 **"It is greatly to be hoped":** Untitled, *Railway Review*, March 24, 1917, 428.

150 **the "ringleader":** "Freight Strike May Grow," *New York Times*, March 10, 1917.

150 **TREASON:** *New York Evening World*, March 14, 1917.

151 **He had learned through back channels:** William Wilson to Tumulty, March 15, 1917, *The Woodrow Wilson Papers*, 41:412.

151 **"I believe that I am honestly a friend":** Willard to Gompers, March 15, 1917, AFL Records.

152 **"They are not blessed with constructive":** Gompers to Fuillet, Feb. 3, 1917, AFL Records.

152 **"preserve order and protect all property":** Hill to Stewart, March 16, 1917, Montana Governors' Papers, Box 17, Folder 2, Montana Historical Society Research Center, Archives.

152 **"shrewder and more astute power":** "Hand of Germany Seen in Decision to Force Strike," *New Orleans Times-Picayune*, March 17, 1917.

152 "I am afraid there will be": Tumulty to Wilson, March 16, 1917, *The Woodrow Wilson Papers*, 41:414.

152 Wilson told him he didn't see: Brahany diary, March 17, 1917.

152 "an immediate accommodation": Wilson to the National Conference Committee of the Railways, March 16, 1917, *The Woodrow Wilson Papers*, 41:414.

153 An Associated Press reporter: Brahany diary, March 19, 1917.

153 "Merciless": Carlisle, "The Attacks on U.S. Shipping," 56.

153 "I am sick at heart": Roosevelt to William Haggard, March 14, 1917, Theodore Roosevelt Papers.

153 "Railroad Strike Called": *New York Tribune*, March 16, 1917.

CHAPTER 11. "COSSACKS, RIDING UP AND DOWN"

155 There were about fifty of them: Harper, *Runaway Russia*, 25.

155 Women had been standing in breadlines: David R. Francis, *Russia from the American Embassy* (New York: Charles Scribner's Sons, 1921), 56.

155 About one-third of the women of Petrograd: Jane McDermid and Anna Hillyar, *Midwives of the Revolution* (Athens: Ohio University Press, 1999), 128–129.

156 they were among the 322,000 soldiers: Burdzhalov, 85.

156 "Keep moving!": Petr Gerasimov, oral interview, May 9, 1917, in Lyandres, 90.

157 "Down with hunger!": Burdzhalov, 107.

157 An army captain, Alexander Chikolini: Aleksandr Chikolini, oral interview, May 5, 1917, in Lyandres, 72.

157 Estimates by the police: Burdzhalov, 113.

157 That evening, radical Bolsheviks gathered: Ibid., 119.

157 Across the Neva, a dinner: Francis, 58.

158 "I was sure they meant business": Harper, *Runaway Russia*, 28.

158 "We slid and slipped and ran": Ibid., 29.

158 By Saturday morning, 300,000 workers: Burdzhalov, 126.

158 "Young Russia is on the march!": Burdzhalov, 126.

159 "Down with the autocracy!": Burdzhalov, 127.

159 The president of the Duma: Mikhail Rodzianko, oral interview, May 16, 1917, in Lyandres, 108.

159 "I felt such calm and peace": Burdzhalov, 147.

160 "The dead were thick": Harper, *Runaway Russia*, 38.

161 "The situation is serious": *The Russian Provisional Government 1917: Documents*, ed. Robert Paul Browder and Alexander F. Kerensky (Stanford, Calif.: Stanford University Press, 1961), 1:40.

162 A Russian journalist spoke with soldiers: Burdzhalov, 166.

162 the Bolshevik Vasily Schmidt: Ibid., 169.

162 **"I knew instinctively that the revolution":** Houghteling, 63.

163 **"halfway between the lines":** Ibid., 68.

163 **"masses of accumulated blackmail":** Ibid., 76.

163 **"watching the flaming spectacle":** Ibid., 71.

164 **"They marched in perfect order":** Ibid., 72.

164 **"Civil war has started":** Browder and Kerensky, 1:42.

164 **"on a still day":** Francis, 83.

165 **"We could not agree to that":** Burdzhalov, 201.

165 **He was immediately named:** Gerasimov interview, in Lyandres, 91.

165 **"But we did not figure that out":** Nikolai Nekrasov, oral interview, May 25, 1917, in Lyandres, 148–149.

165 **"With the Duma":** Houghteling, 74.

166 **"Today begins the long-needed":** Ibid., 76.

166 **The U.S. ambassador:** Francis, 62.

166 **This was the first revolution:** Burdzhalov, 223.

167 **"If only we had one":** Sergei Mstislavskii, *Five Days Which Transformed Russia* (Bloomington and Indianapolis: Indiana University Press, 1988), 31.

167 **"It seemed rather decent":** Houghteling, 80.

167 **"It is absolutely clear to me":** Matvei Skobelev, oral interview, May 29, 1917, in Lyandres, 188.

168 **"Long live the revolution! *Ura!*":** Leon Trotsky, *History of the Russian Revolution*, trans. Max Eastman (New York: Simon & Schuster, 1936), 138.

168 **"one of the Allied sovereigns":** Roman Rosen, "Forty Years of a Diplomat's Life, Part 38," *Saturday Evening Post*, Nov. 20, 1920, 18.

170 **"They were still dazed":** Ibid., 108.

171 **Shulgin was mortified:** Burdzhalov, 295.

171 **"This pitiful excuse for a czar":** Ibid., 297.

CHAPTER 12. "HAPPIER DAYS FOR ALL HUMANITY"

172 **"lovers of freedom":** "Russia the Democratic," *The Outlook*, March 28, 1917, 542.

173 **"It has been very hard":** "Revolt May Make Sloane Pro-Ally," *New York Times*, March 19, 1917.

174 **"all the mysticism and melancholy":** Marguerite Harrison, "Symphony a Triumph," *Baltimore Sun*, Dec. 9, 1916.

174 **"Its weird harmonies":** Marguerite Harrison, "New York Symphony," *Baltimore Sun*, Feb. 8, 1917.

175 **"The concert closed":** Marguerite Harrison, "Paderewski in Recital," *Baltimore Sun*, Jan. 19, 1917.

175 **"intensely nationalistic":** Marguerite Harrison, "Boston Symphony Orchestra," *Baltimore Sun*, Feb. 15, 1917.

175 **"a ploy to seize Danzig"**: House diary, Jan. 6, 1917.

176 **"I again expressed the opinion"**: House diary, Jan. 12, 1917.

176 **"One of the interesting things"**: House diary, Jan. 15, 1917.

176 **"It is not realized that Russia"**: Sir William Wiseman to Sir Cecil Arthur Spring Rice, March 6, 1917, *The Woodrow Wilson Papers*, 41:347.

177 **"I think this country should aid"**: House to Wilson, March 17, 1917, Woodrow Wilson papers, the Library of Congress.

178 **"It would encourage and strengthen"**: Lansing to Wilson, March 19, 1917, Robert Lansing Papers.

178 **"What an hour would be that"**: "12,000 Cheer for Hard-Hitting War," *New York Times*, March 23, 1917.

178 **"We ask our American friends"**: "Root Predicts Fall of Central Rulers," *New York Times*, March 26, 1917.

179 **"I believe if you were to go"**: Pou to Roosevelt, April 2, 1917, Theodore Roosevelt Papers.

179 **"The Russian front is the proper place"**: Symmes to Roosevelt, April 7, 1917, Theodore Roosevelt Papers.

180 **"I should like to say very emphatically"**: "Czar's Abdication Was Talked of Months Ago," *New York Times*, March 18, 1917.

180 **"This, the most significant political change"**: "Hapgood Writes of Russia—A Land Come Into Its Own," *Baltimore Sun*, March 25, 1917.

181 **"the complete triumph of democracy"**: George Kennan, "The Victory of the Russian People," *The Outlook*, March 28, 1917, 546–547.

181 **"The Jews and the Poles"**: "Russia, the Democratic," *The Outlook*, March 28, 1917, 542.

181 **"shouted themselves hoarse"**: "10,000 Jews Here Laud Revolution," *New York Times*, March 21, 1917.

181 **"fettered and tortured"**: "Jewish People Rejoicing Over the New Russia," *Christian Science Monitor*, March 23, 1917.

182 **"magnificent uprising"**: "Jews in Favor of Allies, Says Oscar Straus," *Christian Science Monitor*, March 31, 1917.

182 **the revolution would mean the end**: "Sees Zionism's End in Russian Revolt," *New York Times*, April 5, 1917.

182 **"The Russian revolution has opened"**: Wilson to Rosenwald, March 28, 1917, Woodrow Wilson papers, the Library of Congress.

182 **"It was freely asserted"**: Robert Lansing, "The Conduct of American Foreign Affairs, 1915–1920," Pt. 2, Chap. 7, 137 (unpublished and undated manuscript), Robert Lansing Papers.

183 **"This is a middle class revolution"**: John Reed, "Russia," *The Masses*, May, 1917, 6.

183 **"with renewed confidence and vigor"**: "The Russian Revolution," *The Outlook*, March 28, 1917, 545.

183 **"That there will be some friction"**: Kennan, "The Victory of the Russian People."

184 **"to create conditions"**: Samuel Harper to Richard Crane, telegram, March 16, 1917, Woodrow Wilson Papers, Library of Congress.

184 **"In normal times revolution in Russia"**: "Revolution in Russia," *Springfield Republican*, March 16, 1917.

184 **"It is much too soon for confidence"**: "Russia and Peace," *Springfield Republican*, March 18, 1917.

185 **"Petrograd you know more about"**: Moreton Frewen to Roosevelt, March 22, 1917, Theodore Roosevelt Papers.

185 **"men who would be more sure"**: "Calls People War Weary," *New York Times*, March 16, 1917.

CHAPTER 13. "NOTHING TO LOSE BUT THEIR MISERABLE LIVES"

187 **"If they crush me today"**: C. P. Connolly, "The Fight for the Minnie Healy," *McClure's Magazine*, July 1907, 331.

188 **"98% slave and but 2% free"**: Carrie Wallace to Rankin, April 3, 1917, Jeannette Rankin Papers, MC 147, Box 10, Folder 1.

188 **"The applicants are lined up outside"**: John Doran to Rankin, July 3, 1917, Jeannette Rankin Papers, MC 147, Box 1, Folder 8.

189 **A Rankin ally in Butte**: Mrs. H. N. Kennedy to Rankin, June 23, 1917, Jeannette Rankin Papers, MC 147, Box 1, Folder 8.

189 **He was five feet four, truculent**: Harold Livesay, *Samuel Gompers and Organized Labor in America* (Boston: Little, Brown & Co., 1978), 11, 92.

190 **"There is an immediate critical problem"**: Gompers to Executive Council, Feb. 28, 1917, AFL Records.

191 **"I do not want to see the yoke"**: Woodson to Gompers, Feb. 10, 1917, AFL Records.

191 **"We cannot conceive"**: McGovern to Gompers, March 15, 1917, AFL Records.

191 **"slaughter caused primarily"**: Arthur Meyer to Gompers, March 19, 1917, AFL Records.

192 **"no confidence whatsoever"**: Marsden Scott to Gompers, March 28, 1917, AFL Records.

192 **"Working men have NEVER profited"**: E. J. Buchet to Gompers, March 13, 1917, AFL Records.

192 **"our great President Woodrow Wilson"**: W.A. Goode to Gompers, March 29, 1917, AFL Records.

192 **"raise, in a time of madness"**: Albert Gough to Gompers, March 9, 1917, AFL Records.

192 **"Some three hundred members"**: W. S. Morrow to Rankin, March 3, 1917, Jeannette Rankin Papers, MC 147, Box 10, Folder 1.

193 **"preserve us from the fierce waste"**: R. T. Cookingham to Rankin, April 2, 1917, Jeannette Rankin Papers, MC 147, Box 10, Folder 1.

193 **A group of engineers**: Alpra L. Longley to Rankin, March 30, 1917, Jeannette Rankin Papers, MC 147, Box 10, Folder 1.

193   **Harvey Coit, a rancher:** Coit to Rankin, Feb. 3, 1917, Jeannette Rankin Papers, MC 147, Box 10, Folder 1.

193   **"Remember, we have gone astray":** Cameron to J. H. Price, in Evelyn J. Cameron diary, 1917, MC 226, Box 6, Folder 5, Montana Historical Society Research Center, Archives.

194   *Read XXXVII Psalm:* from the King James Version of the Bible:

Fret not thyself because of evildoers, neither be thou envious against the workers of iniquity.

2 For they shall soon be cut down like the grass, and wither as the green herb.

3 Trust in the Lord, and do good; so shalt thou dwell in the land, and verily thou shalt be fed.

4 Delight thyself also in the Lord: and he shall give thee the desires of thine heart.

5 Commit thy way unto the Lord; trust also in him; and he shall bring it to pass.

6 And he shall bring forth thy righteousness as the light, and thy judgment as the noonday.

7 Rest in the Lord, and wait patiently for him: fret not thyself because of him who prospereth in his way, because of the man who bringeth wicked devices to pass.

8 Cease from anger, and forsake wrath: fret not thyself in any wise to do evil.

9 For evildoers shall be cut off: but those that wait upon the Lord, they shall inherit the earth.

10 For yet a little while, and the wicked shall not be: yea, thou shalt diligently consider his place, and it shall not be.

11 But the meek shall inherit the earth; and shall delight themselves in the abundance of peace.

12 The wicked plotteth against the just, and gnasheth upon him with his teeth.

13 The Lord shall laugh at him: for he seeth that his day is coming.

14 The wicked have drawn out the sword, and have bent their bow, to cast down the poor and needy, and to slay such as be of upright conversation.

15 Their sword shall enter into their own heart, and their bows shall be broken.

16 A little that a righteous man hath is better than the riches of many wicked.

17 For the arms of the wicked shall be broken: but the Lord upholdeth the righteous.

18 The Lord knoweth the days of the upright: and their inheritance shall be for ever.

19 They shall not be ashamed in the evil time: and in the days of famine they shall be satisfied.

20 But the wicked shall perish, and the enemies of the Lord shall be as the fat of lambs: they shall consume; into smoke shall they consume away.

21 The wicked borroweth, and payeth not again: but the righteous sheweth mercy, and giveth.

22 For such as be blessed of him shall inherit the earth; and they that be cursed of him shall be cut off.

23 The steps of a good man are ordered by the Lord: and he delighteth in his way.

24 Though he fall, he shall not be utterly cast down: for the Lord upholdeth him with his hand.

25 I have been young, and now am old; yet have I not seen the righteous forsaken, nor his seed begging bread.

26 He is ever merciful, and lendeth; and his seed is blessed.

27 Depart from evil, and do good; and dwell for evermore.

28 For the Lord loveth judgment, and forsaketh not his saints; they are preserved for ever: but the seed of the wicked shall be cut off.

29 The righteous shall inherit the land, and dwell therein for ever.

30 The mouth of the righteous speaketh wisdom, and his tongue talketh of judgment.

31 The law of his God is in his heart; none of his steps shall slide.

32 The wicked watcheth the righteous, and seeketh to slay him.

33 The Lord will not leave him in his hand, nor condemn him when he is judged.

34 Wait on the Lord, and keep his way, and he shall exalt thee to inherit the land: when the wicked are cut off, thou shalt see it.

35 I have seen the wicked in great power, and spreading himself like a green bay tree.

36 Yet he passed away, and, lo, he was not: yea, I sought him, but he could not be found.

37 Mark the perfect man, and behold the upright: for the end of that man is peace.

38 But the transgressors shall be destroyed together: the end of the wicked shall be cut off.

39 But the salvation of the righteous is of the Lord: he is their strength in the time of trouble.

40 And the Lord shall help them, and deliver them: he shall deliver them from the wicked, and save them, because they trust in him.

194 **sent his old Springfield rifle:** W. Jobes to Roosevelt, Feb. 19, 1917, Theodore Roosevelt Papers.

194 **"The West has been slower than the East":** "Trained Regiments of Volunteers to Be Ready in West," *New York Tribune*, Feb. 28, 1917.

195   "hearty cooperation": "To Raise Army Through West," *Farmington* (Missouri) *Times*, March 30, 1917

195   "one of the best known old time cowpunchers": "Arizonians to Be in Division Roughriders," *Arizona Republican*, April 9, 1917.

196   "Dear Comrade": Butte Local No. 1 to Rankin, April 1, 1917, Jeannette Rankin Papers, MC 147, Box 10, Folder 8.

196   "the horrible European war": J. W. Gillette to Rankin, March 31, 1917, Jeannette Rankin Papers, MC 147, Box 10, Folder 1.

196   "modern war serves to enrich": John Mattson to Rankin, March 21, 1917, Jeannette Rankin Papers, MC 147, Box 10, Folder 1.

197   "I earnestly appreciate your attitude": Rankin to J. W. Hamblock, March 10, 1917, Jeannette Rankin Papers, MC 147, Box 10, Folder 1.

197   "I feel sure we are all anxious": Rankin to James L. Kirby, March 26, 1917, Jeannette Rankin Papers, MC 147, Box 10, Folder 1.

CHAPTER 14. "THE GREAT LIBERAL LEADER OF THE WORLD"

198   "The President has had a bad cold": Brahany diary, March 17, 1917.

198   Lord Nelson, of Trafalgar fame: Edith B. Wilson, 131.

198   "Dammit, he makes me tired": Ibid., March 29, 1917.

199   "It is my belief": Lansing to Wilson, March 17, 1917, Woodrow Wilson Papers, Library of Congress.

199   St. Patrick's Society of Brooklyn: "Patriotism Holds Sway at Dinner of St. Patrick Society," *Brooklyn Daily Eagle*, March 18, 1917.

199   the Irish Party: "America First to Recognize the New Russia," *New York Times*, March 25, 1917.

200   "Look at those faces": "Railway Strike Order Held Up 48 Hours," *Philadelphia Evening Ledger*, March 17, 1917.

200   The deposed Nicholas II: "Ex-Czar Owns $50,000,000 Here," *Philadelphia Evening Ledger*, March 19, 1917.

201   "was good enough to say": House diary, March 17, 1917.

201   House, who once said: Ibid., March 9, 1917.

201   "I have been fearful": House diary, March 17.

202   The twenty-five-year-old ship: Carlisle, "The Attacks on U.S. Shipping," *Northern Mariner*, July 2007, 57.

202   At 10 a.m. the officer of the watch: "Submarine Trailed Vigilancia's Boats," *New York Times*, April 2, 1917.

205   "It is simply war": Lodge to Roosevelt, March 19, 1917, Theodore Roosevelt Papers.

205   "did not seem to be greatly perturbed": Brahany diary, March 19, 1917.

205   Wilson, ever thrifty: Ibid., March 25, 1917.

205 **U-boat attacks hadn't changed:** Lansing to Wilson, March 19, 1917, *The Woodrow Wilson Papers*, 41:425.

205 **"that the sooner we openly admitted":** Memorandum by Robert Lansing, March 20, 1917, Robert Lansing Papers.

205 **"If you agree with me":** Lansing to House, March 19, 1917, *The Woodrow Wilson Papers*, 41:429–430.

206 **"He still hoped to avoid it":** Daniels diary, March 19, 1917.

206 **"I firmly believe that war will come":** Lansing to Wilson, March 19, 1917, Robert Lansing Papers.

209 **"indignation and bitterness":** Memorandum by Robert Lansing, March 20, 1917.

210 **"that the revolution in Russia":** Lansing Memorandum, March 20, 1917.

210 **a quick-tempered, domineering and stingy man:** Brahany diary, March 9, 1917.

210 **"so that those Prussians will realize":** Lansing Memorandum, March 20, 1917.

210 **the United States would be forced:** Daniels diary, March 20, 1917.

210 **"I could almost feel":** Lansing Memorandum, March 20, 1917.

211 **"I do not care for popular demand":** Daniels diary, March 20, 1917.

211 **"Well, gentlemen":** Lansing Memorandum, March 20, 1917.

211 **First, though, he went to see:** Brahany diary, March 20, 1917.

211 **As the president sat in the dark:** "Attractions at the Washington Theaters," *Washington Post*, March 20, 1917.

CHAPTER 15. "IT MIGHT BE ALL RIGHT FOR YOU TO HAVE YOUR LITTLE POCKET GUN"

212 **"That's the stuff":** "Colonel at Flower Show: Urges Preparedness, Drinks Tea, and Has His Picture Taken," *New York Times*, March 21, 1917.

213 **"words are wasted upon Germany":** "War Call Sounded by Col. Roosevelt," *New York Times*, March 20, 1917.

213 **"No man can go into the wilderness":** "Present Medal to Roosevelt; Colonel Tells Geographical Society This Is No Country for Pacifists," *New York Times*, March 21, 1917.

214 **"This city is not half awake":** "Would Strike at Once," *New York Times*, March 21, 1917.

216 **"fatuous cry of 'Stand by the President'":** Lodge to Roosevelt, March 20, 1917, Theodore Roosevelt Papers.

217 **"It is not our war":** "Whose War?" *The Masses*, April 1917, 11.

217 **"our opportunity in the establishment":** Grace Abbott and Fred A. Moore to Woodrow Wilson, undated, Emergency Anti-War Committee (Chicago, Illinois) Collected Records, Peace Collection, Swarthmore College Library.

218 **the Congress of Forums:** Edward F. Sanderson to Roosevelt, Feb. 21, 1917, Theodore Roosevelt Papers.

218   **"I cannot accept your proposal"**: "Roosevelt Scorns Debate with Bryan," *New York Times*, March 5, 1917.

218   **"America's hesitation to go to war"**: "Dr. Grant Challenges Col. Roosevelt's View," *New York Times*, March 25, 1917.

219   **"The favored class"**: "Wall Denounces War Dog Menace," *Quincy (Illinois) Daily Journal*, March 6, 1917.

219   **on March 9, the full house erupted**: Louis Lochner to LaFollette, March 10, 1917, LaFollette Family Papers.

219   **"it called forth a storm of applause"**: C. S. Eckert to LaFollette, March 12, 1917, LaFollette Family Papers.

219   **the Emergency Anti-War Committee**: Emergency Anti-War Committee (Chicago, Illinois) Collected Records, Peace Collection, Swarthmore College Library.

219   **"The alternative to war"**: "A Message from the Religious Society of Friends (Quakers) in America," *Baltimore Sun*, March 20, 1917.

220   **"frank opinion"**: David Starr Jordan to Roosevelt, March 21, 1917, Theodore Roosevelt Papers.

220   **"The action you now propose"**: Roosevelt to Jordan, March 23, 1917, Theodore Roosevelt Papers.

221   **"I think I satisfied them"**: House diary, March 25, 1917.

221   **"We should be asses"**: "Socialists Conservative," *New York Times*, March 5, 1917.

222   **"I have tried to look at this"**: Amos Pinchot, "For 'A Strongly Defensive Policy'" *New York Evening Post*, March 27, 1917.

223   **plea from Franklin Roosevelt's law partner**: Langdon Marvin to Theodore Roosevelt, March 19, 1917, Theodore Roosevelt Papers.

223   **"I am going away"**: "Roosevelt to Hunt Florida Devilfish," *New York Times*, March 24, 1917.

224   **car K-56**: Atlantic Coast Line Railroad Company confirmation, March 1, 1917, Theodore Roosevelt Papers.

224   **Measuring 18 feet 2 inches**: Theodore Roosevelt, "Harpooning Devilfish," *Scribner's*, Sept. 1917, 301.

224   **He had hired a crew**: Coles to Roosevelt, Feb. 22, 1917, Theodore Roosevelt Papers.

224   **Coles had laid in some Mexican hats**: Coles to Roosevelt, March 11, 1917, Theodore Roosevelt Papers.

225   **"most dangerous game"**: Coles to Roosevelt, March 7, 1917, Theodore Roosevelt Papers.

225   **"It might be all right"**: Coles to Roosevelt, Feb. 28, 1917, Theodore Roosevelt Papers.

226   **"I again earnestly ask permission"**: "Correspondence of Theodore Roosevelt and the Secretary of War," *Metropolitan*, August 1917, 23.

226   **"I would like to hear that tune"**: "Colonel Would Lead a Division in France," *New York Times*, March 25, 1917.

226   **Early the next morning**: Theodore Roosevelt, "Harpooning Devilfish," *Scribner's*, Sept. 1917, 296–305.

CHAPTER 16. "LIKE A RIVER AT FLOOD"

229 **"dirty and unwashed":** Nekrasov interview in Lyandres, 150.

229 **"By assuming the throne":** Burdzhalov, 303.

230 **A black snowstorm:** Houghteling, 113–119.

232 **"The meeting flows on":** Trotsky, *History of the Russian Revolution*, 158.

232 **"thin as a candle":** Mstislavskii, 74.

232 **"The members of the Provisional":** Ibid., 64.

234 **"a real factor":** Burdzhalov, 256.

234 **"the single worthy document":** Trotsky, *History of the Russian Revolution*, 276.

235 **"would prosecute the war fearlessly":** Francis, 88.

236 **Streetcar service resumed:** Houghteling, 162–164.

237 **"great test of strength":** Trotsky, *History of the Russian Revolution*, 239–241.

238 **"semi-contraband sovereignty":** Ibid., 144.

238 **"Movement, effort and strain":** Harold Williams, "War Council Runs Russia's Army," *New York Times*, March 28, 1917.

239 **"Lord, what a difference":** Helen Azar, *The Diary of Olga Romanov* (Yardley, Pa.: Westholme, 2014), 90.

240 **The soldiers left almost immediately:** This account is taken from Mstislavskii, 81–106.

CHAPTER 17. "TO SCOLD AN EARTHQUAKE"

243 **Polk, the State Department counselor:** House diary, March 22, 1917.

243 **(House thought it was a mistake):** House to Lansing, March 20, 1917, State Department Records, M367/31, National Archives II.

244 **"Apparently he is not":** Brahany diary, March 21, 1917.

244 **"President Wilson has decided to meet":** "Country's Call for War Before Congress April 2," *Philadelphia Evening Ledger*, March 24, 1917.

244 **"He thinks the president":** House diary, March 22, 1917.

245 **And how important it is:** Ibid., Jan. 6 and Feb. 1, 1917.

245 **"All history teaches us":** "12,000 Cheer for Hard-Hitting War," *New York Times*, March 23, 1917.

247 **The hall erupted in boos and hisses:** "Three Fights Mark Big Peace Meeting," *New York Times*, March 25, 1917.

249 **She had appearances in Indianapolis:** Lee Keedick to Rankin, March 22, 1917, Jeannette Rankin Papers, MC 147, Box 9, Folder 8.

249 **"Wages may be high":** "Congresswoman Is Silent as to War," *St. Paul Daily News*, March 31, 1917.

250 **"the most valuable work":** Harriet Thomas to Jane Addams, March 24, 1917, Woman's Peace Party Records, Swarthmore College Peace Collection, mf reel 113:10, Wilmington, DE: Scholarly Resources, Inc.

250 **"I never heard of anything so bumptious"**: "War Offer Causes War for the Suffs," *New York Sun*, Feb. 9, 1917.

250 **the time was ripe for Wilson**: Carrie Chapman Catt to Joseph Tumulty, Jan. 19, 1917. Carrie Chapman Catt Papers, Library of Congress.

251 **she thought it would be unacceptably hypocritical**: Letter to *Dallas Evening Journal*, June 4, 1917, Catt Papers.

251 **"Attention! Women of America!"**: National Service Schools collection, Woodrow Wilson Presidential Library, Staunton, Va.

251 **a member of the Women's Section**: "Uncle Sam's First Woman Navy Officer Proudly Happy," *Philadelphia Evening Ledger*, March 22, 1917.

252 **"I love peace"**: "Rose Pastor Stokes Quits the Pacifists," *New York Times*, March 18, 1917.

252 **"It was the vote of the women"**: Byron DeForest to Rankin, March 26, 1917, Jeannette Rankin Papers, MC 147, Box 10, Folder 1.

252 **In Missoula**: Gertrude Sloane to Rankin, April 2, 1917, Jeannette Rankin Papers, MC 147, Box 10, Folder 1.

252 **"Jeannette, dear, don't sell us out"**: Swinnerton to Rankin, April 2, 1917, Jeannette Rankin Papers, MC 147, Box 10, Folder 1.

253 **"In spite of the spectacular"**: Welles to Rankin, March 26, 1917, Jeannette Rankin Papers, MC 147, Box 10, Folder 1.

253 **"The women of Pennsylvania"**: Woods to Rankin, March 31, 1917, Jeannette Rankin Papers, MC 147, Box 10, Folder 1.

253 **"I am the mother of an only son"**: Wilson to Rankin, March 31, 1917, Jeannette Rankin Papers, MC 147, Box 10, Folder 1.

253 **"biggest contribution to the race"**: Sissle, "Jim Europe—A Memoir," 48–50.

254 **"Germany was sinking our boats"**: Ibid., 51.

254 **"I believe Germany is responsible"**: Du Bois to Moritz Schanz, Oct. 9, 1914, W. E. B. Du Bois Papers, Special Collections and University Archives, University of Massachusetts Amherst Libraries.

255 **"The negro has always been loyal"**: "Colored Folk Are Loyal, Says Leader," *Washington Post*, April 6, 1917.

255 **"In this great crisis"**: "Says Negroes Are Loyal," *New York Times*, April 6, 1917.

255 **"They are playing with fire!"**: "Loyalty," *The Crisis*, May 1917, 8.

255 **"So some day a black woman"**: "The World Last Month," *The Crisis*, May 1917, 8.

255 **"Grievances I have against this people"**: "Negro's Idea of Loyalty Called Rebuke to Whites," *Louisville Courier-Journal*, March 21, 1917.

256 **complaining that Negroes were barred**: J. W. Hudspeth to Roosevelt, March 9, 1917, Theodore Roosevelt Papers.

256 **"There is widespread apathy"**: Charles W. Anderson to Roosevelt, April 4, 1917, Theodore Roosevelt Papers.

256 **"and his administration of Negro baiters":** "Negro Loyalty in the Present Crisis," *New York Age*, March 29, 1917.

256 **Spingarn wrote a somewhat sheepish letter:** Joel Spingarn to Du Bois, Feb. 26, 1917, W. E. B. Du Bois Papers.

257 **"The ten million colored people":** "Tells Negroes to Wage a Bloodless War for Their Constitutional Rights," *New York Age*, March 29, 1917.

CHAPTER 18. "REEKED WITH PATRIOTISM"

259 **Detectives at the Frankford Police Station:** "See Plot to Paralyze Pennsylvania R.R.," *New York Times*, March 11, 1917.

261 **The state militia was assigned:** "Militia Assigned to Active Duty on River Front," *New Orleans Times-Picayune*, March 29, 1917.

261 **"to neither heed nor circulate":** "Proclamation," *New Orleans Times-Picayune*, March 30, 1917.

261 **A man in New Orleans:** "Flag Insulter Jailed," *New Orleans Times-Picayune*, March 28, 1917.

261 **arrested three Germans in Atlanta:** "Woman Arrested as Spy Suspect," *New Orleans Times-Picayune*, March 24, 1917.

261 **"hanging them from lampposts":** House diary, March 23, 1917.

261 **"Every red-blooded American man":** "Rally to Your Country's Help," advertisement in *New Orleans Times-Picayune*, March 24, 1917.

261 **"born again":** "Bishop Prophecies War," *Baltimore Sun*, March 3, 1917.

262 **"Under Military Regulations":** *New Orleans Times-Picayune*, March 9, 1917.

263 **"if the other players have a desire":** Robert Maxwell, "Bill Killefer, Sailing with Phils, Defies Nor'easter in Low Shoes; Then is Seasick Hugging Boiler," *Philadelphia Evening Ledger*, March 8, 1917.

263 **"the same social standing":** Robert Maxwell, "Paul Fittery, Salt Lake Rookie, Awarded 'P,' Standing for Pitcher, on Phillies' Squad," *Philadelphia Evening Ledger*, March 20, 1917.

264 **"an amusing burlesque":** "Perhaps Training in Military Tactics Will Assure Good Marching on Opening Day," *Philadelphia Evening Ledger*, March 24, 1917.

264 **"He was literally blown to pieces":** *Everyman at War*, ed. Charles Benjamin Purdom (London: J. M. Dent, 1930), 101, 105.

264 **"What chance was there":** Ibid., 121.

265 **"The whole of Europe":** H. L. Mencken diary, Feb. 16, 1917.

266 **"A month in the trenches":** "Tells of War's Horrors," *Baltimore Sun*, March 3, 1917.

266 **"With its gas bombs":** "G.A.R. Commander Calls Europe's War Wholesale Murder," *New Orleans Times-Picayune*, March 11, 1917.

266 **"We must have a stake":** Granville Fortescue, "Why America Must Fight if War Is Declared," *Washington Post*, March 18, 1917.

266 **"arrogance, self-esteem, pride"**: Joyce Kilmer, "How the War Changed a Vorticist Sculptor," *New York Times*, June 25, 1916.

266 **"I thought of all the gentle, kindly Germans"**: Marguerite Harrison, *There's Always Tomorrow* (New York: Farrar & Rinehart, 1935), 66.

267 **"the average man in the United States"**: Ibid., 84.

267 **"Much of the German stuff"**: Ibid., 82.

267 **"I began vaguely to grasp"**: Ibid., 91.

267 **"how appallingly unprepared"**: Ibid., 85.

268 *The Butcher Boy*: https://www.youtube.com/watch?v=OoAD8___Aq4.

269 **Lectures were distributed**: George Creel, *How We Advertised America* (New York: Harper & Brothers, 1920), 84–98.

270 **"we know where to festoon them"**: "Gerard Warns Public War Will Be Serious," *Baltimore Sun*, March 31, 1917.

270 **he realized he'd never find a publisher**: Mencken to Joseph Hergesheimer, March 1917, in *The New Mencken Letters*, ed. Carl Bode (New York: Dial Press, 1977), 71.

270 **"He has reached out for the wires"**: H. L. Mencken, "Ludendorff," *The Atlantic*, June 1917.

270 **"an international expert in morals"**: H. L. Mencken, *A Book of Prefaces*, 3rd ed. (New York: Alfred A. Knopf, 1920), 198.

271 **"Puritanism has become bellicose"**: Ibid., 233.

271 **"American became a sort of braggart"**: Ibid., 236–237.

272 **"But it would be a very evil thing"**: Roosevelt to Wilfred Osgood, Feb. 23, 1917, Theodore Roosevelt Papers.

272 **He protested "emphatically"**: Roosevelt to John Moffat, March 15, 1917, Theodore Roosevelt Papers.

272 **"Do the small duties"**: "Inscription by Colonel Roosevelt," March 10, 1917, Theodore Roosevelt Papers.

CHAPTER 19. "A MENDING OF THEIR TROUBLES"

273 **British authorities took them**: "Russian Radical Detained," *New York Times*, April 11, 1917.

274 **They had seized the commanding admiral**: Harper, *Runaway Russia*, 198–204.

275 **"The responsibilities of office"**: Houghteling, 180.

275 **Residents of apartment houses**: Ibid., 172–173.

276 **Julia Speransky-Grant**: Princess Cantacuzène, *Russian People: Revolutionary Recollections* (New York: Charles Scribner's Sons, 1920), 164.

276 **"When the revolution came"**: Ibid., 317.

277 **"Kolchak's sailors were too"**: Ibid., 234.

277 **"In Bouromka the people"**: Ibid., 61.

278 **"There is a committee"**: Mark D. Steinberg, *Voices of Revolution, 1917* (New Haven, Conn.: Yale University Press, 2001), 138.

278 **"Remaining alive meant"**: Cantacuzène, *Russian People*, 113.

279 **"Please do not decide"**: Pauline S. Crosley, *Intimate Letters from Petrograd* (New York: E. P. Dutton & Co., 1920), 42.

279 **"those whose single aim"**: Ibid., 181–182.

279 **"This is certainly a peculiar people"**: Ibid., 221.

279 **"in an endless chain"**: "100,000 Siberian Exiles, Freed by Duma Government, Dashing Across the Snow to New Russia," *Washington Post*, April 4, 1917.

280 **"Aren't you singing the praises"**: Steinberg, 86–87.

280 **"The Russian Revolution will not allow"**: Skobelev interview in Lyandres, 195.

280 **"The free Russian people must not"**: Steinberg, 107.

281 **at least 1.5 million deserters**: Russian government estimates in the report of the Root Commission, Elihu Root Papers, Manuscript Division, Library of Congress.

281 **"the manifest unwillingness of the people"**: Rosen, "Forty Years of a Diplomat's Life, Part 38," *Saturday Evening Post*, Nov. 20, 1920, 110.

281 **Pacifism among the troops**: Skobelev interview in Lyandres, 204.

282 **"splitting all along its seams"**: Maxim Gorky, essay for *Novaya Zhizn*, July 12, 1917, in Untimely Thoughts (New York: Paul S. Eriksson, 1968), 67.

282 **"Our most merciless enemy"**: Gorky, essays for *Novaya Zhizn*, May 1–6, 1917, in Untimely Thoughts, 6–16.

283 **"So I surrendered my last hour"**: Houghteling, 194.

CHAPTER 20. "THE LID IS KEPT SCREWED DOWN"

284 **Come to Washington immediately**: This account is drawn from Elting Morrison, *Admiral Sims and the Modern American Navy* (New York: Houghton Mifflin Co., 1942), which in turn relied on "Hearings Before the Subcommittee of the Committee on Naval Affairs," United States Senate, 1920.

286 **"With the governments of England"**: "Suffragists in U.S. Buoyed by British Action," *Washington Times*, March 29, 1917.

287 **Eduard Bernstein, a prominent Socialist**: "Socialists Oppose Budget," *Baltimore Sun*, March 30, 1917.

287 **"Germany never had the slightest intention"**: "German Chancellor, Defending U-Boat War, Says That if U.S. Chooses to Enter Conflict German Nation 'Shall Also Overcome This,'" *Baltimore Sun*, March 30, 1917.

287 **"I declared expressly"**: "Defends Attempt to Win Carranza," *New York Times*, March 31, 1917.

288 **"We are watching with interest"**: James O'Donnell Bennett, "Germany Sees War Act by U.S. as 'Foregone Conclusion,'" *Chicago Tribune*, March 31, 1917.

288 "the influence of events in Russia": "Cry for Democracy Rising in Germany," *New York Times*, April 4, 1917.

290 "the president has reached": Brahany diary, March 31, 1917.

290 "If the people of this country": This and subsequent letters are from the La Follette Family Papers at the Library of Congress.

292 "If we have war": Daniels diary, March 10, 1917.

292 On April 1 he announced: "Pinchot Hopes Tax Will Prevent War," *New York Times*, April 2, 1917.

294 "My own mind has been forced": Wilson to Hitchcock, March 31, 1917, Woodrow Wilson Papers, the Library of Congress.

294 "If the president is writing": Brahany diary, March 31, 1917.

CHAPTER 21. "WHEN THE MAN-WORLD IS MAD FOR WAR"

296 "All in black": "House Welcomes Woman Member," *Philadelphia Evening Ledger*, April 2, 1917.

297 "The president is, I believe": "Miss Rankin Stands by the Republicans," *New York Times*, April 2, 1917.

297 "a stunning black satin": "House Welcomes Woman Member."

298 "There should be but one party": "House Elects Clark Again," *New York Times*, April 3, 1917.

299 "well fitted": House diary, March 27, 1917.

299 "Unless he changes his mind": Ibid., March 28, 1917.

300 "of a splendid Bengal tiger": Edith B. Wilson, 67.

301 "to meet all expectations": House diary, April 2, 1917.

302 "he was a damned liar": "Pacifist Is Beaten Following Attack on Veteran Solon," *Washington Times*, April 2, 1917.

302 "At my age": Lodge to Roosevelt, April 4, 1917, Theodore Roosevelt Papers.

302 "white and majestic": Edith B. Wilson, 132.

304 That line created no stir at first: "Must Exert All Our Power," *New York Times*, April 3, 1917.

304 "with his arms folded tight": Ibid.

305 "talked it over": House diary, April 2, 1917.

305 "with some difficulty": "Call for War Stirs All City," *New York Times*, April 3, 1917.

305 "You have done a great thing": McAdoo to Wilson, April 3, 1917, Woodrow Wilson Papers, Library of Congress.

306 "For having seen this": Lippmann to Wilson, April 3, 1917, Woodrow Wilson Papers, Library of Congress.

306 "Your message is not addressed": Nelson Page to Lansing, April 5, 1917, State Department Records, M367 /31, National Archives II.

306 **"Raymond Poincaré, the president":** Poincaré to Wilson, April 5, 1917, State Department Records, M367/31, National Archives II.

306 **An acquaintance in Chicago:** M. K. Northam to La Follette, April 5, 1917, La Follette Family Papers.

306 **"patriotic grounds":** Abbott to La Follette, April 4, 1917, La Follette Family Papers.

306 **"to show their loyalty and patriotism":** Hummer to La Follette, April 4, 1917, La Follette Family Papers.

307 **Catherine Smith:** This letter and those following are in the Jeannette Rankin Papers, Box 10, Folder 1, the Montana Historical Society Research Center, Archives.

308 **Rankin told them about the heavy pressure:** Amelia R. Fry, "Conversations with Alice Paul: Woman Suffrage and the Equal Rights Amendment," 1976, Bancroft Library, University of California/Berkeley, Regional Oral History Office.

308 **Wellington was urging her to vote:** Oral history interview of Jeannette Rankin by Hannah Josephson, 1973, Bancroft Library, University of California/Berkeley, Regional Oral History Office.

309 **"Miss Rankin was evidently":** "Seek to Explain Miss Rankin's 'No,'" *New York Times*, April 7, 1917.

CHAPTER 22. "HISTORY WILL COUNT YOU RIGHT"

311 **"I remember as if":** Harrison, *There's Always Tomorrow*, p. 85.

311 **"While I should have liked":** "Suffrage Leaders Pardon Miss Rankin," *New York Times*, April 7, 1917.

311 **"By the way, our Congress Lady":** Carrie Chapman Catt Papers, Library of Congress.

312 **"History will count you right":** Baldwin to Rankin, April 6, 1917, Jeannette Rankin Papers, MC 147, Box 3, Folder 8.

323 **"We've done all the damage":** Nadine Brozan, "Crusading Forerunner of Women's Lib," *New York Times*, Jan. 24, 1972.

BIBLIOGRAPHY

MANUSCRIPTS AND ARCHIVES

Addams, Jane, Papers, Swarthmore College Peace Collection.

American Federation of Labor Records, Manuscript Division, Library of Congress.

Brahany, Thomas W., Diary, National Archives and Records Service, Franklin D. Roosevelt Library, Hyde Park, N.Y.

Catt, Carrie Chapman, Papers, Manuscript Division, Library of Congress.

Daniels, Josephus, Papers, Wilson Library, University of North Carolina at Chapel Hill.

Du Bois, W. E. B., Papers, University of Massachusetts Libraries, Amherst.

Europe, James Reese, collection, Schomburg Center for Research in Black Culture, New York Public Library.

House, Edward Mandell, Papers, Yale University Library.

La Follette Family Papers, Manuscript Division, Library of Congress.

Lansing, Robert, Papers, Princeton University Libraries.

Mencken, Henry L., Papers, Enoch Pratt Free Library, Baltimore.

Rankin, Jeannette, Papers, Montana Historical Society, Missoula.

———, Swarthmore College Peace Collection.

Roosevelt, Theodore, Papers, Manuscript Division, Library of Congress.

Wilson, Woodrow, Papers, Library of Congress.

———, Papers, Princeton University Libraries.

———, Papers, Woodrow Wilson Presidential Library, Staunton, Va.

BOOKS AND PERIODICALS

Azar, Helen. *The Diary of Olga Romanov*. Yardly, Pa.: Westholme, 2014.

Badger, Reid. *A Life in Ragtime*. New York: Oxford University Press, 1995.

Benjamin, Walter. *Berlin Childhood Around 1900*. Cambridge, Mass.: Belknap Press, 2006.

Berg, A. Scott. *Wilson*. New York: G. P. Putnam's Sons, 2013.

Bode, Carl, ed. *The New Mencken Letters*. New York: Dial Press, 1977.

Browder, Robert Paul, and Alexander F. Kerensky, eds. *The Russian Provisional Government 1917: Documents*. Stanford, Calif.: Stanford University Press, 1961.

Burdzhalov, E. N. *Russia's Second Revolution*. Translated by Donald J. Raleigh. Bloomington: Indiana University Press, 1987.

Cantacuzene, Julia Speransky-Grant. *My Life Here and There*. New York: Charles Scribner's Sons, 1921.

————. *Russian People: Revolutionary Recollections*. New York: Charles Scribner's Sons, 1920.

Carlisle, Rodney. "The Attacks on U.S. Shipping that Precipitated American Entry into World War I." *Northern Mariner* (Ottawa), July 2007.

Carter, Lawrence T. *Eubie Blake: Keys of Memory*. Detroit: Balamp Publishing, 1979.

Connolly, C. P. "The Fight for the Minnie Healy." *McClure's Magazine*, July 1907.

Creel, George. *How We Advertised America*. New York: Harper & Brothers, 1920.

The Crisis, "Loyalty," May 1917.

————, "The World Last Month," May 1917.

Crosley, Pauline S. *Intimate Letters from Petrograd*. New York: E. P. Dutton & Co., 1920.

Curtiss, Thomas Quinn. *The Smart Set: George Jean Nathan and H. L. Mencken*. New York: Applause Books, 1998.

Feinstein, Elaine. *Anna of All the Russias*. New York: Alfred A. Knopf, 2005.

Fortescue, Granville. "Why America Must Fight if War Is Declared." *Washington Post*, March 18, 1917.

Francis, David R., *Russia from the American Embassy*. New York: Charles Scribner's Sons, 1921.

George, Alexander L., and Juliette L. George, *Woodrow Wilson and Colonel House*. New York: J. Day Co., 1956.

Gorky, Maxim. *Untimely Thoughts*. Translated by Herman Ermolaev. New York: Paul S. Eriksson, 1968.

Harper, Florence MacLeod. *Runaway Russia*. New York: Century Co., 1918.

Harper, Samuel N. *The Russia I Believe In*. Chicago: University of Chicago Press, 1945.

Harrison, Marguerite. *There's Always Tomorrow*. New York: Farrar & Rinehart, 1935.

Houghteling, James L. Jr. *A Diary of the Russian Revolution*. New York: Dodd, Mead & Co., 1918.

Kennan, George. "The Victory of the Russian People." *The Outlook*, March 28, 1917.

Kennedy, David M. *Over Here: The First World War and American Society*. New York: Oxford University Press, 2004.

Kilmer, Joyce. "How the War Changed a Vorticist Sculptor." *New York Times*, June 25, 1916.

Kittredge, William, and Annick Smith. *The Last Best Place: A Montana Anthology*. Seattle: University of Washington Press, 1988.

Knightley, Phillip. *The First Casualty*. New York: Harcourt Brace Jovanovich, 1975.

Larson, Eric. *Dead Wake*. New York: Crown Publishers, 2015.

The Letters of Franklin K. Lane. Edited by Anne Wintermute Lane and Louise Herrick Wall. Boston and New York: Houghton Mifflin Co., 1922.

Lewis, Sinclair. *The Job*. New York: Harper & Brothers, 1917.

Lightfoot, Claudia. *Havana: A Cultural and Literary Companion*. Brooklyn, N.Y., and Northampton, Mass.: Interlink Books, 2002.

Likhachev, Dmitry S. *Reflections on the Russian Soul*. Budapest: Central European University Press, 2000.

Literary Digest. "Our Busy 'Congresswoman.'" Aug. 11, 1917.

Livesay, Harold. *Samuel Gompers and Organized Labor in America*. Boston: Little, Brown & Co., 1978.

Lopach, James, and Jean Luckowski *Jeannette Rankin: A Political Woman*. Boulder: University Press of Colorado, 2005.

Lyandres, Semion, ed. *The Fall of Tsarism*. Oxford: Oxford University Press, 2013.

Mannes, David, *Music Is My Faith*. New York: W. W. Norton & Co., 1938.

McDermid, Jane, and Anna Hillyar. *Midwives of the Revolution*. Athens: Ohio University Press, 1999.

McLaughlin, Irene Castle. "Jim Europe—A Reminiscence." *Opportunity*, March 1935.

Mencken, H. L. *A Book of Prefaces*. 3rd ed. New York: Alfred A. Knopf, 1920.

———. *Heathen Days*. New York: Alfred A. Knopf, 1975.

———. "Ludendorff." *The Atlantic*, June 1917.

———. *Prejudices: Second Series*. New York: Alfred A. Knopf, 1920.

Metropolitan, "Correspondence of Theodore Roosevelt and the Secretary of War," August, 1917.

Morrison, Elting, *Admiral Sims and the Modern American Navy*. New York: Houghton Mifflin, 1942.

Mstislavskii, Sergei. *Five Days Which Transformed Russia*. Translated by Elizabeth Kristofovich Zelensky. Bloomington and Indianapolis: Indiana University Press, 1988.

Nabokov, Vladimir. *Speak, Memory*. New York: Vintage International, 1989.

Norton, Albert James. *Norton's Complete Handbook of Havana and Cuba*. Chicago and New York: Rand, McNally & Co., 1900.

Outlook. "Russia the Democratic." March 28, 1917.

The Papers of Woodrow Wilson. Edited by Arthur Link. Vol. 41. Princeton, N.J.: Princeton University Press, 1983.

Pinchot, Amos. "For 'A Strongly Defensive Policy.'" *New York Evening Post*, March 27, 1917.

Purdom, Charles Benjamin, ed. *Everyman at War*. London: J. M. Dent, 1930.

Rankin, Jeannette. "Why I Voted Against War." Unpublished manuscript, 1972. Swarthmore College Peace Collection.

Reed, John. "Whose War?" *The Masses*, April 1917.

Rodgers, Marion. *Mencken: The American Iconoclast*. New York: Oxford University Press, 2005.

Roosevelt, Theodore. "Harpooning Devilfish." *Scribner's*, Sept. 1917.

Rose, Al. *Storyville, New Orleans: Being an Authentic Account of the Notorious Red-Light District*. Tuscaloosa: University of Alabama Press, 1974.

Rosen, Baron (Roman). *Forty Years of Diplomacy*. New York: Alfred A. Knopf, 1922.

Schuller, Gunther. *Early Jazz: Its Roots and Musical Development*. New York: Oxford University Press, 1968.

Slotkin, Richard. *Lost Battalions*. New York: Henry Holt & Co., 2005.

Steinberg, Mark D. *Voices of Revolution, 1917*. New Haven, Conn.: Yale University Press, 2001.

Teachout, Terry. The Skeptic. New York: HarperCollins, 2002.

Therese, Josephine [pseud.]. *With Old Glory in Berlin*. Boston: Page Co., 1918.

Trotsky, Leon. *My Life: An Attempt at Autobiography*. New York: Charles Scribner's Sons, 1930.

———. *History of the Russian Revolution*. Translated by Max Eastman. New York: Simon & Schuster, 1936.

Williams, Harold. *The Baltimore Sun 1837–1987*. Baltimore: Johns Hopkins University Press, 1987.

Wilson, Edith Bolling. *My Memoir*. Indianapolis and New York: Bobbs-Merrill Co., 1938–1939.

Wilson, Joan Hoff. "Jeannette Rankin and American Foreign Policy: The Origins of her Pacifism." *Montana the Magazine of Western History*. Winter 1980.

Wilton, Robert. *Russia's Agony*. New York: E. P. Dutton & Co., 1919.

IMAGE CREDITS

1. *Residents of New York's Lower East Side:* Library of Congress.
2. *Paperboys in Oklahoma City:* Library of Congress.
3. *James Reese Europe:* Courtesy of the Maryland Historical Society, PP301.376.
4. *Rep. Jeannette Rankin of Montana:* Library of Congress.
5. *Two National Service School campers:* Courtesy of the Woodrow Wilson Presidential Library, Staunton, Virginia.
6. *H. L. Mencken:* © Enoch Pratt Free Library, Maryland's State Library Resource Center. All Rights reserved. Used with permission. Unauthorized reproduction or use prohibited.
7. *Teddy Roosevelt:* Library of Congress.
8. *Franklin Roosevelt:* National Archives.
9. *A Russian Farm Family:* New York Public Library.
10. *Revolutionary Russian soldiers man a barricade:* Library of Congress.
11. *Revolutionary soldiers take up position on a car:* Getty Images.
12. *Alexander Kerensky:* Library of Congress.
13. *A banner hailing the Soviet of Workers' and Soldiers' Deputies:* Library of Congress.
14. *Clifford K. Berryman political cartoon about the Russian revolution:* National Archives.
15. *Berryman cartoon about control of the House of Representatives:* National Archives.
16. *Antiwar protesters on the steps of the Capitol:* Library of Congress.
17. *African-American soldiers:* Photography © New-York Historical Society.
18. *The Civarro family assembling patriotic pins:* Library of Congress.
19. *Uncle Sam and Columbia:* Library of Congress.

INDEX